THE EDUCATIONAL SYSTEM OF ISRAEL

Recent Titles in
Contributions to the Study of Education

THE EDUCATIONAL SYSTEM OF ISRAEL

Yaacov Iram
and Mirjam Schmida

Contributions to the Study of Education, Number 70

GREENWOOD PRESS
Westport, Connecticut • London

Library of Congress Cataloging-in-Publication Data

Iram, Yaacov.
    The educational system of Israel / by Yaacov Iram and Mirjam
Schmida.
        p.   cm.—(Contributions to the study of education, ISSN
0196–707X ; no. 70)
    Includes bibliographical references and index.
    ISBN 0–313–30269–3 (alk. paper)
    1. Education—Israel.   2. School management and organization—
Israel.   I. Shemida‘, Miryam.   II. Title.   III. Series:
Contributions to the study of education ; no. 70.
LA1441.I73   1998
378.5694—DC21   97–30127

British Library Cataloguing in Publication Data is available.

Copyright © 1998 by Yaacov Iram and Mirjam Schmida

Library of Congress Catalog Card Number: 97–30127
ISBN: 0–313–30269–3
ISSN: 0196–707X

First published in 1998

Greenwood Press, 88 Post Road West, Westport, CT 06881
An imprint of Greenwood Publishing Group, Inc.

Printed in the United States of America

The paper used in this book complies with the
Permanent Paper Standard issued by the National
Information Standards Organization (Z39.48–1984).

10 9 8 7 6 5 4 3 2 1

Contents

Introduction

The Israeli educational system has many features in common with other national educational systems in developed countries. However, the Israeli educational system also has unique characteristics derived from both Jewish tradition and modern history, as well as from national revival over the last century. Israel's educational system represents a microcosm of many national, political, and social issues resulting from historical developments. Its current geopolitical situation in the Middle East and the multicultural, multiethnic, and multinational composition of its society all have an impact on the educational system. While the Israeli educational system is interesting in its own right, its analysis may contribute to a better understanding of other educational systems from an international perspective.

Since the early 1960s no comprehensive survey of the Israeli educational system has been conducted. This book attempts to provide an analytical review of the Israeli educational system as a whole from the preschool stage through higher education and also addresses special educational issues, such as reforms, changes, multiculturalism, vocationalism, and equity. The following are the main chapters and issues that are discussed in this book.

CHAPTER 1: HISTORY, GEOGRAPHY, DEMOGRAPHY, ECONOMY, AND GOVERNMENT

This chapter describes the context in which the Israeli educational system functions: the geography of the state and its borders, the two populations—Jews and non-Jews—and their ethnic composition. Israel is characterized as a migrant society and the resulting implications on culture, religion, and education are addressed. Israel's economic difficulties are analyzed, as well as its large expenditures on defense, absorption of immigrants, scarcity of water, and lack of other natural resources. Israel's government as a Western parliamentary democracy is described, and the basic characteristics of its educational system are presented. Since Israel's present educational system is based on the foundations that were laid during the prestate period, the historical background of the developments in Palestine during the British Mandate is discussed.

CHAPTER 2: PREPRIMARY AND PRIMARY EDUCATION

This chapter examines two sets of influences on the development of early childhood preprimary education: external universal influences originating in nineteenth-century Europe and the US, and internal influences dominated by particularistic national developments in Palestine-Israel. The first modern kindergartens, besides the traditional religious preprimary schools, were established by German-Jewish and French-Jewish philanthropic organizations during the latter part of the nineteenth century and taken over by the organized Jewish community during the early part of the twentieth century. The developments of these institutions and their objectives are described. The long-standing tradition of preschool education has been reinforced with statehood, and five-year-olds have been included within the Compulsory Education Law of 1949. In disadvantaged neighborhoods, three- and four-year-olds are also provided with free preschool education. The unique role, characteristics, and functions of early childhood education in the development of Israeli society are analyzed.

The foundations of primary education in Israel were also laid by Jewish philanthropic organizations in the mid-nineteenth century. The schools followed various European educational traditions, mainly those of Germany, France, and England, and consisted of five years of schooling. During the British Mandate on Palestine the educational system was under the control of the British government and various national (Arab and Jewish) and religious sectors (Muslim, Christian, and Jewish). The Jewish educational system was further divided into four ideological subsystems. These varied in their ideologies, pedagogical practices, and curricula. The British governmental school provided five to seven years of primary schooling to the Arab population, while the Jewish school system provided eight years of schooling. Between 1949 and 1953 the newly established State of Israel assumed responsibility for primary education of eight years, in addition to one year of compulsory kindergarten. All state schools were required to adopt a uniform basic curriculum in addition to elements reflecting the linguistic division (Hebrew and Arabic) and religious observance. A major change occurred in 1968 with the Reform Act, which changed the schooling structure from a two-level system: primary (K–8), and secondary (9–12) to a three-tier system: elementary (K–6), intermediate (7–9), and secondary (10–12). The main goals of this reform were to raise the academic achievements of all students and to foster social integration. However, at present (1997) the reform has been implemented in about 55–60% of Israeli schools. Thus, the state education system is split between a two-tier and a three-tier schooling structure. This chapter analyzes the effects of the structural changes on alternative structures and curricula orientations in primary schools: pedagogically, ideologically, and academically, as well as the emerging policy trends, such as parental choice and community schools.

CHAPTER 3: POSTPRIMARY EDUCATION

Major developments of the system, from prior to the establishment of the state until the 1990s, are surveyed. The development of postprimary education in Israel reveals a gradual transition from an elitist "class" selective system of gymnasiums to a system of "secondary education for all." Three types of secondary schools have developed at different times and at different rates: agricultural, academic, and vocational. A dynamic process of development of postprimary education is described quantitatively and qualitatively since statehood in the wake of mass immigration. The legal status of postprimary education, and its control, administration, and finances are discussed. Since 1968 the comprehensive high school system comprises about a third of all postprimary schools. Five major stages are discerned in its development: the years 1953–1963, when the essential components of comprehensiveness were experimented with in eleven experimental schools; 1963–1968, the period of institutionalization, when the major guiding principles of comprehensiveness were formulated; 1968–1973, the years when comprehensiveness gained formal legitimization as a result of the parliamentary decision to establish a six-year comprehensive high school; 1973–1984, the period of stagnation; and finally, 1984–1990s, perhaps a period of revival, due to the establishment of more integrated schools and "educational parks."

CHAPTER 4: VOCATIONALISM

Contrary to universal tendencies, vocational education in Israel is expanding. The phenomenon is analyzed in light of being considered appropriate for disadvantaged youth; it is also in line with the policy of secondary education for all and serves Israel's developing economy and technology. The institutional fabric of vocationalism is presented: the ministries in supervisory capacities, the major organizational frameworks, the internal schools' structure, curricula, and diplomas. Since the 1960s, changes and reforms in vocational education have been proposed by several committees. Their recommendations, based upon social changes in Israel and future scientific technological needs, are analyzed. The major characteristics of the proposed changes are: a curricula geared toward more sophisticated industry, the curtailing of training for semiskilled occupations, and the increase in theoretical studies based on technological scientific foundations, as well as horizontal mobility within flexible structures. The dilemma facing the system—integration of weaker students in schools versus the country's need for high-level technical manpower—is discussed. Vocationalism is evaluated in light of its social objectives and economic gains and its major orientations are illustrated in its international context.

CHAPTER 5: HIGHER EDUCATION

The development of higher educational institutions since prestate until the 1990s is discussed. A gradual transition from autonomy to centralization and bureaucratization is described. The division of the system into six distinct subsystems is presented and their differential functions are analyzed. The Law of Higher Education and its three-tier hierarchical administrative bodies are discussed. Since the 1980s four interrelated issues are discerned in the higher education system and their implications on the structure, government, and finance of individual higher educational institutions are analyzed. Major changes are discernible during the 1990s, such as more direct state control applied by means of accountability, productivity criteria, and external survey committees. With the establishment of undergraduate colleges, a process of diversification and democratization of the system is predicted for the twenty-first century. The higher education system in Israel has moved from being "elitist" in the 1940s and 1950s, to being "mass" higher education in the 1960s and 1970s, and is now approaching the stage of "universal" higher education. As a result of these developments, issues of control, finance, access, the structure of the system, governmental intervention, and institutional concern over academic freedom have become subjects of public debate.

CHAPTER 6: INFORMAL EDUCATION

Informal education has played an important role in Israel, both in its own right and as a supplement to formal education. It is examined from the organizational perspective in out-of-school and extracurricular activities, as well as from the sociological pedagogical viewpoint. The informal education system is characterized by a special educational approach, which is based upon structural features, activity contents, sociological characteristics, and mechanisms of control. The historical background of informal education is presented from both the prestatehood period, which is characterized by its social orientation, and the period after the foundation of the state. During the first decade of statehood, out-of-school activities for younger children were predominant; since the 1960s extracurricular activities in schools have been added. The fabric of informal education is surveyed and analyzed through youth movements, compensatory education, community education, the educational work with youth at risk, and extracurricular activities. The formal status of informal education within the system is discussed. The unique contribution of the various informal educational frameworks to social integration and national solidarity as well as future prospects are discussed.

CHAPTER 7: ARAB EDUCATION: DEVELOPMENT VERSUS CONTROL

This chapter, written by Majid Al-Haj, presents a general review of the trends of development in the Arab educational system in Israel. These trends are characterized by rapid expansion of educational opportunities, making it a "mass system" open to all sectors within the Arab population. The review of the developmental trends is followed by an analysis and discussion of the main problems of this system, including inner-local neglect, institutional discrimination, and lack of involvement on the part of the Arab population. Also addressed are debates over the goals underlying Arab education in general and the curriculum in particular.

CHAPTER 8: EDUCATIONAL REFORMS AND CHANGES

This chapter deals with the phenomenon of recurrent reforms and changes in the Israeli educational system, which are apparent in four areas: (1) the structure of the system, (2) curricular policies, (3) patterns of matriculation examinations (*Bagrut*), and (4) the locus of influence on policy making. The underlying base of these reforms are changes in the ideological realm, in which emphasis on excellence in education alternates with emphasis on equality. The changes reflect shifts in the philosophy of "equal education opportunity," to which Israeli society and its educational system have been committed since the latter's inception. The chapter describes and analyzes the different phases of the interpretation of this philosophy and its influences on the four educational areas. The recurrence of reforms and changes is explained by political and institutional perspectives in light of success and failure of structural and pedagogical reforms of national educational systems.

CHAPTER 9: MULTICULTURAL EDUCATION

Israel's multicultural composition is presented and analyzed. The Israeli educational system has to deal with intercultural differences, due to the absorption of immigrants from all over the world, and at the same time with intergroup relations, both within the country and with its neighbors. Israel pledged in its Declaration of Independence to uphold equality of all citizens, and this principle of equality has been incorporated into various acts of legislation. Arab-Muslim, Christian, and Druze minorities enjoy full rights and formal equality in regard to education. The school system has been the major focus of efforts to teach multiculturalism, which is addressed at three major societal divisions: religious and nonreligious Jews, Oriental and Western Jews, and Israeli Arabs and Jews. In spite of the educational system's continuous efforts to cope with multiculturalism, the problems have not been resolved satisfactorily because of socioeconomic and geopolitical implications, which are beyond education. However, major developments may be envisioned in the approach to multiculturalism in the wake of increased immigration from the former Soviet Union states on the one hand and the peace process on the other.

CHAPTER 10: MAJOR TRENDS AND FUTURE DEVELOPMENTS

Like many other countries, Israel has experienced rapid change during the last five decades of its existence as an independent state. Geopolitical developments, particularly the continuous conflict with Arab state neighbors, have affected all spheres of life, including education. Demographically, changing patterns of Jewish immigration have transformed the Jewish population several times from predominantly European in the late 1940s, to Middle-Eastern during the late 1950s and 1960s, and again to European following mass immigration from the former Soviet Union in the late 1980s and 1990s. Demographic changes have raised issues of equality in economic and educational policies. Indeed, the Israeli educational system is on the crossroads of still another transformation as a result of the prospects of peace in the region. The possible impact of these developments on Israeli society in general, and on the educational system in particular, is assessed.

Chapter 1

History, Geography, Demography, Economy, and Government

The area of Israel within its 1949 armistice borders measures 20,700 square kilometers. In addition, Israel controls "administered territories" of about 7,500 square kilometers, occupied since the 1967 Six Days War, that includes territories of Syria, Jordan, and Egypt. They are administered by military government according to regulations in force prior to the occupation, and part of these territories has been relinquished to the emerging Palestinian entity. Since the Oslo agreements in 1993 and 1995, more territories are being transferred. Israel is bounded on the north by Lebanon, on the northeast by Syria, on the east by the Hashemite kingdom of Jordan, as well as by the emerging Palestinian autonomous area in the West Bank, and on the southwest by the Gulf of Aqaba/Eilat and the Egyptian Sinai Desert (*The Middle East and North Africa*, 1996, 530).

Israel's total population in December 1994 was 5,462,300, of whom 82% were Jews and 18% were non-Jews. The non-Jewish population comprised 14.2% Muslims, 2.3% Christians, 1.7% Druze and others (Circassians and Ahmadis) (Central Bureau of Statistics, 1995, 3). The Jewish population is predominantly urban, while the Arab minority is rural.

One of Israel's most striking characteristics is the rapid increase in its population. The main source for growth in Israel's population is immigration, accounting for 58% of the yearly increase between 1948–1977, and for 30% of the yearly increase in the total population, and 46.2% in the Jewish population between 1948 and 1988 (Central Bureau of Statistics, 1989, 39–40). Thus, the ethnic composition of Israeli society changed according to the source of immigration. In 1948 the ethnic division according to parental origin was 80% Ashkenazim, 15% Orientals, and 5% Israeli born. Mass immigration from countries in the Middle East and North Africa caused an "orientalization" of Jewish society in Israel. Thus, ethnic origin division in 1989 was 38%

Ashkenazim, 42% Orientals, and 20% Israeli born. Half a million Jewish immigrants who arrived from the former Soviet Union countries again changed the ethnic mix to 40% Ashkenazim, 37% Orientals, and 23% Israeli born (Central Bureau of Statistics, 1994).

Although Jews have been living in Israel throughout all periods of history, its modern settlement is generally considered to date from the latter part of the nineteenth century. At this time the age-old longing to return to the Land of Israel was reinforced and made definite by the influence of national movements in Europe. Groups such as "Lovers of Zion," *Hovevi Zion,* were formed; Hebrew, the language of the Bible, was revitalized to become a modern language; and immigration to Israel was perceived as a cherished goal. The formation of the Zionist movement in 1897 provided an ideological and organizational framework for further immigration and development of the land.

Indeed, during the years 1882–1903 between 20,000 and 30,000 Jews came to Palestine from Eastern Europe. These immigrants established the first agricultural villages and laid the foundation for the new Jewish community. A second wave of immigration, in the years 1904–1914, brought between 30,000 and 40,000 more people. Its nucleus was a group of intellectuals who had witnessed the abortive 1905 Russian Revolution and had suffered bitter disillusion when this uprising also led to pogroms (the destruction of Jewish communities). Many of these intellectuals were intensely preoccupied with social problems, and they laid the basis for the Jewish Labor Movement and collective settlements *(kibbutzim).*

The third and fourth waves of immigrants arrived mainly from Eastern Europe between 1919–1931, bringing about 115,000 additional Jews to Palestine. These waves were largely precipitated by the increased suffering of Jews during and after World War I, as well as by the hopes aroused by the British government's Balfour Declaration in 1917, which promised the establishment of a national Jewish home in Palestine. This period witnessed the arrival of large numbers of *halutzim* (pioneers), who were motivated by social and national ideals and were prepared to live a life of hardship and sacrifice in order to realize them. Among the immigrants were tradesmen and manufacturers, who established commercial and industrial enterprises and contributed to the development of urban life.

The fifth wave of immigration, which began with the crisis that struck Europe in 1929, and was intensified by the Nazis' rise to power in Germany in 1933 and the consequent persecution of Jews, lasted until the establishment of the State of Israel in 1948. It is estimated that some 370,000 immigrants arrived in this wave, including about 100,000 German Jews. For the first time, substantial capital was brought into the country, which instigated the development of trade and industry.

With the establishment of the State of Israel, immigration received a strong impetus resulting in the arrival of 953,000 immigrants through the end of 1958. The absolute and relative size of this immigration, together with natural increase, tripled the Jewish community of 650,000. Considering the spatial and temporal limits of the State of Israel, the demographic and ethnic composition of this immigration, its social and economic character, its distribution over the country, and the process of its absorption have created many problems and changes in the fabric of Israeli society. Israel has devoted most of its efforts and resources in absorbing this vast immigration since establishment.

From this description of the background of Jewish national revival and the realization of its ideals and objectives in Israel, two major characteristics in the historical development of Israel follow, which are manifested in Israel's society and institutions. First, since Israel is a society of immigrants, its gradual crystallization and consolidation have been accomplished through the continuous clash between the successive waves of immigration. Second, the emergence of the State of Israel was conceived as a spiritual realization of a social-ideological-national movement, Zionism, and its physical embodiment. The Zionist movement was influenced by progressive social ideas and organizational structures prevailing in Europe during the nineteenth and early twentieth centuries. For example, many of the child and youth welfare services, including education, constituted an attempt to give practical expression to social theories developed in the countries from which the Jews had emigrated to Israel (Fajanas-Gluck, 1968; Katerbursky, 1962). Jewish cultural heritage together with the specific characteristics of diaspora Jewry and the reality of Israel have been additional important factors in modifying and shaping these developments.

In the early 1990s, Israel remains a migrant society. Of 2,315,900 Israeli-born Jews, only one-third (33.9%) are second generation Israelis. Of the total Jewish population, only 21.5% are second generation Israelis (Central Bureau of Statistics, 1994, 83).

The large waves of immigration in the early 1990s, which arrived mainly from Russia but also from Ethiopia, resulted in a further cultural and social diversification of Israeli society. This precipitated major problems in economic absorption, social integration, and education. Special programs were introduced to teach the Hebrew language and to impart Israeli culture to new immigrants.

Israel is also a pluralistic society. Nationally there exists a Jewish majority and a non-Jewish, predominantly Arab, minority. Linguistically, there are two official languages: Hebrew and Arabic. As a result of national, religious, and linguistic pluralism, separate educational systems emerged: Jewish, Arab, and Druze (Mari, 1978).

The Jewish majority is diversified ethnically, religiously, culturally, and educationally. From an ethnic perspective, in the sense of country of origin, there are *Ashkenazim*—Jews who originate from Eastern and Central Europe; and *Sephardim* or "Orientals"—Jews from the Mediterranean Basin and other Arab and Muslim countries (Ben-Rafael and Sharot, 1991). Israeli Jews are also divided into "religious" and "nonreligious" categories (Liebman, 1991). From a cultural perspective, diversity arises from the different ethnic groups who brought from their countries of origin different customs, ceremonies, attitudes, values, and ways of life. In terms of education, differences in religious observance have resulted in the emergence of three Jewish school systems: state education, state-religious education, and the independent education of ultra-orthodox Jewry.

Israel's economic development was affected by objective difficulties. These hardships included a heavy defense expenditure (absorbing 25% of the budget) as a result of the continuous Arab-Israeli conflict and the need to absorb immigrants, about half of whom came from underdeveloped, semifeudal, and traditional societies in the Middle East and North Africa, lacking formal education and skills required by a modern industrially oriented economy. Israel's economy was also adversely affected by scarcity of water and natural resources. Despite these difficulties, during the years 1951–1972 the Gross National Product (GNP) and constant prices rose by an annual average of 10%. From 1973 onward the rate of growth decreased considerably to 1.3% in 1976 and 1977, increased to 4.7% in 1978, and registered as static in 1982. The rate of growth increased by less than 1% in 1983 and 1.6% in 1988, and expanded by 5.9% in 1991, 6.6% in 1992, and 6.5% in 1994 (Central Bureau of Statistics, 1994). Defense takes the largest share of the annual state budget, more than 20%, while allocation for education amounts to 7.5% of the state budget in 1993–1994 (Central Bureau of Statistics, 1994).

Israel's government and politics share basic democratic principles and practices derived from, and associated with, Western parliamentary democracies. Israel essentially is a parliamentary democracy. Elections are held every four years. National and local elections are strictly proportional, reflecting multiparty competition. No single party has been able so far to secure a majority of seats in the 120-member Knesset (Parliament). As a result, all governments are formed by coalition between political parties. The Arab and Druze citizens of Israel enjoy full rights of citizenship and formal equality, including equal rights in education (Beilin, 1992). However, in recognizing the identity of its non-Jewish citizens, the state provides a separate Arabic system of education with Arabic as the medium of instruction at all levels, except for higher education. Unlike other levels of the educational system, which are administered directly by the government, the higher educational system is largely autonomous, in spite of governmental funding of 60% to 80% of its budget.

EDUCATIONAL DEVELOPMENTS

Education in the small Jewish community in Palestine (about 25,000 in 1880) resembled traditional schooling prevailing in Jewish communities elsewhere. The Jews of Eastern European tradition maintained the traditional *Cheder, Talmud Torah,* and *Yeshivah,* where Yiddish was the language of instruction. The Oriental (primarily North African Jewry) and Sephardi (descendants of Spanish Jewry) communities sent their boys to the *kutab,* where they studied in Ladino (a Spanish dialect) or Arabic (Nathan, 1937). Hebrew was taught as a theoretical language only and was consequently a dead language. The syllabus in all these institutions was limited to religious instruction: Bible, Talmud, and the commentaries. Secular subjects were not taught, and girls received no formal education whatsoever. During the second half of the nineteenth century, philanthropic Jewish families from Central and Western Europe, who had had relatively modern schooling, attempted to establish similar modern schools for their fellow Jews in Israel. The most well-known Jewish families are the Austrian Laemel family, the English Moses Montefiore family, and the French branch of Edmond James de Rothschild family (*Encyclopedia Judaica*, 1971). In addition, several Jewish national and international organizations came to the fore, not only materially aiding the small Jewish community, but also establishing modern schools, similar to those in Europe. The most important organizations were the French *Alliance Israelite Universelle,* the German *Hilfsverein der deutschen Juden,* the English *Anglo-Jewish Association,* and the Hebrew-National *Hovevi Zion* (Lovers of Zion).

Indeed, the roots of the present-day school system in Israel date back to the second half of the nineteenth century, when Jewish philanthropic organizations founded schools in the Western European tradition for the Jewish community in Palestine. These schools employed their respective sponsor's language of instruction: French, German, or English. Most teachers were natives of these countries. These modern schools at first existed in parallel to traditional Jewish schools, but later gradually replaced them. Jewish immigration to Palestine in the 1880s brought Jews believing in national revival to the newly established villages, and they promoted the spirit of renaissance in all spheres of life. They wanted Hebrew to be the language of instruction in their schools, despite resistance from philanthropic organizations.

The founders of the Technion, the German *Hilfsverein der deutschen Juden,* insisted on adopting German as the language of instruction. As a result of fierce opposition from the Jewish community who supported the implementation of Hebrew, the *Hilfsverein* withdrew its support from most of its schools in Palestine. These schools were subsequently taken over by the Hebrew Teachers' Union, whose members were committed to national renaissance and the revival of Hebrew. These schools became the nucleus of a national Hebrew school system, directed by a board of education, which continued to operate Jewish schools after World War I and throughout the thirty years of the British Mandate in Palestine. This school system was later to provide an important infrastructure for statehood.

THE EDUCATIONAL SYSTEM—AN OVERVIEW

The modern educational system dates back to approximately fifty years before Israel gained independence. Many of the foundations laid during the early years are still evident. The system includes kindergartens, primary schools, secondary schools (including vocational and agricultural secondary schools), teacher training institutions, postsecondary schools for continued and vocational studies, colleges and universities. Hebrew language and culture comprise the basis for studies. The school year is approximately ten months long, from September through July; the study week is thirty to thirty-five hours. Studies take place in homeroom classes staffed by homeroom teachers, who are responsible for class studies and social activities. In the lower grades the homeroom teacher teaches most of the studies, while in the higher grades specialized teachers are employed to teach subjects. Schools maintain close contact with parents, and most classes have a parents' committee. In addition to formal studies, there are an extensive range of extra-curricular activities (informal education) inside and outside of school.

The state educational system includes separate schools for Arab and Druze students. The structure of the Arab school sector is similar to that of the Jewish sector. The main differences are in the language of instruction, (Arabic), and in the curriculum, which is designed to reflect the unique culture and history of the various Arab populations (Muslim, Christian, and Druze) (Al-Haj, 1995).

Israel's educational enterprise is a centralized system financed by the state and directed by the Ministry of Education, Culture, and Sport. It is subdivided into Jewish and Arab schools, which implies that it is a bilingual system embracing Hebrew and Arabic. The Hebrew-speaking schools are divided into two tracks: state schools (*mamlachti*-"state") and state religious (*mamlachti-dati*) schools. Parents have the right to choose between religious and nonreligious schools. Schooling is free and compulsory between ages five to sixteen, and free but not compulsory between the ages three to four and seventeen to eighteen. The educational system is ideologically oriented and performs a dual mission. First, it fulfills the social mission of providing equal educational opportunities to disadvantaged children, mainly of Oriental origin. Second, in recent years it performs the national mission of integrating the various groups of immigrants (i.e., Russians and Ethiopians) into the fabric of Israeli society.

The educational system in Israel copes with dilemmas and conflicts inherent in its historical and sociocultural conditions: tradition and modernity, nationalism and universalism, uniformity and pluralism, elitism and egalitarianism, centralization and decentralization. These dilemmas characterize all spheres of public life and institutions, but have a particular effect on education.

The Structure of the System

Israel's educational system is based on four levels: (1) preschool, (2) primary school, (3) secondary school, and (4) postsecondary and higher education (see Table 1.1).

Table 1.1
Structure of the Education System, 1996

Preprimary Education	Primary Education	Secondary Education		
Kindergarten and Nursery School (ages 2–5)	Primary School (Grades 1–8)	Lower Secondary Schools (Grades 7–9)	Upper Secondary Schools (Grades 9–12)	
		193,000		E / T*
320,000 (90%)	690,000 (96%)		288,000 (90%)	
	Free and Compulsory Education		Free Educ.	

```
 |  |  |  |  |  |  |  |  |  |  |  |  |  |  |  |  |  |  |
 2  3  4  5   6  7  8  9  10 11 12 13 14 15 16 17 18 19 20
```

AGE

* Practical Engineers and Technicians

Source: Ministry of Education, Culture, and Sport, *Facts and figures*, 1996, p. 23.

In 1996 the total number of students in the educational system supervised by the Ministry of Education, Culture, and Sport was about 1,490,000. The first level includes municipal, public, and private nurseries and kindergartens for children aged two to six. The Compulsory Education Law of 1949 and its subsequent amendments (Stanner, 1963) made one year's attendance at a public kindergarten and ten years of primary and secondary school compulsory and free of charge, while two additional years of schooling (grades 11–12), are free of charge although not compulsory (Yifhar, 1984). Preschool education is considered an essential prerequisite for further schooling of all children; particularly for children of new immigrants and disadvantaged families. This explains the growing interest of both government and the private sector in this early stage of education and the high rate of attendance, as will be discussed later.

Until 1968 primary education was mainly comprised of eight grades. It was followed by secondary schools offering academic education of four years, or vocational-technical-agricultural schools of two to four years. Following the 1968 School Reform Act, the traditional school structure of 8 + 4 was replaced by a 6 + 3 + 3 structure. However, due to financial constraints and sociopolitical considerations, this structural reform has been only partially implemented, as will be discussed later. By the 1990s, the reform embraced about 54% of the total school population, while 46% still attended schools of the traditional structure (Ministry of Education, Culture, and Sport, 1996). Thus, both school structures continued to exist concurrently.

After completing six or eight years of primary school, all students transfer to a three-year comprehensive junior high school ("intermediate division"). The third level of education is the senior high school ("upper division"), comprising grades 10–12. Senior high schools are of three major types. The first type is the general academic, which offers a variety of programs both in the humanities and sciences. The academic high school leads toward a matriculation certificate (*Bagrut*)—a prerequisite for higher education. The second type is the vocational technological high school. The technological track also includes a postsecondary program for grades 13–14 leading toward a technicians' or practical engineers' certificate. In 1992 about 55% of high school students attended general academic secondary schools, while 45% were registered in vocational technological secondary schools (CBS 1993, no. 44, 641). This data refers also to students in the corresponding academic and vocational tracks in the comprehensive high school. The third type is the comprehensive high school, which comprises both academic and vocational tracks, which are similar to the corresponding two types mentioned above, but function in a joint institution.

The postsecondary level includes various types of nonacademic institutions for training primary school teachers, nurses, technicians, and a variety of other semiprofessionals. Some of these institutions that train in the semiprofessions are in the process of "academization," namely, they opt for academic recognition and status. In addition, there are some two dozen nonuniversity higher education institutions that offer professional bachelors' degrees and an open university.

There are seven universities. They offer three-year programs that lead to a bachelor's degree. This is followed by a two-year master's degree program and doctoral studies. Admission to all higher education institutions is based on having passed the nationally administered matriculation examinations (*Bagrut*). These exams are usually taken by students from academic secondary schools, as well as in advanced tracks of vocational schools, or by external examinees. An additional requirement for admission to higher education is also the psychometric test, which is administered centrally by the universities. About 67% of the matriculation examinees in 1989–1990 were entitled to matriculation certificates (CBS 1993, no. 44, 641). However, this group constitutes only about 30% of a given age cohort.

Israel's educational system is centrally administered by the Ministry of Education and Culture. The ministry has two main wings: the pedagogical secretariat, and the pedagogical administration. The pedagogical secretariat is responsible for setting educational and policy curriculum and supervising the system. The pedagogical administration is responsible for the implementation of the educational policy in regard to personnel, students, buildings, and finances. The chief executive officer is the director general. Each level of education is regulated by a corresponding unit within the ministry. The administration of the system is conducted through six regions and a nationwide rural education division. Local municipal authorities share the responsibility for the implementation of the compulsory education law. They are responsible for student registration, erecting and maintaining school buildings, and providing equipment and support services.

The universities maintain an independent status. They are financed and coordinated by a separate statutory body: the Council for Higher Education (CHE), and its Planning and Budgeting Committee (PBC), while all other levels of the educational system are jointly financed by the Ministry of Education and the local municipalities.

The Legal Basis for Education

The present-day school system is based on the following laws and regulations: the Compulsory Education Law (1949); the State Education Law (1953); the Council for Higher Education Law (1958); the School Inspection Law (1968); the Special Education Law (1988); the Long School Day Law (1990); certain provisions passed by the Knesset; and amendments to existing laws. The 1949 Compulsory Education Law introduced free compulsory primary education for all children of ages five to thirteen years. This primary education included one year of kindergarten and eight years of elementary school. This law was extended in 1968 to include grades 9 and 10. In 1979 free, but not compulsory, education was extended to grade 12.

The State Education Law abolished the old "trend" education system, which was controlled by political parties, and imposed the responsibility for education upon the government. However, the law still recognizes two main forms of primary education: (1) state education and (2) recognized nonstate education. State education comprises two distinct categories of schools: state schools and state-religious schools, where the language of instruction is Hebrew, and Arab state schools, where the language of instruction is Arabic. The state and local authorities own and control schools and kindergartens of the state system. Recognized nonstate institutions, mainly religious, are privately owned, although they are subsidized and supervised by the state. The largest recognized school system is the *Agudat Israel* (ultraorthodox religious). Other recognized schools are mainly Christian denominational schools.

State primary education is financed by both the government and the local authorities. Since 1953 state teachers' salaries were paid by the central government. However, the cost of maintenance, and the provision of new buildings and equipment were financed by local authorities. The state does not impose an education tax, but local authorities are entitled to levy a rate on parents for special services.

This chapter has provided the background for understanding the developments of the Israeli educational system. The chapter has emphasized the difficulties facing the State of Israel, due to external geopolitical conditions, and the internal raison d'être of the Jewish State, namely, the ingathering of the exiles and the facilitation of their absorption.

The following chapter, "Preprimary and Primary Education," describes and analyzes the implications of the above factors on the structure, contents, and policies of the educational system. These first stages of education, preprimary and primary, play a fundamental role in the long socialization process.

BIBLIOGRAPHY

Ackermann, W. (1982). *Erziehung in Israel*, 2 Bände. Stuttgart: Klett-Cotta.

Al-Haj, M. (1995). *Education, empowerment and control: The case of the Arabs in Israel*. Albany, NY: State University of New York Press.

Becker, H., and L. Liegle (1980). *Israel, Erziehung und Gesellschaf.* Stuttgart: Klett-Cotta.

Beilin, Y. (1992). *Israel: A concise political history.* London: Weidenfeld and Nicolson.

Ben-Rafael, E., and S. Sharot (1991). *Ethnicity, religion and class in Israeli society.* Cambridge, Eng.: Cambridge University Press.

Bentwich, J. (1965). *Education in Israel.* London: Routledge and Kegan Paul.

Central Bureau of Statistics (CBS). *Statistical abstracts of Israel 1989*, no. 40. Jerusalem.

Central Bureau of Statistics (CBS). *Statistical abstracts of Israel 1993*, no. 44. Jerusalem.

Central Bureau of Statistics (CBS). *Statistical abstracts of Israel 1994*, no. 45. Jerusalem.

Central Bureau of Statistics (CBS). *Statistical abstracts of Israel 1995*, no. 46. Jerusalem.

Eisenstadt, S. N. (1985). *The transformation of the Israeli society*. Boulder, CO: Westview Press.

Elazar D., and C. Kalchheim (eds.). (1988). *Local government in Israel*. Lanham, MD: University Press of America.

Encyclopedia Judaica (1971). New York: Macmillan.

Fajanas-Gluck, S. (1968). *Early childhood education*. Tel Aviv: Yavneh Publishing (Hebrew).

Goldstein, S. (ed.). (1980). *Law and equality in education*. Jerusalem: van Leer.

Horowitz, D., and M. Lissak (1989). *Trouble in Utopia: The overburden policy of Israel*. Albany, NY: State University of New York Press.

Katerbursky, Z. (1962). *Thirty-five years of work in nursery schools and kindergartens*. Tel Aviv: Israeli Teachers' Union (Hebrew).

Kleinberger, A. F. (1969). *Society, schools and progress in Israel*. Oxford: Pergamon Press.

Landau, J. M. (1993). *The Arab minority in Israel: 1967–1991*. Oxford: Clarendon Press.

Liebman, C. S. (1991). *Religious and secular: Conflict and accommodation between Jews in Israel*. Jerusalem: Keter.

Mari, S. K. (1978). *Arab education in Israel*. Syracuse, NY: Syracuse University Press.

The Middle East and North Africa. (1996). London: Europa Publications, pp. 530–588.

Ministry of Education, Culture, and Sport (1996). *Facts and figures*.

Nathan, M. (1937). *The Jewish school: An introduction to the history of Jewish education*. London: Eyre and Spottiswoode.

Stanner, R. (1963). *The legal basis of education in Israel*. Jerusalem: Ministry of Education and Culture.

Yifhar, Y. (ed.). (1984). *Laws of education and culture*. Jerusalem: Ministry of Education and Culture.

Chapter 2

Preprimary and Primary Education

The development of early childhood education in Israel was influenced by both external and internal factors. The external factors were related to universal trends prevailing in Europe and the United States during the nineteenth century, which contributed to the development and expansion of educational opportunities for preschool children. Internal factors were dominated by particularistic national developments pertaining to Jewish national revival in Palestine during the latter part of the nineteenth century and its gaining momentum of realization in the early twentieth century.

In recent years early childhood became a field of inquiry from a psycho-historical perspective (Finkelstein, 1979; Hiner, 1983) invoking disagreements among educators in Europe and America as to the appropriate form of kindergartens. These developments in early childhood education were familiar to proponents of preschool education in Palestine-Israel in the late nineteenth and early twentieth centuries, through educational literature or by direct experience and training. Educators in Israel were concerned with educational thought and practice. This is reflected in early educational periodicals in Hebrew (Iram and Krim, 1989), as well as in the pedagogical discussions held in annual conferences of the Hebrew Teachers' Association (Bentwich, 1965). Some of the earlier teachers were trained in Europe, being sent either prior to their immigration to Israel or after their immigration. However, the immediate developments in general education in Israel, and particularly in early childhood education, followed Jewish national revival in Palestine, beginning in the 1880s, and culminating with the establishment of the State of Israel in 1948.

HISTORICAL BACKGROUND

Early childhood education has a lengthy tradition among the Jewish people. The traditional preprimary and primary school since the Middle Ages was known as *Heder* (literally, *room*), in which one teacher would teach boys ages three to thirteen from early morning until sunset. Early age instruction was formal and comprised learning to read Hebrew and knowledge of the prayers, followed by study of the Pentateuch and Talmud (Lifshitz, 1947). However, the establishment of kindergartens in the modern European sense followed the general process of modernization of education in the Jewish community in Palestine during the second part of the nineteenth century. Indeed, Jewish philanthropic organizations opened kindergartens alongside modern elementary schools. Thus, the *Alliance Israelite Universelle* established in Palestine preschool institutions modeled after the French *asile d'enfants,* in which children from three to six years of age were taught to play and sing in French in order to prepare them for formal learning of reading and writing in elementary school (Bentwich, 1965). Similarly, the *Hilfsverein der deutschen Juden* included in its educational enterprises in Palestine the establishment of kindergartens, which followed the Froebelian methods and employed German as its language of instruction (Hewes, 1980).

A third group, who had the most decisive role in the development of early childhood education in Palestine at the turn of the nineteenth century, were Hebrew teachers in the newly established agricultural settlements. They felt the need for an informal preparatory stage during which children between four and five years of age would acquire academic and social skills in addition to proficiency in Hebrew, which was not spoken in their homes.

Education theorists and scholars of child development from Plato to Maria Montessori have lauded early childhood as the optimal developmental stage for the introduction of desired cognitive, affective, and social learning. Many national educational systems have made provisions for preschool children to receive instruction on a continuum with formal education being provided by the schools (Hunt, 1971). Recognizing the importance of early childhood for establishing language proficiency in Hebrew, many preschool institutions were established by the organized Jewish community in Palestine half a century before the establishment of the State of Israel in 1948.

The first Hebrew kindergarten was opened in the first agricultural settlement, *Rishon Letzion,* in 1898. The idea quickly gained in popularity, and soon a network of kindergartens in all parts of the country came into existence. The main purpose of these early kindergartens was the inculcation of the Hebrew language, and an introduction to reading, writing, and arithmetic. Thus, kindergartens served as preparation for school. The seating arrangements, teaching methods, and the general atmosphere were rather scholastic. When the graduates of the Pestalozzi-Froebel school came to Palestine, the atmosphere and methods changed. Suitable equipment was gradually introduced and work was centered around "subjects" taken from the child's surroundings. This work included handiwork, but largely still comprised talks, stories, singing, and rhymes. A ten o'clock meal was introduced and hygienic standards were improved. Over the course of time, elements from the

Montessori, Decroly, and other methods were introduced into kindergartens. Later, the progressive method, as developed in the United States, was adopted in many kindergartens. With the increase in the number of kindergartens and the establishment of Teachers' and Kindergarten Teachers' Training Colleges, methods of work became crystallized and unified. Native elements began to appear; the care of plants and animals was introduced, and trips designed for students to become acquainted with the country were organized. Emphasis was put on Jewish tradition and history, mainly in the form of great preoccupation with holidays and national and cultural events (Smilansky, Weintraub, and Hanegbi, 1960).

Although kindergartens were established and maintained by philanthropic and women's voluntary organizations, they were subject to pedagogical supervision by the Department of Education of the Jewish self-government throughout the period of British Mandate over Palestine. Indeed, preschool education was common during that period. It has been estimated that over 80% of Jewish children who began elementary school in 1945 had previously attended kindergarten (Kleinberger, 1969). This long-standing tradition of preschool education was reinforced with the establishment of the State of Israel in 1948. This rather unusual provision of the law resulted from the particular circumstances and needs of Israel. Due to mass immigration following the establishment of the state, there was an influx of non-Hebrew speaking immigrants. These immigrants were also unfamiliar with the functions and values of the country's institutions and modern education. Thus, many children were unable to receive reinforcement from their families, which is an essential ingredient for school success. Under these circumstances, one year of compulsory attendance in kindergarten became a *conditio sine qua non* for success in primary school.

Indeed, since its establishment in 1948, Israel has used the school system, including preschool education, to cope with its major social and cultural problems, including immigrant absorption. It was widely believed by the public, as well as by educators and policymakers, that "kindergartens were expected to solve problems, since the earlier treatment is applied, the faster the [socioeconomic and cultural] gap is closed" (Ministry of Education and Culture, 1979). The expectation that schools can contribute to solving social problems is deeply rooted in Jewish cultural tradition, which has always valued literacy and learning as the core of Jewish culture, even as a religious duty. This tradition, together with the increasing knowledge of human growth discovered by developmental psychology, has suggested that social interventions are most efficient with young children. This attitude is summarized by the former secretary-general of Israel's Ministry of Education and Culture as follows:

Kindergartens contribute toward the cultural cohesion of the population. Kindergartens prepare young children for school, and this again assumes special importance in Israel. This is because the homes of many immigrants, during the first few years following their arrival, lack the quiet and stable environment which is so vital for the young child's early development. (Avidor, 1957)

This also explains why public opinion in Israel supported compulsory education for five-year-old children in kindergartens within the framework of compulsory education. Furthermore, whenever the issue of extending compulsory schooling was raised, there were always groups who insisted on lowering the attendance age to four and even three years of age.

The national commitment in Israel to early childhood preschool education was stated repetitively by the Ministry of Education: "The encouragement and development of early childhood centers for still younger tots is the avowed policy of the Ministry of Education and Culture, with the intention of admitting the majority of Israel's very young into such programs" (Ministry of Education and Culture, 1981). Since preschool education is considered an essential prerequisite for success in school, particularly for children of new immigrants and disadvantaged families, the declared policy of the Ministry of Education and Culture is to make preschool education universal. Thus, free preschool education is already provided for three- and four-year-olds from culturally and economically deprived homes in "distressed areas" and inner-city quarters. However, according to Amendment 16 to the 1949 Compulsory Education Law, passed on June 13, 1984, and implemented over a six-year period beginning in September 1985, free and compulsory education for all children commences at three years of age (*Government Yearbook 5745*, 1985). Thus, Israel's national involvement in early childhood preschool education has been a consistent commitment since its inception almost a century ago.

In 1993–1994 the kindergarten system numbered 320,000 children, ranging in age from two to six years, who attended municipal, public, and private kindergartens and nursery schools. Increasing interest in the developmental problems of the very young, together with the social dilemmas Israeli society was facing, prompted the education system to pay more attention to the preprimary level. Thus 69% of two-year-olds, 95% of three-year-olds, and 95% of six-year-olds attended day-care centers and nursery schools (Ministry of Education, Culture and Sport, 1995).

The basic assumption of the education system is that education must commence as early as possible in order to ensure that all children are provided with the necessary conditions and opportunities for achieving personal fulfillment. At the preprimary level, goals include teaching educational fundamentals, such as language and thought development, fostering learning and creative abilities, and also social skills. In accordance with the policy of "nurturing" the disadvantaged, the Ministry of Education, Culture and Sport has allocated resources for educating three- and four-year-olds in development towns, immigrant settlements, and urban renewal districts.

PRIMARY EDUCATION

The system of primary education is the largest in the Israeli educational system, in terms of the numbers of students and professional staff involved. Since its inception it has embodied many of the central issues with which the educational system, as a whole, is coping today. Primary schools, prior to statehood and to mandatory requirements, had catered to about 80% of children in the pertinent age groups, thus testifying to the importance of education in the evolving Jewish society. But there were high dropout rates, and in some areas only 20% of the students completed eight years of study (Bentwich, 1965). Primary education in prestate Palestine was the forerunner of "universal free public primary education for all" in the State of Israel.

The major ideological and sociocultural orientation of primary education was toward equality. This involved providing all young children with a common cultural base and, primarily, with knowledge of the Hebrew language. But in parallel, these were already indicators of a more selective and elitist approach toward primary education. This approach preferred particularistic and achievement-oriented values, which have a more divisive impact on society, as opposed to collective and universal values, which unite and enhance social solidarity. The different orientations were identifiable, mainly, in the organizational structure of the primary schools and in the number of years of study, but also in the composition of the student body and the allocation of students into learning groups in schools and in the classrooms. Another central issue related to the different emphasis on traditional religious values as opposed to more liberal and secular ones, which were reflected in the streams of education to which the schools were affiliated. In the general stream the proportion was 40% Jewish studies in the curriculum and 60% secular studies. In the Mizrachi stream, the proportion was 60% to 40% in favor of Jewish studies; and in the labor stream, 70% to 30% in favor of general studies. The differences in streams were recognizable also in the methods of teaching, in the schools' climates, and in the relationships between teachers and students (Arnon, 1948; Ben-Yehuda, 1973).

Another issue focused on the division of power and authority between the central educational agencies during the period of the Yishuv. These agencies included the Vaad Leumi and the boards of education of the educational streams, as well as the individual schools and their communities of parents and students. In the following years, this issue became known as the movement toward centralization of the educational system versus the movement toward decentralization. During prestatehood the foundations of the future powerful teachers' union were laid. In 1904 an assembly of sixty teachers established the Association of the Hebrew Teachers in Palestine, which elected an executive central committee and named it the Center of Teachers—*Merkaz Hamorim*. The political and sociocultural changes that Israeli society underwent during fifty years of statehood and the major educational tensions and conflicts besetting it were reflected in the developmental stages of the primary school system.

Prestatehood

Two major milestones, which have shaped the development of the primary school system during the years, were identifiable already at the beginning of the twentieth century: the foundation of the teachers' union in 1903 and the breakout of the war of languages—the "War over Hebrew"—in 1913 (Lamm, 1985). The aims of the union were to improve the conditions of Jewish education and to imbue it with a national Hebrew character, to revive the Hebrew language, and to raise the professional status of the teacher. The union prepared the curriculum for a four- to six-year elementary school, which was influenced by the European education system, especially that of Germany and Austria. The program was ratified almost without changes by the administration of the Zionist movement in 1923 and served as the officially accepted curriculum of the elementary school until 1945. The second milestone dealt with the priority of the Hebrew language over European languages, especially over the German language, in the educational system. The main conflict involved the "Ezra" movement, which wanted to impose the German language over the Hebrew language. This conflict with relation to languages was serious because of the difficulties inherent in the Hebrew language, which had not been used as a living language for many centuries. The Hebrew language had not been used with general curricular subject matters, especially with those in the scientific realms, such as, chemistry, biology, and mathematics. Due to the intense devotion of the majority of the Yishuv to the Hebrew language and the strong opposition led by the teachers' union to foreign languages, the victory of the Hebrew language over foreign languages was complete. According to J. Azariahu (1929), the school was a crucial factor in the renaissance of the Hebrew language into a living language. In 1880 the first Hebrew school was established in Rishon Letzion—one of the new settlements near Jaffa. In the wake of the victory of the Hebrew language, the establishment of additional Hebrew primary schools was enhanced. At the end of World War I, there were twenty-seven primary schools, and following the waves of immigration, the number of schools rose to ninety-seven with a student population of 10,000 in 1919 (Arnon, 1948).

With the war of languages now over, the educational system began to deal with pedagogical problems, especially with the proper integration between traditional and modern education. Various pedagogical methods were practiced, some of them originating from American influences, which became important during the 1920s, for example, emphasis on school climate and social life of students in the schools; concentration of subject matter around central issues; and the creation of clusters of learning taken from close academic disciplines, with a single teacher appointed to teach them.

During the period of the British Mandate over Palestine, from 1922 to 1948, the Hebrew school system was struggling with two major problems—safeguarding the budget of the schools with the help of the British government, and maintaining the administrative and pedagogic autonomy of the system. The Mandatory administration contributed only a small grant to the expenditures of the Jewish system of education. Since 1933, with the publication of the Ordinance of Education, the British calculated its allowances according to the ratio between the respective school-aged populations of the Jewish and Arab communities, which was very much in favor of the latter, because of their large family size (Kleinberger, 1969). In 1944–1945 the British Mandate's fiscal contribution to the Jewish system of public education was only 8.5% (HMSO, 1946).

Between the two world wars the Jewish society in Palestine crystallized around its administrative organizations, which functioned on a voluntary basis. These organizations were successful because they were oriented toward the satisfaction of all the segments of the Yishuv and their different ideological interests. The most salient demonstration of this policy was visible in the organization of the educational system, which was not determined by the demands of the majority, but empowered also the smaller groups to find satisfactory answers to their ideological and religious demands within the system.

Thus, the four educational trends (Rieger, 1940), in spite of their socially divisive character, and their segregative ideological orientations, which were rooted in the political parties of the Yishuv, nonetheless served as a uniting force. Because of the organization of streams, each family could provide its children with the education of its choice (Lamm, 1973).

The Structure of the Primary School System

The first official assembly of teachers, at the end of the nineteenth century, decided that primary school should be of five years' duration, beginning with six-year-old children. This decision was changed in 1903 by the newly founded teachers' union, which voted on an eight-year school called "public school"—*Bet Sefer Ammami*. In parallel, different educational structures were considered and carried out. In 1905 a private school was established by Dr. Yehuda Leeib Matman-Cohen, named the Herzliyah Gymnasium, after Herzl, the founder of Zionism. The gymnasium was designed as a twelve-year school, consisting of four preparatory grades (*Mechinot*) and eight regular ones. The founder promised to provide students with knowledge of the Hebrew language, national education, as well as general secondary education. He focused mainly on realistic and commercial studies in order to prepare the students for higher studies in the university and the poly-technicum (Ben-Yehuda, 1973; Bentwich, 1965).

The new school was very attractive to parents, who considered it comparable to European schools. The number of students increased from year to year and reached five hundred in 1913. Two additional schools emulated the model of the gymnasium: the Hebrew gymnasium in Jerusalem and the Reali School in Haifa. Consequently, two parallel structures of education were established: an eight-year elementary school, followed by mainly four to five years of seminary for elementary teacher training; and a gymnasium, consisting of four years of preparatory classes for secondary education, followed by an eight-year academic secondary school. The dual structure, which was modeled after the Central European educational system, especially that of Germany, reflected the conception of a stratified society, divided into two social classes. The lower classes, the plebeian, were not interested in higher education, but expected to pursue a living through physical work and business. The minimum education that they considered to be necessary was reading, writing, and arithmetic, which could be acquired in an eight-year popular school. The second social class was comprised of aristocrats, who were expected to strive for academic titles and to be provided with a twelve-year education at least in order to enter institutions of higher academic education. The dual structure was criticized severely from its inception and named a "blunt mistake" (Rieger, 1940).

At the end of World War I, the central administration of the Jewish educational system convened a meeting to discuss the problems inherent in the dual structure. The following principles were adopted: the abolishment of the duality of the system at the lower level of education; the founding of secondary education on the base of primary education and not parallel to it; and the standardization of an eight-year elementary school. As for the articulation of primary and secondary school education, various proposals were made, reflecting the tension between primary and secondary school teachers. The primary school teachers, who were supported by the teachers' union, wanted to strengthen the basic school for all children and even extend the number of its years beyond eight (Twersky, 1963, 33); whereas the academic secondary school teachers were interested in prolonging the secondary school. They relied on psychological arguments, such as the beginning of the period of adolescence at age twelve, which is related to the developmental stage of formal logic reasoning (Inhelder and Piaget, 1958), and the intellectual shallowness of the last two years of elementary schooling, and were supported by professors from the Hebrew University (Rieger, 1940). No decisive resolution was accepted, and the situation did not change drastically. The duality of the educational system was not abolished and only shrunk by means of a formula that was not strictly adhered to. According to the formula, the secondary school would be a five-year school, and the status of the first seven years of the twelve-year gymnasium would be equated to the eight-year public school. The dispute concerning the structure of the educational system continued until the disagreements between the parties came to an end by external interference. The Department of Education of the British Mandate suggested the institution of a six-year elementary school, at the end of which students would receive a Diploma of Elementary Education. In addition, it proposed a six-year secondary school, based on the elementary school. The final examinations of this stage would be prepared by the British Governmental Council of Higher Education, and students successfully passing would receive a British Certificate of Matriculation. The administration of the Yishuv considered these suggestions as dangerous to the desired standards of learning of Jewish schools. In order to prevent this danger, the parties agreed upon the structure of an eight-year elementary school, followed by a four-year secondary school, although a few exceptions still remained.

Since Statehood

In 1948, eighteen months after the inception of the State of Israel, the Law of Mandatory Learning was enacted. This law established nine years of mandatory learning for all children: one year in kindergarten for five-year-olds; and eight-years in elementary school (*Book of Laws*, 1949). The law obligated the central government and the local educational authorities to provide the educational services, and obligated parents to register their children in the schools and to be responsible for their regular attendance. The law provided the legal base for the physical and spiritual absorption of the masses of immigrant children into the schools, as well as the legal framework of primary education for all. The second law of education, which was enacted in 1953, filled the legal framework with pedagogical contents, in regard to the objectives of the educational system and their application in the school curricula. The law is entitled the State Education Law (*Hok Hinuch Mamlachti*) (*Book of Laws*, 1953) because of the general national assumptions underlying it. The law abolished the autonomous educational streams, which were established during the period of the Yishuv, and united the educational system under the auspices of the Central State Administration. The religious educational stream of the *Mizrachi* was to maintain its autonomy to a certain degree. Both streams, the state-general and the state-religious, belonged to the state, but differed with relation to religious beliefs and behaviors. These differences were manifested in the establishment of separate schools, in school curricula, and in school personnel, who were supposed to be religious in the religious stream. The schools of *Agudat Israel*, the ultra-orthodox political party, separated from the mainstream of state education. Upon their commitment to minimal state curricular requirements, they acquired the status of officially recognized schools and enjoyed monetary support from the state.

The enactment of the State Education Law symbolized the victory of the centrist-national orientations in education over the sectorial political orientations. Two different explanations are given for the establishment of the two streams. A. F. Kleinberger (1969) connects the process with its meaninglessness in the eyes of new immigrants, who did not understand the ideological and pedagogical differences between the various educational systems. D. Horowitz and M. Lissak (1972, 280) explain the law as the denouncement of the political leadership of the public service and its transference to central state agencies. The law grounded the goals of state education in the values of the Israeli culture, in the love of the country, and in loyalty to the state. It urged schools to educate students to achieve in science and to promote the establishment of a society based on freedom, equality, tolerance, mutual help, and love of mankind.

Conceptions of Equal Educational Opportunities

During the first decade of statehood, between 1948–1957, primary school education was guided by the conception of formal equality, namely, equal budgetary inputs to the schools and uniform administrative and pedagogic measures with relation to the number of students in classrooms, number of hours and days of learning, and methods of teacher training and teachers' qualifications. The aim of this policy was to create a common and uniform elementary school for all children. The school was designated to serve as a melting pot, in which children shaped their identification with the Israeli-Jewish culture, learned the Hebrew language, and acquired basic educational skills in order to integrate in the evolving Israeli society as productive citizens. The underlying assumption of formal equality in education was that due to the uniformity and equality of educational inputs, educational and achievement outputs were to be equal as well. This approach ignored the heterogeneity of cultures and values of different student bodies and the many difficulties they had to cope with as children of new immigrants. A more differential approach was rejected by the minister of Education and Culture because it was considered to be incompatible with the norms and values of the national consensus, according to which all children are equal and deserve the same treatment. The words of B. Z. Dinur, the Minister of Education and Culture, are illuminating in this context. He claimed that "we do not want to establish two levels of schools. . . . I am convinced that all the children of Israel. . .   are able to reach this program. . . . The intellectual and cultural equality of all children in Israel must be our ideal" (1948). A strong centralized educational administration was developed in order to implement this policy.

The educational output of this policy was twofold. On one hand, the foundations for the physical absorption of 80,000 immigrant children into the school system were laid; the number of schools increased five times and the number of teachers increased four times; 10,000 new classrooms were built and equipped for the student population, which numbered 100,000 in 1948, and increased to 500,000 until 1957 (Avidor, 1958). On the other hand, the failure of educational and academic achievements of immigrant children became apparent. Children who immigrated from Asian and African countries lagged behind children from Western countries. The former did not acquire reading and writing skills during their first years of schooling; a deficiency that accumulated and carried over to the subsequent higher stages of education. It should be noted that the waves of immigration since statehood changed the demographic composition of Israel. Before statehood the proportion of Occidentals (*Ashkenazim*) in the population was 78%, compared to 22% of Orientals (*Sephardim*). Ten years later the percentages changed to 52% Occidentals and 48% Orientals (Sikron, 1960). As the family size of the Orientals was usually bigger than that of the Occidentals, children of Asian-African origin tended to be overrepresented in the primary schools in relation to their numbers in the population. The academic failures of Oriental children in school were attributed to environmental factors, such as, situations of crisis familiar to new immigrants; difficult socioeconomic conditions, such as poverty, density of housing, and different patterns of culture, norms, and values. But the schools themselves were also charged with the responsibility for the failure of the new student population. The teachers, many of whom were unqualified, had no previous experience in dealing with Oriental immigrants; nor were there adequate textbooks available or appropriate methods of teaching known. In 1958, Zalman Aran, the minister of Education and Culture, presented the problem to Parliament, which became acquainted with it for the first time (*The Words of Parliament*, 1959). Since then, the academic failure of Oriental children has become a critical issue, known as the problem of "disadvantaged children" (*teunei tipuach*) (Minkowich, 1969).

During the second decade of statehood, from 1958–1967, the formal equality approach was rejected by the primary school system because of its failure to raise the educational and academic level of the disadvantaged student populations and to narrow the gap between them and children from stronger segments of society, mainly from Occidental origin. The new policy of equality was based on a differential approach to different student groups and set in motion a broad spectrum of affirmative actions in favor of disadvantaged students. They were officially defined as students who needed additional help and attention and more resources than ordinary students. In parallel, the Ministry of Education and Culture identified schools with high percentages of Oriental children, whose levels of academic achievement were below the national median norms and whose teachers were poorly qualified. These schools received special treatment on the administrative level, as well as on the pedagogic level. They received additional hours of education—their school year was extended, and the norms in their passing examination from elementary to secondary school were lowered. Since 1955 the ministry administered a nationwide examination, *seker*, to all students in the last year of elementary school in order to select talented students for secondary education.

On the pedagogical level, new methods in the instruction of reading and writing were developed—homogeneous learning groups were established, a less-demanding curriculum was proposed, and special textbooks were compiled. In addition, many enrichment activities were administered in the areas of art, sport, and social skills (Adiel, 1970). In spite of the new approach to equality in education, and in spite of the various efforts invested in disadvantaged student populations, the results were by no means unequivocal. On the one hand, the new approach testified to the commitment of the state to the ideal of equality in education and to the upgrading of its weaker student population. There was an increase from 6.6% of the government's budget in 1954 to 11% in 1964 (Ministry of Education and Culture, 1974). On the other hand, the new approach stigmatized a whole segment of the student population, as being of lower academic ability and achievement, and worst of all, it linked the phenomenon of disadvantaged students to Oriental ethnicity. An objective evaluation of the outcomes did not show a significant improvement in academic achievements. The educational and academic gap between disadvantaged students and other students neither closed nor narrowed. Even worse, sometimes the new approach fostered expectations for the weaker students, and when these expectations were not fulfilled, as happened often, the students became even more frustrated (Kleinberger, 1969). Many explanations for the failure of the new approach were suggested. Some of these suggestions blamed the administrative measures, which were not accompanied by important pedagogic steps; others thought that the system did not have enough knowledge of the process of teaching disadvantaged student populations, and that compensatory educational interventions might not be the appropriate solution to the problem (Ladson-Billings, 1995). Aran, the minister of Education and Culture, voiced the disappointment of those in the educational system. He focused on the failure to raise the educational and academic level of disadvantaged student populations, in spite of the numerous and varied efforts invested. He initiated a new approach, which resulted in the Reform of Education.

The reform was prepared by a process which continued from the beginning of the 1960s until 1968. It consisted of three stages and was based on political and pedagogical considerations (Schmida, 1987). During the first stage, the consultations took place within the Ministry of Education and Culture. In 1963, Aran appointed a public committee to examine the need and possibility of the extension of the Compulsory Education Law for two additional years. Finally, in 1966, Parliament appointed a committee in order to examine the structure of primary and postprimary education (*The Parliament Report*, 1971). In 1968 Parliament voted by a majority of sixty-nine to three in favor of the reform, with eighteen abstentions (*The Words of Parliament 1968*, 2929), which meant the whole educational system would be overhauled. The implications of the reform were mainly directed at postprimary education, but some of them applied to primary education as well. Primary education was recommended to be of six years duration, followed by six years of postprimary schooling. Another recommendation related to the need to raise the levels of teacher training in order to improve the level of instruction at all stages of the system. The assumption was that the academic and educational achievements of the students would rise in parallel; the educational gap between the various student populations would be narrowed, and the integration of disadvantaged students into the mainstream of society would be enhanced.

The process of the reform had to overcome many obstacles that influenced the change of the primary school structure. At the outset, the process was intense, but it declined from year to year. Actually, in the 1990s the dual structure of primary education still exists: the eight-year primary school functions in addition to the six-year primary school. In the 1990s, only about 60% of students in the 12–15 year age group learn in the new structured schools (Ministry of Education and Culture, 1993) because of the different attitudes, which varied from enthusiasm to strong objection, of the local authorities toward the new educational structure (Schmida and Sherzer, 1991).

Since the Reform

The reform, which was directed mainly toward the stage of postprimary education, influenced the stage of primary education beyond the number of years it entailed. It seems as if this stage, which was imbued mainly with egalitarian orientations and emphasized the uniting mechanisms more than the divisive ones, entered an era of changing orientation. At least the notion of equality in primary school education was not unanimously accepted anymore. The changes were rooted in internal processes of the Israeli society as well as in external influences, especially those originating from the United States. The changes were identifiable in various directions; their common denominator was the parents' will to be more involved in their children's education and to gain more control and power over it. One of the issues was the parents' degree of freedom as to the choice of schools for their children. The laws of education did not confer parents with any official standing; they were restricted to zones of registration, in which they could choose between schools belonging to either the general educational stream, the religious stream, or that of the ultra-orthodox movement. Following the parliamentary decision of the Reform in Education, the zones of registration were determined more strictly, and the freedom to choose between schools was more limited. The limitation which was placed on parents' choice of schools was aimed to ensure greater heterogenization of student bodies within the schools. But this limitation provoked parents' counterreactions, who since the middle of the 1970s were searching for loopholes to circumvent this limitation to be able to choose the "better" schools, in their eyes, than those to which they were assigned (Friedman, 1974).

Parents also attempted to gain control over curricular contents. The process started during the 1970s and intensified during the following decades. It began with "gray education," namely enrichment programs in expressive activities and in academic curricular subjects (Bar-Siman-Tov and Langerman, 1988), and culminated in the establishment of separate and distinctive schools. Gray education was financed by Parents' Associations, mainly in the more established parts of the country. The gray education programs were anchored in the Law of National Education (1953), which authorized the parents to add curricular contents to the official curriculum at their expense. In spite of the legal base, it was not implemented until the 1980s. Students from weaker socioeconomic populations did not always participate in additional studies because of their parents' inability to meet the required payments. The 1980s witnessed an additional phenomenon in the same direction, namely, the establishment of "distinctive schools." They differed from regular public schools because of specially defined curricular contents, such as schools for the arts or natural sciences; on the basis of ideological and moral orientations, such as schools which emphasized the values of the Labor Party or Jewish liberal values; or on the basis of special pedagogic conceptions, such as experimental and open schools (Shapira, 1988).

The distinctive schools were also located in better-off neighborhoods, and although the initiation came from the parents, they were supported by local educational authorities and the Ministry of Education and Culture. The distinctive schools were obliged to absorb 30% of the disadvantaged student population, but due to the high standard of entrance examinations, this requirement was not fully observed. Three phenomena; parental choice, gray education, and distinctive schools, testified to the tension between the two orientations—equality versus excellence—on the primary school level. The advocates of the egalitarian approach conceived these phenomena as segregative mechanisms, which emphasized the socioeconomic differences within the student population and enlarged the academic and educational gap between them. The advocates of a more elitist approach praised the processes as reflecting the new liberal direction of education, which was also prevailing in the United States (Coons and Sugerman, 1980). According to them, these schools were more effective, functioned on a higher level, and created social school solidarity (Levine and Doyle, 1990). In addition these schools gained in pedagogical and administrative authority, and parents' involvement increased.

During the 1990s, because of growing opposition to these initiatives from the wider public, as well as from professional circles, no further steps were taken in this direction.

Disadvantaged Students

Various research projects evaluating the different programs and approaches, which were enacted during the 1950s and 1960s in order to raise the academic and educational level of the weaker student populations in primary schools, did not indicate any significant progress of the target population (Minkovitz, Davis, and Bashi, 1977; Peleg and Adler, 1977; Adler and Sever, 1984). At the end of the 1960s it became evident that the provision of additional help to the existing individual schools by itself was unsatisfactory. Consequently, a more comprehensive approach was considered, namely, changes in the nature of the schools, modifications in the curricula, alternative methods of teaching, changes in the composition of student bodies, and upgrading of teacher training (Bashi, 1985). The underlying working assumption was that the lower the chances of relevant student groups to reach the median level of academic achievement, the more resources the schools required. Concomitantly, not only was the mere fact of disadvantageousness determined, but also its depth. The fact that the vast majority of disadvantaged students were of Oriental origin exposed the society to the danger of identifying Orientals as "low achievers" (Yogev, 1988). In order to determine the eligibility of the schools to be included in the category of disadvantaged schools, three indexes were composed over the years. The first index was implemented during the years 1963–1973; it was based on achievement criteria, namely, the grades in the screening test, the *seker*, and grades in Hebrew, and arithmetic in the fourth grade. The additional criteria were social markers, such as, Oriental origin, years of immigration, and the quality of teaching staff with relation to years of experience and levels of qualifications (Algerbali, 1970). Following the abolishment of the screening examinations, the index was changed and the achievement criteria were eliminated. Since 1974 "disadvantageous" was determined by the father's country of origin, his level of education, and the number of children in the family. Schools were eligible for additional resources on the basis of the percentage of students who were defined as disadvantaged (Egozi, 1977). The index was changed again in 1994, due to changes which the Israeli society underwent, such as, a reduction in the number of children born in Oriental countries, an increase in the general level of education, and a reduction in large-sized families. The new index was composed of the socioeconomic status of the student population, their parents, and the functional distance of the school from the center of the country (Ministry of Education, Culture and Sport, 1994). The last criterion became the cornerstone of the policy of the new department within the ministry—the Department of Educational Care and Welfare. This department focused its activities mainly on new settlements and poor neighborhoods, thus adopting the conception that the criteria for defining the target population should be related to social and ethnic factors. The underlying assumption was that the educational gap was rooted in environmental and cultural factors, which have to be treated directly.

A summary of primary education highlights its major developments. Almost all the children in the relevant age groups attend school, and the percentage of dropouts decreased significantly over the years. The administrative and pedagogical staffs in the schools are better qualified than previously. The educational level of the parents, who were educated in the Israeli school system including the primary school, rose. Investment in weaker student populations increased, in relation to budget, hours of learning, buildings, facilities, and auxiliary pedagogic equipment. Still, schools in well-established areas have priority over schools for the disadvantaged, in spite of the additional resources invested. They have more qualified and experienced resources, and know how to take better advantage of the resources at hand, in addition to the resources which the parents themselves provide.

This chapter has examined some of the historical, philosophical, and social foundations of the first stages of the educational system. These foundations have paved the way to free, compulsory primary education for all, based upon the notion of equal educational opportunities. The following chapter explores the next stage in the educational ladder, namely, postprimary education, as well as its evolving function, structure, and characteristics.

BIBLIOGRAPHY

Adiel, S. (1970). "A decade of activities for the disadvantaged." In *A decade of activities for the disadvantaged.* Jerusalem: Ministry of Education and Culture (Hebrew).

Adler, H., and R. Sever (1984). *Guidelines for the analysis and planning of the educational care (Tipuah) in Israel.* Jerusalem: Research Institute for Innovations in Education, The Hebrew University (Hebrew).

Algerbali, M. (1970). "Dimensions to characterize the social composition of the schools and the method to allocate budget of educational care in Israel." *Megamot, 21,* 219–227 (Hebrew).

Arnon, A. (1948). "The Hebrew education in Palestine and its problems." *The Hebrew education in the exiles.* Jerusalem: Association for Books' Publication of the Hebrew University (Hebrew).

Avidor, M. (1957). *Education in Israel.* Jerusalem: Youth and Hehalutz Department of the Zionist Organization (Hebrew).

Avidor, M. (1958). *Decade of education (1948–1958).* Jerusalem: Publication of the Ministry of Education and Culture (Hebrew).

Azariahu, J. (1929). In D. Kimhi (ed.), *The jubilee book of the teachers' union, 1906–1928.* Jerusalem: The Center of the Teachers' Union in Palestine (Hebrew).

Bar-Siman-Tov, R., and S. Langerman (1988). *Additional curriculum with parents' budget in primary schools.* Jerusalem: Henrietta Szold Institute (Hebrew).

Bashi, J. (1985). "The primary education." In R. Ackerman, A. Carmon, and D. Zucker (eds.), *Education in an evolving society: Schooling in Israel.* Jerusalem: Hakibbutz Hameochad, Van-Lier Institute (Hebrew).

Bentwich, J. (1965). *Education in Israel.* London: Routledge and Kegan Paul.

Ben-Yehuda, B. (1973). "The history of education in Palestine until the establishment of the State." In H. Ormean (ed.), *The Education in Israel.* Jerusalem: Ministry of Education and Culture (Hebrew).

Book of Laws (Reshumot) (1949). Issue 26, 18.9.1949, pp. 287–292, "Law of Mandatory Learning" (Hebrew).

Book of Laws (Reshumot) (1953). Issue 131, 20.8.1953, p. 137, "The State Education Law" (Hebrew).

Coons, J., and M. Sugerman (1980). *Education by choice.* Berkeley, CA: University of California.

Dinur, B. Z. (1948). "Values and ways." *Urim* (Hebrew).

Egozi, M. (1977). *The student composition in primary education according to origin, father education and size of family.* Jerusalem: Ministry of Education and Culture (Hebrew).

Finkelstein, B. (ed.). (1979). *Regulated children, liberated children: Education in psycho-historical perspective.* New York: Psychohistory Press.

Friedman, J. (1974). *Formal and real zones of registration for formal schools.* Jerusalem: Institute for Urban and Regional Studies (Hebrew).

Government Yearbook 5745 (1984–85). (1985). Jerusalem: Government Printer (Hebrew).

Hewes, D. W. (1980). "The Froebelian kindergarten as an international movement." *ERIC*, Ed. 186125.

Hiner, N. R. (1983). "Domestic cycles: History of childhood and family." In John H. Best (ed.), *Historical inquiry in education.* Washington, DC: The American Educational Research Association, pp. 265–281.

HMSO (1946). *The system of education of the Jewish community in Palestine.* Report of the Commission of Inquiry, appointed by the Secretary of State for the Colonies, London, p. 10.

Horowitz, D., and M. Lissak (1972). *From Yishuv to state.* Tel Aviv: Am Oved (Hebrew).

Hunt, J. (1971). "Early childhood learning." In Lee C. Deighton (ed.), *The encyclopedia of education,* Vol. 3. New York: Macmillan.

Inhelder, B., and J. Piaget (1958). *The growth of logical thinking.* New York: Basic Books.

Iram, Y., and S. Krim (1989). "A collective biography of the Hebrew national school teachers during the first aliyah, 1882–1903." *Hebeitim Behinuch (Aspects of Education).* Ramat Gan: Bar-Ilan University, pp. 51–66 (Hebrew).

Kleinberger, A. F. (1969). *Society, schools and progress in Israel.* Oxford: Pergamon Press.

Kremer, L. (1973). "The primary school." In H. Ormean (ed.), *The education in Israel.* Jerusalem: Ministry of Education and Culture (Hebrew).

Ladson-Billings, G. (1995). "Toward a theory of culturally relevant pedagogy." *American Educational Research Journal, 32(3),* pp. 465–491.

Lamm, Z. (1973). "Ideological tensions—Struggles over the aims of education." In H. Ormean (ed.), *The education in Israel.* Jerusalem: Ministry of Education and Culture (Hebrew).

Lamm, Z. (1985). "The Israeli teacher: Routinization of a mission." In R. Ackerman, A. Carmon, and D. Zucker (eds.), *Education in an evolving society: Schooling in Israel.* Jerusalem: Hakibbutz Hameochad, Van-Lier Institute (Hebrew).

Levine, M., and D. Doyle (1990). "Magnet schools: Choice and quality in public education." *Phi-Delta Kappan, 66,* 265–270.

Lifshitz, E. M. (1947). "Haheder." *Ketavim,* Vol. 1 (Hebrew).

Ministry of Education and Culture, Central Committee of the Performance of the Reform. (1970). *The recommendations of the committee of the examination of the primary and postprimary structure of education.* Jerusalem (Hebrew).

Ministry of Education and Culture. (1974). *The education system in the mirror of numbers.* Jerusalem: Department of Planning (Hebrew).

Ministry of Education and Culture. (1979). *Report for the years 1978–1979.* Jerusalem (Hebrew).

Ministry of Education and Culture. (1981). *Report for the years 1979–80 to 1980–81.* Jerusalem (Hebrew).

Ministry of Education and Culture, Administration of Economics and Budgets. (1993). *The education system in the mirror of numbers.* Jerusalem (Hebrew).

Ministry of Education, Culture and Sport, Office of the Chief Scientist. (1994). *The index of educational care, principles of allocation.* Jerusalem (Hebrew).

Ministry of Education, Culture and Sport. (1995). *Report for the years 1994–1995 (5757).* Jerusalem (Hebrew).

Minkowich, A. (1969). *The disadvantaged child: Problems of diagnosis, etiology and rehabilitation.* Jerusalem: School of Education of the Hebrew University and the Ministry of Education and Culture (Hebrew).

Minkowich, A., D. Davis, and J. Bashi (1977). *Evaluation of educational achievements in the elementary school in Israel.* Jerusalem: Hebrew University (Hebrew).

The Parliament Report. (1971). The Parliamentary Committee of the Examination of the Primary and Postprimary Education in Israel (1966–68). Jerusalem (Hebrew).

Peleg, R., and H. Adler (1977). "Compensatory education in Israel: Conceptions, attitudes and trends." *American Psychologist, 32,* 945–958.

Rieger, E. (1940). *The Hebrew education in Palestine: Aim and program.* Tel Aviv: Dvir (Hebrew), pp. 28–40

Schmida, M. (1987). *Equality and excellence: Educational reform and the comprehensive school.* Ramat Gan: Bar-Ilan University Press (Hebrew).

Schmida, M., and M. Sherzer (1991). "Between equality and excellence during the 80s in the educational system in Israel." *Studies in the administration and organization of education,* No. 17. School of Education of Haifa University (Hebrew).

Shapira, R. (1988). "Educational and social distinctiveness." *The planning of the policy of education.* Jerusalem: Ministry of Education and Culture, the Pedagogical Secretariat (Hebrew).

Sikron, M. (1960). "Demographic structure of Israel with emphasis on children and youth." *Child and youth welfare in Israel.* Jerusalem: Henrietta Szold Institute (Hebrew).

Smilansky, M., S. Weintraub, and Y. Hanegbi (eds.). (1960). *Child and youth welfare in Israel.* Jerusalem: Henrietta Szold Institute (Hebrew).

Stanner, R. (1963). *The legal basis of education in Israel.* Jerusalem: Ministry of Education and Culture (Hebrew).

Twersky, J. (ed.). (1963). *Knowledge and practice in education: A book in memory of A. Arnon.* Tel Aviv: The Public Board (Hebrew).

The Words of Parliament. (1959). Vol. 26 (Hebrew).

The Words of Parliament. (1968). Vol. 52 (Hebrew).

Yogev, A. (1988). "The policy of education in Israel toward the advancement of students from weak social groups." Jerusalem: Ministry of Education and Culture, the Pedagogical Secretariat (Hebrew).

Chapter 3

Postprimary Education

The postprimary educational system developed during the period of the Yishuv. By statehood forty academic high schools and seventeen vocational and agricultural schools already existed. From the beginning this stage of education was occupied with two major issues: the type of postprimary schooling, academic or vocational, and the number of years designated to this stage—four, five, or six. The academic high school was based on elitist selective orientations, and only children of parents who were able to pay tuition fees were admitted. At the end of this schooling, students sat for matriculation examinations, which were administered prestatehood by the Educational Department of the Vaad Leumi. Students who successfully passed these examinations were entitled to be admitted to higher academic education, thus turning "matriculation" into a status symbol and a "gatekeeper" of admission to the universities (Yogev and Ayalon, 1986).

Vocational and agricultural high schools were less selective in their policies of admission; they relied less on tuition fees because of financial support that they received from various public foundations. The studies in nonacademic high schools usually terminated with the final examinations, which were administered mainly by the schools themselves, who conceived their task as the preparation of youth for productive work and not for further studies.

The second central issue, the length of the postprimary educational stage, is connected with the structure of the educational system as a whole. This issue was debated in the elementary school system, represented by the Elementary Teacher Union, and in the postprimary educational system, which was supported by the universities. Already in 1907 the evolving Elementary Teacher Union decided upon an eight-year elementary school, whereas the first academic high schools, the Gymnasium Herzliyah in Tel Aviv-Yaffo, the Hebrew Gymnasium in Jerusalem, and the Academic High School, *Hareali*, in

Haifa, which had all been founded at the beginning of the century, functioned on a twelve-year basis. The schools were divided into four years of preparatory grades and eight years of academic high school (Ben-Yehuda, 1973). Consequently, two parallel structures of schooling developed: a highly selective system for the "few," mainly for the well-to-do populations, and another, a public system, for the majority. The dual system was heavily criticized because it reflected the social division of society (Rieger, 1940). After World War I, with the establishment of the central administrative authorities of the Yishuv, the conflict intensified. There was consensus with respect to the social danger inherent in the dual educational system and to the conception that postprimary education should extend the limits of four years. In parallel, the elementary school would be shortened from eight to six years, because it did not live up to the academic disciplinarian demands of the curricular subjects, nor did it answer the psychological developmental needs of youth, thus rendering, it was argued, the last two years of elementary schooling as superfluous. The debate continued until it was decided by the unanimous opposition of the Yishuv to the proposition of the Department of Education of the British Mandate. Consequently the Yishuv agreed on the eight-year elementary school, followed by a four-year postelementary school, whereas only few private academic high schools retained the six-six year structure (Ben-Yoseph, 1974).

THE FIRST DECADE OF STATEHOOD: 1948–58

With statehood and the establishment of the Ministry of Education and Culture, the legal base of postprimary education was rooted in the British Mandatory Ordinance of Education from 1933, which authorized the minister of Education and Culture to issue regulations with regard to schooling in public and supported institutions. The majority of postprimary schools accepted the authority of the ministry with regard to curricula, qualifications of professional staff, and matriculation examinations. But without a solid legal base, postprimary education was optional and expensive. David Ben-Gurion, the first prime minister of the new state, emphasized the need for the Law of Postprimary Education if Israel wanted to raise the educational level of the young generation, regardless of its ethnic origin or socioeconomic group (Ben-Gurion, 1951). Aran, the Minister of Education and Culture, shared Ben-Gurion's opinion, but postponed the actual beginning of the legal process, due to budget shortages, and mainly because he wanted to link the rise of mandatory learning age, which was stated by the Compulsory Education Law of 1949 at the end of the eight-year elementary school, with changes in the overall structure of the educational system, its contents, and framework. Meanwhile, the Ministry of Education and Culture introduced the system of graded tuition fees based on parental income. Since 1955 all graduates of elementary school underwent a screening test, *seker*, which entitled those who successfully passed to be admitted to high school with graded tuition fees. In 1960 the system of graded tuition fees extended to vocational high school, and also benefited students who failed the screening test. Thus, besides the financial advantages for the parents, the new system of payment added prestige to the academic high school, and deflated the already lower prestige of the nonacademic types of postprimary education. Consequently, a hierarchy of prestige was created in the postprimary educational system (Katz and Schmida, 1992). Moreover, students of Oriental background were underrepresented with relation to their percentages in the population, at the postprimary level in general, but especially in academic high schools. This process started during the period of the Yishuv and did not improve during the first decade of statehood. The numbers of Oriental students also decreased in all types of postprimary schooling with the rise in school grades.

THE SECOND DECADE OF STATEHOOD: 1958–68

During this period special attention was given to disadvantaged student populations at all levels of the system, but mainly at the postprimary stage because of its implications on the structure of the evolving Israeli society. The educational gap between Oriental and Western students increased, and consequently, the formal qualifications of the Orientals did not enable them to reach higher occupational positions and higher socioeconomic levels. This situation constituted a serious threat to the unity and solidarity of the young Israeli society. Three affirmative steps were taken during this decade to increase the chances of weaker student populations to achieve higher academic standards. The first step involved making the transition from the elementary to postelementary schools easier for disadvantaged students, by lowering the required norms for success in the screening test. Consequently, higher percentages of disadvantaged students were admitted to more prestigious high schools, but quite often they failed later within the schools.

The second step focused on the establishment of new types of postprimary schools, namely two- to three-year schools, with strong emphasis on vocational orientations. As these schools were planned mainly for the new towns and new settlements, they were stigmatized in a short time as second-rate educational institutions. A more fruitful approach was the first experiments with comprehensive high schools, which functioned as bilateral schools, housing both academic and vocational education under one roof. The main effort during this period was invested in the extension of vocational education, which was considered to suit the needs and talents of weaker student populations better than academic high schooling. Whereas the system of academic high schools increased only nine times, the system of vocational education expanded thirty times. An additional affirmative step was the establishment of enrichment centers and boarding schools for the more talented disadvantaged students. At the end of this period the minister of Education and Culture concluded that in spite of all the efforts invested in the educational system, the academic achievements of Oriental students did not improve significantly, and the gap between them and their Western counterparts did not close. He was convinced that only the change of the educational system's structure by means of a total reform would bring about the needed improvement.

THE REFORM IN EDUCATION: 1968–80

Aran, the minister of Education and Culture, initiated the process of reform in education to reach a twofold aim: to provide postprimary education with a solid legal base, and to change the structure of the educational system, namely, to shorten the period of elementary schooling to six years, and to extend the period of postprimary schooling from four to six years.

In 1966 Aran convinced Parliament to set up a commission to examine the structure of the primary and postprimary educational system. The committee accomplished its mission in 1968 and proposed two major recommendations: to extend the law of compulsory and free learning for two additional school years, grades 9 and 10, and to establish a junior high school, consisting of grades 7, 8, and 9, to be gradually developed into a six-year comprehensive high school. The screening test between elementary and postelementary schools would be abolished, and all students would be admitted to postprimary education without any process of selection. The Israeli Parliament adopted the recommendations with a vast majority and the reform went on its way. In 1977, according to the ministry's decree, two additional years, grades 11 and 12, were exempted from tuition fees, although not designed as compulsory studies (Parliament, 1978a). In parallel, an additional measure was taken to include working youth in postprimary education as well. According to the amendments to the Compulsory Education Law (Parliament, 1979), every employer of sixteen- and seventeen-year-olds and their parents were obliged to inform the local authority.

The reform and its additional appendices suggested a radical change of the whole education system, instead of the partial and more sporadic changes of the previous decades. It offered changes in the allocation of resources for the different stages of education for the percentage of students participating, with special emphasis on disadvantaged student populations (Schmida, 1988). The process of implementing the reform was quite satisfactory during the 1970s, when about twenty-five integrative junior high schools were established in a year, but it declined significantly during the following decades, until it reached almost total stagnation in the 1980s and 1990s. The causes of decline could be pinpointed to three areas. First, the legislative process of the reform was based on a national consensus, which was very difficult to reach in the Israeli pluralistic society. Aran achieved consensus among a vast majority of members from the various political parties in Parliament because of the many concessions he made, which weakened the power of the parliamentary decision. For example, an important concession was made to the local authorities, which granted free choice as to the educational structure within their jurisdiction.

Many of the local authorities, sometimes due to internal circumstances, preferred to adhere to the old structure and reject the new one. The second area was a shift in the climate of the Israeli society during the 1980s and 1990s, from a more egalitarian orientation toward a more elitist one (Iram and Schmida, 1993). Finally, the economic difficulties that the state experienced and the cuts from educational budgets and land shortages restricted the possibility of building new schools. In spite of these drawbacks, statistics indicate that about 60% of the relevant age group attend integrative junior high schools, and 90% of youth attend one of the postprimary educational frameworks (Ministry of Education and Culture, 1992). In summary, postprimary education underwent the process of democratization toward postprimary education for all. This stage was considered the natural continuation of the stage of elementary schooling, crucial for the extension and deepening of a wide cultural and educational base. The common integrative junior high school moderates the allocative function of the school system and postpones it to a later stage, whereas the different types of senior high schools—academic, comprehensive, and vocational—represent the stage of sorting and selection of students.

THE ACADEMIC HIGH SCHOOL

The academic high school is the most notable type of schooling among the three postprimary educational frameworks (Schmida and Katz, 1994). This type of school was founded on the assumption that only a small percentage of the student population has the intellectual talent to cope with academic and abstract subjects, and that only 25% of postprimary education graduates continue their studies in academic higher education. Accordingly, only about 40% of elementary school graduates should be admitted to academic high schools. Furthermore, it is assumed that the desired abilities of academic high school students, such as intellectual talent, curiosity, diligence, and sense of intellectual adventure, are identifiable at an early age. At the outset of the development of academic high schools, the gymnasia selected students at the young age of ten, following four years of primary education. During the 1950's, the age of selection rose to fourteen, when the screening test, *seker*, was administered by the Ministry of Education and Culture toward the end of elementary schooling. Only students who passed the *seker* with success were admitted to academic high schools. Of the remaining students, about 50% pursued vocational or agricultural training, either in schools or as apprentices on the job. The result was a rigid division between two groups of youth: those studying and those working. This division correlated with sociological characteristics, such as socioeconomic level, ethnic origin, and seniority in the country. The academic high schools were populated mainly by students of Western origin who belonged to middle and higher socioeconomic strata. Students from lower socioeconomic levels, mainly of Oriental origin and new immigrants, occupied the nonacademic frameworks of postprimary education, namely vocational schools and vocational learning tracks in comprehensive high schools.

The academic high school is demanding and places heavy intellectual pressure on its student population. Students have a large number of learning hours per week, a heavy homework load, and an increasing number of examinations from year to year, until the final examination, the matriculation examination, at the end of grade 12. In order to cope with these demands, students have to be highly self-disciplined and invest years of hard work, often at the expense of leisure activities.

The assumptions underlying postprimary education changed with the parliamentary decision on the Reform in Education in 1968, which delayed the allocation of students to different types of postprimary educational frameworks until the age of fifteen, at the end of grade 9. According to the Law of Postprimary Education, every student was entitled to receive a broad and comprehensive general education in the curricular areas of literature, languages, mathematics, and the sciences, at least until the end of junior high school. Consequently, increased numbers of weaker student populations aspired to gain entry to academic high schools, which tried to adapt themselves to a certain degree to these students' needs and capacities. In parallel, vocational schools added more prestigious routes of training for manual labor occupations, which prepared students for middle-range occupations, such as technicians and electricians.

But still the academic route of high school remained the most eminent type of postprimary education, mainly because of the matriculation examination. This examination is the sine qua non for admission to a university and serves as the basis for acquiring higher occupational positions, which are accompanied by higher socioeconomic status.

From the beginning the academic high school was charged with a twofold mission: namely, to raise its students to universal cultural and scientific standards, and to provide them with norms of modern behavior and proper social skills for formal and informal social relations. In addition, these highly educated students were to be imbued with values of responsibility and commitment to the evolving Israeli society. Between these two sets of values existed an inherent conflict, which was dealt with differently over the years. During the prestate period, the idea of academic studies being mandatory in order to reach scholarship was considered contradictory to the concept of "pioneer"—*halutz*—which was cherished by the political leadership of the Yishuv (Eisenstadt, 1967; Horowitz and Lissak, 1977). The halutz was devoted to hard physical labor, mainly in agriculture, and was quite opposed to values of academic learning, especially learning toward diplomas. The professional high school teachers, who were highly educated, strongly advocated the idea of scholarship. They were instilled with responsibility for their intellectual mission and assumed their vocation to be highly prestigious, well beyond their real status in society (Ben-David, 1957).

During the first decade of statehood, a compromise between the universal intellectual and the social national missions was suggested and coined by the phrase, "the serving elite." According to Ernst Simon (1962), professor of education at Hebrew University, the aim of the academic high school is to educate the intellectual as an "elite," who rather than serving his own interests, serves those of society as a whole. Simon acknowledges various other types of elite groups—such as moral, artistic, technical, and social—but he ranks them in a hierarchical order, with the intellectual academic elite at the top. Chen and Segal (1985) draw attention to the fact that the sociocultural gap between the various ethnic groups was completely ignored by the academic high school system during the 1960s, although it was already well known that Oriental students and new immigrants did not attend this type of school.

The different approaches to high school education were also manifested in the educational terminology. The advocates of "secondary education for all" argued that all educational frameworks of postprimary education should be called "secondary schools," whereas the elitists were ready to confer this title upon academic secondary schools only. The different orientations toward the second stage in education alternated throughout the decades of Israeli statehood and shifted concomitantly with societal changes, moving back and forth between more egalitarian orientations to more elitist ones. But in spite of the recurrent changes in these orientations, the academic high school maintained its place at the top of postprimary education.

From the beginning, academic schooling was highly centralized, first by the educational administration of the Yishuv, and since statehood, by the Ministry of Education and Culture. In 1957 the first official curriculum was published (Ministry of Education and Culture, 1957) with the purpose of engaging the schools in a uniform national curricular framework. The highly demanding curriculum tried to balance between a universal scientific orientation and a Hebrew national orientation, as well as between a broad, comprehensive knowledge and values of tradition and renewal (Chen and Segal, 1985).

In 1976 the Ministry of Education and Culture issued a special curriculum, which specified the number of weekly hours in each subject, the amount of curricular material and its contents, the curricular demands of each unit, and its level of difficulty. By means of the many detailed instructions and regulations, which were to be overseen by supervisors within the school, the Ministry of Education and Culture played a decisive role in the daily life of academic high schools. The most central influential factor is the matriculation examination, which students take at the end of academic high school. The questions on the matriculation examination were composed by ministerial officials who act in the capacity of supervisors. The ministry also supervised the various functions of the schools, by evaluating students' academic achievements. The correlation between marks awarded by the schools' teachers and marks awarded in the external matriculation examinations were calculated, and with the increase in correlation, the academic prestige and independence of the school increased in parallel.

The Matriculation Examination

The first academic high schools, which were established before statehood, administered final examinations independently. According to the results, the schools issued final certifications. With the establishment of the British Mandate in Palestine, the schools requested its academic acknowledgment of these final examinations. The recognition was granted in 1926 and withdrawn in 1929, due to unsatisfactory standards of the examinations, according to the British. Instead, they recommended that students sit for the British Palestinian matriculation. This proposal was rejected by the Yishuv, and a special Board of the Jewish Academic High Schools was established, consisting of representatives from universities, the Jewish Agency, and the British Mandate. When negotiations with the British failed, their representatives were excluded, and in 1935 the board assumed the responsibility for writing matriculation questionnaires, evaluating them, and issuing matriculation certificates. With statehood, the format of the examinations from the Yishuv period was maintained, namely four obligatory examinations in Hebrew, Bible, English, and Mathematics, in addition to two other examinations in optional subjects. During the following decades, these examinations underwent many changes, reflecting the oscillations between egalitarian and elitist orientations toward secondary education (Levy, 1990). The changes were based on the recommendations of various committees which examined the topic (Ministry of Education and Culture, 1973, 1979, 1989, 1994). The recommendations centered mainly around the distribution of examinations over the years; the substitution of examinations for term papers; the balance between examinations administered by the ministry and those administered by the schools; the various combinations of subjects to be examined; and the degree of students' freedom to choose their subjects. The recommendations evolved in a circular fashion: after suggestions in 1978 to liberalize the process, namely to enlarge students' options to choose their subjects and not to have to study mathematics and chemistry as obligatory subjects, the process changed again in 1986, based upon the recommendations of another commission (Ministry of Education and Culture, 1979). The number of optional choices was restricted, and emphasis was put on students rendering services to the community. These restrictions were explained by the financial and technical difficulties that were involved in the preparation and evaluation of hundreds of different exam papers. Moreover, as a result of the process of liberalization, two categories of matriculation certificates were established: one prestigious, which was accepted by universities, and the other less prestigious, due to fewer units of learning and choice of easier subjects. The universities rejected the second type of matriculation. In 1993 an additional commission was established, that suggested a more equal balance between the examinations administered by the ministry and those by the schools themselves. The maximum number of examinations was set as seven—five examinations being obligatory and two being optional. Each subject was divided into three levels of difficulty: basic, regular, and accelerated. The overall structure of the system was modular and incremental, thus enabling students to progress from one level to another.

The recommendations of the various commissions were aimed at improving the system of matriculation examinations. No commission suggested their abolishment, despite the knowledge of their inherent disadvantages. Already Ben-Gurion (1954) was suspicious of the pursuit of high marks, which might be at the expense of a valuable education and the commitment to ideals. D. Pur (1989) identifies the negative effects of examinations on students' intrinsic motivation to study, on teacher–student relations and school climate, and on social aspects of education. Still, this system of examinations is considered overall to be the best and most reliable indicator of the levels of students' academic achievement. Moreover, all types of postprimary educational frameworks evaluate their achievements according to the standards of the matriculation exams. Seemingly, these factors outweigh the disadvantages inherent in the system, namely, the highly centralized curriculum; accelerated studies in order to cover the required material at the expense of depth and enrichment; feelings of anxiety and tension evoked in students; and psychological harm inflicted upon those students who fail. Each alternative suggested, such as examinations prepared by the universities, was considered worse than the already existing matriculation examination.

According to the latest statistics (personal communication with Chaim Navon, 1997), 75.3% of the total age group attend the final grade of high school, 61.2% are permitted by the schools to write the matriculation examinations, out of which only 37.9% pass. The majority of the successful students live in the centers and big towns of the country, whereas the percentage of failing students increases with distance from the center. These distant areas are populated mainly by weaker student populations and new immigrants. During the 1990s, various programs were developed to assist failing students to acquire the matriculation certificate. These programs were not very attractive to students, mainly because of their social stigma and the universities' hesitance to accept their graduates. Consequently, academic high schools remain the most prestigious type of postprimary education, and students who acquire the matriculation certificate are considered to be the future elite of Israeli society.

THE COMPREHENSIVE HIGH SCHOOL

Five major stages are identifiable in the development of the Israeli comprehensive high school. The years 1953–1963 can be considered the first stage, during which the essential elements of comprehensiveness were examined and the first experiments in comprehensiveness were administered in eleven high schools (Ministry of Education and Culture, 1966). The second stage covers the years 1963–1968, during which comprehensive schools were established by the state and its municipalities. Several committees of the Ministry of Education and Culture decided upon the establishment of comprehensive schools in settlement towns, and money was collected around the world for this purpose. Concomitantly, experts in comprehensiveness were invited. Professor Robin Pedley from Great Britain and Dr. Jonas Orring from Sweden came to teach a seminar addressing problems in comprehensive schooling. The period between 1968–1973 constituted the third stage in the history of comprehensive schools in Israel. In 1968 Parliament decided upon the Reform in Education, which changed the structure of elementary and postelementary education in Israel. The focus of this reform was the establishment of a six-year comprehensive high school. The years 1973–1988 represented a period of stagnation in the development of comprehensiveness. And 1988 heralded a new developmental stage with the establishment of integrated schools and educational parks. In the following discussion, the various stages of the development of the comprehensive high school will be presented and analyzed.

1953–1963: Decade of Investigation and Experimentation

During this decade, the first experiments with the new model of comprehensive schooling were conducted. The director general of the Ministry of Education and Culture described these experiments as "intuitive tourism of the comprehensive route" (personal communication with Chanoch Rinot, 1966). Eleven experimental high schools were established, which differed from the typical academic high schools in both their intake of more heterogeneous student populations, as well as their diversity of curricula. This differing structure was designed in order to meet the different talents and various areas of interests of students. The new type of schooling was usually the only type of postprimary schooling in the new towns and settlements, which were populated mainly by new immigrants.

Aran, the minister of Education and Culture between 1957–1961, expressed at a principals' conference in 1959 the fear that if students in new towns would not continue their studies in postprimary education, a hidden social bomb would explode in the state. Ben-Gurion (1962) also declared that the new State of Israel must provide the entire young generation with postelementary education, regardless of parents' socioeconomic status or ethnic origin.

1963–1968: The Institutionalization of Comprehensive Schools

During this period the Ministry of Education and Culture declared comprehensiveness its official education policy, particularly in the new settlements. Comprehensive schools were defined by the Standing Committee for postelementary education as institutions that accept almost all students in the relevant age groups and base their curriculum on various learning tracks and differing levels of studies. Thus, the Israeli comprehensive school became in essence a multilateral school, which is actually its name in official documents (Schmida and Katz, 1993).

In 1963 the ministry decided to carry out its policy of comprehensiveness and established more comprehensive schools in order to absorb 100,000 children from new towns in postprimary education. In 1964 the Israeli Education Fund was founded in the United States (The United Jewish Appeal, 1964) in order to raise money for new school buildings and to provide them with necessary facilities, such as libraries and laboratories. However, the development of the comprehensive school system was stalled, both by lack of funds and by the conflict of interest within the Ministry of Education and Culture, especially between the established departments of academic and vocational education. This conflict focused on issues such as the subordination of comprehensive schools within the ministry, the responsibility for the composition of curricula and their implementation, the composition of examinations, and the issuance of diplomas. When no agreement was reached, Aran, who gave high priority to the development of the new schools, disqualified the existing departments from dealing with the comprehensive schools and established a new administrative unit to take care of them. The policy of this unit was to base the comprehensive high school on six years, and to unify it as regarding supervision, principalship, teachers' qualifications, and salaries. Due to potent resistance from other ministerial departments, the new unit was denied its pedagogic responsibilities, which were divided between the departments of academic and vocational high schools, and which apparently affected the development of the new schools in the future. The new unit was limited to administrative aspects, such as budgets and physical facilities. This arrangement, which was initially considered as temporary, is still operating in the 1990s.

In 1964 an international symposium on comprehensiveness was convened in Jerusalem, which ushered this type of schooling into the center of educational thinking. Indeed, this symposium may be considered an important landmark in the development of comprehensive high schools. The symposium was documented by the Ministry of Education and Culture, and its final report formulated the essential elements of comprehensiveness and its guiding principles in practice. Comprehensiveness was now defined as a nonselective type of schooling in the intake of its student population; its curriculum was rich and diversified in order to advance heterogeneous student bodies according to their talents, abilities, inclinations, and areas of interest. Parity of esteem was to exist between academic and vocational study tracks, and mobility of students among the various tracks and levels of studies was to be made feasible, thus lowering the percentages of dropouts. Comprehensive schools were recommended not only for newer towns and settlements, but also for more established towns. Finally, the process of school integration was to be intensified, mainly by means of extracurricular activities. The practical guidelines that were derived from this educational approach referred to the change in the structure of the educational system; the determination of regional zones for students' enrollment in the schools; the diversification of curricula and the development of extracurricular activities; special in-service training programs for teachers; and the establishment of guidance programs for students. The main mission of comprehensive schools was the integration of various social groups into the mainstream of the evolving Israeli society.

During this decade the preparation for the reform in education began. The minister of Education and Culture was aware of the need to change the structure of the educational system, to raise the age of compulsory learning, and to integrate general studies with vocational training in one school (Words of Parliament, 1966). Two committees were established, the recommendations of which were ratified by the Israeli Parliament on July 2, 1968.

1968–1973: The Reform in Education—Legitimization of Comprehensiveness

The parliamentary decision to adopt the reform in education gave momentum to the development of comprehensive high schools. According to this decision, postprimary education would span a period of six years, divided into three years of junior high school and three years of senior high school. All the students would be transferred from the six-year primary school into the high school, without the processes of examination and selection. The decision recommended the six-year comprehensive high school as the most "suitable" and "desirable" structure of postprimary education, and preferred it to any other organizational framework. Student intake to the school would be based on predetermined zones of registration in order to ensure a heterogeneous student body for social integration. The curriculum would consist of diversified learning tracks of differing levels of ability. By the end of 1971 there were twenty comprehensive high schools in the educational system, and each of them comprised at least two academic and two vocational tracks, thus enabling learning on different levels. Characteristic of these schools was a strict division between the academic and vocational tracks. The first years following the parliamentary decision on the reform in education were years of momentum for comprehensiveness, but the process gradually slowed down to stagnation.

1973–1988: Period of Stagnation

During this period few new comprehensive schools were established. The existing postelementary schools absorbed junior high schools graduates, and the high achievers among them continued their studies in the academic high schools. Lower-achieving students presented a problem, since they were obliged by law (*Book of Laws*, 1978) to complete an additional year of studies and were not admitted to prestigious academic high schools. Consequently, local authorities, as well as the Ministry of Education and Culture, sought solutions to enable students of all levels of achievement to remain in school until the end of grade 12.

1988–1990s: A New Developmental Era

During this period plans were made to minimize the phenomenon of dropouts from high schools and to assist weaker student populations in passing their matriculation examinations successfully. Various experiments were conducted with integrated schools, which consisted of a three-year junior high school, affiliated with three-year senior high schools: academic, vocational, and comprehensive. The monolateral schools added new tracks of learning to the curriculum in order to retain their students for as long as possible. Monolateral schools also offered various options to prepare lower achievers for matriculation examinations. Plans were also made to construct large school campuses, modeled after educational parks, especially those in England (Pohland, 1988). This model is based upon a number of junior high schools, that feed into a senior high school, either academic, vocational, or comprehensive, and where each student is given the opportunity to fulfill his or her potential. The advocates of this program perceive the advantages as a big enterprise, whereas the opponents point to the dangers of solitude and alienation of students (Ish-Shalom and Schmida, 1993). At the end of the 1990s the educational parks have not yet materialized, and only about three campuses are functioning.

At the end of the 1990s only about two-hundred high schools, from a total of 602, are registered officially as "multilateral schools." The distinction between multilateral and comprehensive schools is rooted in the proximity or distance of the essential characteristics of the school from the ideal type of comprehensiveness (Schmida and Katz, 1993). The common denominator of both types of schooling—the multilateral and the comprehensive—is the nonselective intake of heterogeneous student populations and the offering of diverse curricula, both in contents and level of difficulty. The Israeli multilateral school fulfills both these conditions, but distances itself from ideal comprehensiveness by its strict division between academic and vocational learning tracks, thus inhibiting the process of social integration. A notable development is the incorporation of the spirit of comprehensiveness in the monolateral types of schooling, namely academic and vocational. These schools also try to adapt themselves to the needs of lower-achieving students and to keep them at school by means of various curricular programs. In parallel, they offer weaker students alternative learning options in order to assist them in passing all matriculation examinations successfully.

This chapter dealt with the transition from a mainly elitist and selective system of postprimary education to a system of secondary education for all. While this chapter discussed the first two types of secondary education, the academic and comprehensive high schools, the next chapter will address the third type of senior high school, namely, the vocational high school.

BIBLIOGRAPHY

Ben-David, Y. (1957). "The social status of the teacher in Israel." *Megamot, 8* (3), 221 (Hebrew).

Ben-Gurion, D. (1951). "High schooling for all," *Hed Hahinuch, 19*, 4–11 (Hebrew).

Ben-Gurion, D. (1954). *The mission of the young generation.* Tel Aviv: Alumim (Hebrew).

Ben-Gurion, D. (1962). "The project of our generation and its mission." *The Governmental Year Book.* Jerusalem: Government Printing Office (Hebrew).

Bentwich, J. (1960). *Education in the State of Israel.* Tel Aviv: Zezik.

Ben-Yehuda, B. (1973). "To the history of education in Palestine until statehood." in H. Ormean (ed.), *The education in Israel*, Ministry of Education and Culture, Jerusalem (Hebrew).

Ben-Yoseph, J. (1974). *Changes and chances in postprimary education.* Tel Aviv: Private Publication (Hebrew).

Book of Laws, 895, (April 14, 1978).

Chen, M., and H. Segal (1985). "The Hebrew academic education." In W. Ackerman, A. Carmon, and & D. Zucker (eds.), *Education in an evolving society: Schooling in Israel.* Tel Aviv: United Kibbutz and Van-Lier (Hebrew).

Eisenstadt, S. N. (1967). *Israeli society: Background, development, and problems.* Y. L. Hebrew University, Jerusalem: Magnes Publications (Hebrew).

Horowitz, D., and M. Lissak (1977). *From Yishuv to State.* Jerusalem: Am Oved, 149 (Hebrew).

Iram, Y., and M. Schmida (1993). "Recurring reforms and changes in the Israeli educational system: An analytical approach." *International Journal of Educational Development, 13(3)*, 217–226.

Ish-Shalom, H., and M. Schmida (1993). *Social revolution in Israel and in the world, secondary education for all: Essence, history and patterns of functioning.* Tel Aviv: Ramot (Hebrew).

Israel Education Fund. *Memorandum, explanation of USA capital fund campaign for education in Israel*, October 22, 1964.

Katz, Y. J., and M. Schmida (1992). "Institutional prestige and students' social orientations." *Education and Society, 10* (2), 93–97.

Levy, J. (1990). *Changes in the matriculation examination in Israel.* Jerusalem: Ministry of Education and Culture (Hebrew).

Ministry of Education and Culture. (1957). *Proposals for the curriculum of the academic high school.* Department of Academic Secondary Education, Jerusalem (Hebrew).

Ministry of Education and Culture. (1966). *The comprehensive school: Report of the debates concerning the comprehensive schools.* Jerusalem (Hebrew), 202–259.

Ministry of Education and Culture. (1973). *The report of the commission of the introduction of changes in the format of the matriculation examinations.* Jerusalem (Hebrew).

Ministry of Education and Culture. (1976). *The senior high school—Principles of studies and examinations.* Issue of Director General, Special Issue I, Jerusalem (Hebrew).

Ministry of Education and Culture. (1977). *The circular of the Director General, special circular A, the senior high school.* Jerusalem. (Hebrew).

Ministry of Education and Culture. (1979). *The report of the commission of the examination of the topic of the matriculation examinations and the matriculation diplomas (the Shield Commission),* Jerusalem (Hebrew).

Ministry of Education and Culture. (1986). "The circular of the commission of postprimary education." *Proposal for changes in the format of the matriculation examinations.* May 1986 (Hebrew).

Ministry of Education and Culture. (1989). *The circular of the Director General, special circular13, the Format of the matriculation examinations.* Jerusalem. (Hebrew).

Ministry of Education and Culture. (1992). *The educational system in the mirror of numbers,* Jerusalem.

Ministry of Education and Culture (1994). "Report of the commission of the examination of the format of the matriculation and final examinations." *Matriculation 2000,* Jerusalem (Hebrew).

Navon, C. (1997). Personal communication. Ministry of Education and Culture, Wing of Educational and Social Services, Head of Department of Educational Centers, Jerusalem.

Parliament. (1971). *The Report, the parliamentary committee for the examination of the primary and postprimary education structure, 1966–68.* Jerusalem, 122–123 (Hebrew).

Parliament. (1978a). "Mandatory law of studies," *Reshumot,* 895 (Hebrew).

Parliament (1978b). "Amendment No. 11 to compulsory law of education." *Book of Laws,* 895.

Parliament. (1979). *Amendments of compulsory state education* (Hebrew).

Pohland, P. A. (1988). "English Village College: Rural education alternative." *Journal of Rural and Small Schools, 2(3).*

Pur, D. (1989). *In favor of equality in education.* Jerusalem: Bet Berl College (Hebrew).

Rieger, E. (1940). *Hebrew education in Palestine: The aim and the program.* Tel Aviv: Dvir Publications (Hebrew).

Rinot, C. (1966). Personal communication. Jerusalem: Ministry of Education and Culture, Director General.

Schmida, M. (1988) "The educational reform in Israel: Twenty years later." *Journal of International and Comparative Education, 3(8),* 325–352.

Schmida, M., (ed.), (1965). *The comprehensive school: A report on the discussions about comprehensive schools with Dr. Pedley and Dr. Orring.* Jerusalem: Ministry of Education and Culture (Hebrew).

Schmida, M., and Y. Katz (1993). "A Guttman scale factor structure of comprehensiveness." *Educational and Psychological Measurement, 53(1),* 225–232.

Schmida, M., and Y. J. Katz (1994). "School prestige and students' social orientations." *Studies in Education,* 59–60, 125–132 (Hebrew).

Simon, E. A. (1962). "On the goals of secondary education in Israel." In M. Shapira (ed.), *Theory and practice in secondary education.* Jerusalem: Secondary School of the Hebrew University (Hebrew).

The United Jewish Appeal. (1964). *National leadership conference on education in Israel.* Biltmore Hotel, New York City.

Words of Parliament. (March 28, 1966) (Hebrew).

Yogev, A., and H. Ayalon (1986). "High school attendance in a sponsored multi-ethnic system: The case of Israel." In A. C. Kerckhoff (ed.), *Research in the sociology of education and socialization,* Vol. 6. Greenwich, CT: JAI Press.

Chapter 4

Vocationalism

HISTORICAL BACKGROUND

Modern education in Israel commenced in the middle of the nineteenth century mainly with the establishment of schools with vocational orientation (Elboim-Dror, 1986; Iram, 1977; Kleinberger, 1969). At the turn of the century, as a result of immigration from European countries and improving economic conditions, schools with a more academic orientation became dominant, such as the gymnasium and the real-schule, at the expense of vocational schools. Indeed, very few vocational schools existed in pre-state Israel (Rieger, 1945; Yonai, 1992). In 1948 vocational education comprised 20% of all secondary schools (Avidor, 1957). Following the establishment of the State of Israel in 1948, which brought large waves of immigrants, particularly from the Middle East and North Africa, the entire educational system rapidly expanded, especially the vocational system. The reason for the unproportional growth of vocational education was rooted in the understanding, which prevailed in the middle of the 1950s, that a traditional academic education was apparently inappropriate for a larger number of youth from Oriental and lower socioeconomic backgrounds, and unsuccessful in providing them with the avenues for upward social and occupational mobility.

The expansion of vocational education in Israel was in contradiction with universal tendencies that predominated during the years 1950–1975. A general decline in vocational education was discernible, and the educational system was moving away from the training of a more differentiated workforce, toward the preparation of a more generally educated citizenry. In less-developed countries, such tendencies were even greater than in developed countries (Ben-Avot, 1983).

The marked expansion of vocational education in Israel corresponded to the concept of providing a secondary education for all, which was embodied in the Reform Act of Education in 1968. It was also assumed that the expansion of vocational education would serve the needs of the newly established state's growing economy.

The expansion of vocational education during the 1960s was also in response to the industrial and defense sectors, which demanded a more technology-oriented labor force. There was a need for experts in specialized fields, such as electronics, metal work, and mechanics. The vocational educational system was now expected to provide training in these skills.

During the following decades, vocational education underwent many changes, but did not decline in terms of student enrollment. In 1991 postprimary education comprised about 60% vocational education (Ministry of Education and Culture, 1992). However, since the beginning of the 1990s, the existence of vocational schools as separate institutions has been questioned, and proposals for more multifunctional schools are being considered.

THE INSTITUTIONAL FABRIC OF VOCATIONALISM IN ISRAEL

Before the establishment of the state until the beginning of the 1960s, the vocational system was supervised by the Ministry of Labor and Welfare. Since 1962 the system was transferred to the authority of the Ministry of Education and Culture, leaving only peripheral vocational frameworks under the supervision of the Ministry of Labor and Welfare. This change was not only administrative, but also reflected an essential change in the conception and function of vocational education in the direction of providing secondary education for all (Iram, 1986).

The Ministry of Education and Culture

Vocational education under this authority functions in two major organizational frameworks. The largest one is the full-time vocational school, comprising about 80% of the students enrolled in vocational education. These institutions are owned primarily by voluntary organizations, such as ORT (the Organization of Labor and Vocation), Amal (Hebrew for *labor*), and Amit (Women's Volunteer Organization for Israel and Torah). Some institutions are owned by large municipalities, such as Tel Aviv and Haifa, and a few are owned by the government itself. The Ministry of Education and Culture is responsible for the curricula of all schools, and for the provision of supervisors, final examinations, diplomas, and teacher training (Karmi, 1986).

At the beginning of the vocational education system, schools were of two to three years' duration, but since the 1970s, the majority of schools continue for four years. Since the 1970s vocational schools are divided into four "tracks" of study: (1) the secondary vocational course (*Masmat*), which culminates in matriculation examinations in technological electives and the matriculation certificate (*Bagrut*), which opens the way to tertiary education; (2) the regular vocational course (*Masmar*), which leads to a final certificate and appropriate trade diplomas without matriculation; (3) the practical vocational course (*Masmam*), which leads to a certificate of completion and vocational certifications by the Ministry of Labor and Welfare; and (4) "guidance" classes for the weakest student population. Each course of study trains toward different occupations and different levels within each occupation. There are more sophisticated technological occupations, such as computers and dataprocessing, which are taught only at the highest level of study (*Masmat*), and other occupations, such as car mechanics, which are taught only at lower levels of study (Ministry of Education and Culture, 1984; Karmi, 1986). The distribution of students among the different courses of study shows an increasing tendency toward the higher level of study, from about 30% in the mid-1970s to 60% in the 1990s; and a decreasing tendency toward the lower levels; from 50% in the mid-1970s to less than 30% in the early 1990s for the regular course, and to 15% in the practical course. The "guidance" classes have almost disappeared (Ministry of Education and Culture, 1992).

The second framework consists of vocational electives within the comprehensive high schools, which include an academic course of study together with vocational courses. The latter is under the authority of the Division of Technological Education within the Ministry of Education and Culture and functions as full-time vocational school. These two full-time educational-vocational frameworks train a workforce for different levels of occupations in the Israeli job market.

The Ministry of Labor and Welfare

The first of two remaining frameworks are part-time vocational schools, which are supervised by the Ministry of Labor and Welfare. These frameworks place more emphasis on practical occupational training of their students, rather than their general education. Their students are mainly of lower academic ability and low socioeconomic strata of Oriental origin. Essentially these frameworks serve as semiformal systems of education (Hecht, 1977). The contents of training programs has changed over the years in response to the diverse demands of the labor market. However, they mainly serve the needs of commerce and industry for semiskilled and skilled workers.

The other main framework of part-time vocational education is the industrial school, which is operated by public governmental and industrial organizations. However, the expenses are shared by the Division of Training and Development of Manpower in the Ministry of Labor and Welfare. Industrial schools and other forms of on-the-plant training combine vocational training in the form of apprenticeship together with general education. The industrial schools are affiliated with specific military and industrial enterprises and enable students to acquire an occupation while working at the plant. The graduates of these schools are entitled to governmental vocational certificates. Similar to students in the full-time vocational schools, students in the industrial schools are divided into three curricular tracks: (1) the highest is the technical industrial track (*Matan*); (2) the regular industrial track (*Matar*); (3) and the practical industrial track, (*Matam*), which is the lowest level. These tracks represent different levels of training and are designed to provide students with flexibility and mobility. The fourth framework is the apprenticeship, which serves mainly working youth and dropouts from other vocational frameworks. There are other additional frameworks consisting of short vocational courses, known as peripheral vocational frameworks (Kahane and Starr, 1984), since they do not represent the mainstream in vocational education. Nonetheless, peripheral vocational frameworks fulfill an important social role due to their pragmatic and informal structure and their specific way of functioning, which aims to rehabilitate youth, return dropouts to the mainstream of society, and facilitate transfer between learning tracks of differing difficulty.

Changes and Reforms in Vocational Schools

Vocational frameworks within the two ministries continued to train semiskilled and skilled workers for the labor market in traditional trades, such as metal work, mechanics, carpentry, and printing. Over the years, as a result of changes in industry and commerce, a lack of skilled workers was apparent, as well as a lack of technicians in textiles, electronics, quality control, and robotics. The vocational system made moderate adaptations to these demands by introducing new training programs. Since the mid-1960s, provisions for training middle-level skilled workers was expanded by adding one to two years of training to the vocational schools (grades 12 and 13), in which technicians and practical engineers (*handasai*) were trained. Although the continuous changes in vocational schools were incremental, they did not meet the pace of economic and industrial changes in Israel, which rapidly moved toward a modern economy based on the advanced processes of production, finance, and commerce.

In order to cope with the lagging progress of vocational education, the Ministry of Education and Culture appointed a committee in 1983 to review different aspects of the vocational education system. Its main goal was to adapt the objectives, contents, and methods of training to the changing social, technological, and economic developments. The committee presented its recommendations in 1985 (Ministry of Education and Culture, 1985). The committee made a distinction between vocational education for all as part of all schools' curricula, and special occupational training in vocational schools leading to vocational occupations. This new concept of vocational education for all included two elements: teaching technology as part of general culture, and understanding the basic concepts of technological developments, as well as their effects on man-machine interactions. As for students in vocational education, the recommendations focused on new methods of training, as well as imparting appropriate attitudes and social skills. The emphasis of training was shifted from narrow skills-training to understanding principles, processes, and problems. Motivation for work, open-mindedness, professional responsibility, and team work capability were also fostered. The curricular implication of these recommendations was the interdisciplinary clustering of related general and applied technological areas of studies. This change was particularly applicable to students in higher tracks, since it provided a base for advanced learning. The committee based its recommendations on projected developments in the coming century, such as new materials in microelectronics, computers, communication systems, and data processing (Ministry of Education and Culture, 1985).

Another committee (Ministry of Education and Culture, 1987) addressed the matriculation examinations in the sector of vocational education. The committee recommended intensifying the study of science, enlarging the number of subject choices, and postponing studies in areas of specialization in order to raise students' chances of attaining the matriculation certificate (Ministry of Education and Culture, 1988). Indeed, as a result of these changes, the number of students completing vocational education with matriculation increased. In response, universities made their entrance requirements more demanding by disqualifying students whose courses of study were based on only three units in English and mathematics, which met the requirements of graduation from vocational schools (Ministry of Education and Culture, 1987). The new regulations were unfavorable toward vocational students. Thus, matriculation in vocational education was a failed enterprise. This stigmatized the sector as a whole, particularly its system of examinations and diplomas, as educational services for weaker student populations.

The recommendations of the Tamir Committee (1985) and the Committee of the Reform of Matriculation Examinations (1987) served as a base for a steering committee, whose function was to propose a comprehensive reform in technological education. This committee was jointly established in 1988 by the Department of Science and Technology, and the postprimary education department in the Ministry of Education and Culture. The committee submitted its recommendation for a comprehensive reform in 1991.

The assumptions underlying the reform were based on an examination of changes in Israeli society and economy as well as its scientific and technological needs in the future. The vocational educational system was required to update its curricular structure in order to meet individual and social needs for the benefit of students and the societal needs for vocational training. This reform was aimed at all stages of the educational ladder: elementary school—by exposing students to modern technologies; junior high school—by providing students with experience in different technological subjects; and high school—by helping students realize their potential, updating occupational training according to future needs, and expanding the scientific base at the expense of practical workshop-level experiences. The reform also emphasized the needs of the weaker student population by expanding the basis of general education. The overall objective was to restructure the educational, technological system in order to meet modern educational, social, and training needs, and to provide all students with more flexibility in their choices of occupation, according to their individual potential. Instead of fixed tracks and frameworks, individual learning programs would be planned, thus deferring specialization to the two upper grades of high school. In addition, the number of training occupations (electives) was reduced from almost ninety to twenty-five aggregates or main electives, in order to eliminate obsolete areas of training and to introduce new areas.

These changes in perception of the world of technology led to a need for developing new curricula, improved study materials and teaching aids, and expanded in-service training of vocational teachers. The new program was endorsed in 1988 by the Ministry of Education and Culture, and two steering committees were assigned to its implementation in ten vocational schools during the period 1989–1990.

Another dimension in the development of technological education was the recommendations of the Harari Committee, which was appointed in 1990 by the Minister of Education and Culture "in order to advance the scientific and technological education in Israel toward the 21st century" (Ministry of Education and Culture, 1992). The committee was chaired by Professor H. Harari, president of the Weizmann Institute of Science, which added prestige to the committee. In 1992 the committee presented its final report, "Tomorrow 98," emphasizing the importance of scientific education at all levels in all types of education. The report states a historical fact that "technology" previously implied a practical craft, which required mainly manual skills without scientific knowledge; whereas today every technological occupation requires a wide scientific background as a basis for professional specialization. The imparting of technical skills and manual technologies is useless due to rapid change. Instead, basic principles of science and technology should be taught. Practical training should be provided for a short period toward the end of schooling and geared to industrial and other labor market needs. The report also recommends to broaden and improve the base of general academic studies in order to prepare students for matriculation examinations and tertiary education.

The Harari report recommends to transform the system from vocational to technological, and into a scientific technological system toward the year 2000. This transformation would be achieved by strengthening the scientific components of the system throughout all levels of schooling.

Dilemmas Facing Vocational Education

The educational system in Israel is facing serious dilemmas. On one hand, it has to cope with the problem of integrating a large number of Oriental youth, mainly from low socioeconomic backgrounds and low academic ability, into mainstream society. On the other hand, it has to maintain high academic standards in the general secondary school system in order to fulfill the country's defense and economic needs for a high-level technical workforce. The need for social integration and the ambition to narrow the socioeconomic, cultural, and educational gap between students from different ethnic backgrounds requires that the problem mainly be resolved within the framework of the vocational full-time school system, and only marginally by apprenticeships or other forms of training with a strong job market orientation (Neuman and Ziderman, 1989; Iram, 1986).

The educational policy of training in full-time vocational schools was supported by the fact that there was no industrial tradition of on-the-job training in Israel. In addition, the policy is rooted in established Jewish tradition, which attaches importance to learning (Iram and Balicki, 1980). The tendency toward full-time schooling, rather than on-the-job training, was reinforced by the 1968 parliamentary decision to reform the school system and provide secondary education for all. The main burden of implementing this provision fell on the shoulders of vocational education, since it absorbed the weaker student population. Many of these students, who were rejected from academic high schools, turned to the vocational system. Thus, the vocational educational system suffered from a well-known phenomenon: the expansion of one part of the system exceeding the other. Moreover, when the more rapidly expanding part absorbed students who were rejected from the other stream, its academic level decreased even more. Indeed, rapid social changes affected vocational schools more than other segments of the educational system (Kahane & Starr, 1976).

In order to meet the conflicting demands of economic development and the student needs, the system became rigidly stratified. It classified students according to their scholastic aptitude, degree of sophistication of occupations and their level of prestige. However, the overall framework of vocational schools was preserved through "tracking." Oriental students of lower socioeconomic background were overrepresented in the lower tracks, which trained their graduates for less prestigious and economically unrewarding occupations (Shavit, 1984).

The system that worked well during the 1960s was questioned in the following decades, as a result of both the Educational Reform of 1968 and accelerated economic and industrial developments. Consequently, major changes in the curriculum were introduced since the 1970s. These changes were geared toward more sophisticated industries, such as electronics, computers, robotics, and electrical engineering, which required the highest level of skilled work. On the other hand, training for occupations, such as metal work, fashion, and hotelkeeping, which required semiskilled workers, was curtailed. Consequently, the dilemma intensified: the system leveled its demands, increased differentiation, and only admitted students of higher academic standing. Areas of training for weaker students were limited, in spite of their increased population in the system.

These developments precipitated the appointment of various committees in the late 1980s and early 1990s. The recommendations of all these committees indicate common trends: the weakening of differentiation between levels of students; an increase in theoretical studies; and vocational education being based on technological scientific foundations.

Evaluation and Discussion

The Israeli educational technological system should be evaluated in light of two major criteria: the social objective of the system, and economic gain. As for the social objective, mainly in the realm of equal educational opportunities, opinions are divided. The line of division crosses between supporters of vocational technological education and its opponents. According to its supporters, from a social perspective the system succeeded in developing unique educational frameworks that meet all students' needs and are conducive to social integration. Its graduates are integrated into civil industry and the military as technicians and engineers (Zuk, 1991). According to the Ministry of Education and Culture report (1991b), the number of students who received the matriculation diploma increased by 63% between 1966–1976. Whereas the annual increase of matriculation in general was 12%, in vocational education it increased by 16.5%, and 86% of its student population are enrolled in grades 10 through 12. Opponents of the vocational educational school system question its occupational contribution to socioeconomic upward mobility, as well as its validity in achieving social integration (Swirski, 1990; Yogev and Ayalon, 1986).

As for economic criteria, mainly cost effectiveness of vocational technological education, Neuman and Ziderman (1991) appraise the outcomes of secondary school vocational education in relation to educational alternatives of general academic secondary schools. Their study was based upon traditional human capital outcomes. In terms of labor, market success was measured by earnings, analyzing data from a 20% subsample of the 1983 Census of Population and Housing. They found vocational schooling to be more cost-effective in terms of higher earnings than general academic education. These results are not in concordance with the predominantly economist view that vocational schooling is an inefficient form of education. Indeed, a large number of cost-benefit analyses, based on labor-market earnings and follow-up studies of vocational and academic secondary school graduates, have shown that the higher costs of vocational school education are not usually offset by any positive and sizable earnings accruing to vocational school graduates. Usually, general secondary schools are considered to be a more cost-effective investment (Foster, 1965; Psacharopoulus and Woodhall, 1985; White, 1988; Psacharopoulus, 1988). However, it should be noted that Neuman and Ziderman's findings refer to "those vocational school attendees who work in occupations related to course study pursued at school." These graduates earn more than both their peers employed in occupations nonrelated to their vocational studies and graduates of academic secondary schools, by up to 10% per month. Indeed, Neuman and Ziderman conclude that "the cost effectiveness of vocational secondary schools . . . must be seen. . . in a 'second best' context, once the full range of educational and training programs for youth are taken into account."

Vocational secondary schools are not cost-effective in comparison to alternative nonformal training modes, such as traditional apprenticeship and factory-based vocational schools. They constitute the most expensive skill-training mode without offering any earnings or productivity advantage to vocational school graduates over those from alternative on-the-job training forms (Borus, 1977; Ziderman, 1989). Therefore, it was suggested that from an economic perspective, training efforts should be transferred from vocational schooling to more job-related training modes outside the formal educational system. This is also consistent with the World Bank's recent position on vocational and technical training. The authors of the World Bank's policy paper (1991) argue that rapid technological and economic changes drive vocational training into apprenticeship, industry-based, and employer-based training, both public and private: "training institutions in the private sector—by private employers and in private training institutions—can be the most effective and efficient way to develop skills of the workforce." This policy paper assigns the government the role of strengthening *general education* at the primary and secondary levels. However, a contrasting view argues that apprenticeship and other industry-based training programs are too narrow in a period of increased industrial and commercial developments. In addition, privatization and deregulation raise the issue of equity, leaving governments without a means to cope with inequalities. Thus, rapidly changing economics require the introduction of vocational education in schools, although it should be based on a broader foundation in scientific and general education and continued government responsibility, as with other kinds of education (Lauglo, 1992).

In Israel vocational secondary education is the dominant provider of skilled workers for skilled trades, notwithstanding issues of economic efficiency. National consensus on the importance of providing a school framework for social and cultural integration acts as a major constraint on the development of training alternatives, which are the norm in other countries (Iram, 1986). Indeed, Israel maintains expensive vocational schools that are not aimed directly at vocational training, but more to general postprimary education. The budget for academic secondary school students is 1.6 hours per student, whereas for the vocational school student, 2.2 hours on average, including materials and equipment (Ministry of Education and Culture, 1991b). Vocational schools in Israel were expanded to provide weaker student populations, mainly of Oriental origin, with secondary education, in order to narrow the gap between their academic achievements and those of stronger student populations, mainly of

Western origin, and to promote social integration (Iram, 1986). If vocational education in Israel had been linked to the economy, it could fulfill a productive role in its economic development; but in Israel, vocational development is not part of the production process, unlike Germany and Switzerland (Iram and Balicki, 1980).

An additional criterion that may be applied to the evaluation of vocational education relates to the issue of equity: are students in vocational schools provided with equal education opportunities, compared with academic secondary school students? The expansion of full-time vocational schools was intended to provide secondary education to youth of lower economic status, mainly new immigrants of Oriental origin, in order to minimize economic, cultural, and educational inequalities. However, according to Swirski (1990), vocational schools in Israel do not perform the role of high schools in facilitating upward mobility, but serve as "holding frameworks" for students. Two-thirds of these students are of Oriental origin, who from the onset despair of the concept of further studies and who are designated for lower-level occupations. Half the vocational tracks do not lead to the matriculation certificate. In 1988, out of 45% of students who passed the examinations, only 39% were Oriental students, compared to 45% of Western origin students. Also, a substantial proportion of students in vocational schools who prepare for matriculation do not write examinations in all subjects, but only in a few (Swirski, 1990). According to Swirski, general schooling in Israel, and vocational schooling in particular, plays an important role in the creation and implementation of stratification and socioeconomic inequalities in Israeli society. A similar tendency was observed in other countries as well (Ben-Avot, 1983).

The most thorough criticism of vocational education, from the perspective of equity, comes from Yogev and Ayalon (1986, 1991). According to them, vocational education exerts a long-term effect on social reproduction and occupational stratification in Israel. The expansion of vocational education since the 1960s was due to the planned policy to improve the educational attainments of lower-status groups, mainly from Oriental background. The allocation to specific vocational training frameworks may serve as a "fine tuning" of social reproduction by tracking, due to the high probability of curricular segregation by social origin. The stratification by curriculum constitutes a "hidden curriculum," with regard to socialization, values and knowledge transmission, corresponding to the ideology of dominant classes. Vocational high school students may be exposed to different types of knowledge, which may consequently result in the differential commodity value of their curriculum in the labor market. Yogev and Ayalon hypothesize that secondary vocational education contributes to social reproduction by curricular allocation according to students' ethnicity, status of origin, and gender (Yogev and Ayalon, 1986). Tracking studies show the disadvantage of vocational school students, compared with academic track students, regarding postsecondary and tertiary education and subsequent occupational attainments (Yogev and Ayalon, 1991). It should be emphasized that if vocational training does not provide economic gain, then equity is not achieved.

Criticism of vocational technical education from the socioeconomic perspective was recently raised by officials within the Ministry of Education and Culture. It is important to note that this criticism came from ministry officials who are responsible for units comprising a large proportion of students from weaker socioeconomic backgrounds, namely, the State Religious Education Sector (Dagan, 1991, 1993), and the southern developing district (Melitz, 1990).

Dagan, the director of State Religious Education, argued that vocational technical education fulfilled its function twenty-five years ago, when it addressed the schooling needs of a growing student population and helped in its cultural transition. Today vocational education is dysfunctional and has become a place for students whose parents cannot afford better schools (Nahon, 1987). The educational climate in vocational schools is neither conducive to general knowledge nor to religious education. Dagan proposed to eliminate the workshops, or at least to reduce the number of hours of practical work by two-thirds and to postpone practical training, which failed. Only 20% of students in vocational schools who wrote examinations earned a matriculation certificate, and even these students were not admitted to universities because of their low grades. Dagan concludes that vocational education harms individuals' chances for socioeconomic mobility and endangers both the Jewish character of the state and its scientific and economic future (Dagan, 1993).

Similar criticism of the vocational education system was voiced by Melitz (1990), a chief officer in the southern district of the Ministry of Education and Culture. He describes the system as a trap into which many students are lured against their will, which results in poorly motivated students and teachers. Better teachers are assigned to academic schools, or to academic tracks within comprehensive schools, while less-qualified teachers are assigned to the vocational schools and the education of vocational students suffers. Their achievements in mathematics, science, and general knowledge are low and do not enable them to earn a matriculation certificate. Melitz (1990) observes that the gap between vocational schools and industry increases. Heads of industrial enterprises prefer graduates with a basic general education, and training them on the job for three to six months, rather than accepting low-level graduates from vocational schools. Vocational schools are populated by weaker students who lack the basic skills required to succeed in theoretical studies. Vocational tracks of comprehensive schools are on a low level and lag behind industry. Teachers also lack modern technological knowledge and qualifications. Melitz recommends improving the modes of instruction and strengthening academic subjects and students' achievements in basic skills in grades 10–12. He recommends providing general education to more students to increase the number of students who would qualify for matriculation and raising the level of basic technological education, thus making it a challenge for strong students and not a shelter for weaker students.

It is interesting to note that the arguments of Dagan (1991, 1993) and Melitz (1990) in favor of strengthening the general education components in all schools and for transferring vocational education to employer-based training are consistent with World Bank's policy paper (1991). Their arguments also echo Foster's classic argument on the "vocational school fallacy," which was raised over thirty years ago (Foster, 1965). Commenting on Adams, Middleton and Ziderman's (1992) article, which overviews the findings of the World Bank's policy paper that they coauthored, Foster (1992) reiterates his position anew: "Just as vocational training is complementary to, and not a substitute for, general education, so state policy should attempt to complement, not replace, potentially viable private initiatives." It seems that Foster's balanced view on these major issues could be useful, if adopted by Israel to cope with the dilemmas previously discussed.

This chapter analyzed the dilemma of vocational education in Israel, namely, its dual role in providing both equal educational opportunities and secondary education for all, as well as the social and economic price which society pays for it. The chapter on "Vocationalism" concludes the vertical analysis of the educational stages within the legal framework of free and compulsory education. The following chapter discusses higher education, which is a public, but not governmental, system.

BIBLIOGRAPHY

Adams, A. V., J. Middleton, and A. Ziderman (1992). "The World Bank's policy paper on vocational and technical education and training." *Prospects, 22,* 127–140.

Avidor, M. (1957). *Education in Israel.* Jerusalem: Youth and Hachalutz Department, Zionist Organization (Hebrew).

Ben-Avot, A. (1983). "The rise and decline of vocational education." *Sociology of Education, 56,* 63–76.

Borus, M. (1977). "A cost-effectiveness comparison of vocational training for youth in developing countries: A case study of four training modes in Israel." *Comparative Education Review, 21,* 1–13.

Dagan, M. (1991). "On the need for changes in technological education." *Maalot, 91* (Hebrew).

Dagan, M. (1993). "The need for policy and structural changes in religious post-elementary education." *Bisdeh Hemed (Religious State Education), 36,* 20–29 (Hebrew).

Elboim-Dror, R. (1986). *Hebrew Education in Eretz Israel, 1.* Jerusalem: Yad Izhak Ben-Zvi Institute, 1854–1914 (Hebrew).

Evans, K., and W. R. Heinz (1993). *Becoming adults in England and Germany.* London: Anglo-German Foundation.

Foster, P. (1965). "The vocational school fallacy in development planning." In A. C. Anderson and M. J. Bowman (eds.), *Education and economics development.* Chicago: Aldine.

Foster, P. (1992). "Vocational education and training—A major shift in World Bank policy." *Prospects, 22,* 149–155.

Hecht, Y. (1977). *Work ideology and vocational education.* Jerusalem: Hebrew University (Hebrew).

Iram, Y. (1977). *Theory and practice in Jewish education.* Tel Aviv: Gomeh Scientific Publications, Tcherikover (Hebrew).

Iram, Y. (1986). "Social policy and education for work in Israel." *Issues in Education, 4,* 259–271.

Iram, Y., and C. Balicki (1980). "Vocational education in Switzerland and Israel: A comparative analysis." *Canadian and International Education, 9,* 95–105.

Kahane, R., and L. Starr (1976). "The impact of rapid social change on technological education: An Israeli example." *Comparative Education Review, 20,* 165–178.

Kahane, R., and L. Starr (1984). *Education and work: Vocational socialization processes in Israel.* Jerusalem: Magnes Press (Hebrew).

Karmi, S. (1986). *Problems of technological education and vocational counselling.* Tel Aviv: ORT (Hebrew).

Kleinberger, A. F. (1969). *Society schools and progress in Israel.* Oxford: Pergamon Press.

Lauglo, J. (1992). "Vocational training and the banker's faith in the private sector." *Comparative Education Review, 36,* 227–236.

Melitz, A. (1990). *Another perspective: A proposal for the organization of post-elementary education in development towns.* Jerusalem: Ministry of Education and Culture, Southern District (Hebrew).

Ministry of Education and Culture. (1984). *Technological education in Israel.* Jerusalem (Hebrew).

Ministry of Education and Culture. (1985). *Technological education in Israel toward the year 2000* (Tamir Report). Hulon: Center for Technological Education (Hebrew).

Ministry of Education and Culture. (1987). *Format of matriculation examinations.* Jerusalem (Hebrew).

Ministry of Education and Culture. (1988). *Structure and organization of the technological and scientific studies in the upper high school.* Jerusalem (Hebrew).

Ministry of Education and Culture. (1991a). *Reform in technological education.* Jerusalem (Hebrew).

Ministry of Education and Culture. (1991b). *Technological education in Israel—A view of the future.* Jerusalem (Hebrew).

Ministry of Education and Culture. (1992). *"Tomorrow 98"—Report of the supreme committee for scientific and technological education.* Jerusalem, Harari Report (Hebrew).

Nahon, Y. (1987). *The patterns of education increase and structure of occupational opportunities— The ethnic aspect.* Jerusalem: Jerusalem Institute (Hebrew).

Neuman, S., and A. Ziderman (1989). "Vocational secondary schools can be more cost-effective than academic schools: The case of Israel." *Comparative Education, 25,* 151–163.

Neuman, S., and A. Ziderman (1991). "Vocational schooling occupational matching and labor market earnings in Israel." *Journal of Human Resources, 26,* 256–281.

Psacharopoulus, G. (1988). "Curriculum diversification, cognitive achievement and economic performance: Evidence from Tanzania and Columbia." In J. Lauglo and K. Lillis (eds.), *Vocationalizing education: An international perspective.* Oxford: Pergamon Press.

Psacharopoulus, G., and M. Woodhall (1985). *Education for development: An analysis of investment choices.* New York: Oxford University Press.

Rieger, E. (1945). *Vocational education in Israel.* Jerusalem: Hebrew University (Hebrew).

Schmida, M. (1987). *Equity and excellence: Educational reform and the comprehensive school.* Ramat Gan: Bar-Ilan University (Hebrew).

Shavit, Y. (1984). "Tracking and ethnicity in Israel secondary education." *American Sociological Review, 49,* 210–220.

Swirski, S. (1990). *Education in Israel: Schooling for inequality.* Tel Aviv: Breirot (Hebrew).

White, M. (1988). "Education policy and economic goals." *Oxford Review of Economic Policy, 4,* 1–20.

World Bank (1991). *Vocational and technological training: A World Bank policy paper.* Washington, DC.

Yogev, A., and H. Ayalon (1986). *Vocational education and social reproduction: Students' allocation to curricular programs in Israeli vocational high schools.* Tel Aviv University, The Pinhas Sapir Center for Development, Discussion Paper No. 14/86 (Hebrew).

Yogev, A., and H. Ayalon (1991). "Learning to labor or laboring to learn? Curricular stratification in Israeli vocational high schools." *International Journal of Education and Development, 2,* 209–219.

Yonai, J. (1992). *Education for work and vocation—documents.* Jerusalem: Ministry of Education and Culture (Hebrew).

Ziderman, A. (1989). "Training alternatives for youth: Results from longitudinal data." *Comparative Education Review, 33,* 243–255.

Zuk, U. (1991). *Vision of the future.* Jerusalem: Ministry of Education and Culture (Hebrew).

Chapter 5

Higher Education

BACKGROUND

Two small institutions of higher education and one research institute were in existence in Israel before the proclamation of the state in 1948. These were the Technion—the Israel Institute of Technology—opened in 1924; the Hebrew University of Jerusalem founded in 1925, and the Weizmann Institute of Science, established in 1934. The number of students in higher education in 1948 was about 2,450. The universities enjoyed academic self-government, including a decisive role for faculty in administrative matters. All positions of power were held by temporary elected officials from within the ranks of senior faculty. The locus of power rested with the academic community, rather than with the appointed administrative hierarchy. Excessive participatory democracy of senior faculty and the veto power of their assemblies and senates prevented the emergence of effective academic administrative leadership (Ben-David, 1986). The 1950s and 1960s were decades of massive expansion of higher education in many countries, as well as in Israel. Enrollments grew rapidly. New universities were founded, and new types of sectors of higher or postsecondary institution were founded or upgraded. National expenditure for higher education increased to meet growing enrollments.

Indeed, during the 1950s two new universities, Bar-Ilan and Tel Aviv, were opened and during the 1960s an additional two were opened in Haifa and Beer Sheva (Ben Gurion). The growth of the system was accompanied by a dramatic rise in student enrollment, from 2,450 in 1949–1950 to 18,368 in 1964–1965, and 36,239 in 1969–1970. New departments in the social sciences and humanities faculties were added, and professional schools in the fields of law and medicine were established in both the old and new universities (see CHE, 1988b; Tables 5.1 and 5.2).

Table 5.1

Students in Universities by Academic Years

Year	1969/70 = 100.0	1964/5 = 100.0	Annual Percentage of Growth	Total*
1948/49	–	–	–	1,635
1949/50	–	–	–	2,450
1959/60	–	–	14.8**	10,202
1964/65	–	100.0	12.4**	18,368
1969/70	100.0	197.3	14.6**	36,239
1974/75	143.7	283.6	8.2	52,088
1979/80	158.7	313.0	3.1	57,500
1984/85	179.5	354.1	0.7	65,050
1987/88	187.4	369.7	1.1	67,900

* Including foreign students and students in special programs.
** On the assumption of linear growth within the years.

Source: Compiled from Council for Higher Education, Planning and Grants Committee, *Higher education in Israel — Statistical abstracts 1983/84; 1986/87*. Statistical Abstracts of Israel, No. 39, 1988.

The small and elitist institutions of higher learning, prior to the establishment of the State of Israel, were isolated from social, political, and ideological controversies within the small Jewish self-autonomous community in Palestine. This safeguarded their autonomy from the Zionist organization, which created and financed the universities. The newly independent State of Israel called the universities to meet the demands of the expanding economy for skilled manpower and growing student enrollments. In this way the universities participated in solving economic, political, and cultural problems in the new state. The postindependence decade saw the few, small, and relatively weak Israeli universities grow in size and quality. But concurrently, the power of the state grew over them. Indeed, initial government support of universities, which was welcomed as supportive, inducing growth and stabilizing funding uncertainties, proved to have quite different consequences from those originally anticipated by academics. Thus, a gradual process of centralization, rationalization, and bureaucratization started in the Israeli higher education system, similar to the process that Trow (1984) accounts for in other higher educational systems.

Table 5.2
Academic Staff in Academic Institutions

Year	Academic Staff	Professors and Lecturers
1948/49[1]	293	118
1959/60[1]	1,531	511
1964/65[1]	2,628	1,207
1969/70[1]	5,977	3,122
1975/76[1]	8,148	3,988
1981/82[2]	8,068	4,463
1985/86[2]	7,756	4,114

1.   Number of persons including part-time staff.
2.   Number of full-time equivalent posts.

Source: Statistical Abstracts of Israel, No. 29, 1978.

From the mid-1950s to the mid-1960s Israeli universities expanded in parallel with the increase in demand for higher education. The government spent immense resources to support the increasing needs of the existent universities and to build new ones. The universities were designed to provide professional training for a growing industrialized state, and the government developed mechanisms and structures to coordinate the growth of the universities. These structures and basic relationships continue to form the foundations of higher education in Israel. However, structures and mechanisms that were originally designed to support and coordinate growth were employed in the 1970s and 1980s, in the wake of recession and government fiscal restraint, to constrain and control growth. Government initiatives during the late 1980s attempted to stimulate change within the confines of the existing and relatively stable structure, and to introduce new structures, such as regional colleges, only outside of the university structure.

THE INSTITUTIONAL STRUCTURE

"Higher education" in Israel, as defined by law, "includes teaching, science, and research which are conducted in universities and other academic degree-granting institutions" (Stanner, 1963, 244). Within the higher education system there is a clear distinction between "universities" and "other institutions of higher education." In practice the system is divided into six distinct subsystems, which included in 1995 the following institutions:

1. Six universities which are authorized to grant all academic degrees—bachelor's, master's and doctorate's.
2. An open university which awards only a bachelor's degree.
3. Seven specialized "institutions of higher education" that are neither universities nor teacher-training colleges and are authorized to award only professional bachelors' degrees. The Planning and Budgeting Committee (PBC) of the Council for Higher Education (CHE) is responsible for the budgets of all the institutions of these three subsystems as will be discussed later.
4. Nine teacher-training institutions that have received or are in the process of acquiring academic status, and are accredited by the Council for Higher Education to award bachelor of education degrees either for the entire institution or for certain programs of study. These institutions are financed by the Ministry of Education and Culture.
5. Eleven regional colleges, which in addition to serving as centers of adult education, provide academic courses under the academic responsibility of one of the existing universities, which also appoint their teachers and award their degrees. The regional colleges are financed by the Ministry of Education and Culture and by various local and regional authorities that are supported by the Ministry of the Interior. The Council for Higher Education has appointed a subcommittee to deal with academic courses at regional colleges "in order to make higher education more accessible to broader segments of the population" (CHE, 1988, 78), and as of 1985, made direct allocations to their academic programs.
6. Three extensions of academic institutions from abroad that were granted a permit from the Council for Higher Education to offer academic programs in Israel, but the degrees will be conferred by the parent-institutions abroad (CHE, 1991).

Only the six universities (excluding the open university) are authorized to award degrees beyond the bachelor's in a variety of fields of study and advanced professional training. The other institutions of higher education are authorized to award the bachelor's degree only in specified fields of study or training as shown in Table 5.3. Out of the nine teacher-training colleges, seven institutions award the B.Ed. to teachers for primary and junior high schools (K–9), one awards the B.Ed. tech degree (Teaching Technology), and still another the degree of BScTE (Teaching of Science).

Israel does not have liberal arts colleges that specialize in teaching undergraduates, except at the open university. This function is performed by research universities that train professionals in law, medicine, engineering, business, and other fields. The typical bachelor's program in the humanities and social sciences is designed for three years of study specializing in two disciplinary fields (departments) of the student's choice, provided they meet the admission criteria of the departments. Professional education in law, medicine, and engineering commences in the first year for undergraduate students for a duration of 3.5–5 years. Three additional years are generally required for the completion of a master's degree. The Ph.D. degree has minimal formal

Table 5.3
Fields of Study in the Institutions of Higher Education

	Hum-anities	Social Sci.	Law	Arts	Social Work	Teach. Train.	Math, Nat. Sci.	Eng, Tech-nology	Agri-cult.	Med-icine	Dent-istry	Para-Med Profs.
Hebrew University	*	*	*	*	*	*	*	*	*	*	*	*
Technion–IIT	.	*					*	*	*	*		
Tel-Aviv University	*	*	*	*	*	*	*	*	*	*	*	*
Bar-Ilan University	*	*	*	*	*	*	*					
University of Haifa	*	*		*	*	*	*					
Ben-Gurion University	*	*			*	*	*	*		*		
Weizmann Institute of Science							*					
Everyman's (Open) University	*	*					*					
Bezalel Academy Arts				*								
Jerusalem Academy of Music				*		*						
Jerusalem College Technology						*		*				
Shenkar–Textile & Fashion				*				*				
Ruppin Institute		*										
College of Administration		*										
Teacher Training Colleges						*						

Source: Council for Higher Education, Report No. 14, 1988a, p.60.

requirements; it is a research degree designed individually according to the candidate's research project.

The number of students at the seven university-level institutions (including the open university) reached 73,500 in 1992; an increase of more than 24% over the last ten years, and an increase of about 10% in the last two years (CHE, 1992). Some 60% of students are studying humanities, social sciences, and law, 25% are studying natural sciences, agriculture, and medicine, and 15% are studying engineering. Some 72% are studying for their first degree (bachelor's), 21% for their second degree (master's), 5% for their doctorate's, and 2% for academic diplomas, mainly secondary-school teaching diplomas. At the thirteen nonuniversity institutions of higher education, there are 5,800 students enrolled. Some 15,000 were enrolled in academic courses at the open university; this number being equal to some 5,000 students in full-time study programs at a regular university, an increase of 10% over the last year (CBS, 1988; CHE, 1992).

It is difficult to compare the rate of study in Israel with the rate in Western countries because of variations in the division between university and postsecondary education in different countries. Also, the principal age-group attending universities in Israel is twenty to twenty-nine years. This differs from other countries due to three years of mandatory military service for men and two years for women. It may, however, be said that in Israel this rate—about 20% of the twenty to twenty-nine age cohort received university education, and 26.4% received some form of higher education—is higher than in most developed nations, similar to New Zealand, France, and Japan, but lower than in the United States and Canada (Shprinzak and Bar, 1991, 74; CHE, 1995, 1). The rate of admission to universities in 1993 was as follows: about 65% of applicants applied to departments of humanities; about 50% of applicants applied to social science departments; and about 20% of those applying to law schools, medicine, and engineering were admitted. At the bachelor's degree level 31.4% studied exact sciences (medicine, mathematics, natural sciences, agriculture, and engineering), for the master's degree 36.9% studied exact sciences, and 64.8% studied exact sciences for the doctorate's degree (CHE, 1995, 2). Tuition fees are set by the government and they range from about 10% of the ordinary budget of universities in the mid-1970s, to 4% in 1982, and about 20% in 1995 (CHE, 1995).

The principal sources of income for the higher education system are: (1) allocations from the government, determined and paid to individual institutions by the PBC; (2) income from current donations; (3) revenue from endowment funds; (4) tuition fees; (5) research contracts and research grants from government and private sources, at home and abroad; (6) sale of services (including teaching services). The share of each is shown in Table 5.4. Government participation in the ordinary budget of higher education is 80%, including tuition fees. This rate remained unchanged in real terms over the past decade in relation to the Consumer Price Index. It did not, however,

Table 5.4
Ordinary Budget of the Higher Education System by Sources of Income and Academic Years

Academic Year[1]	Various[2]	Donations from Abroad	Tuition Fees	PBC Allocations				Ordinary Budget
				Earmarked Allocations and Various[3]	Matching Allocations[4]	Direct Allocations	Total	
NIS THOUSANDS, AT CURRENT PRICES								
1979/80	159	126	64	52	50	867	969	1,318[5]
1980/81	450	260	133	108	225	2,228	2,561	3,404[5]
1981/82	1,132	505	272	150	400	4,138	4,688	6,597[5]
1982/83	3,754	1,205	1,405	569	600	13,326	14,495	20,859[5]
1983/84	25,763	5,944	3,290	3,702	1,363	36,623	41,688	76,685[6]
1984/85	43,387	42,199	29,603	24,079	8,820	153,075	185,974	301,163[7]
1985/86	43,503	57,741	99,256	38,629	38,254	253,037	329,920	530,420[7]
1986/87	89,179	80,087	124,085	49,540	43,904	324,625	418,069	711,420[7]
PERCENTAGES								
1979/80	12.1	9.6	4.8	3.9	3.8	65.8	73.5	100.0
1980/81	13.2	7.6	3.9	3.2	6.6	65.5	75.3	100.0
1981/82	17.2	7.6	4.1	2.3	6.1	62.7	71.1	100.0
1982/83	18.0	5.8	6.7	2.7	2.9	63.9	69.5	100.0
1983/84	33.6	7.7	4.3	4.8	1.8	47.8	54.4	100.0
1984/85	14.4	14.0	9.8	8.0	3.0	50.8	61.8	100.0
1985/86	8.2	10.9	18.7	7.3	7.2	47.7	62.2	100.0
1986/87	12.5	11.3	17.4	7.0	6.2	45.6	58.8	100.0

[1] From October 1 to September 30; [2] Includes deficits; [3] Including allocations for research and special subjects (earmarked allocations, inter-university activities, aid to students, budgetary transfers and miscellaneous subjects); [4] To endowment funds at the institutions; [5] According to the balance sheets of the institutions; [6] According to financial reports received from the institutions; and [7] Final budget updated prices. *Source:* CHE, *Higher Education in Israel — Statistical Abstracts, 1986/87,* p.56.

compensate the universities for the growth in student population by almost 25% (see Tables 5.1 and 5.4), and for the significant increase in wages and salaries of university staff, which is determined by government. National expenditure on higher education in Israel is 1.8% of the GNP, and expenditure per student is $11,100, which is higher than in most developed countries (CHE, 1995, 3).

At present a three-tiered hierarchy administers higher education in Israel. At the apex is the Council for Higher Education (CHE), which is appointed by the president of the state, and chaired by the minister of Education and Culture. The CHE possesses extensive legal power to regulate the higher education system. Below the CHE is the Planning and Budgeting (Grants) Committee (PBC/PGC), which is the executive arm of the CHE. The PBC is responsible for planning and budgeting the overall operation of the system. At the bottom stream are the individual institutions, which are expected to handle their own affairs through their presidents, rectors, and deans, the latter two being elected by senior faculty members.

EXPANSION AND CENTRALIZATION

In the wake of the expansion of the higher education system and the increased demand for public and governmental funds, four interrelated issues surfaced: creating criteria for the accreditation of new universities, deciding on ways of channeling public funds to the individual institutions, democratizing access and governance, and developing ways to make university studies more relevant to the economy and career planning. These developments augmented governmental influence over the magnitude, cost, and future direction of the higher education enterprise. To cope with these developments, new structures of organization, government, and finance had to be formed.

Indeed governmental involvement became apparent in Israel in 1958 with the establishment of a statutory body, the CHE, to serve as "the state institution for matters of higher education in the State" (Stanner, 1963, 244). The CHE is the sole authority that recommends the government to grant a permit in order to open a new institution of higher education, as well as to grant an institution recognition and accreditation, authorizing it to confer academic degrees. In an apparent attempt to safeguard academic freedom, Section 4a of the Council for Higher Education Law of 1958 states that "at least two thirds of its CHE members must be persons of standing in the field of higher education," namely, full professors, and Section 15 of the law is meant to guarantee institutional autonomy: "An accredited institution shall be at liberty to conduct its academic and administrative affairs within the framework of its budget. This liberty includes the determination of a program of research and teaching, the appointment of the authorities of the institution, the appointment and promotion of teachers, the determination of a method of teaching and study, and any other scientific, pedagogic or economic activity" (Stanner, 1963, 244–

249). Thus, the CHE let the governing bodies of each university decide its developmental policy, without interfering with its decision, or coordinating, either with other universities or with the government. As a result, almost all of the universities incurred increasing deficits, and after creating faits accomplis, the state was asked for additional financial resources.

The continuous growth of the higher education system was accompanied by a massive increase in the proportion of public funding, which rose steadily to 45.5% in 1959–1960, and to almost 80% in 1974–1975 (see Table 5.5). Following increased government funding of higher education, the basic issue that emerged was how to reconcile the inherent conflict between academic freedom and accountability to the public. Various proposals were made to make government funding more rational and the universities more accountable to the public. An amendment in 1972 to the Council for Higher Education of 1958 also specifically charged the council with the responsibility for planning higher education. An equitable system for financing higher education, however, was still lacking.

In 1974 the Council for Higher Education appointed the first Planning and Grants Committee (PGC) "based on the model of the British University Grants Committee (UGC)," as a buffer between the Ministry of Education and Culture, the Ministry of Finance, and the universities. As of 1991, the Planning and Grant Committee was renamed as the Planning and Budgeting Committee (PBC), which is a more literal translation of the Hebrew name of the committee. The term PGC will be used throughout this paper, since all publications until 1991 are under this name. The PGC has six members, including its chairman. At least four of the members, including the chairman, must be full professors appointed as persona, the other two members can be from business and industry. "The four professors represent the two cultures; two from the natural sciences, engineering, medicine, or agriculture" (CHE, 1985, 95). To safeguard against state intervention, all PGC members are appointed by the minister of Education and Culture only after approval by the Council for Higher Education in a secret ballot. The chairman of the PGC is employed fulltime and is ex-officio a member of the council. He is assisted by an administrative and professional staff of eighteen to nineteen members (Government Decision No. 666 of June 5, 1977). Thus, the PGC is an independent body coming between the government and the national institution, on the one hand, and the institutions of higher education, on the other in all matters relating to allocations for higher education, taking into account the needs of society and the state, while safeguarding academic freedom (CHE, 1987).

The PGC is essentially a collegial organization. Its members are appointed on the basis of individual merit, and not as representatives of their own institutions. They view as their prime interest defending the essential characteristics of the traditional institutional fabric of the universities as a whole and the autonomy of the individual institution. The PGC submits annual reports to the

Table 5.5

Public Participation in Recurrent Budget of Higher Education

Year	No. of Students	Total Recurrent Budget (in millions of Israeli pounds)	Public Participation*	Percent
1959/60	10,202	28.1	12.8	45.5
1964/65	18,368	78.3	40.2	51.0
1969/70	36,239	241.3	162.1	67.0
1974/75	52,088	1,075.0	852.0	79.8

*From 1967 to 1968 the Jewish Agency allocated funds to universities for their recurrent budgets.

Source: Council for Higher Education, Planning and Grants Committee Report for 1974 (Hebrew): *Higher Education in Israel—Statistical Abstract 1986/87.*

CHE at the end of each academic year.

The forming of the PGC marked a gradual withdrawal of government from direct involvement in financing higher education, and also the universities' concession of power to the authority of the PGC in fiscal and planning matters. This made the PGC the single most powerful central organization in Israel's higher education system in matters of planning, development and funding of individual institutions, and the system as a whole. However, individual higher education institutions are at liberty to conduct their academic and administrative affairs autonomously within the limitation of their approved budgets. The budget of each institution is determined by its authorities after negotiations with the PGC.

THE 1990s AND BEYOND

Higher education in Israel has retained its traditional central European elitist character (Iram, 1992b), despite more than forty years of rapid growth, which has brought it beyond Trow's "15% enrollment threshold" (Trow, 1976) into the range of "mass" higher education. However, at the beginning of the 1990s there were growing signs that Israel's higher education system is undergoing major changes. Basic concepts, such as institutional autonomy and long-cherished tenets such as academic freedom and elitism, which were the foundations of the system, are being reassessed. Awareness of inadequacies, such as equity, quality of instruction, and effectiveness of training, were growing both by internal self-evaluation and external critiques, as well as by increased governmental intervention and politicization.

During the 1980s institutional autonomy of higher education in Israel was infringed on by legal enactments and by administrative actions in all five constituents of academic freedom, as defined by the Robbins Committee (Iram, 1987).

1. Freedom of appointment of academic staff remained, but the right of an institution to attract the best candidates was limited by national salary scales imposed on universities by the government, though a university is free to determine the position and rank of the appointee.
2. Freedom to determine curricula and standards are generally maintained by departments and faculties, but the introduction of new programs, or any structural or curricular changes in existing programs, are subject to the approval of the PGC, even though no funds are required.
3. Universities have full discretion in setting criteria and methods of selecting student applications for admission, however, these criteria and methods have been subject to continuous public concern and pressure, demanding relaxation of admission requirements.
4. The freedom of an individual institution to determine the balance between teaching and research was infringed on in recent years by the PGC's "productivity" formula, in which the PGC evaluates the scope and quality of research, the "output" of an institution, and then uses this evaluation to determine budgetary allocation.
5. The freedom of a university to determine the direction and scope of its own development is limited by what it can negotiate with the PGC.

Thus, the autonomy of each university is considerably less than it was intended in 1974 when the Planning and Grants Committee was founded.

Growing participation in higher education since the 1950s and concomitant growth in its share of public finance, which was followed by economic recession and fiscal restraints by the government since the mid–1970s, raised concerns about accountability in Israel, as in many other countries (Iram, 1992a). In Israel these demands were introduced both on the system level and the institutional level. Thus, demands for accountability were expressed in Israel by proposing that existing needs for higher education could be met only through greater efficiency and a more vocationally oriented system. Furthermore, it was proposed that any expansion be measured by the same criteria. These demands were followed by growing pressure for higher "productivity" and "efficiency," or "joint utilization" of facilities and equipment. The productivity criteria, applied by the PGC to determine the range of budgetary allocation to individual institutions, added an accountability dimension on the system level. In addition, the periodic inspection of units within universities by external review committees, as well as the appointment of survey committees of entire fields of studies, such as the Schools of Education in 1987 and Life Sciences in 1988 (CHE, 1990a), might have far-reaching restructuring effects on both the system and interinstitutional levels. Indeed, university faculty and administrators tended to see some of these demands as a disguise for more direct state control at the expense of institutional autonomy and academic freedom.

In 1990, following increased immigration from the Soviet Union, the issue of access became more pressing, and the PGC changed its former policy of opposition to the establishment of undergraduate colleges (CHE, 1991). Thus, the decision to establish undergraduate colleges will necessarily influence the policies of the higher education system in the direction of further diversification and differentiation (CHE, 1992). Indeed, in 1990 new proposals to establish independent undergraduate colleges were submitted to the Knesset (Parliament). This decision found immediate expression in the expansion of the number of regional colleges between 1990 and 1995 (Iram, 1996). The chairman of PGC announced that some of these colleges might be upgraded soon into independent undergraduate institutions (*Ha'aretz* daily newspaper, June 9, 1992; June 16, 1992). This process is indeed expanding as of 1993 (CHE 1994).

As of the late 1980s there has been growing public discontent over restricted access to higher education, in general, and to highly desired professional studies, in particular. As an example of restricted access, while about 65% of applicants to humanities departments and 50% of applicants to social sciences departments were admitted during the 1987–1988 and 1988–1989 academic years, only 20 to 30% of applicants to law, medicine, paramedical, and engineering faculties were granted admission. These admission restrictions resulted in public pressure, which led in turn to political intervention and legislative initiatives by the Knesset. In 1990 the Knesset approved a resolution to open new law colleges. Although the law colleges were to be associated with existing law schools, they were not to become an integral part of universities and would not grant academic degrees, but rather, legal training. Another legislative proposal, which was approved by the Knesset, dealt with opening private "extrabudgetary" independent undergraduate institutions outside the aegis of the Council for Higher Education and the Planning and Grants Committee, and its budget. The CHE and the PGC opposed this proposal. These developments confirm Cerych and Subatier's (1986) argument that it may often be easier to set up entirely new institutions than to modify, let alone reform, existing ones. Such was the case with the creation of the open university in the United Kingdom and in other countries including Israel, the founding of the network of regional colleges in Norway and Israel, and the development of IUTs (Instituts Universitaires de Technologie) in France.

CONCLUSION

A more detailed analysis of these policies is required to predict the future course of the higher education system in Israel as a result of public pressure for democratization, pressures for expansion, legislative intervention, and the government's role in recent developments. It seems a reasonable speculation, however, that Israel's higher education system is on the threshold of two major and interrelated changes, which will affect the development of the system beyond the 1990s. The first, a changing relationship between government and universities, for example, more direct government involvement in higher education, and reduced authority for the Council for Higher Education and for the Planning and Budgeting Committee, and even possible abolition of these institutions, as exemplified by the fate of the University Grants Committee (UGC) in Britain (Watson, 1989). The second major issue that the higher education system may have to face in the 1990s and beyond is public concern over restrictions of access to higher education. Mounting public pressures are expressed by the media, enlisting political and parliamentary involvement. At present, various proposals are being debated by Parliament, that are aimed at democratizing access to existing institutions. These proposals include abolishing the psychometric entrance examination, introducing new professional and regional colleges, and establishing private higher education institutions that are not dependent on governmental or public funding. Another development is the increased involvement of foreign universities, particularly British and American universities, which have opened branches in Israel. These proposals and developments will affect the future course of Israeli higher education in structure and content.

Another development is in the direction of moving from "elite" to "mass" to "universal" access, that is, providing postsecondary education to every person wishing and able to benefit from it (Trow, 1970, 1976). Israel, like other industrialized nations (with the exception of the United States, Canada, and to some extent Japan) has paused at the threshold of a "mass" system, and may start to move toward the "universal" stage in higher education. It is too soon to predict, with confidence, what the outcomes of the present developments will be. It is likely that in the decade of the 1990s, significant changes in all these areas will remain an integral component of Israel's higher education system and that its structure will be significantly diversified as the twenty-first century approaches.

Higher education represents the last stage in the hierarchy of the formal Israeli educational system. The following chapter, "Informal Education," addresses some specific educational issues in the system of informal education. Informal education is related to formal education in the sense that it is provided in schools and is interdependent with the formal curriculum.

BIBLIOGRAPHY

Albert, C. (1982). *Technion: The story of Israel's Institute of Technology*. New York: American Technion Society, Israel Institute of Technology.

Aranne, L. (1970). *Government policy toward higher education in Israel*. Jerusalem: Center for Policy Studies.

Ben-David, J. (1983). "Research on higher education in Israel." *Higher Education in Europe, 8*, 76–79.

Ben-David, J. (1986). "Universities in Israel: Dilemmas of growth, diversification and administration." *Studies in Higher Education, 11*, 105–130.

Bendor, S. (1977). "University education in the State of Israel." In A. S. Knowles (ed.), *International Encyclopedia of Higher Education*. San Francisco: Jossey-Bass, 2331–2341.

Beytan, M., S. Cuenin, and J. Elcher. *L'evolution de l'enseignement superieur en France et en Israël (1972–1983)*. Dijon, France: Institute de Recherche sur l'Economie de l'Education, Université de Dijon.

CBS, Central Bureau of Statistics. (1988). *Statistical abstract of Israel*, No. 39. Jerusalem: Government Printer.

Cerych, Ladislav, and P. Sabatier. (1986). *Great expectations and mixed performance: The implementation of higher education reforms in Europe*. Trentham: European Institute of Education and Social Policy.

Council for Higher Education (CHE). (1984). *The Planning and Grants Committee: The higher education system in Israel—Guidelines on the development of the system and its planning for 1988 with a first glance at 1995*. Jerusalem: Planning and Grants Committee.

Council for Higher Education (CHE). (1985). *The Planning and Grants Committee annual report no. 12, academic year 1983–1984*. Jerusalem: Planning and Grants Committee.

Council for Higher Education (CHE). (1987a). *The Planning and Grants Committee annual report no. 13, academic year 1985–1986*. Jerusalem: Planning and Grants Committee.

Council for Higher Education (CHE). (1987b). *Report No. 2, The Sixth Council 1981–1986*. Jerusalem: Council for Higher Education.

Council for Higher Education (CHE). (1988a). *The Planning and Grants Committee annual report no. 14, academic year 1986–1987*. Jerusalem: Planning and Grants Committee.

Council for Higher Education (CHE). (1988b). *The Planning and Grants Committee. Higher education in Israel—Statistical abstract 1986–1987*. Jerusalem: Planning and Grants Committee.

Council for Higher Education (CHE). (1989). *The Planning and Grants Committee annual report No. 15, academic year 1987–1988*. Jerusalem: Planning and Grants Committee.

Council for Higher Education (CHE). (1990a). *The Planning and Grants Committee annual report No. 16, academic year 1988–1989*. Jerusalem: Planning and Grants Committee.

Council for Higher Education (CHE). (1990b). *The Planning and Grants Committee: The first degree in Israel—Guidelines, facts and data*. Jerusalem: Planning and Grants Committee.

Council for Higher Education (CHE). (1991). *The Planning and Budgeting Committee annual report No. 17, academic year 1989–1990*. Jerusalem: Planning and Budgeting Committee.

Council for Higher Education (CHE). (1992). *Newsletter of the Planning and Budgeting Committee* (Hebrew).

Council for Higher Education (CHE). (1994). *The Planning and Budgeting Committee annual report No. 28, academic year 1993–1994*. Jerusalem: Planning and Budgeting Committee.

Council for Higher Education (CHE). (1995). *Newsletter of the Planning and Budgeting Committee* (Hebrew).

Gamson, Zelda, and T. Horowitz. (1983). "Symbolism and survival in developing organizations: Regional colleges in Israel." *Higher Education, 12*, 171–190.

Globerson, A. (1978). *Higher Education and Employment: A Case Study of Israel*. New York: Praeger.

Ha'aretz daily newspaper, June 9, 1992; June 16, 1992.

Halperin, S. (1984). *Any home a campus? Everyman's university of Israel*. Washington, DC: Institute of Education Leadership.

Hebrew University. (1950). *The Hebrew University of Jerusalem 1925–1950*. Jerusalem: Hebrew University.

Iram, Y. (1983). "Vision and fulfillment: The evolution of the Hebrew University 1901–1950." *History of Higher Education Annual, 3*, 123–143.

Iram, Y. (1987). "Quality and control in higher education in Israel." *European Journal of Education, 22*, 145–159.

Iram, Y. (1992a). "Centralization trends in higher education: Israel's Planning and Grants Committee." *Higher Education, 23*, 33–43.

Iram, Y. (1992b). "Curricular and structural developments at the Hebrew University, 1928–1948." *History of Universities, 11*, 205–241.

Iram, Y. (1996). "*Michlalot ezeriot*—Regional colleges in Israel: Challenges, promises and prospects of an alternative model in higher education." In R. Latiner Raby and N. Tarrow (eds.), *Dimensions of the community college: International, intercultural and multicultural perspectives*. New York: Garland Publishing, 291–301.

Kleinberger, A. F. (1969). *Society schools and progress in Israel*. Oxford: Pergamon Press.

Klinov, R. (1988). *Allocation of public resources to Israel's education system: Issues and options*. Jerusalem: Center for Policy Studies.

Schatzker, C. (1987). "Tradition and reform at the universities of Israel." In H. Röhr's (ed.), *Tradition and reform of the university under an international perspective — An interdisciplinary approach*. Frankfurt: Verlag Peter Lang, 185–202.

Shprinzak, D., and E. Bar. (eds.) (1991). *Ministry of education and culture, 1991*. Jerusalem: Ministry of Education and Culture.

Silberberg, R. (1987). *The studies for the first degree in the higher education system*. Jerusalem: CHE, PGC.

Stanner, R. (1963). *The legal basis of education in Israel*. Jerusalem: Ministry of Education and Culture.

Technion (Israel Institute of Technology) (1953). *History of the Technion in the beginning: 1908–1925*. Haifa: Technion.

Trow, M. A. (1970). "Reflections on the transition from mass to universal higher education." *Daedalus, 9*, 1–42.

Trow, M. A. (1976). "Elite higher education: An endangered species?" *Minerva, 14*, 355–376.

Trow, M. A. (1984). "The analysis of status." In B. R. Clark (ed.), *Perspectives on higher education*. Berkeley, Los Angeles: University of California Press, 132–164.

Watson, K. (1989). "The changing pattern of higher education in England and Wales — The end of an era?" *International Review of Education, 35*, 283–304.

Zadok, M. (1984). "The Israeli Planning and Grants Committee at the crossroads: From shock absorber to steering wheel." *Higher Education, 13*, 535–544.

Chapter 6

Informal Education

The informal educational system falls into two categories based on an organizational viewpoint: "out of school activities," which include programs conducted outside the school, and "extracurricular activities," which include those activities conducted within the school.

Another approach to informal education emphasizes the unique features of the informal educational system, which enable it to fulfill socioeducational tasks. These tasks are not fulfilled by schools and other educational institutions. According to this approach, informal education is neither incidental nor unintentional, but rather a unique educational method that integrates contents, forms of action, and principles of structure.

Kahane (1988) developed ten theoretical dimensions of informal education, which sometimes are referred to as the "ten commandments." These dimensions are: voluntarism, multidimensionality, moratorium, trial and error, symmetric relationships, collegial supervision, structural flexibility, symbolism, expressive orientation, and ambivalence of meanings. The dimensions cluster around four major axes. One cluster emphasizes structural features, such as voluntarism and structural flexibility. The importance of voluntarism lies in the fact that students may join or leave the activity program whenever they want. Due to their freedom, students' power to bargain with adults is strengthened, and the opportunities to pursue activities suited to their capabilities and areas of interest are increased. In order that voluntarism be realized, a flexible and modular program structure is required, and that program structure should be open to changes and improvisations with regard to timing, contents, and composition of student bodies.

The second cluster of dimensions focuses on the contents of activities, which should be multidimensional and cover many various areas of students' interests. This enables students to ease tension, as well as to build resources, such as feelings of strength, positive self-image, and the capability to internalize the norms and values of society (Coleman, 1971). The different activities within the program should be of the same social status and prestige to enable large numbers of participants to foster their individual capabilities and to attain excellence in numerous fields. This in turn may contribute to the strengthening of students' personalities. Effects may be immediate for the individual student, such as improved personal feelings, but they may also have long-term implications, such as the development of intellectual and emotional skills. On the group level, these dimensions create a sense of solidarity based upon the mutual dependence of the participants in the program.

The third cluster relates to the sociological characteristics of the dimensions, namely moratorium (Erikson, 1953), symbolism, and ambivalence of meanings. These activities provide students with trial and error situations in which students may fail in their actions without bearing full responsibility; but through a second effort they may gain experience within their peer groups. Symbolism refers to the development of skills to integrate between the symbolic and value meanings of activities and their practical uses. The ambivalence of the activities aims to create the environment in which participants are protected, because they are judged by particularistic criteria, similar to the environment in the family. Yet at the same time, participants are exposed to universalistic criteria, such as in society, which is dominated by free and open competition. Consequently, the activity program serves as a bridge for students progressing from childhood through adolescence to adulthood.

The fourth cluster of dimensions deals with mechanisms of control; namely autonomy, symmetric relationships, and peer-group supervision. The common denominator of these dimensions is a more balanced division of power between adults and youth. Autonomy allows children to participate in the process of decision making and, by means of trial and error, to learn principles of mutual responsibility, subordination, and leadership. The relations within the group are symmetrical, based upon equivalency of resources, which reduces adult use of coercion and power (Coleman, 1967). The social interactions among members of peer groups are based upon universal norms and values, which embody the injunction "not to inflict upon your neighbor what you hate yourself." Finally, social control is based upon positive means, such as giving explanations and exerting influence in order to reach group consensus, as well as refraining from the use of threats and sanctions.

The ten dimensions suggest a unique educational approach by means of which two main objectives might be reached. Children, as well as adults, are able to spend time in an environment that is both pleasant and educational. In addition to leisure activities, the unique educational environment also provides participants in programs with important intellectual and emotional resources. Even youth at risk who have not been exposed to a nurturing environment, mutual feelings of trust, and positive role-models at home may profit from such an educational program (Bronfenbrenner, 1970; Goodman, 1970). It should be noted, though, that these dimensions suggest the ideal type of informal education, which is realized only partially in reality.

HISTORICAL BACKGROUND

The interval between the British Mandate over Palestine (1919) and the establishment of the State of Israel (1948) can be divided into two major periods. The period 1918–1935 was characterized by the social orientation of informal education, especially by work with younger children, and was conducted mainly by voluntary women's organizations. These children were known as "nighttime shoe lace-sellers in coffee-shops." Concomitantly, youth movements were active, which were influenced by Zionist youth movements in Central Europe and the English Scouts Movement. During the second period, 1936–1948, the youth branch was established within the Department of Education in the Vaad Leumi. The new unit was responsible for the Hebrew Scouts Movement, playgrounds of the Hadassah movement, clubs of Israeli voluntary groups, organization of courses for personnel training, and finally, the foundation of youth hostels and summer camps (Meyuhas, 1975).

After the establishment of the state, the youth division was taken over by the youth department within the Ministry of Education and Culture. The new institution did not limit itself to coordinating existing activities and initiating new ones. The number of voluntary activities decreased, and informal education became a national municipal service known as complementary education. It included all informal educational services for children and youth during their leisure time or after school or work, without regard for economic status or political orientations (Meyuhas, 1970).

During the first decade after statehood, 1948–1958, a time of mass immigration from developing countries, informal education continued to focus on younger children. Many "houses for pupils" (*batei talmid*) were established in new development areas, branches for youth services were initiated on the local level, and special supervisors for informal education were appointed. In addition, the number of summer camps and youth hostels was increased, and the youth leaders' training institutions were established.

With the exception of youth movements, which were active within schools, the majority of informal activities were separated from school programs. This situation changed during the 1960s with the increase in the number of schools and the heterogenization of student populations. Out-of-school informal activities were initiated by the government and later adopted by the municipal authorities, whereas within-school activities were initiated within schools, later adopted by the municipalities, and only then recognized by the government. Since 1965 the organizations that deal with informal education were institutionalized within the Ministry of Education and Culture. Since this time financial resources have been reserved and a special function within the school, known as the coordinator of extracurricular activities, was planned.

During the last decade, with the development of the orientation toward community education, informal educational activities have undergone additional changes. Many activities have become integrated within community centers, school buildings, or in separate buildings. These activities include youth as well as adults. Concomitantly, the educational orientation toward involvement in the community of children and youth has intensified.

THE FABRIC OF INFORMAL EDUCATION

Youth Movements

One of the earliest informal educational systems in Israel is the youth movement, which is associated with political parties and supported ideologically and financially by them. The first movements were established at the beginning of the 1930s, and today there are fourteen active youth movements. These youth movements are democratic organizations, that are based upon decentralized authorities and integrated by countrywide leadership. The functions of this leadership include decision making on questions of policy, preparation of training programs for youth leaders, mobilization of man power, and organization of countrywide projects. Heading the movements are non-professional youth leaders, who are appointed by the respective political parties.

Youth movements differ from other educational institutions, both formally and informally, by nature of their goals. In youth movements education is not a goal by itself, but serves as a means to reach general national and political objectives. The youth leaders are members of their respective political movements. They are trained by older members, during a period of two to four years, and are usually in charge of youth who are younger than them by only two or three years.

Activities are based on age and divided into three age groups: ten to fourteen years, fifteen to sixteen years, and seventeen to eighteen years. The process of political socialization within the movement gradually intensifies in proportion to the increase in age. The programs focus on topics related to general world perspectives, national Zionist issues, and ideologies of the individual movements. Methods of conducting the programs vary from games with younger groups, to more academic activities with older groups. All movements, for all ages, create a special social atmosphere and involve sports and excursions. Thus, youth movements develop a unique subculture of youth, which is reinforced by symbols, such as, uniforms, flags, and ceremonies. The movements require a high degree of commitment to their ideals and much effort in terms of time and devotion. Consequently, the membership of youth movements is quite selective and comprises only about one-third of the pertinent age groups. Only members who fulfill the requirements of the movement continue to remain affiliated. Such members are mainly associated with elite social groups of Western origin and established socioeconomic strata and study in academic high schools.

Youth movements apply major dimensions of informal education in their programs. Activities are based on voluntary participation of members and are diverse and multidimensional in order to address the needs of participants. The interaction between the leaders, who are young and nonprofessional, and the members is based on equal terms and mutuality. The leader-participant relationship is controlled, to a large degree, by the participants themselves. Activities are loaded with symbolic meanings: they provide immediate expressive effects, by means of leisure activities, but also long-term effects which contribute to the development of intellectual and social skills.

Two major periods are prominent in the development of youth movements: the period of pioneering, from the 1920s until the War of Independence in 1948, and the individualistic period, which has continued from statehood until today. The first period corresponds to the idealistic period of the Yishuv, which was characterized by collectivist values. These values were realized through voluntary projects in the realm of security and the establishment of new settlements. During this period young people were more influenced by youth movements than by their families and schools.

The main aims and functions of youth movements were to build a new society and protect it, while negating the ethos of Exile and its negative characteristics as envisaged by the *halutz*, such as scholastic attitudes toward life, unproductive occupations, and detachment from nature. The ideal was to be achieved by physical labor, mainly agricultural, and the establishment of new settlements (*Kibbutzim*) near to nature, where a meaningful and simple life could be fostered. In addition, the social and psychological needs of youth were addressed by expressive activities, which provided for leisure time in order to relieve tension, but also to promote socialization into the new society and ensure continuity of leadership.

During the second period, the orientation of youth movements became more individualistic, with more emphasis on leisure and social activities. Many functions that were previously fulfilled voluntarily were now taken over by formal and public state authorities. The army now oversaw functions in state protection, central and local authorities supervised education, and political systems professionalized leadership training. Thus, the unique synthesis that combined the missionary spirit of youth movements with their objectives of socialization changed. In addition to conceptual changes, structural and practical changes also occurred. Schools gained priority over youth movements as a result of intensive industrial and scientific developments, which demanded more formal diplomas. Furthermore, central and local informal educational systems, besides the multimedia, competed with youth movements for young people's leisure time.

In order to adjust to the new situation, youth movements became less selective and absorbed new populations from lower socioeconomic levels, mainly of Oriental origin. They emphasized activities with more immediate effects, such as games and sports, at the expense of value education requiring ideological commitment. Because of the high adolescent dropout rates, youth from fourteen years of age and older, as well as children as young as seven years of age, were drawn to the youth movements. The attrition of older youth was probably due to the academic pressure placed on them, as well as the fact that the youth movements no longer fulfilled their needs. New developments have recently emerged, such as sixteen- and seventeen-year-old students volunteering to complete their studies in new settlement towns, thus assisting the local pupils. But the new movement is limited in number of participants and selective by character.

Compensatory Education: Informal Education for All

These frameworks, established for youth by adults, have no predetermined objectives. Their only goal is to address the needs of participants. The various frameworks offer diverse activity programs in which younger children and youth may participate, without any ideological commitment. Leadership is mainly professionally trained and supervised by the local authorities. The relevant unit within the Ministry of Education and Culture directs the activities and provides them with partial financial support.

Until the middle of the 1930s, voluntary organizations founded seventy-one youth clubs, which took care of about four thousand children. Significant developments occurred after the establishment of the state, following mass immigration and child neglect. Since the end of 1950, with the development of the formal infrastructure of the educational system, it became evident that the formal educational system alone was unable to address the needs of children and youth. Consequently, the Ministry of Education and Culture, together with local educational authorities, developed special informal educational frameworks, trained professional leaders, and allocated special budgets. The central institute for primary school children was the "House for the Student," which aimed to help new immigrants integrate into the new society. This was achieved by means of group games, social meetings, enrichment clubs, and help in school work between three to four days a week, for two to three hours in the afternoon. These activities were coordinated by the schools and took place mainly in school buildings.

A more independent framework was the Youth House, which was located in neighborhoods, rather than in schools. About 200–250 youth participated in the programs of each house. Over the years this institute gained in importance, especially the Central Youth House in large cities, which developed prestigious programs, such as orchestras and choirs. Similar to the Central Youth House is the Community Center, which was established in 1968 by the Governmental Society for Centers of Culture: Youth and Sports, and is affiliated with the Ministry of Education and Culture. The centers are active mainly in new towns and in poorer neighborhoods of older cities and include programs for the elderly, adults, adolescents, and younger children during the school year.

No exact data are available as to the number of participants in informal educational activity programs. But apparently, participation does not exceed 30% of the relevant age group. Younger children participate more than older children, and children from lower socioeconomic backgrounds participate more than children from higher socioeconomic backgrounds, especially in out-of-school frameworks (Schmida, 1979; Central Bureau of Statistics, 1993).

Objectives. The main objectives of complementary programs, as stated by their founders, are to provide students with the following: relief of emotional tensions due to school competition; opportunities for the expression of emotional life; promotion of the unique talents of each individual; opportunities for the development of youth culture; facilitation of meetings between students of the opposite sex; and the promotion of leisure time and social integration. It is argued that formal schooling fails to fulfill these tasks due to its strict rules. Compensatory education is based on the conception that children's needs should be addressed in accordance with their internal growth pattern, without external restrictions and ideological commitments. Educators disagree as to the importance of these activities: are they useful only to "have a good time," or do they also contribute to the building of new and important future resources? Due to the unique educational philosophy of informal education, no structured programs exist, the leaders are not always competent, and the rate of turnover among them is very high. Leaders tend to improvise the activity programs according to the changing situation. As a result, the participants do not feel committed to the programs and act often without feelings of reciprocity and involvement. The programs focus more on the contents of the various clubs, sometimes for purposes of shows and social events, and less on social activities and free expression of feelings.

Following proposals by educators from the academy and the Ministry of Education and Culture, serious changes have been introduced since the beginning of the 1970s. More emphasis was given to weaker populations, children received help with their homework, and families were supported within their communities. In addition, systematic efforts were made to develop educational contents for the activity programs. In order to intensify participants' commitment, a staff of young leaders was trained, who helped the professional leaders.

Working with Youth at Risk

"Youth at risk" includes fourteen- to eighteen-year-old adolescents, who do not study or work at a steady base. These young people are mainly of Oriental origin, that live either in new settlement towns or in peripheral neighborhoods of more established cities. Their social values and norms are removed from those of the mainstream population, and they are often embroiled with the police, due to drugs and other related crimes. There is no exact data as to the range of the phenomenon, but it reaches approximately 8% of the relevant age cohort (Ministry of Education and Culture, 1992).

At the beginning, work with youth at risk aimed to prevent delinquency. However, since the end of the 1960s, programs became more education-oriented, to make youth conscious of their situation and to strengthen their motivation for change of values, attitudes, and modes of behavior. It was believed that if these young people were to be provided with basic learning skills and vocational training, the process of normative socialization would be strengthened, and the social gap between them and the mainstream population would be narrowed.

The professional work with youth at risk serves as an alternative option to families and schools. Methods are flexible and sensitive, and change is gradual according to the situation and the individuals involved. The most popular program is centered around youth gangs, mainly boys who are also known as "street-corner youth." They meet with the youth leader in a location the youth chooses and on their conditions. Thirty percent of this category of youth are girls, who are treated on a more individual level. Only after the leader has gained the confidence of these youth, would he attempt to introduce changes; gradually he works on their medical problems, deals with difficulties at work, and problems with the police. Usually he encounters difficulties in procuring the cooperative support of the relevant social services. Moreover, the personality and the training of youth workers are sine qua non to their professional success. Although the level of general education of these leaders is usually higher than that of other youth leaders, their special professional training is poor and their rate of turnover is high, reaching even 40% per year.

New developments in working with youth at risk are evident in the establishment of youth centers, where needed services are concentrated and located in one place, and through boarding schools, where solitary youth are being integrated.

EXTRACURRICULAR ACTIVITIES

Extracurricular activities are informal educational activities within schools, which aim to fulfill goals that remain unfulfilled by schools due to their formal structural features. These activities are defined as within-school programs and events, that do not award students any academic credit. The activities are planned and conducted by students themselves or in cooperation with school authorities. They aim not only to entertain students but also to enable them to express themselves in various realms of interests and talents (Good, 1959). They contribute to the development of the student's whole personality, as well as to his or her ability to make judgments and choices. The development of these abilities is very important for youth in Israeli society, because of the many problems with which they struggle. These problems include Jewish-Zionist identity, cultural pluralism and social gaps, the Arab-Israeli conflict, and the duty to serve in the army. Schools, especially high schools, are formal systems based on division of labor and professional specialization of staff. Their main orientations are toward academic and professional achievements, which limit their capacities and time to address immediate problems and events as well as more comprehensive processes in students' development.

During the prestate period, schools served as "cultural pioneers" of national aims. Teachers contributed to the renewal of the Hebrew language and literature and inspired their students with enthusiasm for national developments, such as building new settlements and laying the foundation for a new society. However, this orientation changed after statehood, when schools began to concentrate mainly on formal teaching in order to prepare students for professional and economic success. An additional educational program was needed, which was aimed at social education in school and the development of more rounded personalities of students. Schools were supported by special divisions within the Ministry of Education and Culture and began to develop a network of clubs in the areas of arts, sport, entertainment, and academic subjects, which were not included in the formal curriculum. In addition, schools experimented with various forms of education in democracy and established student councils and committees, student newspapers, and yearbooks. These activities were supervised by the program coordinator, who was specially trained and received pedagogical and financial support from the ministry. The coordinator's task was not easy, as he competed with formal schooling for students' time and institutional prestige.

Due to the fact that extracurricular activities are part of a school's formal structure, they actually act as a semiinformal educational system by partially and uniquely applying the dimensions of informal education. As the formal educational orientation is dominant in schools, the effectiveness of the informal approach is reduced. Often the informal approach adopts the dimensions of formal education, with the exception of examinations and grades, and only rarely does it influence the formal educational approach, serving as a mechanism for change (Schmida, 1979).

The activity program offers a wide range of options and, depending on the size of the school, students may choose among various activities. Some activities, like homeroom and student assemblies, are mandatory. The autonomy of students and their self-control are less evident in these programs than in independent informal institutions. Schools co-opt students and may confer them with the status of secondary leadership. Thus, a better interaction between adults and students is attained as students gain in power, but adults still remain the domineering group.

The importance of the program is based on its free and democratic atmosphere. Activities are unstructured, without predetermined curricula. Students who fail in academic subjects may excel in activities, thus improving their self-confidence and self-image. The approach of adults to students is more spontaneous, which helps students to relieve tension and give free expression to their feelings.

CONCLUSION

In addition, the following peripheral, informal educational frameworks should be mentioned: permanent camp sites, which mainly serve youth movements according to a fixed schedule; youth hostels, which are located in various regions of the country and also host study groups; country schools, which integrate nature protection, guidance activities, and research; and special institutes for Zionist education, which teach grade 11 high school students seminars on social and national topics.

The informal educational system is not legally based, and responsibility for it among various public and governmental agencies is not defined. Usually, the local authority is in charge of the program, on the condition that its citizens are ready to give the needed political and financial support. In weaker local authorities, governmental agencies increase their involvement. Often, during budgetary crises, informal educational services are the first to be reduced. In addition to the financial weakness of these services, they suffer from pedagogical ambiguity. This ambiguity derives from the relationships between formal and informal education, as well as the definitions of informal educational activities suitable to various student populations.

The following chapter deals with Arab education. "Arab Education: Development versus Control" was written by an Arab educator at the special request of the authors. Although Arab education in Israel is an integral part of the state educational system and shares most of its characteristics, it merits special discussion because of the unique status of the Arab minority within the predominantly Jewish majority in Israel.

BIBLIOGRAPHY

Bronfenbrenner, U. (1970). *Two worlds of childhood, US and USSR*. New York: Russell Sage Foundation.

Central Bureau of Statistics. (1993). *Extracurricular activities of 9th–12th grade pupils, Hebrew and Arab education*, 1990/91, Part I, Special Series No. 946, Jerusalem.

Coleman, J. S. (1967). "Game models of economic and political systems." In S. Z. Klausner (ed.), *The study of total societies*. Garden City, NY: Doubleday/Anchor Books.

Coleman, J. S. (1971). *Resources for social change*. New York: Wiley and Sons.

Erikson, E. H. (1953). "Growth and crises in the healthy personality." In C. K. Kluckhon and H. A. Murray's (eds.), *Personality in nature, society and culture*. New York: A. Knopf, pp. 185–225.

Good, C. V. (ed.). (1959). *Dictionary of education*. New York: McGraw-Hill.

Goodman, M. E. (1970). *The culture of childhood*. New York: Teachers' College Press.

Kahane, R. (1988). "Multicode organizations: A conceptual framework of the analysis of boarding schools." *Sociology of Education, 61*, pp. 211–226.

Meyuhas, Y. (ed.). (1970). *35 years of complementary education*. Jerusalem: Ministry of Education and Culture, Youth Department. (Hebrew).

Meyuhas, Y. (ed.). (1975). *The book of complementary education*. Jerusalem: Ministry of Education and Culture, Youth Department, pp. 218–219, 223 (Hebrew).

Ministry of Education and Culture. (1992). *In the mirror of numbers*. In D. Sprinzak, E. Bar, and D. Levi-Mazlom (eds.), Department of Economy and Statistics, Jerusalem, Table No. 12 (Hebrew).

Schmida, M. (1979). *Social education in high school*. Tel Aviv: Ahiasaf Publishing (Hebrew).

Chapter 7

Arab Education: Development versus Control

Majid Al-Haj

INTRODUCTION

Since the establishment of the State of Israel, both qualitative and quantitative changes have occurred in Arab education. This includes the development of educational institutions, teachers' training, women's education, and most important, the conversion of the educational system to a "mass system" that is open to all population levels. However, along with these changes, Arab education still faces severe problems in various areas resulting from neglect, institutional discrimination, and lack of involvement from the Arab population. This chapter presents a general review of the trends of development in the Arab educational system in Israel.

ARAB EDUCATION AFTER 1948: QUANTITATIVE CHANGE

Following the 1948 Arab-Israel War (War of Independence), the Arab population remaining in the country became a small minority without political, social, or religious leadership. The Arab cultural and educational institutions in the big cities collapsed, while the majority of the urban Palestinian population became refugees in Arab countries.

Indeed, the starting point of Arab education in Israel was low in comparison to Jewish education. At the time of the establishment of the State of Israel there were only forty-five Arab elementary schools and one high school in Nazareth (see Table 7.1). However, within ten years the number of elementary schools tripled and the trend of development continued. In 1993, there were 335 elementary schools, 89 intermediate schools, and 94 high schools, spread over most of the Arab settlements (SAI, 1993).

Table 7.1

Schools in the Arab and Jewish Educational System, 1948–1996

Year	Elementary Education			Secondary Education			
	Total	Regular Schools	Special Schools	Total	Intermediate Schools	High Schools	Total Elementary + Secondary
Arab Schools							
1948/49	45	45	–	1	–	1	46
1959/60	139	138	1	7	–	7	146
1969/70	219	207	12	37	4	35	(256)
1979/80	312	294	18	59	43	49	(371)
1995/96	369	325	43	(149)	104	101	(518)
Jewish Schools							
1948/49	467	467	–	98	–	98	565
1959/60	1,051	1149	352	353	–	353	1,854
1969/70	1,519	1,235	284	(545)	32	544	(2,064)
1979/80	1,475	1,261	214	(521)	248	478	(1,996)
1995/96	1,568	1,355	203	(746)	371	621	(2,314)

References: Central Bureau of Statistics, Statistical Abstract of Israel 1986, No. 37, p. 522; 1989, No. 40, p. 606; 1993, No. 44, p. 638; 1996, No. 47, p. 487.

Note: Schools with more than one level of education (e.g., junior high and high school) were counted in the table separately, but in the total were counted as one institution (in parentheses).

SCHOOL ATTENDANCE

Parallel to the growing number of educational institutions, the number of students also increased. In 1949 there were 11,129 students in Arab schools, compared to 269,364 students in 1996; an increase by twenty (see SAI, 1996). An important development in the Arab educational system was the increase in regular attendance of female students.

In the early 1950s female students constituted only 18.6% of all Arab students. Today female students constitute 47% of all Arab students. In 1995 female attendance was higher than male attendance in both Arab and Hebrew schools. In conclusion, regular attendance of Arab high school students is lower than their Jewish peers—673 compared to 959 for 1,000 students in 1994–95.

The discrepancy in regular attendance between Arab and Jewish students begins in the pre-elementary stage. Sixty-seven percent of two-year-old Jewish children attend nursery school, while in the Arab sector there are almost no nurseries. Only 20% of all three-year-old Arab children attend a precompulsory kindergarten as opposed to 96% of their Jewish peers. Fifty-five percent of all four-year-old Arab children attend kindergarten, as opposed to 99% of their Jewish peers. In other words, Jewish and Arab children begin their education with a discrepancy of two to three years, in favor of Jewish children. This discrepancy is revealed later in the disparities of learning achievements between Arab and Jewish children.

According to a 1985 report on Arab education, 20% of Arab students drop out of school prior to completing eight years of learning, 32% drop out before completing compulsory education at the end of grade 10, and 50% drop out prior to the end of high school (Ministry of Education and Culture, 1985). These statistics explain the increase in juvenile delinquency among Arab children. A 1984 report of the Ministry of Education and Culture indicated an increasing rate in juvenile delinquency in the Arab sector, a finding which is directly related to the rate of dropouts from school (Toledano, 1984).

QUANTITATIVE CHANGE

An impressive change in learning standards at Arab high schools occurred in the middle of the 1970s. It was expressed, among other things, in the higher rate of grade 12 students studying obligatory subjects toward at least four units in their matriculation. Nevertheless, a wide discrepancy still existed between the achievement levels of Arab and Jewish students, based on ethnic or religious factors. Among Arabs, Muslims constitute the highest rate of underprivileged children. Only 45% of Muslim students passed the regular matriculations in 1995, compared with 52.5% of Druze and 61.7% of Christian students. The passing rate of the most successful group among Arabs, the Christians, is equal to the weakest group among Jews, those coming from North Africa and Asia. A similar discrepancy can be found in vocational education (SAI, 1996). The rate of Arab high school graduates indicates a more serious situation than the results of the matriculation certificate. Only 45% of Arab students graduated from high school, compared to 81.6% of Jewish students (Israel State Comptroller, 1992). From children attending 1st grade in 1978, only 13.7% of Arab students obtained a matriculation certificate, compared to 42.3% of their Jewish peers (Israel State Comptroller, 1992).

EDUCATION SERVICES

Although Arab schools are maintained in reasonable physical conditions, the gap between them and Jewish schools has grown larger in other areas. Many services that naturally exist in Jewish schools cannot be found in Arab schools (National Committee of Arab Local Authorities, 1986). Psychological counseling is provided in 85.5% of Jewish schools, while in the Arab sector such service exists only in nine local authorities, in which less than 10% of Arab students attend (SAI, 1991). General doctors, dentists, nurses, and social workers visit most Jewish schools. These kinds of services hardly exist in Arab schools. The Jewish educational system offers a variety of social, cultural, and educational activities with governmental support. Arab students are limited to the routine curriculum (Ministry of Education and Culture, 1985). A variety of services exist, almost only in Jewish schools, that include libraries, enhanced study programs, homework help, a long school day, computerized diagnosis and guidance, instrumental enrichment, plays, concerts, and museum visits, reading centers, and extracurricular activities, such as music, dance, and arts and crafts classes.

The majority of Arab schools do not offer students lessons in music, arts, or sports. As a result of constant cutbacks in regular curriculum hours, to which Jewish schools are also subjected, Arab schools are forced to secure time allocation for the main subjects, such as languages and mathematics, on account of other more "luxurious" subjects (National Committee of Arab Local Authorities, 1986). An official report of the Ministry of Education and Culture stated that even if Arab education was to undergo affirmative action, ten to fifteen years will have to pass until equality between Arab and Jewish schools is attained (Ministry of Education and Culture, 1985).

It is noteworthy that the state of services in Arab schools improved during the Labor–Meretz government (1992–96). According to data received from Dr. Gideon Ben-Dror, the Ministry of Education and Culture adopted a policy of preference for Arab education. This is evident in the allocation of funds to the Arab sector, which received relatively larger amounts in proportion to the total student population.

In the years 1992–1994 Arab schools were given an extra 58,499 hours above basic allotment, in addition to 6,000 hours to enhance "special care" students. During this time, 609 classes were established, inadequate buildings were replaced, and, in addition, thirteen kindergarten classes were built in 1994 (Ben-Dror, 1994). Nevertheless, there is a wide gap between Jewish and Arab schools. For example, in 1995 Arab students constituted only 1.9% of those who participated in a special project aimed at increasing the number of students eligible for the matriculation certificate. In addition, the proportion of Arab localities in the "holistic project," which was implemented in thirty disadvantaged communities was only 5% of the total budget (Adva Center, 1996).

ARAB TEACHERS—NUMBERS AND EDUCATIONAL LEVEL

One of the basic problems of Arab education from the beginning was the lack of teachers with adequate training. In the last twenty years, there has been a considerable improvement in the educational level of Arab teachers. In 1997–1998, for the first time since the establishment of the state, there was no shortage of Arab teachers. Arab schools managed to fill all their positions and to absorb seminar and university graduates (*Davar*, 1977). The main change occurred during the 1970s. Between 1970–1980, the percentage of Arab teachers with academic degrees increased from 4% to 21%, while at the same time the percentage of unqualified teachers decreased from 55% to 22%. Since then, an increase in the educational level of Arab teachers is slowly observed in the academic education area.

The ratio between students and teachers in Arab schools is higher than the ratio in Jewish schools. In 1990 the student-teacher ratio in Arab schools was 31.1, compared to 27.9 in Jewish schools. The average number of students per school was 475 in Arab schools, compared to 412 in Jewish schools (SAI, 1991). A report of the Ministry of Education and Culture confirmed that in order to raise Arab teaching conditions to the same level existing in the Jewish sector, it required an additional 5,000 teaching positions (Ministry of Education and Culture, 1985).

Another aspect of criticism is related to the quality of training given to Arab students in teachers' seminaries. The Peled Committee recommended to increase the level of Arab seminars to an academic level, as well as increasing admission requirements (Ministry of Education and Culture, 1975). These recommendations were gradually applied, and in 1980 teacher training was prolonged to three years. In addition to written and oral admission examinations, it was determined that a matriculation certificate would be needed as an admission requirement (Ministry of Education and Culture, 1985). Moreover, seminars developed special training areas tailored to suit the needs of the Arab educational system (Roseberg, 1985). Also, the College of Arab Teachers in Haifa was recently recognized by the Council for Higher Education in Israel, and the Arab Teachers' College in Bet Berl is in the process of receiving full academic recognition. Nevertheless, there is room for further development in the curriculum and teacher training methods. The Teachers' Association appointed a special committee to examine teachers' training programs in the Arab sector. The committee report criticized the methods of teacher training in the Arab sector. The report recommended to open a new teachers' seminary in the Galilee, instead of the existing seminary in Haifa (Teachers' Association of Israel, 1988). The report also emphasized that the lack of teaching positions in Arab schools is one of the main obstacles for teachers in properly accomplishing their task (Teachers' Association of Israel, 1988).

Another severe problem is teachers' extension studies. There is complete chaos in the existing system, and currently the gaining of qualification scores is mainly a guide for teachers. There is neither coordination between the organizing elements of studies, nor a complete strategy guiding the contents of extension studies. A survey conducted by the author in a few Arab schools found that teachers are discontent with regard to extension studies and their contents. It is reasonable to assume that if this situation continues, with a lack of professional organizations supporting schools with new ideas and qualified human resources, all funds thus far invested will be wasted. Indeed, this type of training has failed and was eventually abolished by the Ministry of Education and Culture.

THE TEACHER, THE ESTABLISHMENT, AND THE COMMUNITY

Since 1948, Arab teachers were in a position of contradicting expectations. On one hand, they were under the inspection of the military government and were forced to cease all political involvement due to fear of dismissal (Cohen, 1951; Jiryis, 1976). On the other hand, as the remnant of the educated elite of the Arab population at that time, the community perceived them as role models ready to join the ranks of leadership (S. Mari, 1978). These pressures made the Arab teacher's role as an educational leader almost impossible. State authorities tried to hold control over Arab schools and create a peaceful atmosphere, in an attempt to rule the Arab population in general and strengthen the feelings of affiliation to Israeli citizenship.

Along with the abolishment of the military government in 1966, the intervention of the security system declined. A security classification was held as an effective controlling tool over Arab teachers and the Arab educational system. Thus, teachers who did not comply with the political consensus of the authorities were not employed. An Arab teacher applying for a teaching position was required to fill out, in addition to the regular questionnaire, a personal questionnaire, which had nothing to do with professional skills. According to this additional questionnaire and other examinations, the office decided if the applicant is "of suitable qualifications" for teaching (Al-Haj, 1995a). Security classification also served as a criterion in choosing applicants for Arab teachers' schools. Officially there is no discrimination in this act, since the applicant completes a questionnaire for security reasons. In the case of rejection, applicants are not given the real reason (Al-Haj, 1995b). It should be noted that the former Ministry of Education and Culture canceled the additional questionnaire for Arab teachers in 1994, according to an interview with Abd el-Halim Zuabi, the minister's advisor.

As opposed to elementary and junior schools, the appointment of high school teachers is not completely under the supervision of the Ministry of Education and Culture. The local authority has a major part in hiring and firing teachers. Before the end of each academic year, the mayor announces the required positions in the municipal high schools (in private schools, the executive council announces the available positions). A professional committee, represented by the local authority and the Ministry of Education and Culture, which sometimes includes representatives from the parents committee, interviews applicants and selects successful candidates. However, the professional decision of the committee does not suffice; the applicants' list is sent for final certification to the Ministry of Education and Culture. Thus, intervention in Arab high schools is not solely on the part of the government, but also on the part of local authorities. On certain occasions the mayor of the local authority uses his power to promote members of his family or supporters.

Due to lack of local resources the local authority is an important channel in allocating resources and providing benefits. Since the government cannot accept all university graduates into office, the local authority is the main employer of a considerable part of Arab academics, who are forced to compete over positions in their localities (Al-Haj and Rosenfeld, 1990). High school teachers are the main occupation source for Arab academics, a position which is exploited by people whose interests do not always comply with those of the school. For a long time Arab teachers were forbidden to discuss political issues in class. Consequently, Arab teachers lost much of their credibility and were considered government servants in the eyes of their students, while their image as educational leaders was damaged. The students searched for answers from political groups outside of school. The *intifada* (literally, uprising) that broke out in the Palestinian territories in 1987 further confused the educational system in Israel as a whole; particularly in Arab schools. In the face of the dynamic events of the *intifada*, Arab teachers found themselves in a delicate situation. They did not know whether or not to deal with those events and if so, how far they could go in expressing a sincere position (M. Mari, 1988).

The discrepancy between school and society within the Arab population is not only political, but also sociological. The school lags far behind the enhanced process of modernization, which the Arab community has experienced. Therefore, the role of the formal educational system to create social change has declined (Al-Haj, 1989). Already, in the early 1960s, Arabs were concerned about the role of teachers. Following the failure of most Arab students to receive the matriculation certificate, public trials were held to investigate the deterioration of the situation (*Haboker*, April 4, 1964). These assemblies concluded that one of the explanations as to the deterioration of teachers' status was that they perceive their task mainly as a source of income, not as a social vocation.

One of the main problems that the Arab school is facing today is the lack of inner democratization. Teacher-student relationships in many schools are still based on obedience and the concept that the teacher is always right. In a discussion a student cannot convey a different view that of his or her teacher. The frontal teaching method still exists in most Arab schools. The hierarchy among those who work in the Arab school system is based upon a number of levels: (1) Ministry of Education and Culture administration, (2) inspector, (3) principal, (4) teacher, (5) student. This rigid hierarchy limits the teacher's initiation, which is supposed to educate for democracy. This situation has changed over the last years due to the change in the quality of Arab teachers and multilevel supervision. Nevertheless, this situation is still far from creating basic conditions for a democratic regime within the Arab schools.

Instead of being the dominant element in the community, the school is vulnerable and not able to withstand exterior pressure. Tensions within the community penetrate easily into the school and affect its atmosphere. The struggling of Arab kinship groups, *hamulas*, over the control of the local power system, frequently finds its way into schools. This affects the relationship between teachers and the school management on one hand, and the relationship between teachers and students on the other hand. The demographic centralization of families within settlements creates a division of students and teachers by *hamulas* within one school. Therefore, it is not rare that a dispute between *hamulas* outside the school enters the school and increases intergroup tension. "Tensions exist also in Arab schools as well as in any other social institute," writes S. Mari. "Teachers of one *hamula* join against teachers from another hostile or rival *hamula*. In this way groups of teachers form on the basis of a *hamula* or inter-*hamula* coalition basis. These groups are active and apply pressure, both inside and outside the school. In this context it is possible to understand tensions and misunderstandings that often take place in schools among teachers themselves and between teachers and the administration." Tension and conflicts of this kind harm the educational atmosphere in school, since even if a teacher is not affiliated to a certain family, his immediate society tends to regard his motivations as based on familial considerations; shown in his relations with students and other teachers (S. Mari, 1974).

SCHOOL CURRICULUM, 1949–1974: CONTROL AND ASYMMETRY

The formation of Arab education in Israel is characterized by centralization and control. The curriculum was imposed upon Arab educators, who had little involvement in shaping it. In 1949 a committee for Arab education was appointed to deal with the goals and curriculum in Arab schools. This committee was authorized to reject books found politically or socially defective, and to print new, more fitting study books in their place (Ministry of Minorities, 1949). Instead of books from the Mandatory period, Arab teachers and Arabic speaking Jewish teachers wrote new books, under the supervision of the Ministry of Education and Culture. Arab teachers received strict instructions to omit sections of history and geography books having a nationalistic orientation (Ben-Or, 1951). These steps were intended to hasten the state's control on the content of Arab education. During the years 1950–1958 only twenty new books were prepared for Arab schools, compared with 720 books for Jewish schools (*Al-Hamishmar*, May 31, 1960). The existence of Arab books did not necessarily imply that they were of much Arab substance. These books were a far cry from the Arab national spirit and ignored the special contribution of Arab and Muslim civilization to mankind. Only in 1967 did

Arab schools obtain study books for all subjects (*Mabat Chadash*, January 1, 1967).

The critique on the Arab curricula began in the 1950s. It was asked why students in Arab schools were learning the Bible and not the Koran, and why the teaching of Arabic, Arab literature, and history did not receive proper attention. Peres, Erlich, and Yuval-Davis conducted a comparative study on the goals of the curricula in Arab and Jewish schools (Peres et al., 1968). Their main conclusion called for policymakers to find a compromise between contradicting trends: equality vis-à-vis existence of Jewish superiority; development of general values as opposed to national values; and the granting of autonomy to Arab education vis-à-vis the desire to fully merge with the Jewish educational system. These objectives were not achieved, since policymakers ignored them (Peres et al., 1968). The Arab curriculum failed to create a balance between "sense of Arab nationality" and "loyalty to the State of Israel." Instead, Arab national identity was concealed, and Arab students were taught inferiority and self-denial in face of the Jewish majority (*Hed Hahinukh*, December 12, 1968; *Al-Hamishmar*, August 13, 1968). The same conclusions can be derived from an analysis of history, language, and religious studies in Arab schools during the first decades of the State of Israel's existence.

History Studies

A comparison between history teaching objectives in Jewish and Arab high schools reveals that while Jewish schools stress national contents, the Arab curriculum overlooks them. Values of Arab–Jewish coexistence, together with Jewish superiority, are planted in the Arab student by repeatedly stressing the role that Arabs and Jews shared during history and the common fate of both peoples. However, values of coexistence are not passed down to Jewish students. Moreover, an Arab student is expected to know the importance of the State of Israel to the Jewish people, not to both Jews and Arabs.

Language Studies

The basic objective, according to the Ministry of Education and Culture, for teaching Arabic was to "provide the child a tool for self expression" (State Archives, 145/1292/GL). Seemingly, this is a simple task to do and easy to implement. But, since self-expression implies also national expression, the Ministry of Education and Culture made utmost efforts to ensure that teaching Arabic would not be used as a channel for transmitting national emblems (State Archives, 145/1292/GL). The teaching of Arab objectives in Arab schools was defined mainly technically, but apparently ignored any national element in language and literature teaching. The objectives were as follows: proper reading and understanding of oral and written language; clear, precise, and logical phrasing of ideas and feelings, written and orally; and the ability to understand

and appreciate good literature; thus opening a gateway to knowing literary culture in both the past and the present (State Archives, 145/1292/GL). However, the objectives of Hebrew teaching in Arab schools were not defined as solely technical. From the beginning, emphasis was made on exposing the Arab student to the culture and heritage of the Jewish people, and promoting the sense of Israeli citizenship (State Archives, 145/1292/GL). A trend of strengthening Hebrew teaching in Arab schools, on account of the mother tongue, was evident for a long time. In 1965 students learned 824 hours of Arab literature and language, while in 1973 they were granted only 732 hours for these subjects. A different trend was seen in the teaching of Hebrew. In 1965, 512 hours were designated to Hebrew teaching, whereas in 1973, 732 hours were designated. In analyzing the curriculum, S. Mari (1978) concludes that Jewish religious studies play a large part in the curriculum of Arab schools, while Islamic studies are categorized as "history and literature," with no reference to national identity.

Religious Studies

Arab students learned more about the Jewish religion than they did about their own religion (Peres et al., 1968). The amount of hours designated to the teaching of Jewish religion was greater than the amount allocated to the Islamic religion: 256 hours of biblical and Jewish studies, in comparison to thirty hours of Islamic studies. In secular Jewish schools, 640 hours were designated to Jewish studies, as opposed to none for Islamic studies. The Koran was not taught as a holy book, but rather as a piece of literature, while biblical and Jewish studies were studied as national religious subjects (S. Mari, 1978).

1975–1990: REDEFINITION OF OBJECTIVES AND CURRICULA

Since the mid-1960s, Israeli Arabs experienced a rapid process of social and political change, which strengthened their national awareness and enhanced their politicization. Officials in the Ministry of Education and Culture realized that if the existing objectives and curricula in Arab schools did not change, alienation of the younger generation would increase. Israeli officials marked the new style of Arab students as disturbing and anti-Israeli (*Zu-Haderekh*, February 14, 1971). A study conducted by Peres verified these fears (*Haaretz*, February 21, 1971). Peres' study maintained that the lack of national contents in Arab curriculum might be responsible, at least partly, for the alienation that Arab youth felt toward the country, a trend that grew after the 1967 war (*Haaretz*, February 21, 1971).

In order to renew the objectives of Arab education, the Ministry of Education and Culture appointed in 1971 a special committee chaired by the minister deputy, Aharon Yadlin. In 1972 the committee gave Minister of Education and Culture Yigal Alon recommendations for Arab education, including a proposal of principles to formulate new educational objectives. According to this proposal, Arab education must be based on the following principles: (a) education in the spirit of peace; (b) education for loyalty to the state, with emphasis on the common share of all citizens, while stressing the uniqueness of Israeli Arabs; (c) imparting Arab, Israeli, and universal cultural values, as well as the development of a plan aimed to ease the social and cultural absorption of Arabs in Israel; and (d) education of female students toward autonomy and improvement of their position.

The importance of the Yadlin proposal lies in the fact that for the first time wide public attention was given to the uniqueness of Arab education and to the need to set special objectives for Arab students. Nevertheless, the document contains many internal contradictions and did not express all the needs and aspirations of Israeli Arabs. Arab educators criticized the document for not dealing with the Arab national identity. They also criticized the attempt to create a "unique Israeli Arab," one divorced from his or her original national and cultural roots, which are closely connected with the Arab world and Palestinians (S. Mari, 1978).

Prior to the implementation of the Yadlin proposal, the director general of the Ministry of Education and Culture appointed a new committee of seven Arabs and eight Jews, chaired by Dr. Mati Peled (the Peled Committee). The task of this committee was to formulate the educational objectives in Israel for the 1980s (Ministry of Education and Culture, 1975).

The Peled Committee maintained a few perspectives of Arab education, including services, objectives, and curricula. Although the committee appreciated the importance of the Yadlin proposal, the Peled Committee criticized it for ignoring the conflict that Arabs in Israel were facing between their identification with the Arab nation and their loyalty to the State of Israel (Ministry of Education and Culture, 1975). The Peled Committee emphasized the need to implement substantial changes in the Arab school curriculum on the basis of the committee's objectives. The committee divided the curriculum in Arab schools into three main categories: (a) curricula similar to those in Jewish schools, such as, English, mathematics, and biology; (b) curricula adapted to the needs of Arab schools, such as, geography and history; (c) curricula developed for Arab schools, such as, Arab language and culture, Hebrew language and culture, religious, and civil studies. The first category was not considered problematic, since the difficulties were of implementation, not of contents. The other two categories were much more complex and demanded a substantial change in objectives and contents (Ministry of Education and Culture, 1975).

The Peled Committee suggested that the objectives of state education should base Arab education on Arab culture, scientific achievements, the love of the country shared by all citizens, and loyalty to the State of Israel by emphasizing common interests while indicating the uniqueness of Arabs in Israel. Arab education would also be based upon knowledge of the Jewish culture, respect for creative work, and a desire for a society based upon liberty, equality, mutual aid, and love for humanity (Ministry of Education and Culture, 1975).

The official objectives proposed for Arab education were repeatedly criticized by Arab and Jewish researchers (Tzartzur, 1981; Al-Haj, 1989; S. Mari, 1978; Nakhleh, 1977; Smooha, 1989). A main point in their criticism is that there is neither explicit nor implicit recognition that the Arabs in Israel are a national minority that is inseparable from the Palestinian people (S. Mari, 1978; Nakhleh, 1977). The objectives for Arab education relate to striving for peace between Israel and her neighbors, as well as a common love for the homeland, which is shared by all her citizens. Yet these issues are absent from the objectives of Jewish education (S. Mari, 1978; Nakhleh, 1977; Tzartzur, 1981). Nakhleh concludes that the guidelines in the process called "redefinition" of education objectives are: how to portray Zionism and the State of Israel in the best light; how to minimize animosity to the state; and how to deal with Arab nationalism without producing nationalistic students (Nakhleh, 1977).

In 1976 the minister of Education and Culture revised the objectives recommended by the Peled Committee. He actually changed the main sentence "the love of the country shared by all citizens," by omitting the word "shared," and declaring the goal as just the "love of the country" (Ministry of Education and Culture, 1977). This implied a withdrawal to the spirit of the former objective, in which Arab students were educated to love the country, not as their own, but as the homeland of the Jewish people. While it is not possible for Arab students to be educated in Israel as full partners, Jewish students are largely educated to love Israel as their homeland and state for all the Jewish people. Nevertheless, the Peled Committee report served as a starting point for revising the Arab school curriculum (*Adult Education in Israel*, 1977).

History Studies

Since the early 1970s, the Ministry of Education and Culture began to revise the former curriculum of history studies in Arab schools. In 1973 the ministry appointed a committee to devise a new curriculum, and in 1976 it published the curriculum for elementary and intermediate school, following in 1982 with the curriculum for high school (Bargut, 1991). The main change in the history curriculum was the mention of identification with the Arab nation as a central objective. However, this version was also ambiguous, carefully phrased, and far from being equivalent to the history teaching objectives of the Jewish schools. The identification with the Arab nation is not necessarily connected to the deepening of the national consciousness. Moreover, the Arab nation was mentioned generally, without relating to the Palestinian people.

It is noteworthy that the revised curriculum for high schools emphasized Jewish-Arab coexistence, along with the contribution of the Jewish nation to culture and mankind. The Jewish schools' curriculum does not include parallel objectives. The Arab curriculum only mentions the principle of coexistence and the shared efforts of Arabs and Jews in building the country for all citizens.

The marginal place of Arab history in general, and of the Palestinian people in particular, is even more conspicuous when analyzing the hourly division by subjects. Only four out of twenty-five subjects in the curriculum are obligatory subjects for matriculation, while all other subjects are optional. Actually, no substantial changes were made in the new curriculum. The component of Jewish history even grew from 20% to 22%. Contemporary Palestinian history and the history of the Arab national movement are optional not obligatory subjects. Those who do not study an extended program in history do not have the opportunity to learn things concerning the Israeli-Arab conflict and the relationships between Israelis and Palestinians. General history is the main focus of obligatory subjects, since it is included in history of the twentieth century and the contemporary Middle East (Ministry of Education and Culture, 1982).

The advantage of the new curriculum is its optional subjects, which include: the development of the national Arab Movement, minorities in the Middle East, oil in the Middle East, modernization and developments in the Arab world, Jewish history from the days of Abraham to King Solomon, life and status of Jews in Islamic countries, anti-Semitism, the uniting and separating powers within the Jewish nation in the past, the ancient Orient, history of the United States, colonialism in the past one hundred years, the industrial revolution, Jerusalem, the Catholic church, Palestine in the Ottoman era, and Jews and Arab relations during the past one hundred years (Ministry of Education and Culture, 1982).

The asymmetry in which the teaching objectives for the Israeli–Arab conflict were formed is most prominent. For Jewish students it is biased in order to strengthen the identification of Jewish students with the Zionist Movement: "To deepen the student's belief in the just struggle of the Jewish people to a national renewal in their homeland." The Arab-Israeli conflict is presented to the Arab student in a balanced manner to strengthen his understanding of both national movements: "To understand the history of the national Arab movement and of the Zionist movement, to know the elements behind them, including developments which occurred as a result of the encounter between the two movements, which led to the present situation" (Farah, 1991). This revision ignores the Palestinian point of view, which is merged with the overall Arab position. Furthermore, it is presented to Arab students in a neutral way, which does not invoke national dignity or strengthen national identification.

Arabic Language and Literature

The new objectives of Arabic teaching are more progressive. They refer to the importance of Arab literature in forming the student's personality and teaching his national heritage. Yet, only one of the twelve new objectives of Arabic teaching in Arab schools relates clearly to the strengthening of the student's pride in Arabic as a national language and as a major part of his personality (Ministry of Education and Culture, 1981). The other objectives are general and are aimed at improving the student's knowledge of classic Arabic; his ability to read and understand literature; his ability at self-expression; librarian skills; exposure to human culture; and the acquisition of human values through Arabic world literature (Ministry of Education and Culture, 1981).

It should be mentioned, however, that the student will find a wide coverage of central trends in Arab modern literature. Likewise, works of Palestinian writers and poets are included in the curriculum and are part of the materials required for the matriculation exams. Some major deficiencies remain in the new curriculum, especially regarding the Palestinian issue. Even though major Palestinian writers and poets are included, others are missing and the choice of works is biased. The works chosen do not represent faithfully the national spirit. These kinds of poems and novels were omitted although they were approved by the committee in charge of the curriculum (Abu-Hanna, 1988). The hours assigned for the study of Palestinian literature are insufficient and barely cover one-third of the required material (Boulus, 1989).

The changes of curriculum in Arabic language and literature were introduced in reverse order: first the curriculum for high schools was prepared in 1981, and only in 1985 was a special committee appointed to take care of the curriculum for intermediate schools. Elementary schools still use the old unrevised curriculum (Boulus, 1989). The redefined objectives of the intermediate school recognized the teaching of Arabic as a means of tightening the connection between Arab students and their social heritage, as well as their attitudes toward Arabic as a national language. Arab educators strongly protested against the fact that Palestinian literature was still included in the Arab literature taught in Arab schools, in spite of students' strong desire to learn about their national heritage (Boulus, 1991). Merely 14% of teaching hours in intermediate schools were assigned to Palestinian literature. As a whole, out of 561 hours of literature studies during the six years of postelementary education, Arab students studied only fifty-six hours of Palestinian literature; merely 10% of the total hours assigned (Boulus, 1991).

Hebrew Language Studies

The curriculum of Hebrew language and literature was published in 1977, as one of the first curricula to be prepared according to the Peled Committee recommendation (Ministry of Education and Culture, 1977). The objectives of the new curriculum were as follows: (a) the imparting of a thorough, precise, and comprehensive knowledge of the Hebrew language in order to facilitate proper communication with Jewish citizens, and to enable students to use it as a vehicle for promoting other goals, including the understanding and friendship between Arab and Jews in the country; (b) facilitation of the integration of students in the social, cultural, economical, and political life of the state; (c) preparation of high school graduates toward integration among higher education institutes in Israel; (d) opening the gate for pupils to become acquainted with the basis of cultural heritage of the Jewish people and appreciation of the Hebrew culture; (e) development of the student's aesthetic judgment by knowing the roles of linguistic forms in poetry and prose, the conveyance of ideas, and the correlation between the two (Ministry of Education and Culture, 1977). Compared to the old curriculum, the main change in the Hebrew curriculum in high school was its emphasis on Hebrew teaching as a means of attaining Jewish-Arab coexistence and the integration of Arabs in Israel. The objectives in the old curriculum were mainly intended to strengthen Arab students' appreciation toward the Hebrew heritage and culture.

Civil Studies

In 1984 new objectives were proposed to teach civil studies in Arab high schools (Ministry of Education and Culture, 1984). These objectives were divided into three levels: cognitive, mental capabilities, and mental attitudes. At the cognitive level, the curriculum was meant to expose students to the options available to Arabs in influencing the events in the country, as well as in building Israeli-Arab connections with the rest of the Arab world. The curriculum was also supposed to encourage students to contribute to Israeli society in general and to Arab society in particular; to actively participate in society; and to have a sense of belonging and loyalty toward the State of Israel and also toward the Arab society in Israel.

An analysis of these objectives indicates a significant change compared to the old curriculum. These objectives related, for the first time, to political issues; to the bond between Israeli Arabs and other Arabs; to the understanding of the problems facing Israeli society, as well as those problems facing the Arab population; and to the opportunities for influencing events and claiming rights. However, these objectives are still ambiguous in a few target issues, which influence the relationship between Jews and Arabs in Israel, such as, the contradiction existing between the democratic character of Israel and its Jewish-Zionist character. Although these objectives relate to non-Jewish groups as minorities, they tend to obscure the uniqueness of the Arabs as a national minority. These objectives attribute great significance to state loyalty and to affiliation to Israeli society, but they fail to deal with the differences between Jews and Arabs, and with the fact that Arabs are second-class citizens.

Nevertheless, the new objectives furnished the way to a progressive social studies curriculum in Arab high schools, which included discussions of actual issues. A textbook titled *Arab Citizens in Israel*, based on these objectives, was copublished in 1987 by Haifa University, the Ministry of Education and Culture and the Van-Leer Institution in Jerusalem. It states, for the first time, that

Israeli Arabs are an inseparable part of the Palestinian people. Issues that until now had been described as "sensitive," such as, identity and expropriation of lands and human rights, are openly dealt with in this book. However, this book is used only in Arab high schools. Arab students in elementary and intermediate schools are still using books published in the mid-1970s.

Religious Studies

Since the end of the 1970s, few attempts were made to develop curricula for teaching the Islamic religion. In 1987 a special committee was appointed, whose members were Arab educators and judges of the *shari'a* courts. The objectives of Islamic teaching distinguish between the general view, emphasizing the cultural educational message, and aspects that highlight knowledge of Islamic principles (Ministry of Education and Culture, 1987). An analysis shows that these general objectives are mainly aimed toward the development of personality; love of humanity; respect of other religions; love of work and science; the development of social responsibility; and the creation of a well-balanced personality by faith in God, in the prophet Mohammed, and in principal personalities in the history of Islam. Only two of the nineteen general objectives relate, for the first time, to the development of a sense of national religious affiliation, though in a very general and carefully phrased manner. The first objective deals with the development of a sense of national affiliation among students in terms of religion, history, and culture. The other objective deals with building the students' Islamic personality, which is well-balanced, whole, and open to culture and science.

There is a significant change in the new curriculum compared to the previous curriculum. The national religious education in the new curriculum is vague and not properly expounded. The fact that the new curriculum is implemented only in high schools deepens the gap between the high schools and elementary schools, in which the old curriculum is still valid, at least to some extent.

CONCLUSION

Education is considered as an economical and political resource, as well as a symbol of social status and national dignity among Israeli Arabs. Since the establishment of the State of Israel, quantitative and qualitative changes have occurred in Arab education, including an impressive growth in number of students, increasing rate in attendance of female students, improvement of teachers' formal training, and a significant development in buildings and educational services.

Yet, several obstacles have remained in materializing the role of education as a catalyst for social change, which have furthered the gap between the school and society in general. One of these obstacles was that Arab education served as a mechanism of control, as part of the policy of supervising the Arab minority. The Ministry of Education and Culture's policy came into practice by invoking "security considerations" in hiring, firing, and promoting teachers in the Arab educational system. It also shaped the curricula in a manner that legitimized the culture and ideology of the majority and emptied Arab education of Arab national contents.

In addition to the policy of control that was directed by the central government, Arab local authorities also used the local educational system for internal political disputes and competition. The local authorities played an active role in the appointment of teachers and principals, particularly in high schools based on familial and sectarian competition. This political weaponry further limited the role of the educational system as a source of modernization and social change.

The school itself is partly responsible for turning education into a conservative, rather than dynamic system. The regime of Arab schools is mostly undemocratic, and students, instead of being at the center of the educational process, remain in the margins without their needs and expectations addressed. Moreover, the Arab educational system is moving very slowly in terms of initiatives and changes. The gradual decrease in the role of teachers as "educational leaders" has weakened teacher status and self-esteem and negatively affected the school's role within the community.

This analysis leads to the conclusion that there is a need to adopt a global strategy of change in the Arab educational system. This will satisfy the needs of the Arab population as well as enable schools to play a significant role in the fast social change that occurs in society.

This strategy requires a change in the control policy of both the Ministry of Education and Culture and the Arab local authorities. It also requires an intensification of the policy of bridging the gap, which has been adopted by the Ministry of Education and Culture, and a basic global change in training and appointing teachers, principals, and superintendents. Most important, it requires the redefinition of objectives and curriculum of Arab education. It should also lead to the establishment of a special Pedagogical Secretariat for the Arab population, which will act with the present one within the Ministry of Education and Culture. In light of the peace process in the area, it is also required to redefine the educational objectives and content of Jewish, as well as Arab education, toward the establishment of a genuine multicultural education in Israel.

The following chapter, "Educational Reforms and Changes," surveys the ongoing process of educational reforms and changes in the educational system as a whole. Reforms have altered all stages of education in Israel, and have been precipitated by a variety of reasons.

NOTE

This chapter is an expanded version of the paper: "Trends for change and continuity in Arab education in Israel." *Hamizrah Hehadash, 27*, 87-107 (1995) (Hebrew). Majid Al-Haj is Associate Professor of Sociology and the Director of the Center for Arab Education at the University of Haifa. He is a member of the Council for Higher Education in Israel.

BIBLIOGRAPHY

Abu-Hanna, H. (1988). "Coexistence and identity: Curricula for Arabic, Hebrew and history." In *Identity, coexistence and contents education*. Haifa: Al-Karmah (Arabic), pp. 48–58.

Adult Education in Israel. (1977). Jerusalem: Ministry of Education and Culture (Hebrew).

Adva Center. (1996). "An overview on the budget of the Ministry of Education 1990–1996." Tel Aviv: Adva Center (mimeographed).

Al-Haj, M. (1988). "Arab university graduates in Israel: Characteristics, potential and employment situation." In M. Al-Haj (ed.), *The employment distress of the Arab university graduates in Israel*. Haifa: University of Haifa, Jewish-Arab Center (Hebrew), pp. 9–22.

Al-Haj, M. (1989). *Education for democracy in the Arab schools: The dilemmas of a changing national minority*. Givat Haviva: The Institute of Arab Studies.

Al-Haj, M. (1994). *Arab education system in Israel: Issues and trends*. Jerusalem: Floersheimer Institute (Hebrew).

Al-Haj, M. (1995a). *Education empowerment and control in the case of Arabs in Israel*. Albany, NY: State University of New York Press.

Al-Haj, M. (1995b). "The status of the Arab teacher in Israel." Haifa: Center for Arab Education in Israel.

Al-Haj, M., and H. Rosenfeld. (1990). *Arab local government in Israel*. Boulder, CO: Westview Press.

Al-Hamishmar. May 31, 1960; August 13, 1968 (Hebrew).

Bargut, S. (1991). "The new history curriculum for Arab schools." In M. Habib-Allah and A. Kupty (eds.), *Education for the Arab Minority in Israel: Issues, problems and demands*. Haifa: Al-Karmah (Arabic), pp. 114–123.

Bashi, Y., and Z. Sas (1991). *Results of the achievement tests in reading comprehensive and mathematics in the fourth and fifth grades*. Jerusalem: Ministry of Education, Culture, and Sport.

Ben-Dror, G. A. (1994). Personal letter about the Arab education system, July 29, 1994.

Ben-Or, J. L. (1951). "Arab education in Israel." *Hamizrah Hehadash, 3* (9), 1–8 (Hebrew).

Boulus, H. (1989). "The Palestinian literature in the curricula of the Arab schools in Israel." Unpublished paper presented in the study day: *The curricula of the Arab* schools, organized by the Follow up Committee for Arab Education. Haifa, June 30, 1989.

Boulus, H. (1991). "The Palestinian literature in the Arabic curriculum in Israel." In M. Habib-Allah and A. Kupty (eds.), Education for the Arab Minority in Israel: Issues, problems and demands. Haifa: Al-Karmah (Arabic), pp. 89–97.

Central Bureau of Statistics, Statistical Abstract of Israel (SAI) 1986. No. 37, p. 522.

Central Bureau of Statistics, Statistical Abstract of Israel (SAI) 1989. No. 40, p. 606.

Central Bureau of Statistics, Statistical Abstract of Israel (SAI) 1990. No. 41.

Central Bureau of Statistics, Statistical Abstract of Israel (SAI) 1992. No. 43.

Central Bureau of Statistics, Statistical Abstract of Israel (SAI) 1993. No. 44, p. 638.

Central Bureau of Statistics, Statistical Abstract of Israel (SAI) 1996. No. 47, p. 487.

Cohen, A. (1951). "Problems of education for Arab children in Israel." Megamot, 2 (2), 126–137 (Hebrew).

Davar. July 11, 1977 (Hebrew).

Farah, N. (1991). "Teaching of history: Curriculum and textbooks." In M. Habib-Allah and A. Kupty (eds.), Education for the Arab Minority in Israel: Issues, problems and demands. Haifa: Al-Karmah (Arabic), pp. 109–113.

Haaretz. February 21, 1971 (Hebrew).

Haboker. April 4, 1964 (Hebrew).

Hed Hahinukh. December 12, 1968 (Hebrew).

Israel State Comptroller. (1992). "State Comptroller's Report." Annual Report, No. 42, part 1. Jerusalem: State Comptroller's Office, pp. 429–490.

Jiryis, S. (1976). The Arabs in Israel. New York: Monthly Review Press.

Mabat Chadash, January 1, 1967.

Mari, M. (1988). "The Arab school and actual issues." In Identity, coexistence and contents of education. Haifa: National Committee of Chairmen of Arab Local Authorities and the Follow-up Committee for Arab Education (Arabic), pp. 95–103.

Mari, S. (1974). "The school and society in the Arab village in Israel." Iyonim Bahinukh 4, 85–104 (Hebrew).

Mari, S. (1978). Arab education in Israel. Syracuse, NY: Syracuse University Press.

Masalhah, M. (1991). Report to the Minister of Education about the Five Year Plan. Jerusalem: Ministry of Education, Culture, and Sport (Hebrew).

Ministry of Education and Culture. (1975). Report of the Arab education team (mimeographed). Jerusalem: Planning Project of Education in the Eighties, Ministry of Education and Culture (Hebrew).

Ministry of Education and Culture. (1977). The Hebrew language and literature for the high grades of the Arab secondary school (mimeographed). Jerusalem: Ministry of Education and Culture (Hebrew).

Ministry of Education and Culture. (1981). Curriculum for Arabic in the Arab schools (mimeographed). Jerusalem: Ministry of Education and Culture (Hebrew).

Ministry of Education and Culture. (1982). The curriculum of teaching history in the Arab high schools. 1st ed. Jerusalem: Center for School Curricula (Arabic).

Ministry of Education and Culture. (1984). *The curriculum of teaching civics and social studies in the Arab high schools for the tenth-twelfth grades* (mimeographed). Jerusalem: Ministry of Education and Culture (Arabic).

Ministry of Education and Culture. (1985). The Committee of the Directors General for Educational Alternatives. *Report of the committee for the examination of the Arab education* (mimeographed). Jerusalem: Ministry of Education and Culture (Hebrew).

Ministry of Education and Culture. (1987). *The curriculum for teaching Islamic religion for Arab secondary schools* (mimeographed). Jerusalem: Ministry of Education and Culture (Arabic).

Ministry of Education and Culture. (1988). *Report on the education system in Israel* (mimeographed). Jerusalem: Ministry of Education and Culture (Hebrew).

Ministry of Minorities. (1949). *Report on the Minorities Ministry activities, May 1948–January 1949* (mimeographed). Jerusalem (Hebrew).

Nakhleh, K. (1977). "The Goals of Education for Arabs in Israel." *New Outlook* (April–May), 29–35.

The National Committee of Chairmen of Arab Local Authorities and the Follow-up Committee for Arab Education (1986). *A Memorandum to the Minister of Education about Arab education in Israel.* Shefar-Am (Hebrew).

New Outlook. January 18, 1967.

Peres, Y., A. Erlich, and N. Yuval-Davis (1968). "National education for Arab youth in Israel: A comparative analysis of curricula." *Megamot, 17* (1), 26–36. (Hebrew).

Roseberg, A. (1985). "The development of Arab education in Israel." Unpublished MA thesis. Haifa: Department of Middle Eastern History, University of Haifa (Hebrew).

Smooha, S. (1989). *Arabs and Jews in Israel: Conflicting and shared attitudes in a divided society,* vol. 1. Boulder, CO: Westview Press.

State Archives. Files No. 1351/1616/GL; 145/1292/GL.

Teachers' Association of Israel. (1988). *The report of the committee for the investigation of teachers training programs in Colleges* (mimeographed). Tel Aviv: Teachers' Association.

Toledano, S. (1984). *The report of the committee for the investigation of delinquency in the Arab Sector* (mimeographed). Jerusalem (Hebrew).

Tzartzur, S. (1981). "Arab education in a Jewish State: Central dilemmas." In *One of every six Israelis: Mutual relations between the Arab minority and the Jewish majority.* Jerusalem: Van leer Institute (Hebrew), pp. 113–131.

Wergift, N. (1989). "A school for discrimination." *Kol Hair* (Jerusalem). June 2 (Hebrew).

Zu-Haderekh. February 14, 1971. (Hebrew).

Chapter 8

Educational Reforms
and Changes

The Israeli educational system is characterized by the universal phenomenon of recurrence of reforms and changes. These are manifest in four areas: the structure of the educational system; curricular policies; patterns of matriculation examinations (*Bagrut*); and locus of influence on policy making.

The underlying basis for educational reforms in Israel is change in ideology, whereby the value of excellence in education alternates with emphasis on equality. This change reflects shifts in the philosophy of "equal educational opportunity," to which the Israeli system has been committed since its inception. However, the interpretation of this philosophy has undergone several phases.

During the first decade of Israel's statehood (1948–1957) equal educational opportunity implied formal equality, which was consistent with the prevailing "melting pot" absorption policy (Eisenstadt, 1967). Soon it became evident that this approach did not narrow the scholastic gap between students of Oriental (North African and Middle Eastern) and Western origin (European and American), especially at the secondary school level (Iram, 1986; Schmida, 1987). Consequently, during the second decade (1958–1967), the "formal" approach was replaced by the compensatory approach of national protectionism. This implied that extra resources were diverted to disadvantaged student populations, mainly of Oriental origin (Smilansky, 1957; Adler, 1984). The failure of this approach also motivated the Ministry of Education and Culture to introduce another approach in the education system's philosophy. Indeed, during the third decade (1968–1977), educational equality emphasized the recognition of existing individual differences and the need to realize students' potential. This aim was to be achieved by providing differentiated educational opportunities within newly established integrative junior high schools (Schmida, 1987).

During the fourth decade (1978–1988) yet another change in the philosophy of education became discernible in the education policy. The orientation toward equality in education weakened, and a more elitist approach, stressing excellence, dominated. This trend was evident in the diminished number of junior high schools that were opened and the expansion of private, semiprivate, and specialized ("distinctive") schools within the public state school system. This public system adhered to the forces of the open market, competing for stronger student populations (Schmida, 1988; Shapira, 1988). Similar trends can be observed in other Western countries, especially in the United States and Western Europe (Leschinsky and Mayer, 1990).

CHANGES IN THE STRUCTURE OF THE EDUCATIONAL SYSTEM

The change in the conception of equal educational opportunity in the Israeli educational system is evident in the changes within the educational structure. This issue is relevant especially at the secondary school level, since in primary schooling the Compulsory Education Law (1949) provides equal educational opportunities to all children, from ages five to fourteen (K–8). As for secondary education the orientation was elitist during the first decade of statehood (1948–1957). Only those with academic abilities were admitted to the few existing academic high schools and were charged tuition fees (Bentwich, 1965); the situation even worsened with the introduction of the national screening examination in 1965, in which the percentage of failures was proportionately high among students of Oriental origin. Consequently, this led to their underrepresentation at the high school level, when compared to their percentage in their corresponding age group. Indeed, the median school attendance in 1961 was 5.9 years for students of Oriental origin, compared to 9.1 years for students of Western origin aged fourteen and above (CBS, 1963). As a result, their access to higher education and higher occupational positions was also impeded (Iram, 1986).

The second decade of the State of Israel was characterized by national pedagogical efforts to raise the educational level of students, particularly those of Oriental origin, in order to reduce the gap between them and students of Western origin. These compensatory efforts, including affirmative pedagogical measures as well as administrative ones, were motivated by national and social considerations. They were also rooted in the concern for the nation's social solidarity, which was threatened by socioeconomic gaps, as well as the need to cope with social and ethnic unrest, which occurred at the end of this decade (Cohen, 1980).

These measures paved the way to a major educational reform, which the Israeli Parliament passed during the third decade of the state's existence (Words of Parliament, 1969). The main features of the structural changes and the legal measures of the reform process and its achievements have been discussed extensively in literature (Amir, Sharan, and Ben-Ari, 1984; Peled,

1982; Peled and Glasman, 1990; Schmida, 1987, 1988). The main purpose of the structural reform was to democratize secondary education by means of raising the compulsory withdrawal age to sixteen (Rimalt, 1971). Furthermore, the reform aimed to precipitate two major changes within the system: to raise the level of academic achievements of all students, while closing the educational gap between students from different ethnic backgrounds and different socioeconomic strata, and to accelerate the processes of social integration among all groups (Ministry of Education and Culture, 1971, 1972a).

CURRICULAR POLICIES

The role of curriculum is twofold: to provide the educational means to convert ideology into social objectives, and to facilitate individual needs and intellectual mastery. Reforms in curriculum are responses to changes in philosophy of education and social circumstances. Contradictory tendencies, namely individualistic versus intellectual and ideological versus social, are the dual goals of education and curriculum. This tension exists latently and emerges to the surface whenever curricular changes are considered.

Indeed, the observed phenomenon of recurring changes in educational practice in general, and in the field of curriculum in particular, are partially caused by this dual set of goals. Instances of such changes include the tension between stresses on academic, vocational, and more general fields of study.

During the first decade of Israel's existence, until the end of the 1950s, the tendency was toward a uniform and rigid academic curriculum (Smilansky, 1957). A unified mandatory curriculum was developed. About 90% of elementary and junior high school classroom hours, and 76% of academic high school hours were mandatory. More structured processes of teacher qualification and accreditation were introduced by the Ministry of Education and Culture, while textbooks were either published by the ministry or given its approval if published by others (Peled and Glasman, 1990). The analysis of the stated aims of the 1953 State Education Law and the specific goals set to various subjects, as well as the study of their content and construct, indicate that curriculum construction was guided by the concepts of "academic rationalism" and "structure of knowledge" (Eisner and Vallance, 1974). These concepts were consistent with the overall aim of schooling, which was oriented exclusively toward cultural transmission and national solidarity (Eisenstadt, 1967). But soon it became evident that the approach of "formal equality" (Smilansky, 1973) left behind pupils from the lower socioeconomic strata, who were largely of Oriental origin. A large gap in academic achievement manifested between students of Oriental origin and students of Western origin and higher socioeconomic level (Smooha and Peres, 1974).

In order to narrow the gap in academic achievement, but also to maintain standards of academic excellence, another curricular approach was taken. The assumption during the second decade, in the 1960s, was that disadvantaged students require compensatory curricular programs in order to reach higher academic achievements. This curricular orientation, which was aimed at weaker students populations, was consistent with the concept of "development of cognitive processes" (Eisner and Vallance, 1974). However, the outcome of this approach was disappointing, and the educational gap narrowed only slightly, particularly at the high school level. Indeed, in 1975 the median school attendance of Orientals was 7.1 compared to 9.8 for Westerners aged fourteen and over (Smooha and Peres, 1980; Iram, 1987).

Israeli society was confronted with economic, national security, and social problems. On the one hand, it had to cope with the continuing Arab–Israeli conflict and with problems of a modern technological society, which demanded high standards of academic excellence. On the other hand, there existed a real social danger of Israeli society disintegrating into ethnic sectors, because of the consistent correlation between ethnic origin and economic, occupational, educational, and political power to the disadvantage of the Orientals (Kleinberger, 1969). This was the background for the third decade of the Israeli educational system.

The educational policymakers adopted a sociopolitical orientation, which was more inclined toward equality (Peled, 1982). The new approach was embodied in the Educational Reform Act of 1969, which depended not only upon structural changes, but also upon the construction of new curricular programs. During the 1970s the curriculum was conceived as "technology," and aimed at the "self-actualization" of students' individual potential and skills (Eisner and Vallance, 1974). The supremacy of academic subject matter declined and was replaced by a more practical curriculum (Eden, 1973). Multiple and ability- differentiated curricular programs were introduced in comprehensive high schools, and the vocational school system with a wide curricular program was expanded to comprise about half of the secondary school age group (Iram, 1986).

The fourth decade of the Israeli educational system, the 1980s, again witnessed a shift from the more egalitarian ideology to one of excellence. In accordance with this shift, academic orientations in school curriculum regained momentum at the expense of more practical orientations.

MATRICULATION EXAMINATIONS

The oscillation between excellence and equality in education, as represented in the different approaches to curricula, are also reflected in the approach to the national matriculation examinations (*Bagrut*). The examinations are conducted at the end of high school and reflect standards of academic achievement in the system in general, as well as the achievements of individual students. Although secondary education schools, and especially the prestigious academic high schools, were rather selective in the intake of students, the rate of success in examinations has been quite low from the beginning. The percentage of students of Oriental origin who passed the examinations successfully was lower than the national mean. Only about 6% of Oriental students passed compared to 33% among students of Western origin (Adler, 1986).

Following the implementation of the Reform Act (1969), which made the first stage of secondary education compulsory and universal, more students entered the second stage of secondary education. These were heterogeneous student bodies, characterized by different interests and competencies than the more selective student bodies of previous years. Students and their parents exerted pressure on academic high schools, to allow more students to be able to sit for matriculation examinations and pass them with success. In response to these demands, and in line with the orientation toward quality in education, more flexible policies regarding the matriculation examinations were implemented (Ministry of Education and Culture, 1972b, 1976; Lewy, 1990). Indeed, the number of students of Oriental origin who passed the examinations increased from about 6% in the late 1960s to about 15% in the early 1980s. The rate of success of students of Western origin increased slightly to about 33% (Bilezki and Turki, 1982; Adler, 1986).

During the 1980s the tendency toward liberalization regarding examinations changed again, in accordance with the shift from a more egalitarian approach in education toward an approach encouraging excellence. Thus, the number of optional subjects for examination was reduced by half to increase the uniformity of various matriculation diplomas and to attain greater balance between various subjects (Lewy, 1990). The most crucial decision regarding the weaker students was whether to raise English and mathematics to the level of obligatory subjects for examination. In these subjects the chances of weaker students succeeding are quite low. The inevitable consequences of these changes in the matriculation examinations was the decrease in the number of students, mainly of Oriental origin, who passed the examination and gained access to further academic studies. This was also a result of the fact that students of weaker socioeconomic background were compelled to rely mainly on school services provided by the government and could not support themselves by their own private resources. These weaker students could not fulfill their aspirations to continue with higher education, partly because of the "sponsored" mobile character of secondary schooling in Israel, "which regulates the participation in the schooling process from its early stages" (Yogev, 1981; see also Yogev and Ayalon, 1986) within rigidly differentiated secondary schools of college-bound and noncollege-bound tracks (Yuchtman and Samuel, 1975; Shavit, 1989). Indeed, while the enrollment rate for twelve years of primary to secondary schooling in Israel reached 93% in 1987, and the rate of participation in higher education was 34% in general, among Orientals the rate was less than 20% (Shprinzak, Segev, Bar, et. al, 1996; UNESCO, 1989). Thus, the ethnic gap in higher education persists, largely because of the "gatekeeping" function of the matriculation examinations.

POLICY MAKING —NATIONAL VERSUS SECTORIAL

The prestate educational system was characterized by the influence of political parties, which instilled the schools with partisan ideologies. The political parties established their own school "trends" and directed them according to their ideologies and beliefs (Bentwich, 1965). The state education law of 1953 replaced the partisan trends with a national system of education divided into two sectors: state and state-religious (Stanner, 1963). During the following decades until the mid-1970s, the influence of political parties on the educational system weakened and a much stronger national centrist orientation dominated.

As of the late 1970s, sectorial tendencies in the educational system reappeared. In that decade the central instrument for the implementation of equality was the integrative junior high school, which was negatively affected. During the decade 1980–1989, less than 10% of the students from the relevant age group joined integrative junior high schools (Ministry of Education and Culture, 1989). It became common for parents from better socioeconomic backgrounds to buy additional educational services within the framework of public education, and sometimes outside of it. This phenomenon of "gray education" spread especially in elementary schools. Gray education was partly a response to drastic budgetary cuts in education. Thus, economically more stable groups of parents added at their own expense supplementary programs to enrich their children in the arts as well as in academic subjects, which had been reduced by the government.

Another reflection of the growth of sectorial influence on education was the establishment of specialized ("distinctive") schools within the public state schools. Some of these schools emphasized particular content areas, such as the arts and sciences. Other schools stressed ideological value orientations, such as Labor Party values or special religious values, or they emphasized special pedagogical approaches, which were directed toward more experimental and open education. The common denominator of these schools was that they attract mostly a selective student population with stronger academic background and ability, than those students from higher socioeconomic strata.

The phenomenon of gray education can be dismissed as the reaction of frustrated parents to a slimmed-down curriculum that was poor in various enrichment courses. Since the mid-1970s the funding of public social and educational services was reduced, due to economic difficulties, high inflation, and budgetary restrictions that prevailed in Israel (Kop, 1985). Indeed, between 1980–1990 classroom hours were reduced by 13–17% in primary schools; 22–24% in junior high schools; and 7–12% in senior high schools (Shprinzak, Segev, Bar, et. al, 1996).

The national authority, namely the Ministry of Education and Culture, encouraged stronger population segments, directly or indirectly, to supplement public educational services by their own means, while reducing support to weaker population segments. This resulted in the strengthening of sectorial influence on education. Various interest groups exerted pressure on the system, demanding rights for parental choice of schools (Shapira and Goldring, 1990; Iram, 1994; Danilov and Inbar, 1994). This approach circumvented and altered accepted policies of social integration and equality in a variety of ways. As a result, schooling conditions in well-to-do neighborhoods are considerably better. This happened despite the existence of a wide consensus regarding the stated policy of school integration and equity, and the allocation of additional resources for the education of disadvantaged student populations (Minkowich et al., 1977; Elboim-Dror, 1989; Inbar and Sever, 1989).

The appearance of various pressure groups and their regaining power and influence in the public educational system is discernible in both the state and state-religious school sectors. These groups claim legitimization for their own schools, based on ideological or religious convictions, or on the basis of demands for higher academic standards. However, it should be noted that most of the sectorial tendencies supported by the pressure groups are less of a political or partisan nature, but are more motivated by ideological, religious, and socioeconomic interests. Nevertheless, if the tendency of establishing "distinctive schools" or unique educational units within existing schools intensifies, as indicated by the recent "Report of the Public Committee of Inspection of Non-Regional Educational Frameworks" (Kashti, 1991), the stated policies of social integration and equality of educational provisions may be negatively affected.

The recurrency of changes and reforms in the educational system is a universal phenomenon. In the Israeli educational system this recurrency occurs in issues of policymaking, structure, curricular contents, and final examinations. Another characteristic feature of the educational system, which is shared by other countries that absorb large-scale waves of immigration, is its pluralistic and multicultural character. The following chapter, "Multicultural Education" deals with the changing meanings and conceptions of multiculturalism and their implications on the educational system.

BIBLIOGRAPHY

Adler, C. (1984). "School integration in the context of the development of Israel's education system." In Y. Amir, S. Sharan, and R. Ben-Ari (eds.), *School desegregation: Cross-cultural perspectives*. Hillsdale, NJ: Lawrence Erlbaum, pp. 21–45.

Adler, C. (1986). "Israeli education addressing dilemmas caused by pluralism: A sociological perspective." In D. Rothermund and J. Simon (eds.), *Education and integration of ethnic minorities*. London: Pinter, pp. 64–87.

Amir, Y., S. Sharan, and R. Ben-Ari (eds.). (1984). *School desegregation: Cross-cultural perspectives*. Hillsdale, NJ: Lawrence Erlbaum.

Bentwich, J. S. (1965). *Education in Israel*. London: Routledge and Kegan Paul.

Bilezki, P., and C. Turki (1982). *The educational system in the mirror of numbers*. Jerusalem: Ministry of Education and Culture (Hebrew).

Central Bureau of Statistics (CBS). (1963). *Language, literacy and educational attainment*. Jerusalem: Government Printer.

Cohen, E. (1980). "The black panthers and Israeli society." In E. Krausz (ed.), *Migration, ethnicity and community*, pp. 147–164. New Brunswick, NJ: Transaction Books.

Council for Cultural Cooperation (1989). *Trends in European educational system: An overall picture*. Strasbourg: Council of Europe.

Danilov, Y., and D. Inbar (eds.). (1994). *Choice in education in Israel*. Jerusalem: Ministry of Education and Culture and Hebrew University (Hebrew).

Eden, S. (1973). "The school curriculum as an instrument for the implementation of educational objectives." In H. Ormian (ed.), *Education in Israel*. Jerusalem: Ministry of Education and Culture (Hebrew), pp. 187–194.

Eisenstadt, S. N. (1967). *The Israeli society, background, development and problems*. Jerusalem: Magnes (Hebrew).

Eisner, E., and E. Vallance (eds.). (1974). *Conflicting conceptions of curriculum*. Berkeley, CA: McCutchan Publishing.

Elboim-Dror, R. (1989). "Conflict and consensus in educational policy making in Israel." In E. Krausz (ed.), *Education in a comparative context: Studies of Israeli society*, vol. 4. New Brunswick, NJ: Transaction Books, pp. 45–58.

Inbar, D., and R. Sever (1989). "The importance of making promises: An analysis of second-chance policies." *Comparative Education Review, 33*, 232–242.

Iram, Y. (1986). "Social policy and education for work in Israel." *Issues in Education, 4*, 259–271.

Iram, Y. (1987). "Changing patterns of immigrant absorption in Israel: Educational implications." *Canadian and International Education, 16*, 55–72.

Iram, Y. (1994). "Parental choice of schools—A comparative perspective." *Megamot (Behavioral Science Quarterly), 2–3*, 197–219 (Hebrew).

Kashti, Y. (1978). "Stagnation and chance in Israeli education." *Comparative Education, 14*, 151–161.

Kashti, Y. (1991). *Report of the public committee of inspection of non-regional educational frameworks*. Jerusalem: Ministry of Education and Culture (Hebrew).

Kleinberger, A. F. (1969). *Society, schools and progress in Israel*. Oxford: Pergamon Press.

Kop, Y. (1985). "Social services in the eighties—a turning point?" In Y. Kop (ed.), *Israel's outlays for human services*. Jerusalem: Center for Social Policy Studies in Israel, pp. 7–18.

Leschinsky, A., and K. Mayer (eds.). (1990). *The comprehensive school experiment revisited: Evidence from Western Europe*. Frankfurt: Verlag Peter Lang.

Lewy, J. (1990). *Changes in the matriculation examinations in Israel*. Jerusalem: Ministry of Education and Culture (Hebrew).

Ministry of Education and Culture. (1971). *The junior high school: Principles, guidelines and instructions for implementation.* Jerusalem: Ministry of Education and Culture (Hebrew).

Ministry of Education and Culture. (1972a). *Integration in elementary school and junior high school.* Jerusalem: Ministry of Education and Culture (Hebrew).

Ministry of Education and Culture. (1972b). *The report of the committee for the implementation of changes in the matriculation examination patterns.* Jerusalem: Ministry of Education and Culture (Hebrew).

Ministry of Education and Culture. (1976). *Circular of the Director-General: Special circular A for the 1976–7 school year—The upper division.* Jerusalem: Ministry of Education and Culture (Hebrew).

Ministry of Education and Culture. (1989). *The education system—statistics.* Jerusalem: Ministry of Education and Culture (Hebrew).

Minkovich, A., D. Davis, and Y. Bashi (1977). *Evaluation of the educational achievements of the elementary school in Israel.* Jerusalem: Hebrew University (Hebrew).

Peled, E. (1979). "The hidden agenda of educational policy in Israel: The interrelationship between the political system and the educational system." Unpublished doctoral dissertation. Columbia University.

Peled, E. (1982). "The educational reform in Israel: The political aspect." In E. Ben-Baruch and Y. Neumann (eds.), *Educational administration and policy making: The case of Israel.* Herzliyah: Unipress.

Peled, E., and N. Glasman (1990). "Reforms in Israeli education: The authority distribution dimension." Paper presented at the Comparative and International Education Society Conference, Anaheim, CA.

Rimalt, E. (ed.) (1971). *The structure of elementary and secondary education in Israel: Report of the parliamentary committee on the structure of education in Israel.* Jerusalem: The Knesset (Hebrew).

Schmida, M. (1987). *Equality and excellence: Educational reform and the comprehensive school.* Ramat Gan: Bar-Ilan University (Hebrew).

Schmida, M. (1988). "The educational reform in Israel—Twenty years later." *Journal of International and Comparative Education, 8,* 325–352.

Schwarzwald, J., and Y. Amir, Y. (1984). "Interethnic relations and education: An Israeli perspective." In N. Miller and M. Brewer (eds.), *Groups in contact: The psychology of desegregation.* New York: Academic Press, pp. 53–76.

Shapira, R. (1988). *Social-educational distinctiveness: Distinctive schools—background, development, problems.* Tel Aviv: School of Education, Tel Aviv University (Hebrew).

Shapira, R., and E. Goldring (1990). *Parental involvement in distinctive schools.* Tel Aviv: School of Education, Tel Aviv University (Hebrew).

Shavit, Y. (1984). "Tracking and ethnicity in Israeli secondary education." *American Sociological Review, 50,* 62–73.

Shavit, Y. (1989). "Tracking and educational spirit: Arab and Jewish patterns of educational expansion." *Comparative Education Review, 33,* 216–231.

Shprinzak, D., Y. Segev, E. Bar, and D. Levi-Mazlom (eds.). (1996). *Facts and figures about education in Israel*. Jerusalem: Ministry of Education, Culture and Sport.

Smilansky, M. (1957). "The social aspect of the Israeli educational structure." *Megamot, 8*, 233–239 (Hebrew).

Smilansky, M. (1973). "The challenge of disadvantaged children in the educational system." In H. Ormian (ed.), *Education in Israel*. Jerusalem: Ministry of Education and Culture (Hebrew), pp. 335–352.

Smooha, S., and Y. Peres (1974). "Ethnic gap in Israel." *Megamot, 20*, p. 17 (Hebrew).

Smooha, S., and Y. Peres (1980). "The dynamics of ethnic inequalities: The case of Israel." In E. Krausz (ed.), *Migration, ethnicity and community*. New Brunswick, NJ: Transaction Books, pp. 165–181.

Stanner, R. (1963). *The legal basis of education in Israel*. Jerusalem: Ministry of Education and Culture.

UNESCO (1989). *Statistical year book*. Paris: UNESCO.

Words of Parliament (1969). Vol. 51, No. 36, pp. 3037–3039 (Hebrew).

Yogev, A. (1981). "Determinants of early educational career in Israel: Further evidence for the sponsorship thesis." *Sociology of Education, 54*, 181–194.

Yogev, A., and H. Ayalon (1986). "High school attendance in a sponsored multi-ethnic system: The case of Israel." In A. C. Kerckhoff (ed.), *Research in Sociology of Education and Socialization*, vol. 6. Greenwich, CT: JAI Press.

Yuchtman, E., and Y. Samuel (1975). "Determinants of career plans: Institutional versus interpersonal effects." *American Sociological Review, 40*, 521–531.

Chapter 9

Multicultural Education

The need and the will to absorb Jews from the various exiles of their dispersion was the raison d'être for the establishment of the State of Israel in 1948. The ideology of the "ingathering of the exiles" characterized Israel's official policy and was embodied in the constitutional Law of Return of 1950 (Eisenstadt, 1967; Elazar, 1985), according to which, every Jewish immigrant was entitled to Israeli citizenship.

Israel experienced massive and rapid growth of its Jewish population, which doubled during the first years of statehood and tripled over the first twelve years (*Statistical Abstract of Israel*, 1977). This change was not only in terms of numbers, which turned veteran citizens almost into a minority, but also profoundly affected the social fabric of the new state. The ethnic and geocultural composition of society diversified, and the religious and cultural character, as well as the socioeconomic structure, changed. Immigrants varied in their countries of origin. Fifty percent of immigrants came from Western countries (Europe and America), whereas the other half came from Middle Eastern and African countries (Iran, Iraq, Yemen, Morocco, and Algiers). Toward the end of the 1970s, Oriental Jews comprised about 45% of the Jewish population (SAI, 1977). The Jewish settlers of modern Palestine, who began the process of immigration in the late nineteenth century, came predominantly from European countries with a Western culture. The phenomenon of mass immigration changed the situation and created an almost numerical balance between Western and Oriental Jews in Israel. Due to the ongoing process of immigration, the population of Israel rose from 600,000 inhabitants at its inception to about 5.5 million in the 1990s.

Chronologically, various waves of immigrants are identifiable. Bein (1952) describes the common features of waves of immigrants before statehood: 90% originated from Western countries; they were young, mainly single, unaccompanied by parents, and well educated. Their motives for immigration were rooted in their rebellion against Jewish life in the diaspora and their ambition to establish a new society in the Jewish homeland (Eisenstadt, 1954). Immigrant arrivals after statehood were motivated mainly by situations of persecution and distress, which Jews had suffered in their host countries. During 1948–1951 survivors from the Nazi Holocaust, who were scattered in various displaced persons camps in Europe, arrived in Israel. During the 1950s and early 1960s mass immigration occurred from Middle Eastern and African countries. These immigrants brought large families with them, many of whom were poor and not formally educated. They also lacked productive occupations suited to Israel's modern, urban, and industrially oriented economy. Consequently, a socioeconomic gap was created between Oriental immigrants and "Westerners" regarding occupational distribution, socioeconomic status, political power, and academic achievements (Peres, 1976; Smooha, 1978).

The mass immigration from Eastern countries was succeeded during the coming decades by immigrants from the Soviet Union, and after its dissolution, from Russia and the newly independent republics. These immigrants came from different parts of Russia and differed accordingly in their general sociocultural level, their occupation and family size, and their attachment to Jewish ways of life (Horowitz, 1986). The big wave of Russian immigrants arrived during 1972–1974 and consisted of 82,000 immigrants. The first wave of Russian immigrants originated in the center of the Soviet Union; they were of higher occupational levels, and deeply involved in Russian culture. However, any close attachment to Jewish tradition was lacking, especially among the younger members of the group.

The second wave of 37,000 immigrants occurred at the end of 1980 (Gitelman, 1982). This wave originated in the Baltic States, which had been annexed to the Soviet Union after 1939. These countries, which included Moldavia, Galicia, and Byelorussia, were centers of Jewish life from 1919–1939, and consequently, immigrants from these places had a higher level of Jewish knowledge and commitment (Iram, 1985). The third wave of immigrants came from countries in Central Asia, and the non-Western parts of the Soviet Union, Georgia, and Caucasus. They had lower general cultural and occupational levels, but were closer to Jewish religion and tradition than their counterparts from the center of the Soviet Union.

Immigration from Ethiopia commenced in small groups during the 1960s. Massive waves, which arrived in the early 1980s and 1990s, occurred within the framework of two large operations: Operation Moses and Operation Solomon, effectively airlifting almost the entire Jewish population of Ethiopia to Israel. These immigrants were conspicuous not only by nature of their dark skin, but also by their different values and rituals that they had practiced in Judaism (Abbink, 1983). Their immigration to Israel forced them to make a transition from a tribal, rural, and traditional society to an urban, industrialized, and democratic Israeli society (Newman, 1985).

The big waves of immigrants, who came to Israel from all parts of the world, turned the rather homogeneous Jewish society prior to statehood into a heterogeneous and multicultural society. The newcomers differed in their motives for immigrating. The majority escaped their countries of origin mainly because of limitation of their rights, rejection, discrimination, and even persecution. Other immigrants came because of Zionist or religious ideals. These immigrants came from modern industrialized countries, as well as from rural and underdeveloped areas. They differed in language, socioeconomic level, and in their level of attachment to Jewish religion and Jewish ways of life.

Israel committed itself, since its inception, to respect the multicultural character of the various sectors of the evolving society. Israel declared this policy officially in the Declaration of Independence on May 14, 1948, which promised to maintain the full social and political rights of all citizens, without distinguishing between race, creed, or sex. Several items of legislation succeeded this declaration and bestowed equal rights upon the different sectors of the new Israeli society, including Arabs, Muslims, and Christians, as well as Druze minorities (Masemann and Iram, 1987).

THE EDUCATIONAL SYSTEM

In Israel the educational system was charged with the responsibility of absorbing immigrant children into the social fabric and cultural norms of the new society, thus paving their way into mainstream society. The educational system was chosen for this task, since it was considered to be the most potent organization, encompassing large groups of children who could be affected and changed. The schools also comprised a qualified and professional personnel and controlled a large budget and material resources.

The primary and most important task of schools was to teach children the Hebrew language, which is one of the basic symbols of Jewish nationalism and the means for cultural assimilation. Moreover, the Hebrew language is the critical base for the whole process of learning at school.

The various waves of immigrant children confronted the educational system with different problems. For example, the main problem facing children from Eastern countries was to close, or at least to narrow, the educational and academic gap between them and Western children. Children originating from European countries, or Soviet republics, did not encounter difficulties in the natural and physical sciences, in which they sometimes had an advantage over their native peers. After a short period, they also performed well in the humanities (Horowitz and Frenkel, 1976). Their main problems were in the difference between the social context in which the schools functioned (Bronfenbrenner, 1970) and their remoteness from a traditionally Jewish way of life. Children who emigrated from Ethiopia were in need of psychological support, due to both their different outward appearance and their requirement to adapt to a completely new way of life in the modern and technological Israeli society.

The Policy of the "Melting Pot"

Over the course of Israel's existence, the educational system has utilized different approaches in absorbing immigrant children. These approaches differ in their underlying assumptions and methods of implementation. During the first decade of statehood, the dominant policy was the "melting pot policy." This policy disregarded the multitude of differences between groups of immigrants, which were rooted in the heterogeneous characters of their cultures, systems of values, and norms of behavior. The objective of this policy was to mold all children into one unified social entity. In addition to the Hebrew language, an additional mechanism was employed, namely the national mandatory school curriculum of the elementary school system. The curriculum was issued by the Ministry of Education and Culture in 1954, following the Compulsory Education Law of 1949, and the Law of State Education of 1953. The policy was guided by the conception of formal, equal administrative and pedagogical approaches. The underlying assumption was that equal educational inputs would facilitate the adjustment of all children to school requirements, shape their primary identification with the evolving Israeli society, and increase their ability to integrate in the future within mainstream Israeli society. The difficulties that immigrant children encountered were explained as characteristic features of the general process of immigration, and they were expected to be temporary.

A more differential approach to the different problems of heterogeneous groups of immigrant children was rejected and considered to be contradictory to the norms and values of the national consensus to which Israel committed itself in the Declaration of Independence (Schmida, 1987). The minister of Education and Culture, Ben-Zion Dinur, publicly expressed the following objection to a more differential approach: "all Israeli children are capable of mastering this program [of curriculum]; the intellectual and cultural equality must be our ideal" (Dinur, 1958). The minister was concerned that two standards of schools would be established that would create two separate nations. But the results of the melting pot policy were disappointing. Children of Oriental origin did not attain the educational and academic standards of their Western counterparts. They lagged considerably at the elementary school level, and their situation deteriorated with the increase in school levels, due to the accumulation of academic deficits. Oriental immigrants were underrepresented in academic high schools, as well as on the tertiary level. They became known as disadvantaged, or culturally deprived, children (*teunei tipuah*), who were in need of special educational treatment due to their unsatisfactory school record of achievement and their high dropout levels (Minkovitz, Davis, and Bashi,

1977). Consequently, the policy of the melting pot was substituted for the "social integration policy" in the educational system.

The Policy of Social Integration

The main challenge surrounding the integration of new immigrants during the 1950s was physical absorption, such as, housing conditions and economic security, which created tension between established citizens and newcomers. These problems were more or less solved, and the general situation of immigrants, with regard to levels of income and housing, improved. Yet the absolute gap remained, and the homogeneity of the weaker immigrant populations intensified. During the 1960s it became evident that these problems were rooted in sociocultural differences, with the main tension stemming from the rift between Oriental and Western Jews. Oriental Jews came from countries where the standard of living did not enable them to attain the degree of modernization and social mobility attained by Western Jews. Oriental Jews had received little or no formal schooling at all, and few of them had technical training that met the demands of a modern economy. Consequently, they were unable to compete with Western immigrants with regard to economic standing and knowledge, and their integration into the higher occupational and social levels of Israeli society lagged behind (Smooha and Peres, 1974).

By the mid-1960s most elementary school children were already native-born, and due to the Compulsory Education Law, the general rate of school attendance increased. Yet, Oriental children still occupied mainly the lower and less prestigious levels of schooling (Eisenstadt, 1969). This situation contradicted the ideals of the founding fathers of the Israeli state, who envisioned an egalitarian society in which the ascriptive differences between groups were kept to a minimum. The ethnic cleavage between Eastern and Western Jews endangered national cohesiveness and solidarity and threatened the development of a modern, industrial economy and civilization (Adler, 1984).

The policy of social integration was based on the assumption that Oriental children, due to their impoverished home environments, would improve their educational and academic achievements if their school environments were enriched. No theory of hereditary inferiority, based upon genetic differences between groups, was accepted.

Social integration was defined in the Israeli educational context as the intake of all students into a common school system, regardless of their ethnic origin, socioeconomic level, intellectual talents, and areas of interest, which mixed them in heterogeneous schools and integrated classrooms (Kleinberger, 1973b). The aims of this policy were twofold: to develop social cohesiveness of different ethnic groups, and to raise the low academic achievements of the weaker student population, especially those of Oriental origin. The process should facilitate the entry of the lower-status ethnic subgroups into the mainstream Israeli society (Amir, Sharan, and Ben-Ari, 1984).

Social integration was conceived both as an end in itself—namely the realization of the ideals of social equality and national unity, but also as a means to achieve these goals in the school system (Blass and Amir, 1984). Blass and Amir identify three stages in the policy of school integration. During the first years of statehood, 1948–1962, Israeli society was not fully aware of the problems created by its multiethnic composition, becoming aware of them only during the 1960s. During the second period, 1963–1968, when the problem of disadvantaged student populations became salient, the main principles of the policy were formulated within the preparations of the educational reform, namely, multiethnic composition of classes, the establishment of comprehensive high schools, and the adoption of the regional principle, as opposed to the neighborhood principle, of student registration.

During the third period of implementing the policy, mainly during the 1970s, social integration became the national approach to education, which was also accepted by rulings of the Supreme Court. When parents tried to avoid their zones of registration and enlist their children in nonintegrative schools, judges gave preference to the interests of the state and society; namely they enacted the policy of social integration against the will of individual parents (Gal, 1985).

In spite of the general public consensus regarding the need and significance of a social integration policy, its implementation in the school system lagged behind. Reasons for this included political, demographic, and financial pressures. During the 1960s the Israeli government adopted the policy of "population dispersion," which was aimed at the geographical distribution and social integration of new populations (Karmon, 1975). This policy was a valid demographic means of security and was also justified by economic considerations to strengthen settlements in remote and unpopulated areas. However, the implementation of this policy interfered with the process of interethnic social integration. The economically comfortable Orientals and the majority of Western populations moved to the center of the country in order to improve their standard of living, leaving mainly weaker Oriental populations behind them (Bashi, 1968). Additional reasons were anchored in the division of the school system into the religious and the secular sectors, between which no social integration occurred. The *kibbutzim* (singular *kibbutz*, collective agricultural settlement), which adhered to a distinctive ideologies, were considered as exterritorial settlements with regard to social integration and were hesitant to implement this policy due to its potential influence on their unique way of education (Kleinberger, 1973a). Finally, during the 1970s, financial governmental resources were scarce, and money for busing of children and building of new schools was not available.

Disjunction also became evident between the policy decided upon at the macrosocial level, and the problems that its implementation encountered in schools. The policy mainly dealt with ideological aspects and tried to predict parental reactions. As to the socioeducational technologies crucial to the policy's success, they were delegated to the individual schools. But the schools lacked both the human and material resources to implement the complex programs of multiethnic education and social integration (Sharan et al., 1984).

The policy of social integration differed from the melting pot approach in its emphasis on the social mixing of various ethnic groups within the school, which was considered as the sine qua non of "equal educational opportunity." Similar to the American situation, the approach of "separate, but equal" was rejected, since it was considered to be "inherently unequal," denying children the benefits of an improved educational system (Fellman, 1962). Minkovitz and his colleagues (1977) conducted an extensive study in which they evaluated the Israeli elementary school system. They found that segregated schools for disadvantaged student populations were awarded first preference in allocation of resources. In spite of this, the gap between segregated schools and other schools did not narrow because of their poor ability to utilize additional resources. The researchers reached the overall conclusion that "education for the poor is poor education." The new approach stresses the direct social contact between heterogeneous groups of students and expects interpersonal and intergroup interactions to occur. Consequently, the groups will be open minded toward each other, stereotypes will be eliminated, and changes in attitude will be generated (Amir, 1969, 1976). In addition, the increase of academic achievement in the weaker student population was predicted because of their will to imitate the stronger students; their motivation was expected to increase, as well as their teachers' expectations regarding their abilities (Ministry of Education and Culture, Interdisciplinary Seminar, 1979).

The Multicultural Approach

Since the end of the 1970s, the implementation of the social integration policy weakened, although the Ministry of Education and Culture did not cancel it officially. A more pluralistic approach was introduced alongside the former policy in the educational system. The main shift was from a monocultural orientation, rooted in Western culture and values, to cultural pluralism with greater awareness of the variety of cultures and traditions in multiethnic Israeli society. This shift was urgent due to the need to reinforce the nation's feelings of unity and the sense of identification and solidarity of the various sectors comprising Israeli society. Despite Israel's Middle Eastern location, the country was oriented toward a modern Western civilization, together with the characteristic elements of rationality, planning, future-mindedness, and technological and scientific progress (Iram, 1987; Kleinberger, 1969). Furthermore, Israel tended to overlook the non-Western ethnic groups of the evolving society.

Israel's multicultural policy addressed three major cultural divisions in society: the ethnic division between Oriental and Western Jewry, the division between religious and nonreligious Jewry, and the division between Israeli Arabs and Jews (Masemann and Iram, 1987). The Israeli scenario may shed light on the more general quest of whether the process of modernization of people from non-Western countries evolves successfully, and to what extent, without interfering with their indigenous traditional culture (Adler, 1984).

The philosophical assumptions underlying the pluralistic approach to education are based on respect for each human being, as well as his or her intrinsic rights and liberties. The educational system, based on these values, accepts the legitimacy of different cultures of various groups comprising Israeli society; acknowledges the importance of becoming acquainted with them, and is committed to developing the uniqueness of each individual and his or her group (Scolnicov, 1995). The state is responsible for the educational system, and although it has the power and monopoly to exert coercion over it, it must do so only to a minimal degree. The state must attempt to maintain the necessary balance between individuals' perspectives, aspirations and world views, and the crucial interests of society. Whereas the social integration policy preferred the interests of society—namely, its cultural and national unity as opposed to individual uniqueness—the pluralistic approach assumed a more balanced position between the two orientations. According to the pluralistic approach, the role of the educational system is to create a common denominator as a base for various ethnic and religious groups to live together. In order to accomplish this process, a common base has to be created by the educational system, which is rooted in different world perspectives and the lifestyles that derive from them. All parts of Israeli society adhere to the nation's unity and desire to coexist. Yet in order to promote these basic orientations, the different needs of the various groups must be fulfilled.

The reasons for a shift in orientation to a more pluralistic approach are multifaceted. The outcomes of the social integration policy were not unanimous and were hotly debated. In the early 1970s, social tension and ethnic protest, which began at the end of the 1950s, were renewed, marking the emergence of a new ethnicity (Shama and Iris, 1977; Cohen, 1980). Oriental Jews demanded equal status within the evolving society and recognition of their unique culture as distinct, but equal to, the dominant Western culture. In response to these demands, the Ministry of Education and Culture launched a series of multicultural programs (Ministry of Education and Culture, 1976b). In 1977 the ministry established the Oriental Jewish Heritage Center, which was responsible for "the cultivation, preservation, and advancement of the Oriental communities' heritage and their cultural assets" (Ministry of Education and Culture, 1979a). The center prepared materials dealing with Oriental creations and productions, supervised their distribution, and coordinated the various ministerial programs. The multimedia increased Oriental performers' presentations and allocated more time to Eastern music, literature, and folklore.

Another step in this direction was experimentation with distinctive schools—*Kedmah*—(literally, *east/orient*), in which teachers and students were mainly of Oriental origin and curricula focused on Oriental contents in order to keep the ancient heritage of Oriental Jewry alive.

These schools protested against the public school system, which was blamed for teaching a monoethnic curriculum that emphasized the contents and values of a Western culture at the expense of a more multiethnic curriculum. But the schools were not very successful, sometimes due to administrative problems, and in other cases, due to the small number of parents and children, as in South Tel Aviv, who opted for them.

An additional development in the same direction was the establishment of an ultra-orthodox political party, *Shass*, (acronym for the Hebrew *Oriental guardians of tradition*), which consisted primarily of Oriental Jews. This new movement departed from the other ultra-orthodox party, *Agudat Yisrael*, which was controlled mainly by Western Jews of Lithuanian origin. The new movement was not satisfied with the option of "religious state education," and established an additional network of schools. This network was independent of the state, yet partially subsidized by it, and functioned as a "recognized educational system," like the other ultra-orthodox schools. In addition, the party established centers for the publication of its special religious and cultural heritage, named *El Hama'ayan* (literally, *to the source*), which was also supported by the Ministry of Education and Culture.

An additional demand for a more individualistic approach within the educational system came from groups of parents, mainly from middle-class Western origin, who demanded greater consideration of their individual rights and liberties. Since the establishment of integrative schools, groups of parents were afraid of a decline in their children's academic achievements due to heterogeneous student bodies. In addition, since the political changes in Israel in 1977, which ushered a right-wing government into power and administered a more liberal economic policy, more money accumulated in the upper socioeconomic levels of society. One channel into which these monetary resources was directed was education. Children of higher socioeconomic levels were provided with private lessons out of school. Within school, the phenomenon of gray education expanded, comprising about 38% of the elementary school system, mainly in large cities in the country's center. The system of gray education was instigated by parents' associations, which provided students with enrichment programs in the arts, but also reinforced central curricular programs in the English language, computers, and mathematics (Bar-Siman-Tov and Langerman, 1988).

Parents also demanded the establishment of distinctive schools, which were founded in the 1980s. Some of these new schools were ideological in character and emphasized political orientations, such as the ideals of the Labor Movement, or those of the National Religious Movement, which emphasized unique norms of religious behavior. Other schools represented more modern educational approaches, such as the "open" and "experimental" schools. Other distinctive schools concentrated on special curricular contents, such as schools for the arts and sciences (Shapira, 1988). An additional outcome of the more individualistic approach was the permission some large local authorities, especially the city Tel Aviv, granted to parents—namely, the right to choose a school for their child. Since the Reform in Education, parental choice of schools was limited by the ministerial policy of planned zones of registration, in order to facilitate the process of social integration. Since the 1980s this limitation was under public attack. The shift in balance from more collectivist orientations toward more individualistic orientations, with regard to the place of education in the life of the individual and society, was also reflected in Supreme Court decisions. During the 1970s, decisions were based on the concept that educational integration is an important social value in itself, and in the case of conflict between the interests of society and individual parents, those of society prevail. During the 1980s and 1990s judges conceived the process of integration as a policy that demands compromise on the part of the individual. Parents' involvement in their children's education, including their choice of school according to individual priorities, gained in recognition and was accepted by judges (Gal, 1985).

Remarks of Evaluation

The main burden of the cultural absorption of immigrants was placed upon the educational system. However, the state also supported the process of immigrant absorption from the beginning with effective social welfare policies, which provided basic needs, such as, housing, food, employment, insurance of births, additional allowances for large families, and free, mandatory education for all. The importance of the government's support was based on the multidimensional character of the process of absorption, in which political, social, and cultural problems have implications beyond the educational realm.

Still, the three major divisions that have disquieted Israeli society since the inception of the state continue to persist in an even more intensified manner. One division is the sociocultural gap between Eastern and Western Jews. In spite of the improvement in Orientals' socioeconomic conditions, the relative gap between them and Western groups did not diminish and spilled over to the succeeding generation. Moreover, during the years ethnic differences have correlated with educational, cultural, economic, and political disadvantages (Adler, 1984). The situation deteriorated with the success of small percentages of Orientals in breaking through the limitations of their group to compete with Westerners on equal footing.

During the 1980s the government initiated a special program, the Education Welfare Program, in order to improve housing conditions in areas of distress and to enrich sociocultural activities. The program was characterized by intensive intervention at all levels of education, including family and community, and also comprised a neighborhood renovation project (Ministry of Education and Culture, 1976b, 1979b; Iram, 1992).

The second division is between religious and nonreligious Jews, whose norms of life are not guided by traditional religious laws and values. During the last two decades, a deep schism also developed between the religious groups themselves; namely between orthodox, conservative, and reform religious groups on the one hand, and ultra- and modern orthodox groups on the other.

The third division is rooted in the Arab-Israeli conflict, an issue that is addressed in Chapter 7 of this book.

Each of the strategies utilized in order to alleviate the difficulties created by these divisions was insufficient, as each group of immigrants provided a strict test of its ideologies, conceptions, and methods of implementation. The melting pot policy, which was administered in the 1950s during mass immigration from Middle Eastern and North African countries, was later declared as misguided; a mistake that should not be repeated in the absorption of later groups (Ashkenazi, 1985). The policy did not consider the adaptive role of ethnic subcultures in the process of immigration and required Oriental immigrants to deny their ethnic culture, sometimes even their religious lifestyle, in favor of a Western and mostly nonreligious culture and lifestyle. This policy was based on the assumption that a process of resocialization of Oriental Jews was required (Bar-Yosef, 1980), since their culture and value systems seemed to be unworthy of the modern Israeli society (Cohen, 1985).

Failures of this approach became evident early on. Oriental immigrants developed feelings of inferiority in relation to their cultural heritage and began to doubt its legitimacy. Generational conflicts between parents and children developed, since parents were reluctant to internalize the values and norms of Western culture. On an individual level, feelings of confusion and insecurity were generated; on the group level, feelings of alienation and marginalization.

The melting pot policy was alternated with the social integration policy, the latter emphasizing direct social contact between children from different ethnic groups. The evaluation of the outcomes of this policy was not clear-cut and highly debated. There was a national consensus that social integration was one of Israel's central mechanisms to achieve goals on the macro-social level, namely, the unity of Israeli society and the solidarity of all its citizens. But already on the national level, there existed social and political circumstances that hindered the policy's overall implementation. Consequently, pockets of "nonintegration" were created, which complicated the necessary dialogue between groups (Adler, 1984). Still, the main doubts focused on the policy's implementation within schools. In fact, the dominant and actual intraschool process is based on *desegregation*, rather than *integration*. The former is a necessary precondition for the success of the latter, but not sufficient in itself. The crucial conditions for the development of a genuine process of integration within schools are lacking.

The primary responsibility for implementing social integration policy has been borne by the three-year junior high school, without extending it to earlier or later years of schooling. But even in desegregated schools, the classroom level is resegregated through *ability grouping*, which serves as the prominent strategy of instruction. Direct social contact, by means of various social technologies that are suitable to the creation of a learning environment conducive to social integration, is neglected (Sharan, Amir, and Ben-Ari, 1984). In parallel, the necessary psychological conditions for social integration were not created, such as, equal status contact between interacting groups; intergroup cooperation in pursuit of common goals; and the enlisting of school authorities' support (Amir, 1969).

Teachers were not qualified for their new teaching conditions, which required major accommodations in defining their roles. They also required new competencies in applying innovative teaching methods, as well as knowledge in subject matters dealing with social and cultural needs of different ethnic groups (Sharan, Amir, and Ben-Ari, 1984). In view of these deficiencies, opponents of the approach highlight its negative results, which inflict psychological damage upon minority groups of school children.

The policy of the pluralistic approach seems to be the most suited to a multiethnic and heterogeneous society, since it is based on assumptions that legitimize different systems of culture and values. However, in reality it appears that the stronger socioeconomic groups take advantage of this policy, exploiting it to their particularistic benefits. This is at the expense of the weaker groups, which consist mainly of Oriental immigrants, including Ethiopian immigrants.

Yet additional and even stronger constitutional provisions and government decrees, as well as experiments with alternative strategies, will be insufficient as long as the disparity in sociocultural status divides the different groups. The most pressing issue is the need for a fundamental change in the philosophical and psychological orientations of the various groups within Israeli society.

This chapter discussed the importance of education in the diversified absorption of immigrants, who differ in their cultural and religious values and socioeconomic attainment, as well as in their educational, technical, and social competencies. These differences were addressed in regard to the educational system. The next chapter, "Major Trends and Future Developments," attempts to outline forthcoming trends in the Israeli educational system.

BIBLIOGRAPHY

Abbink, J. (1983). "Seged celebration in Ethiopia and Israel: Continuity and change of a Falasha religious holiday." *Anthropos, 78,* 789–810.

Adler, H. (1984). "School integration in the context of the development of Israel's educational system." In Y. Amir, S. Sharan, and R. Ben-Ari's (eds.), *School desegregation: Cross-cultural perspectives.* Hillsdale, NJ: Lawrence Erlbaum.

Amir, Y. (1969). "Contact hypothesis in ethnic relations." *Psychological Bulletin, 71,* 319–342.

Amir, Y. (1976). "The role of intergroup contact in change of prejudice and ethnic relations." In P. Katz (ed.), *Toward the elimination of racism.* New York: Pergamon.

Amir, Y., S. Sharan, and Ben-Ari, R. (1984). "Why integration?" In Y. Amir, S. Sharan, and R. Ben-Ari's (eds.), *School desegregation: Cross-cultural perspectives.* Hillsdale, NJ: Lawrence Erlbaum.

Ashkenazi, M. (1985). "Studying the students." *Israel Social Science Research, 3,* 85–96.

Bar-Siman-Tov, R., and S. Langerman (1988). *An additional school curriculum in elementary schools, financed by parents.* Jerusalem: Henrietta Szold Institute.

Bar-Yosef, R. (1980). "Desocialization and resocialization: The adjustment process of immigrants." In E. Krausz (ed.), *Migration, ethnicity and community.* New Brunswick, NJ: Transaction Books.

Bashi, R. (1968). *Population distribution and internal migration in Israel.* Project H-1 (Third Ford Grant, mimeograph).

Bein, A. (1952). *Return to the soil: History of Jewish settlement in Israel.* Jerusalem: Zionist Organization.

Blass, N., and Y. Amir (1984). "Integration in education: The development of a policy." In Y. Amir, S. Sharan, and R. Ben-Ari's (eds.), *School desegregation: Cross-cultural perspectives.* Hillsdale, NJ: Lawrence Erlbaum.

Book of Regulations (1975). No. 3388. Jerusalem: Government Printer, p. 2520.

Bronfenbrenner, U. (1970). *Two worlds of childhood: US and USSR.* New York: Russell Sage Foundation.

Cohen, E. (1980). "The black panthers and Israeli society." In E. Krausz (ed.), *Migration, ethnicity, and community.* New Brunswick, NJ: Transaction Books.

Cohen, E. (1985). "Ethnicity and legitimization in contemporary Israel." In E. Krausz (ed.), *Politics and society in Israel.* New Brunswick, NJ: Transaction Books.

Dinur, B. Z. (1958). *Values and methods.* Tel Aviv: Urim (Hebrew).

Eisenstadt, S. N. (1954). *The absorption of immigrants.* London: Routledge and Kegan Paul.

Eisenstadt, S. N. (1967). *Israeli society: Background, development and problems.* London: Weidenfeld and Nicolson.

Eisenstadt, S. N. (1969). "The absorption of immigrants, the amalgamation of exiles and the problems of transformation of Israeli society." In *The integration of immigrants in Israel from different countries of origin.* Jerusalem: Magnes Press (Hebrew), pp. 6–15.

Elazar, D. J. (1985). "Israel's compound policy." In E. Krausz (ed.), *Politics and society in Israel.* New Brunswick, NJ: Transaction Books.

Fellman, D. (ed.). (1962). *The supreme court and education.* New York, NY: Columbia University Teachers' College Press, pp. 85–90.

Gal, N. (1985). *The individual, authority, and the letter of the law: The Israeli supreme court's position on parental choice of school*. Jerusalem: NCJW Research Institute for Innovation in Education, Hebrew University.

Gitelman, Z. (1982). *Becoming Israelis: Political resocialization of Soviet and American immigrants*. New York: Praeger.

Horowitz, T. R. (ed.). (1986). *Between two worlds: Children from the Soviet Union in Israel*. Lanham, MD: University Press of America.

Horowitz, T. R., and E. Frenkel (1976). *Adjustment of immigrant children to the school system in Israel*. Jerusalem: Henrietta Szold Institute.

Ichilov, O., and M. Chen (1973). "The political and social foundation of education." In H. Ormian (ed.), *The education in Israel*. Jerusalem: Ministry of Education and Culture.

Iram, Y. (1985). "The persistence of Jewish ethnic identity: The educational experience in interwar Poland and Lithuania, 1919–1939." *History of Education, 14*, 273–282.

Iram, Y. (1987). "Changing patterns of immigrant absorption in Israel: Educational implications." *Canadian and International Education, 16*, 55–72.

Iram, Y. (1992). "Educational integration of immigrants in Israel." In D. Ray and H. Poonwassie Deo's (eds.), *Education and cultural differences: New perspectives*. New York and London: Garland, pp. 509–529.

Israel Information Center (1996). *Facts and figures about Israel 1996*. Jerusalem: Hamakor Press.

Karmon, N. (1975). "Attaining social goals through housing policy: The evolution of the aspiration and an empirical study of the implementation." Unpublished doctoral dissertation, Haifa: Technion (Israel Institute of Technology) (Hebrew).

Kleinberger, A. F. (1969). *Society, schools and progress in Israel*. Oxford: Pergamon Press.

Kleinberger, A. F. (1973a). "Legislation, politics and directives in the realm of education." In C. Ormean (ed.), *The education in Israel*. Jerusalem: Ministry of Education and Culture (Hebrew).

Kleinberger, A. F. (1973b). "Social integration as a main purpose and justification of the educational policy in Israel." *Policy Planning and Administration in Education, 3*, 11–25 (Hebrew).

Masemann, V. L., and Y. Iram (1987). "The right to education for multicultural development: Canada and Israel." In N. Bernstein-Tarrow (ed.), *Human rights and education*. Oxford: Pergamon Press.

Ministry of Education and Culture. (1976a). *Education in Israel in the eighties*. Jerusalem: Ministry of Education and Culture (mimeograph).

Ministry of Education and Culture (1976b). "Integration of Oriental Jewish heritage in educational institutions." *Director-General Circulars, 37/2*. Jerusalem: Government Printer.

Ministry of Education and Culture. (1979a). "Integration of Oriental Jewish heritage in educational institutions." *Director-General Circulars, 39/4, 39/5*. Jerusalem: Government Printer.

Ministry of Education and Culture. (1979b). *Integration and promoting the goals of education in Israel* (mimeograph).

Minkowich, A., D. Davis, and J. Bashi (1977). *Evaluation of educational achievement in Israeli elementary school.* Jerusalem: Hebrew University.

Newman, S. (1985). "Ethiopian Jewish absorption and the Israeli response: A two-way process." *Israel Social Science Research, 3,* 104–111.

Peres, Y. (1976). *Ethnic relations in Israel.* Tel Aviv: Sifriat Poalim and Tel Aviv University (Hebrew).

Schmida, M. (1987). *Equality and excellence: Educational reform and the comprehensive school.* Ramat Gan: Bar-Ilan University.

Scolnicov, S. (1995). "Education for pluralism incompatible with real disagreement." Paper presented at conference on Education and Change, Pretoria.

Shama, A., and M. Iris (1977). *Immigration without integration: Third-world Jews in Israel.* Cambridge: Shenkman Publishing.

Shapira, R. (1988). "Educational social uniqueness." In *Planning of educational policy: Position papers and decisions of the standing committee of the pedagogical secretariat.* Jerusalem: Ministry of Education and Culture (Hebrew).

Sharan, S., Y. Amir, and R. Ben-Ari (1984). "School desegregation: Some challenges ahead." In Y. Amir, S. Sharan, and R. Ben-Ari (eds.), *School desegregation: Cross-cultural perspectives.* Hillsdale, NJ: Lawrence Erlbaum.

Smooha, S. (1978). *Israel: Pluralism and conflict.* Routledge and Kegan Paul.

Smooha, S., and Y. Peres (1974). "Ethnic gap in Israel." *Megamot, 20.*

Statistical Abstract of Israel (1976, 1977). Jerusalem: Israel Government Printing Office.

Chapter 10

Major Trends and Future Developments

Israeli society has always considered education as one of its most important functions. This concept is in line with Jewish tradition, which ranks education high in its value structure. Since the inception of the State of Israel, and indeed prior to statehood in Palestine, education has been a cornerstone in the building of the evolving Israeli society. After statehood, with the ongoing waves of mass immigration to Israel, the educational system has been charged with the responsibility of immigrant absorption and their social and cultural integration. Thus, the educational system has assumed the responsibility of fulfilling this task.

The primacy of absorption has been embodied in the new state within a series of laws and amendments, and it has been provided with vast human and financial resources, second only to security. From the beginning, the educational system has faced dilemmas and conflicts, the roots of which are anchored in historical, philosophical, and sociocultural developments, beliefs, and attitudes. One of the dilemmas focuses on issues related to the organization and administration of the educational system: whether it should be uniform and therefore centralized, or whether it should allow for a more pluralistic system, and consequently tend toward decentralization and autonomy of smaller educational units, such as, local educational authorities and individual schools. Another conflict lies in the realm of school curricula: whether it should emphasize modern and universal content, or Jewish traditional and Israeli national content. An additional deep-rooted division lies between the fluctuating orientation of education toward either equality or excellence. Israel, being a democratic society, is committed to the ethos of social equality and to the democratization of the educational system in order to provide equal educational opportunities for all children. On the other hand, the educational system is committed to the preparation and training of a highly skilled workforce for the labor market, in order to advance the scientific and technological base of the Israeli modern economy. In order to reach the necessary high standards, one must aspire to excellence. During the five decades of the existence of the State of Israel, the educational system oscillated between the differing assumptions underlying the dilemmas and alternated its emphasis in quite cyclic movements, as far as social and educational policy are concerned.

The oscillation from one orientation to the other in educational systems is a universal phenomenon. Thus, the two perspectives that L. Cuban (1990) suggests, the political and the institutional, for explaining the recurrence of reforms and changes in the American educational system might also be relevant in explaining these phenomena in the Israeli educational system.

The political approach assumes that hidden tensions exist between competing social values inside the schools. When these values are triggered by external events, individuals and groups demand changes that are eventually reached by political trade-offs. However, the institutional perspective analyses schools as organizations, which try to be responsive to the values and demands of their constituencies. On the other hand, schools are organizations that promise teachers a satisfying autonomy, which is insulated from externally driven pressures.

The political perspective of education in Israel is induced by socioeconomic dimensions, namely, socioeconomic gaps between ethnic groups of Oriental and Western origin. The development of inequalities in income, occupation, political power, and education (Smooha and Peres, 1980) posed a threat to the solidarity of the evolving Israeli society. These hidden tensions erupted in ethnic riots during the 1950s and 1960s (Cohen, 1980). However, they reached the forefront of the central political scene, following the gradual transition of young Orientals from their peripheral positions of power in the local municipalities to more central positions on the national level (Peled, 1979). Thus, the ethnic socioeconomic and educational gap became a "salient issue" (Dawson, 1973) on the national agenda, with which the Ministry of Education and Culture had to cope during the 1960s.

Because of the persistence of the gap between ethnic groups, the Israeli Parliament decided upon the Reform of Education in 1968 after many intensive deliberations (Schmida, 1987). In order to reach political consensus, the reform needed to be decisive, which it was not, as far as its orientation toward equality and integration was concerned. The inherent weakness of this decision facilitated its ambiguous interpretation, which in turn led to ambiguity in its implementation. Nevertheless, during the initial stages, the implementation of the reform was ambitious in its depth, breadth, and level of implementation. However, the political coalition that the reform mobilized was not large enough or strong enough to implement the changes and to protect them from their opponents. Various groups were not content with the spirit and the practical implications of the reform, thus weakening the spirit of consensus, which was crucial for the reform's success. This paved the way for its later decline. In addition, the parliamentary decision granted the local authorities freedom whether to introduce or to reject the reform in their localities. Some local authorities ceded to pressure groups, mainly well-situated parents, who feared educational dilution and declining standards, which were attributed to the reform and its policy of social integration. In order to evade the reform there was even a shifting of populations among schools in some localities (Coleman, 1989). The end result was that in the 1990s only 55% of the relevant age group attended reformed schools. Individual schools, too, retained a fair amount of autonomy in their implementation of the reform. Some of these schools based instruction on curricular tracking and ability grouping, which are segregative mechanisms highly correlated with ethnicity, thus avoiding the ministry's directive of social integration.

The various tactics adopted by schools in order to prevent school integration can be explained also by teachers' opposition to the basic social, psychological, and organizational premises upon which the reform was based. Teachers were not involved in the political process of planning the reform, and the teachers' union opposed the reform throughout (Peled, 1982). Indeed, the European Council for Cultural Cooperation (1989) states that "many educational reforms in Europe have not been successful because the teachers had not been involved right from the start, and had not been fully convinced." Teachers may have been afraid of lowering standards of students' academic achievements (Schwarzwald and Amir, 1984). It is also possible that teachers were incompetent to cope with an integrative and heterogeneous student population in the classroom, because they were not provided with appropriate training in new methods of instruction, proper facilities, or learning materials (Dar and Resh, 1986). Thus, the incongruence between the national political level, which decided upon the educational reform, the opposition of the teachers' union, the reluctance of some local authorities, and the conduct of individual schools that did not comply with the spirit of the reform, may explain the decline of the reform and the recurrence of prereform phenomena, including practical "resegregation." Besides these "internal" educational factors, "external" ideological developments also weakened the ethos of striving toward social justice and solidarity, which characterized Israeli society (Horowitz and Lissak, 1989). These developments were consistent with rising trends, such as liberalism, which replaced socialism; economic competitive enterprenuity, which replaced state-regulated initiatives and regulations; individual rights for self-realization, which replaced communal solidarity; and the increased power of the community and local authority, which replaced national-central authority (Horowitz and Lissak, 1989; Kashti, 1991).

During the 1980s a decline in the reform process was witnessed, simultaneously with recurrent changes in other spheres. The changes occurred in the structural, curricular, and sectorial orientations in education, as well as in the matriculation examinations. These developments marked a break in national consensus, which was agreed upon in the 1970s, and constituted a process of "external transaction," by which groups outside the public educational system made efforts to obtain more and better services and to provide additional resources directly to educators (Archer, 1979). This was conducted in Israel within the framework of "gray education" within state schools, by providing additional educational services paid for by parents and the establishment of segregated distinctive schools; a form of "magnet schools."

The retreat from the reform may be viewed as an outcome of an ongoing struggle between groups, conflicting interests, and inherently contradictory social relations. Indeed, the reform may be analyzed in terms of the struggles between ethnic, racial, and economic status groups competing for scarce resources. Thus, parental choice of schools in the 1990s became a driving force for school improvement (Iram, 1994). This demand was voiced by both parents and some local educational authorities who confronted the criticism and dissatisfaction with the present state of schooling. These tendencies added a new dimension for school change, the outcome of which is not yet known.

"Vocationalism" in the Israeli educational system, as a movement encompassing both technical and academic curricula, especially in the postprimary school system, may also be considered a universal phenomenon in education.

In surveying "vocationalization" trends in an international context, Lauglo and Lillis point out that "curriculum change in a practical or vocational direction is an old and recurring policy theme in many countries. [It] transcends the division between rich and poor countries and between different political systems" (1988, p. 3). An analysis of the Israeli experience should be of interest both in its own right and as a case study on these issues from an international perspective. It seems that the recent proposals to reform vocational technical schooling in Israel follow a dual aim. On the one hand, these proposals aim to strengthen technical scientific education, and on the other hand, they postpone vocational technical specialization to the upper stages of high schools and transfer it from school to the workforce. The changing balance between the technical vocational and the technical scientific trends are relevant to many educational systems.

The problems revealed in the study of vocationalism in Israel are consistent with the wider ongoing debate over the existing models of vocational and technical education. The debate is on the relative merits of the "mixed model" common in England (Evans, 1990), versus the "schooling model" adopted in Sweden (Husen, 1989), or the "dual model," which is practiced in Germany (Blossfeld, 1990). The proposed development of the Israeli vocational system is in line with that of Husen (1989), who proposed the Swedish comprehensive schooling model. This model integrates academic and vocational elements of curriculum for all students and embraces continuity of experience from education to employment, with vocational education increasingly replacing academic elements of the curriculum for those students not planning to enter higher education. Regarding the issue of interdependence in the relationship between general education and vocational education, Husen concluded that "one should postpone organizational differentiation as far up in the system as possible, and try to keep all students in a common core program" (1989, pp. 12–13). This model was recently proposed in Israel.

The reform proposals in Israel may also be viewed from the perspective of "liberal vocationalism" (Silver and Brunar, 1988), which was defined as education for work in its broader social, economic, and technological aspects. Thus, by guaranteeing all students access to wider social, technological, humanistic, and linguistic studies, one may anticipate to "bridge the failure of narrow vocationalism" and to integrate the academic and practical, the general and vocational (Funnel and Muller, 1991). Indeed, "liberal vocationalism" following Silver and Brunar (1989) implies a broader and extended curriculum, which encompasses studies selected from several disciplines; problem-solving methods of instruction and training related to real-world problems; breadth of courses and outcomes; care with long-term employment needs; concern to educate questioning and critical adults and openness to external influences (Schweitzer, 1989). Thus, for example, in recent years in England there have been moves toward bridging and even ending the academic vocational divide, including the idea of a new "British baccalaureate." This program has three domains of study. Each student is required to select one subject from each of the following areas: the social sciences, economics and industry, mathematics or technology, or the linguistic and aesthetic disciplines (Evans and Heinz, 1993).

An analysis of the prevailing trends of the vocational educational system in Israel suggests that individual and social considerations were given priority over economic and technological factors. The present challenge facing Israel, as in other countries, is to integrate all these elements for the benefit of the individual, as well as to promote the social integration and economic advancement of the country.

Future developments in the Israeli educational system are very difficult to predict, not only because of the unstable external political conditions, which characterize the existence of the State of Israel and threaten its security, but also because of internal political changes within the Ministry of Education and Culture. The Israeli government is based upon a coalition of political parties, and each new minister of Education and Culture molds the policy of the office according to his political affiliations and individual preferences and aspirations. Thus, Zalman Aran, who was Minister of Education and Culture in the 1960s, fought for social equality; Yigal Allon, who succeeded him in the 1970s, emphasized higher education; Yitzhak Navon in the 1980s focused on social integration; Amnon Rubenstein in the 1990s addressed the democratization of matriculation and higher education; and Zevulun Hammer, as of 1996, stresses the importance of imparting both universal and Jewish values to students. Still, the ethos of equality and excellence has been adhered to by all ministers, but they interpreted the orientations differently, resulting in different emphases and methods of implementation. Another potent internal factor is the socioeconomic factor, which affects the interrelations between different segments in Israeli society: immigration, ethnicity, ideology, and religion.

It might be predicted that one of the major future trends will be the continuation, and even the intensification of the process of democratization of higher education. With the expansion of existing colleges and the establishment of new regional colleges, higher education will move toward "higher education for all," similar to the process of "secondary education for all," which has been in force since the 1970s. This prediction is based on changes in two major areas: the increase in the number of students who obtain their matriculation certificate after twelve years of study, in spite of the fact that compulsory education ceases after ten years of study, and the legal provisions that have been made for the expansion of and admission to college.

Since the 1980s, the Ministry of Education and Culture has initiated a variety of actions to keep students in school until the end of grade 12 and to help them obtain the matriculation certificate (Brandes, 1996b). Learning hours have been increased, curricula have been updated, professional teaching skills have been improved, and individual schools and teachers have been encouraged to conduct experiments with new and modern educational approaches. In addition, affirmative action has been taken with relation to disadvantaged student populations and with the investment of additional financial and pedagogical resources. High school principals have been instructed to discourage students from dropping out, and to keep all students at school until the end of grade 12. Principals were even differentially compensated according to the decrease in the dropout rate in their schools.

Indeed, the administrative and pedagogical efforts of the ministry were successful: the average percentage of students in grade 12 reached about 90% in 1993, compared to about 60–65% in the 1960s. In 1990 51.8% of the population sat for matriculation examinations, compared to 61.2% in 1995. The success in examinations also increased, from 31.4% in 1990 to 37.9% in 1995. The prediction is that in the year 2000, 50% of the relevant student population will obtain the matriculation certificate. It should be noted, however, that the distribution of the percentages of successful students is uneven in various parts of the country. The rate of success is higher for student populations who live near the center of the country and among students who are of Western origin (Brandes, 1996a).

The growing number of graduates, among them immigrants from Russia, exert heavy pressures on the higher educational system, especially on universities. The number of students in universities between 1990–1995 increased by 43%, from 21.3% (68,000) in 1990 to 37.9% (97,000) in 1995 (Volansky, 1996). Universities could not admit more students without the investment of many additional fiscal resources, which the public authorities, namely the Council for Higher Education, could not afford. The establishment of regional colleges, which were designated to be institutions of higher education focusing on teaching and training without research, were less expensive by 30%. But in addition to economic considerations, there were also inherent deliberations with regard to the unique character of the colleges. The labor market demanded at least the first academic degree in more practical occupations, such as, tourism, communication, and the performing arts, which the colleges were prepared to supply. These colleges were also considered to be more suitable than universities, since the new higher education consisted of student populations of new immigrants and students with lower academic achievements, especially from the northern and southern outskirts of the country. Indeed, in 1996 27% (28,000) of bachelor degree students learn in colleges, and the percentage is predicted to reach 40–50% at the beginning of the coming millennium.

The development of the colleges is ensured by the provision of a solid legal base. In 1993 the Council of Higher Education (1993) prepared the master plan, which was ratified by the government in 1994 and adopted by Parliament in 1995. Thus, the most salient future trend is the process of democratization of higher education.

In opposition to the orientation toward equality in higher education, orientations toward excellence are discernible at lower stages of the educational system, especially in the primary and junior high schools. Tel Aviv, the largest metropolitan area in Israel, has implemented processes of parental choice, which are accompanied by the abolishment of predetermined zones of student registration and the establishment of distinctive schools (Shavit and Shapira, 1996). The policy has been implemented in spite of the reservations pointed out in the recommendations of the Inbar Committee (1994) to pursue the policy of parental school choice with a general renewal of schools and especially to improve the weaker schools. The educational system of Tel Aviv has always served as an educational role model for the rest of the country (Schmida, 1964), therefore, it might be predicted that additional local authorities will follow the Tel Aviv model. Consequently, the academic gap between stronger and weaker schools might increase, unless compensation measures are adopted. Moreover, stronger student populations, largely Westerners and veterans, will profit from better educational services, leaving the Orientals and new immigrants far behind.

The opposing trends at the different stages of the educational system testify to the lack of coordination between them. This situation might lower the effectiveness of the system as a whole, since the emphasis and actions of one stage may counteract those of another. If, for example, the lower stages concentrate on processes of early selection, the aim of the higher stages to fulfill the potential of each individual student may not be obtained. This phenomenon should be judged in light of the deep schism that divides Israeli society into different ethnic groups, veterans and newcomers, as well as into religious and secular sectors. To cope with this growing schism between religious and secular Jews, a committee was appointed (Shinhar Committee, 1994). It recommended that Jewish studies should be expanded and intensified at all levels of the general school system, not only in religious schools. The underlying assumption is that more and better knowledge of Jewish tradition might bridge the deep gap regarding Jewish heritage between the two parts of society. It is too early to predict the outcomes of the recommendations of the Shinhar Committee.

In summary, it might be concluded that if the educational system serves as one of the most important social mechanisms, it should multiply its efforts in the direction of unifying policies and actions and refrain from those policies whose impact might strengthen the divisive powers that threaten the existence of Israeli society from the inside.

BIBLIOGRAPHY

Archer, M. (1979). *Social origins of educational systems*. London: Sage.
Blossfeld, H. P. (1990). *Is the German dual system a model for a modern vocational training system?* Paper presented at conference on the Role of Vocational Education and Training in International Comparison, Berlin.
Brandes, O. (1996a). "Equal educational opportunities—The realization of the potential of each student." In O. Brandes (ed.), *The third jump: Changes and reforms in the educational system in the 90s*. Ministry of Education, Culture and Sport (Hebrew).
Brandes, O. (1996b). "There is a chance—The advancement of academic achievements and the raise in the percentage of [students] who are entitled to matriculation." In O. Brandes (ed.), *The third jump: Changes and reforms in the educational system in the 90s*. Ministry of Education, Culture and Sport (Hebrew).
Cohen, E. (1980). "The black panthers and Israeli society." In E. Krausz (ed.), *Migration, ethnicity and community*. New Brunswick, NJ: Transaction Books.
Coleman, J. (1989). Introduction. In E. Krausz (ed.), *Education in a comparative context: Studies of Israeli society*. New Brunswick, NJ: Transaction Books.
Council for Higher Education. (1993). *The master-program for the development of academic frameworks*. Educational Institutions, Document 206 (Hebrew).
Cuban, L. (1990). "Reforming again, again, and again." *Educational Researcher, 19*, 3–13.
Dar, Y., and N. Resh (1986). "Classroom intellectual composition and academic achievement." *American Educational Research Journal, 23*, 357–374.
Dawson, R. E. (1973). *Public opinion and contemporary disarray*. New York: Harper and Row.
European Council for Cultural Cooperation. (1989). *Trends in the European educational system: An overall picture*. Strasbourg: Council of Europe.
Evans, K., and W. R. Heinz (1993). *Becoming adults in England and Germany*. London: Anglo-German Foundation.
Evans, R. (1990). "Post-16 education, training and employment." *British Journal of Education and Work, 3*, 41–59.
Funnel, P., and D. Muller (1991). *Vocational education and the challenges of Europe*. London: Kogan Page.

Horowitz, D., and M. Lissak (1989). *Trouble in utopia: The overburdened polity of Israel*. Albany: State University of New York Press.

Husen, T. (1989). "Integration of general and vocational education: An international education—An international perspective." *Vocational Training, 1*, 9–13.

The Inbar Committee (1994). *The report of the committee for choice in education*. Pedagogical Secretariat of the Ministry of Education, Culture and Sport (Hebrew).

Iram, Y. (1994). "Parental choice of schools: A comparative perspective." *Megamot, 36* (2-3), 197–219 (Hebrew).

Kashti, Y. (1991). *Report of the public committee of inspection of the non-regional educational framework*. Jerusalem: Ministry of Education and Culture (Hebrew).

Lauglo, J., and K. Lillis (eds.). (1988). *Vocationalizing education: International perspective*. Oxford: Pergamon Press.

Peled, E. (1979). "The hidden agenda of educational policy in Israel: The interrelationship between the political system and the educational system." Unpublished doctoral dissertation, Columbia University.

Peled, E. (1982). "The educational reform in Israel: The political aspect." In E. Ben-Baruch and Y. Neuman (eds.), *Educational administration and policy making: The case of Israel*. Herzliyah: University Press (Hebrew).

Schmida, M. (1964). "Major assumptions underlying universal, free public secondary education in the United States and the high school system of the municipality of Tel Aviv." Unpublished doctoral dissertation. New York: Teachers College, Columbia University.

Schmida, M. (1987). *Equality and excellence: Educational reform and the comprehensive school*. Ramat Gan: Bar-Ilan University (Hebrew).

Schwarzwald, J., and Y. Amir (1984). "Interethnic relations and education: An Israeli perspective." In N. Miller and M. Brewer (eds.), *Groups in contact: The psychology of desegregation*. Orlando, FL: Academic Press.

Schweitzer, J. (1989). "Integration of vocational and general education: An educational task and political challenge for the future." *Vocational Training, 1*, 35–37.

Shavit, R., and R. Shapira (1996). *Principles and changes in integration in education in Israel—Toward a system approach*. Working paper (Hebrew).

Shinhar Committee (1994). *The nation and world: Jewish education in a changing world*. Committee for the Examination of Jewish Studies in the National School System. Jerusalem: Ministry of Education, Culture and Sport (Hebrew).

Silver, H., and J. Brunar (1988). *A liberal vocationalism*. London: Methuen.

Smooha, S., and Y. Peres (1980). "The dynamics of ethnic inequalities: The case of Israel." In E. Krausz (ed.), *Migration, ethnicity and community*. New Brunswick, NJ: Transaction Books.

Volansky, A. (1996). "Opening the gates—Democratization of higher education." In O. Brandes (ed.), *The third jump: Changes and reforms in the educational system in the 90s*. Jerusalem: Ministry of Education, Culture and Sport (Hebrew).

Glossary

Agudat Israel: (literally, Association of Israel). A political party representing ultraorthodox Jews, which maintains its own separate school system.

Alliance Israelite Universelle: (French: Universal Alliance of Jews). An international Jewish organization founded in 1860 in France to represent Jewish interests and to engage in philanthropic activities, mainly by establishing educational and vocational institutions for Jews.

Amal: (literally, labor). A voluntary organization which partly owns vocational institutions in Israel.

Amit: acronym for *Irgun Mitnadvot Israel Torah*, the Women's Volunteer Organization for Israel and Torah, which partly owns vocational institutions in Israel.

Ashkenazim: (singular, *Ashkenzai*). Jews of European origin and their descendants in other countries.

Asile d'enfants: (French: children's shelter). An institution where 3–6-year-old children were prepared for formal learning in elementary school. Following the French model, the Alliance Israelite Universelle established the first kindergarten in Israel at the end of the 19th century.

Bagrut: (literally, maturity). A secondary school leaving examination administered nationally by the Ministry of Education, as a prerequisite for entry to higher education.

Batei Talmid: (literally, Houses of the Student). Informal educational organization which is closely tied to elementary schools, for students to prepare their homework and to engage in leisure and recreational activities. These houses were particularly active during the 1960s and 1970s.

Bet Sefer Ammami: (literally, public school). This was the name of the 8-year elementary public school, as distinguished from the private school, until the 1968 Reform in Education.

El Hama'ayan: (literally, to the fountain). An organization of *Shass*, an ultraorthodox political party, which provides young children with both formal and informal education.

Halutzim: (singular, *halutz*; literally, pioneer). Settlers in collective agricultural settlements, known as kibbutzim.

Hamula: (Arabic). Extended family that functions as a socioeconomic unit.

Handasai: Hebrew for technicians and practical engineers. Since the mid-1960s, these engineers have been trained in grades 12 and 13 of the extended vocational schools.

Hareali: An academic highschool, which was founded at the beginning of the century in Haifa, and has been functioning ever since on a 12-year basis.

Heder: (literally, room). A traditional single-teacher Jewish religious primary school in Europe.

Hilfsverein der deutschen Juden: (German: German Jewish Support Association). A Jewish philanthropic association founded in 1901 in Berlin in order to support Jewish political, financial and educational causes.

Hok Hinuch Mamlachti: (literally, State Education Law). This law was passed in 1953 and provided 5–6-year-old children with universal, free and compulsory kindergarten education, as well as 6–14-year-old children with free elementary school education.

Hovevi Zion: (literally, Lovers of Zion). An ideological and political movement, which inspired the national revival of Jews and their resettlement in their ancient homeland. In 1897 it became part of the Zionist movement.

Intifada: (Arabic: uprising). Palestinian resistance against Israeli authorities in the West Bank and Gaza Strip.

Kedmah: (literally, eastward). A network of schools established during the 1990s for children of Oriental origin, with a strong emphasis on Oriental curricular contents. Due to minimal support from the Ministry of Education and low appeal to the student population, this type of school is decreasing in number.

Kibbutz: (plural, *kibbutzim*). A collective farm or settlement cooperatively owned and managed by its members, and organized on a communal basis.

Kutab: a religious single-teacher primary school common in Oriental Jewish communities.

Mamlachti: State school system, which follows the 1953 State Education Law.

Mamlachti Dati: State religious school system. This school system maintains educational autonomy in curricular and personnel issues.

Masmam: (acronym for *Maslul Miktzoi Ma'asi*). The practical vocational course, which leads to a certificate of completion and vocational certification by the Ministry of Labor and Welfare.

Masmar: (acronym for *Maslul Miktzoi Ragil*). The regular vocational course, which culminates in a final certificate and the appropriate trade diplomas without matriculation.

Masmat: (acronym for *Maslul Miktzoi Tichoni*). The secondary vocational course of studies, which ends with matriculation examinations in technological electives, as well as academic matriculation examinations. This course was established during the 1970s.

Matam: (acronym for *Maslul Ta'assiyati Ma'asi*). The practical industrial track, which is the lowest of the vocational schools. Graduates of the three industrial learning tracks are entitled to government vocational certificates.

Matan: (acronym for *Maslul Ta'assiyati Nivchar*). The elected industrial track, which is the highest learning track in the industrial schools.

Matar: (acronym for *Maslul Ta'assiyati Ragil*). The regular industrial track in the industrial schools.

Mechinot: (literally, preparatory classes). These classes comprise 4–6 years of elementary education in private schools, which are connected to secondary schools.

Merkaz Hamorim: (literally, Teachers' Center). The elected central committee of the Association of the Hebrew Teachers in Palestine, which was established in 1904.

Mizrachi: (acronym for the Hebrew "spiritual center"). A political party of moderate Orthodox Zionist Jews, founded in 1902. In 1956 it became the National Religious Party (NRP).

ORT: (acronym for Russian Organization of Labor and Vocation). A voluntary Jewish international organization established in 1880 in Russia, which partly owns vocational institutions in Israel.

Seker: (literally, survey). A screening test which was enacted in 1955 by the Ministry of Education, and administered to all students upon completing 8 years of elementary school. This test was given as a means of assessing students' eligibility for postprimary school.

Sephardim: (singular, *Sephardi*). Originally, Jews of Spanish and Portuguese origin and their descendants, mainly living in the Middle East and North Africa.

Shari'a: (Arabic: the way). The religious law of Islam.

Shass: (acronym for *Shomrei Torah Sephardi'im*; literally, Sephardi Torah Guardians). An ultraorthodox political party, which was founded in the mid-1980s, and consists mainly of members of Sephardic, or Oriental, origin.

Talmud Torah: (literally, study of the Torah Law). A traditional religious Jewish communal school.

Teunei Tipuach: (literally, in need of care). A positive term for disadvantaged school children. A special unit within the Ministry of Education was responsible for this project since the 1960s. The criteria defining this student population underwent many changes during the years of statehood.

Torah: The Pentateuch, namely, the first five books of the Bible. It also broadly refers to the entire body of the traditional religious teaching and study of Judaism.

Yeshivah: (plural, *yeshivot*). Traditional rabbinical academy devoted primarily to the study of Talmud (the Jewish Oral Law).

Annotated Bibliography

GENERAL OVERVIEW

Bentwich, J. S. (1965). *Education in Israel*. London: Routledge and Kegan Paul.

This book gives an account of the various forms of education in Israel, as well as their present organization and curricula. The book attempts to give some idea of the motion in the unfolding drama of education in Israel, with its roots in the distant past, and reaching out toward a new way of life in a rapidly developing world. Israel is presented as a microcosm, coping with problems, such as, how to break down class barriers; the provision of equal educational class opportunities; how to maintain values in a pleasure-seeking world; how to build a new synthesis of religion and science; and how to create a new and better way of life in a technological society.

Gaziel, Haim (1993). *Educational policy at a crossroads between change and continuity: Education in Israel in the past decade*. Jerusalem, Israel: Institute for the Study of Educational Systems.

The Institute for the Study of Educational Systems has from its inception set itself the goal of analyzing all aspects of the Israeli education system in the 1980s as the basis for follow-up studies in subjects of concern to the system's decision-makers. This research report is intended to complete the analysis of the trends in the education budgets of the 1980s carried out in a previous study. That report examined how the allocation of resources to education reflects the policy of the government and local authorities, and expresses national and local priorities and the various manifestations of the decline in the level of education services. When combined with that report, this monograph, which monitors the changes in education policy over the last decade and analyzes the motivations behind the pronouncements and decisions of the system's policymakers, unfolds a comprehensive picture of education in Israel, its problems, structure, sectors, and trends. Divided into five chapters, Chapter 1 discusses efficiency as an economic value versus equality as a social value, equality in education, educational equality versus educational elitism, and educational choice as a basis for education policy. Chapter 2 describes the landmarks of education policy in Israel, the strategies of formal equality, differential resources, and reform and integration in education. Chapter 3 focuses on the conflicting aims of the previous decade, describing state religious education, technological education, education reform, and Arab education. Chapter 4 describes what actually took place in the decade. Chapter 5 discusses trends for the future.

Gaziel, Haim (1996). *Politics and policy-making in Israel's education system.* Sussex: Academic Press.
This book describes and analyzes the structure of Israel's educational system from a political and policymaking perspective. It explains how education policy in Israel is shaped by the political agenda, and how the fluid balance of power lies between vested political interests in education policy.

Kleinberger, Aharon F. (1969). *Society, schools and progress in Israel.* Oxford: Pergamon Press.
This book surveys the development of the educational system in Israel since the inception of the State of Israel. The chapter on Historical Background is followed by a description of Israeli society, its policies, and economy. After the general overview, the book deals with the major issues of education, its legislation, and politics; the schools at various levels; teacher education; and finally discusses some major problems.

Krausz, Ernest (ed.). (1989). *Education in a comparative context: Studies of Israeli society,* vols. I–IV. Publication series of the Israel Sociological Society. New Brunswick, NJ: Transaction Books.
This book belongs to the series which identifies the major areas of sociological research being conducted on Israeli society. It focuses on education and represents a milestone in the development of the sociological analysis of the socialization and educational processes at work in Israeli society. The book is introduced by an article by James Coleman, and followed by an overview of policy perspective by E. O. Shield. The book is divided into five parts: the social state of educational policies; structural varieties and social change in education; achievement and the issue of equal opportunity; integration and ethnic disparities in education; and finally, students, teachers, and social climates.

STRUCTURE OF THE EDUCATIONAL SYSTEM

Goldring, Ellen B. (1992). "System-wide diversity in Israel: Principals as transformational and environmental leaders." *Journal of Educational Administration, 30,* (3), 49–62.

Israeli principals are actively redefining their role and are evolving from routine managers to leader managers. This role change is reflected in four pivotal areas: resource allocation, organizational framework, governance, and market structure. Israeli principals are required to be environmental managers who mobilize resources and manage professional organizations with pluralistic governance in a competitive market structure.

Levin, Benjamin. "Government planning and decision-making in education and other social policy fields." Conference paper at the Canadian Studies Programme of the Hebrew University of Jerusalem, Israel, January 8, 1987.

Major trends in social policy and the public service fuel the change with regard to the entire perspective. They include shifting needs of social services; inflexibility of institutions; increasing domination by narrow-viewed pressure groups; declining faith of the people in government; increasing gap between expenditures and revenues and growing interdependence in the policy system that cause implementation difficulties. Greater government flexibility in use of resources and a more integrated approach to policy development are required. Given time, governments will make the change in spite of the barriers of status and pay.

PRIMARY EDUCATION: PARENTAL INVOLVEMENT

Chen, M. (1993). "Sponsored privatization of schooling in a welfare state." Conference Paper. Annual Meeting of the University Council for Educational Administration, Houston, TX. 18 pp.

Examines the emergence of privatization in Israel's educational system. Privatization of educational services in a welfare state such as Israel expands the role of central government in educational affairs. The two emerging forms of privatization are the Culture Youth and Sports Community Centers and the "Gray Education" movement. Privatization may disguise the central government's increased involvement in the managements of some educational services that are demanded by powerful pressure groups.

Goldring, Ellen, B. (ed.). (1991). "Parental involvement and public choice in education." *International Journal of Educational Research, 15* (3-4), 229–352.

Eight papers discuss the public choice model of education in an international context and the implications of choice for parental involvement in schools. Perspectives and dilemmas in the United States, Great Britain, Japan, and Israel are considered. Conflicting views of schools as service organizations and as commonwealth organizations are illustrated.

Menahem, Gila et al. (1993). "Parental choice and residential segregation." *Urban Education, 28*(1), 30–48.
Examines motivation and residential distribution of parents who enrolled their children in Special Program Non-Neighborhood schools in Tel Aviv, Israel. Results suggest that enrollment may serve as an alternative to residential mobility for families with high educational and professional status relative to residential area.

Shapira, Rina, and Flor Hayman (1991). "Solving educational dilemmas by parental choice: The case of Israel." *International Journal of Educational Research, 15*, (3-4), 277–291.
Examines the organizational, educational, and social characteristics of elementary schools of choice in Israel; focuses on whether and how these schools constitute a solution to educational problems or create new dilemmas. Two types of schools are studied: those which emphasize particular subjects, and those which are ideologically oriented. Results suggest that schools of choice in Israel permit a dynamic balance between the central state system that emphasizes equality and integration and the parents who wish to satisfy their needs.

POSTPRIMARY EDUCATION

Comprehensive High School

Egozi, Moshe et al. (1984). *Inputs and outputs of sponsored comprehensive schools in Israel.* Jerusalem: Hebrew University of Jerusalem. National Council of Jewish Women Research Institution for Innovation in Education.
This book examines specially funded comprehensive secondary schools in Israeli development towns during the 1960s. Forty-five schools and 31,000 students were examined during the years 1976–1977 and 1978–1979 on the following school variables: type of school, comprehensiveness, teachers' qualifications, and pupil composition. Pupil variables included background, academic, and military achievement. Findings indicate that the sponsored comprehensive schools provide their students with different opportunities than academic, mixed, and vocational urban schools.

Schmida, Mirjam. (1987). *Equality and excellence, educational reform and the comprehensive school.* Ramat Gan: Bar-Ilan University (Hebrew).
This book discusses the dilemma confronting modern educational systems in Israel and in Western Europe, which aim simultaneously for equality and

excellence. The book describes the transition from elitist educational systems for "the few" to populist systems for "all." The democratic approach is accompanied by the meroticratic approach in order to answer the needs of the modern technological society. The comprehensive high school is presented as the ideal type to cope with the dilemma. The book traces developments of this type in Western Europe and Israel, defines its guiding principles, and analyzes its functional difficulties.

VOCATIONALISM

Bagan, Jack. "The pulse of a nation: ORT Israel and vocational-technical training." *Intellect, 106* (2395), 404–407.
The basic purpose of the Organization for Rehabilitation through Training (ORT) is to teach and train people in working skills in order that they live free from charity. Describes ORT's efforts.

Borus, Michael. (1977). "A cost-effectiveness comparison of vocational training for youth in developing countries." *Comparative Education Review, 21* (1), 1–13.
This article presents a case study of youth training in Israel and seeks to measure the economic returns associated with the costs incurred for different types of vocational training. The findings point in favor of nonformal modes of training for the most cost effective preparation of semiskilled and skilled workers. The findings are highly tentative.

Doron, Rina, and A. Lederer (1967). *Vocational training and industrial needs: Report on a pilot study in the metal work industry.* Jerusalem, Israel: Henrietta Szold Institution.
This study determines if vocational school graduates leave school trained for their jobs. Opinions and suggestions of industrial engineers and administrators were elicited by a questionnaire. Opinions were divided as to the need to provide a broad theoretical basis versus the need to devote more time to practical work. It was concluded that vocational schools should be diversified to include additional "streams" and levels.

Hoffman, Alice M. (1980). "Worker's education in Israel." *Lifelong Learning: The Adult Years, 3* (9), 4–7.
Description of the educational and cultural activities of the *Histadrut*, the General Federation of Labor, responsible for workers' education in Israel. Additional topics discussed are immigrants' and women's education, as well as Israeli Arab and cooperative Third World programs.

Iram, Yaacov. (1986). "Social policy and education for work in Israel." *Issues in Education, 4* (3), 259–271.

Analyzes education for work in Israel, focusing on vocational education in the light of cultural, social, and economic variables, related to social and educational policies. The training program is criticized because of emphasis on general education instead of providing skilled workers for industry, commerce, and civil service.

Kaniel, Shoshana. *The social background of students and their prospect of success at school.* Israel National Commission for UNESCO, May 1971 (available in CEAS Abstract Series No. 1-4 (ED'060 227).

A reply to an IBE questionnaire. The goal of the Israeli educational policy was to raise the educational level of backward immigrants to Israel while maintaining a high standard education for other population segments. In spite of enrichment programs for underprivileged students, the gap between the children has magnified. The reasons defined are poverty, lack of experience, and poverty of language.

Karayanni, Mousa. (1987). "Impact of cultural background on vocational interest." *Career Development Quarterly, 36* (1), 83–90.

Compared vocational interests of Jewish and Arab students in Israel from the same region and about the same socioeconomic level. Cultural biases emerged in the construction of the Arabic version of the interest inventory. Results showed interests of Arab students becoming modern and Western.

Meir, Elchanan, J. et al. (1990). "Vocational, avocational, and skill utilization congruencies and their relationship with well-being in two cultures." *Journal of Vocational Behavior, 36* (2), 153–165.

Examines interrelationship among congruence aspects and their relationship to well-being measures. Inventories administered to Jewish and Arab teachers found various kinds of congruence being related, not only to reported satisfaction but also to reported physical and distress symptoms.

Neuman, Shoshana, and Adrian Ziderman (1989). "Vocational secondary schools can be more cost-effective than academic schools: The case of Israel." *Comparative Education, 25* (2), 151–163.

Compares labor market outcomes for graduates of academic and vocational schools among 15,846 25–49-year-old male Israeli workers. Concludes that vocational schools are more efficient than academic schools in terms of worker earnings in relation to educational costs.

Neuman, Shoshana, and Adrian Ziderman (1991). "Vocational schooling, occupational matching, and labor market earnings in Israel." *Journal of Human Resources, 26* (2), 256–281.

This paper examines the efficacy (in terms of labor market outcomes) of vocational school education in Israel as compared with that of academic schools. Using data from the 1983 population census, the study shows vocational schooling, which accounts for half of secondary school enrollment in Israel, to be more cost-effective than general school education for those students who do not go on to higher education. In particular, those who complete vocational school and who work in occupations related to a course of study pursued at school earn more (by up to 10% annually) than their counterparts who attended general secondary schools or those from vocational schools who are employed in noncourse-related occupations. These results provide strong reinforcement of recent, broadly similar studies for the United States.

Shavit, Yossi. (1984). "Tracking and ethnicity in Israeli secondary education." *American Sociological Review, 49* (2), 210–220.
In Israel, academic track placement enhances eligibility for higher education for all but the least able students. Vocational track placement inhibits *Sephardis'* (students from Oriental background) already low likelihood of receiving higher education.

Shavit, Yossi. (1990). "Segregation, tracking, and the educational attainment of minorities: Arabs and Oriental Jews in Israel." *American Sociological Review, 55* (1), 115–126.
Explores the pattern of Arab-Israeli men attending postsecondary schools at higher rates than Oriental Jews in Israel. Tests and corroborates the explanation that Arabs benefit from separate, predominantly college preparatory school system while Oriental Jews must compete with European-origin Jews and are disproportionately tracked into vocational programs.

Shirom, Arie, and Joel Goldberg (1974). "Adjusting to work: Workplace mobility of young male workers in Israel," *Journal of Educational Behavior, 5* (1), 67–76.
This study focuses on some of the correlates of workplace mobility of male workers aged fifteen to seventeen. Results suggest that the early stages of a young worker's process of occupational socialization are of importance in determining his future career decisions.

Silverman, Robert E. (1969). "Educational technology in Israel: Open to the future." *Educational Technology, 9* (11), 33–35.
Focuses on ORT Israel, which is a project that develops and tests programmed materials for Israel's vocational high schools that successfully introduced programmed instruction.

Ziderman, Adrian. (1987). "Initial vs. recurrent training for skilled trades in Israel—Results of a 7-year follow-up study." *Economics of Education Review, 6* (2), 91–98.
The earnings of former trainees for the skilled trades in Israel were monitored over a seven-year period. While no significant differences were found between graduates of one year adult training courses and similar programs for teenagers, postponement of training until the twenties is not a paying proposition.

Ziderman, Adrian. (1989). "Training alternatives for youth: Result from longitudinal data." *Comparative Education Review, 32* (2), 243–255.
Analyzes annual earnings data from 1969–1975 for 1,233 Israeli skilled workers, born 1947–1948 and trained in vocational secondary school or in one of three nonformal work-related training programs. No differences in earnings by training modes were found. Suggests that vocational secondary schools are not cost effective.

SOCIAL PERSPECTIVE: DISADVANTAGED STUDENTS

Boarding Schools

Aviram, Ovadia. (1993). "Appearance and reality in a stressful educational setting: Practices inhibiting school effectiveness in an Israeli boarding school." *International Journal of Qualitative Studies in Education, 6* (1), 33–48.
The objectives of this study were to understand the observed behavior of personnel in a stressful educational setting and to consider the impact of such behavior on the effectiveness of the organization. The perspective taken is that of the phenomenological paradigm. The case study included participant observation followed by interviews. "Generating appearances," namely, mental constructs to substitute for unrealized appearances, were discovered. This phenomenon emerged within a framework of factors, such as, frustration due to paucity of rewards, inadequate training, and low expectations of students.

Kahane, Reuven. (1986). "Informal agencies of socialization and the integration of immigrant youth into society: An example from Israel." *International Immigration Review, 20* (1), 21–39.
Less formal and more voluntaristic socialization agencies seem to facilitate the absorption of immigrant youth into the Israeli society more effectively. Symmetry and voluntarism, which are the agency's structural character-istics, allow newcomers to maintain their sense of dignity and increase their capacity to integrate economically and politically on their own terms.

Kahane, Reuven. (1988). "Multicode organizations: A conceptual framework for the analysis of boarding schools." *Sociology of Education, 61* (4), 211–226.
Delineates six types of boarding schools based upon different modes of conduct or "codes." The ideal boarding school would be a hybrid type maximizing pedagogical potential providing students with a high degree of freedom and fostering commitment to universal values and responsible elite orientations. Cites examples from Israel, Britain, and the United States.

Kashti, Yitzhak. (1988). "Boarding schools and changes in society and culture: Perspectives derived from a comparative case study research." *Comparative Education, 24* (3), 351–364.
Boarding schools are presented as educationally integrative and culturally innovative. Historical examples of Eastern Hungarian Kollegium, England's eighteenth century public schools and Israeli youth villages are examined. Boarding schools, their autonomy and power of survival, are conceived as potential accelerators of change in social structure and culture.

Smilansky, Moshe et al. (1971). "Secondary boarding schools for gifted students from disadvantaged strata." *Technical Report No. 2, The socio-economic background of students and their success in secondary school: A follow-up study*. Tel Aviv University, Research and Development Lab for the Study of the Disadvantaged.
This report is one of a series on studies conducted to understand and assist culturally disadvantaged pupils. After a brief historical background, the theoretical basis of the study is presented. Students' socioeconomic background, as well as their success in secondary schools, is analyzed. Findings show that the State of Israel strives toward defined goals by absorbing a "culturally disadvantaged population," distinguished by ethnic and social characteristics.

Compensatory Education

Adler, Chaim et al. (1975). "The education of the disadvantaged in Israel: Comparisons, analysis and proposed research." Research/technical report. Hebrew University of Jerusalem (Israel). National Council of Jewish Women, New York, NY.
Education for disadvantaged children is overviewed in Israel and some Western nations, and procedures and programs applied are evaluated. Vocational and technical education in Israel are discussed, as well as informal educational organizations. It is concluded that educational methods and techniques are emphasized at the expense of institutional structural and cultural aspects. More educational intervention is needed, as

well as greater focus on informal education. Other systems' failures should be studied.

Eisenberg, Theodore et al. (1983). "A follow-up study of disadvantaged children two years after being tutored." *Journal of Educational Research*, *76* (5), 302–306.
The study shows that the lasting effects of tutoring seem to be more value-related than behavioral according to a follow-up study of 324 tutored disadvantaged children. Lasting effects were shown only in academic aspirations.

Goldberg, Harvey, E. (1984). "Disadvantaged youngsters and disparate definitions of youth in a development town." *Youth and Society*, *16* (2), 237–256.
Sketches the development, achievements, and reception of a community-based educational program for disadvantaged Israeli youths. Stresses the importance of the youths' view of their own developmental cycle and the significance of the youths' brief adolescence.

Inbar, Dan, and Nura Resh (1983). "Learning of the disadvantaged and school climate." Publication No. 89. Hebrew University of Jerusalem (Israel), School of Education, National Council of Jewish Women, New York, Research Institution.
This study analyzes the relationship between the school climate of five integrated junior high schools in Israel and different students' educational outcomes. Two distinctive climates were revealed on the school level: an achievement-conservative one and an integrative-open one. The type of climate was related to students' variables, such as, achievement, aspirations, locus of control, self-image, and anxiety. Results showed that classes are differentially sensitive to school climate's effects, according to their ethnic composition.

Iram, Yaacov (1992). "Educational integration of immigrants in Israel." In Douglas Ray and Deo H. Poonwassie (eds.), *Education and cultural differences: New perspectives*. New York: Garland Publishing.
The article discusses the need to change strategies of absorption and educational policies, because of the changing nature of immigration to Israel since 1948. Flexible and imaginative strategies are crucial to the successful absorption of Ethiopian and Russian immigrants.

Jaffee, Eliezer, D. (1985). "Trends in residential and community care for dependent children and youth in Israel: A policy perspective." *Child and Youth Services*, *7* (3-4), 123–141.

Reviews policy and ideological trends within three Israeli institutions for disadvantaged youth: Youth Aliyah, the Ministry of Labor and Social Affairs, and the Ministry of Education and Culture. Recommends policy initiatives, research, differential diagnosis, program assignment, and planning accountability.

Landau, Erika, (1987). "The gifted disadvantaged." *Gifted International, 4,* (1), 65–69.
Describes an enrichment program for five- to fifteen-year-old gifted disadvantaged children in Israel. The program included neighborhood and outside-neighborhood activity programs. Evaluation indicated substantial IQ increases after three semesters.

Lassar-Cohen, H., and Amos Dreyfus (1991). "Obtaining meaningful feedback from disadvantaged pupils' essays concerning their attitudes toward tutorial activities." *Urban Education, 25* (4), 454–465.
Discusses a tutoring project employing student-teachers in a rural residential school; appreciates the sympathetic companionship of tutors close in age to the students.

Lerner, Natan. (1984). "Affirmative action in Israel." Conference paper. ED249301. For conference proceedings, see UD023798.
This paper examines equality, discrimination, affirmative action, and preferential treatment in Israel. It discusses policies of the state in relation to Arab minorities, disadvantaged Oriental communities, and women. The role of affirmative action is analyzed, focusing on the legal status, privileges and economic situation of Western and Oriental Jews and Arabs. It is concluded that inherent differences between Israel and other countries account for the low profile of Israeli affirmative action.

Peleg, Rachel, and Chaim Adler (1977). "Compensatory education in Israel: Conceptions, attitudes and trends." *American Psychologist, 32* (11), 945–58.
Various approaches and perceptions concerning the progress of disadvantaged students in Israel are presented. Activities aimed at rehabilitation and achievements are discussed.

Schwarzwald, Joseph et al. (1979). "Israeli teachers' outlook on the necessity and feasibility of teaching values to advantaged and disadvantaged children." *Journal of Psychology, 101,* 3–9.
The attitudes of seventy Israeli elementary school teachers were examined as to teaching scholastic, social, and personal values to advantaged and to disadvantaged children. As hypothesized, teachers rated this instruction

higher for disadvantaged students. Teachers' dogmatic scores correlated with attitudes about the need to teach social values to both groups.

Sharon, Nachman. (1985). "A policy analysis of issues in residential care for children and youth in Israel: Past, present, future." *Child and Youth Services*, 7 (3-4), 111–122.
Presents an overview of the development of Israel's dependency on residential placement for child welfare. Recent trends reflect heavier reliance on community based services. Efforts to coordinate and improve services for disadvantaged youth are at their beginning.

Shmueli, Eliezer, (1977). "Problems in educating Oriental Jewish children in Israel." *Integrated Education, 15* (3), 3–5.
Explains the reason of a big disparity in academic achievement between Ashkenzai and Oriental Jews and the educational programs promoted to narrow this disparity.

Stahl, Abraham. (1991). "Teachers' prejudices: A perennial problem in Israeli education." *Urban Education, 25* (4), 440–453.
Discusses Israeli teachers' negative attitudes toward Jews of North Africa and Middle Eastern origin, who constitute about 50% of Israel's Jewish population and about 90% of Israel's disadvantaged children. Describes several countermeasures and predicts their influence.

Weiss, Sol. (1972). "Educating the disadvantaged, Israeli style." *Urban Education 1* (2), 181–197.
Both in Israel and the United States research on disadvantaged children is most advanced, showing parallel, as well as distinct, characteristics. Reasons for low academic performance of Israeli Oriental children are discussed, such as, poor teaching and sociocultural conditions of parents. Three approaches for their advancement are discussed.

Books

Adler, Chaim, and Rita Sever (1994). *Beyond the dead-end alley of mass education*. Boulder, CO: Westview Press.
The book explores the aims and strategies of EFO—the Educational Fostering movement—which intends to narrow the gaps in educational opportunities and achievements between ethnic minorities and majorities. Policies aim at marginalized students, either contextually or personally. Findings show social inequality to be reversible and EFO effective. To avoid stigmatization, EFO should target social, rather than ethnically or racially, defined groups. A theoretical typology of intervention is proposed: bypass strategies that equalize rewards of target groups, fill-in strategies that

replenish missing rewards, and reinforcing rewards possessed by groups. Policy of class homogenization is rejected.

Chazan, Maurice (ed.). (1973). *Compensatory Education.* Butterworth and Co.
The book originates in a symposium on compensatory education at the 1970 Annual Conference of the British Psychological Society. Complex concepts, such as "disadvantaged," "deprivation," and "compensatory education" are discussed and are illustrated by projects conducted both in the United States and Israel.

Frankenstein, Carl. (1972). *They think again . . . . Summary of an educational experiment with disadvantaged adolescents.* Jerusalem: Hebrew University.
The book originates in an experiment conducted at the Hebrew University High School in Jerusalem to determine if adolescents of impaired cognitive ability, caused by social and/or cultural deprivation, could be rehabilitated through proper teaching and counseling methods. Findings show rehabilitation to be successful, but social integration to be much harder.

Smilansky, Moshe, and David Nevo (1979). *The gifted disadvantaged: A ten-year longitudinal study of compensatory education in Israel.* Gordon and Breach, Science Publishers, Inc.
Reports on compensatory education in Israel and presents results of a ten-year evaluation of the "Boarding School Fostering Program," a secondary school project of culturally disadvantaged gifted students. The book presents a "General Orientation to Compensatory Education in Israel," and examines disadvantaged children in Israeli society; it describes a "Fostering Program for the Gifted Disadvantaged," and presents a ten-year longitudinal evaluation of it, discussing the program's significance and suggestions of improving it.

REFORMS AND CHANGES IN THE EDUCATIONAL SYSTEM

Doctoral Studies

Glasman, N. N. (1969). "Developments toward a secondary education act: The case of Israel." Unpublished doctoral thesis, University of California, Berkeley.
Analyzes developments in Israeli educational administration during 1960–1967, especially the expansion of provisions for free and/or compulsory secondary education and the school structural reform. The findings show that the 1961 extension proposal was a political response to societal demands. Purely pedagogical issues becoming politicized attest to the ministry's administrative strength and political weakness. The link between the extension of the educational system and a structural change was a brave

administrative move, but questionable as to effectiveness. A public bureaucracy, which was given up on statehood, strongly centralized administrative powers in order to carry out political decisions, created a mechanism by which bureaucratic activities were effectively checked by politicians.

Peled, Elad. (1979). "The hidden agenda of educational policy in Israel: The interrelationship between the political system and the educational system." Unpublished doctoral dissertation, Columbia University, N.Y.

This study purports to analyze Israel's educational policy regarding disadvantaged students, to emphasize its political aspects, and to extend the Eastonian model of system analysis. The study is a four-case study exploring the pioneering nonissue era (1940s), the formal equality education era (1950s), the compensatory era (1960s), and the structural reform and ethnic integration (late 1960s, 1970s). The findings show how the growing political power of the Orientals enhanced the social learning of the policymakers and developed their responsiveness to the demands of the disadvantaged and the cumulative findings of educational researchers.

Schmida, Mirjam. (1964). "Major assumptions underlying universal, free public secondary education in the United States and the high school system of the municipality of Tel Aviv." Unpublished doctoral dissertation, Teachers College, Columbia University, New York.

The project purports to identify and interpret major assumptions underlying the secondary educational enterprise of the municipal corporation of Tel Aviv-Yafo, Israel. On the assumption that the American and Israeli societies are similar, a comparison with the American secondary public education system was pursued. Findings show that the Tel Aviv high school system, which serves as an example for the country, is based upon rigid differentiation between highly talented students; the average, and slower ones. Accordingly, a hierarchical postelementary system has been established with strong preference for the academic schools. The model of the American comprehensive high school is recommended.

Articles

Ben-Dror, Gideon. (1986). "Structural reform in the Israeli educational system: Lessons of experience." Conference Paper.

The Israeli Parliament decision in July 1969 instigated an educational reform, focusing on curriculum development, teacher education, new buildings, and equipment and change in structure. The reform was necessitated because of dropouts, useless curricula, job market demands, and demands for integration. Teacher and parent resistance, as well as financial restrictions, obstructed the government's objectives.

Blass, Nachum. (1982). "The evaluation of the educational reform in Israel: A case study in evaluation and policy making." *Studies in Educational Evaluation, 8* (1), 3–37.
The implementation and evaluation of the 1968 Reform in Israel's educational system are reviewed, highlighting trends and problems in the relationships among researchers and policymakers. The multifaceted aspects of these relationships, their ramifications, and the various groups' ambivalent attitudes toward the reform are discussed.

Friedman, Helen et al. (1978). "Research review of equal education: A second report on Israeli education." *Research Review of Equal Education, 2* (3), 35.
Illustrates the inequality of education in Israel by means of problems confronting Oriental Jews, includes interviews with Israeli educators, and describes selective events in Israel during March–July 1978. Integration in schools, educational background of Afro-Asian children and their state of discrimination, rise in inflation, housing, and dental problems are also discussed.

Gaziel, Haim, H., and David Taub (1992). "Teacher's unions and educational reform—A comparative perspective: The cases of France and Israel." *Educational Policy, 6* (1), 72–86.
Examines the impact of teacher unions in two centralized educational systems—France and Israel—on school reforms. Document analysis and interview data show that since 1970 teacher unions have more say in policy reforms. Despite similar tactics, the French unions are more politically oriented than the Israeli ones.

Iram, Yaacov, and Mirjam Schmida (1993). "Recurring reforms and changes in the Israeli educational system: An analytical approach." *International Journal of Educational Development, 13* (3), 217–226.
Recurring reforms of the Israeli educational system are examined in terms of curriculum, matriculation examinations, and national versus sectoral orientation. The sociopolitical, economic, and ideological basis of the changes in educational policy and goals at various periods since Israeli independence can be explained in terms of the need to build a unified state and the demands of various interest groups.

Levy, Josef. (1990). "Stages in the reform of the matriculation examinations in Israel." ED322193.
Four major changes in the system of matriculation examinations since the early 1950s are discussed. The changes are explained by means of sociopolitical circumstances, school autonomy, parents' and teachers'

attitudes, the Ministry of Education and Culture, universities, and psychometricians.

INTEGRATION

Amir, Yehuda, and Shlomo Sharan (eds.). (1984). *School desegregation: Cross-cultural perspectives.* Hillsdale, NJ: Lawrence Erlbaum Associates.
The book deals with the desegregation of schools attended by Jewish children in Israel from various ethnic backgrounds, following Israel's Parliament decision in 1968. The chapters, written by participants in an interuniversity and multidisciplinary seminar, are ordered from discussions on the macrosocial level and progress to the various components of the microsocial level.

Dar, Y., and N. Resh (1986). *Classroom composition and pupil achievement: A study of the effects of ability-based classes.* New York: Gordon and Breach.
This book examines student body composition from a sociological perspective and is specially concerned with the dilemma whether groups should be integrated in schools and classrooms. A detailed review of research on the problem is presented, followed by an analysis of the macro- and microsocial processes that explain educational achievements resulting from the segregation or integration of student groups. A conceptual framework is formulated. Focusing on the interaction between class composition and the personal resources of individual students, the framework is applied to the analysis of data from two Israeli studies.

Klein, Z., and Y. Eshel (1980). *Integrating Jerusalem schools.* New York: Academic Press.
The book reports the results of a research project in school integration that encompassed more than seven-hundred elementary school children in Jerusalem. The progress was followed over a five-year period (1971–1975). The manner in which the project was implemented allowed for structuring a quasi-experimental design to evaluate its outcomes. Findings are presented and discussed separately for achievement, academic self-image, sociometric standing and classroom observations. The contrast between Israel and the United States uncovers a number of theoretical and practical issues.

ARAB EDUCATION

Abu-Saad, Ismael (1991). "Towards an understanding of minority education in Israel: The case of the Bedouin Arabs of the Negev." *Comparative Education, 27,* (2), 235–242.
This article presents an overview of the educational system of the Bedouin Arab minority in southern Israel. Inequities between the Jewish and Arab

schools include inadequate school facilities, an insufficient number of qualified teachers and administrators, and an unacceptably high student-to-teacher ratio. A clear reform policy for Bedouin Arab schools is needed.

Abu-Saad, Ismael (1995). "The assessment of organisational climate in Bedouin Arab schools in Israel." *Educational Management and Administration, 23*(4), 260–270.
This article summarizes the results of a study designed to identify organizational climate factors in Israel's twenty-nine Bedouin Arab elementary schools, and to explore their relation to certain teacher and school-level variables, including sex, educational level, tenure, teachers' origin, school type, and school size. The most important organizational climate factor was principal leadership.

Al-Haj, Majid. (1994). *Education empowerment and control in the case of Arabs in Israel.* Albany, NY: State University of New York Press.
This book describes and analyzes various aspects of Arab education in Israel from a sociological perspective. The development of Arab education in Israel is also traced from a historical perspective and compared to the Hebrew education system. Issues of modernization and social change, control and empowerment, ethnicity and nationality are explored. The economic, political, demographic, and social changes in Arab society in Israel are the background for this analysis of Arab education.

Ichilov, Orit, and André Elias Mazawi. (1996). *Between State and Church : Life history of a French-Catholic school in Jaffa.* Frankfurt: Peter Lang.
This book tells the story of a French-Catholic school founded in Jaffa in 1882, from the Ottoman period until today. The study illuminates issues such as the social origins of educational systems and the motive for their transformation, education and social stratification, and conditions for peaceful coexistence of rival groups in one school.. The book represents an important contribution to the study of social and political aspects of Arab-Christian education and society, which is a minority within a minority.

Mari, Sami Khalil (1978). *Arab education in Israel.* Syracuse, NY: Syracuse University Press.
The author argues that Arab education in Israel is at a cultural crossroads. On the one hand, it is influenced by the socioeconomic forces and cultural transformations which are occurring within Arab society itself, and on the other hand, it is affected by political and socioeconomic dynamics which operate within Jewish society. Arab education is also sensitive to the cultural and political movements which exist in the Arab world in general, and among Palestinians in particular. Consequently, Arab education in Israel is caught in the middle of this triangle.

Saad, Ismael Abu, and Isralowitz, Richard E. (1992). "Teachers' job satisfaction in traditional society within the Bedouin Arab schools of the Negev." *Journal of Social Psychology, 132,* 771–781.
This article describes an article of job satisfaction among 373 elementary teachers in Bedouin schools in southern Israel. The study found that the two most significant job satisfaction factors were teachers' satisfaction with work itself, and teachers' satisfaction with social needs. The study also found that female teachers and teachers with higher educational levels were more likely to be satisfied with their jobs.

Shectman, Zipora et al. (1994). "Principal leadership style and teacher feelings and behavior: Arab schools in Israel." *School Community Journal, 4,* (2), 53–66.
This article summarizes a study testing relationship patterns among principal, teacher, and student variables. Participants were randomly selected Arab students and teachers from twenty schools in northern Israel. Democratic leadership appears to be a central factor of positive school climate in Arab schools in Israel. The social and professional mobility of students graduating from democratic schools is more open than for graduates of more authoritarian schools.

Tibawi, Abd Al-Latif (1956). *Arab education in mandatory Palestine: A study of three decades of British administration.* London: Luzac and Company.
The author was a supervisor of the Arab educational sector during the British mandate. He surveys the development of Arab education from 1920 to 1948, the year the Jewish State was established, from political and social perspectives.

Name Index

Subject Index

About the Authors

YAACOV IRAM is Professor of comparative and international education at the School of Education of Bar-Ilan University, Israel. He is also Chairman of the Josef Burg Chair in Education for Human Values, Tolerance and Peace, and President of the World Association for Educational Research (WAER).

MIRJAM SCHMIDA has retired as head of the School of Education of Bar-Ilan University in 1995. She has written extensively on the sociology of education and is the author of *Equality and Excellence: Educational Reform and the Comprehensive School*. She was awarded the Prize of Education by the Tel Aviv Municipality and the Prize of Informal Education by the Ministry of Education and Culture.

ISBN 0-313-30269-3

90000>

EAN

9 780313 302695

HARDCOVER BAR CODE

WHO'S IN CHARGE OF AMERICA'S RESEARCH UNIVERSITIES?

A Blueprint for Reform

Thomas J. Tighe

State University of New York Press

Cover image: © PhotoDisc

Published by
State University of New York Press, Albany

© 2003 State University of New York

For information, address State University of New York Press,
90 State Street, Suite 700, Albany, NY 12207

Production by Judith Block
Marketing by Anne Valentine

Library of Congress Control Number

Library of Congress Cataloging-in-Publication Data

Tighe, Thomas J.
    Who's in charge of America's research universities: a blueprint for reform/Thomas J. Tighe.
        p. cm.
    Includes bibliographical references and index.
    ISBN 0-7914-5741-9 (alk. paper)–ISBN 0-7914-5742-7 (pbk. : alk. paper)
        1. Universities and colleges–United States. 2. Research–United States.
    I. Title.

LA227.4 .T56 2003
378.73–dc21

                                                                    2002029183

10 9 8 7 6 5 4 3 2 1

Love talks with better knowledge, and knowledge with dearer love.

–Shakespeare
Measure for Measure

Contents

❧

Preface

This book is intended for the broad audience that has an important stake in the future of our research universities and of higher education in general, including university faculty, administrators, trustees, legislators and the public at large. While the focus is the research university, in a larger sense the book is about knowledge creation in our society, since our research universities are the primary means for the production and dissemination of knowledge in the public interest. As such they play a major role in our technological, economic, and cultural development, while also preparing much of the country's leadership, particularly in the sciences, engineering, medicine and other professions. However, there is now a pervasive sense that something is seriously wrong with our universities, as attested by a spate of recent books and articles highly critical of higher education and particularly of the faculty culture. Unlike other analyses, this book posits internal division and specifically dysfunction in governance as a major cause of the problems of higher education. The book traces the current strains in the university to societal and internal changes over the past several decades that together have created a growing schism between the concerns and objectives of faculty, which traditionally have stressed disinterested inquiry, basic education, and the broad and balanced pursuit of knowledge, and those of governing authorities, which tend to be short-term in nature and oriented toward economic and political interests. Accompanying this split has been a weakening and virtual disengagement of faculty from the governance of their institutions and a growth in the power and activism of nonacademic administrations and governing boards. The text describes how this fundamental disconnect, to which faculty and governing authorities alike have contributed, now threatens the basic mission of the university. To address this state of affairs, a new university structure is proposed that would re-engage faculty with the governance and welfare of their institutions while helping to focus governance authorities on the truly unique strengths of the university.

A number of people should be acknowledged for their contribution to the writing of this book. I am particularly grateful for the assistance provided by professors Herbert Pick of University of Minnesota and Bert Moore of the University of Texas at Dallas who served as reviewers of the manuscript, and also for the review provided by an anonymous member of the editorial board of the State University of New York (SUNY) Press. Their comments and suggestions were very helpful in composing the final version of the book. I am also grateful for the support provided by members of the SUNY Press. SUNY Press acquiring editor Priscilla Ross, production editor Judith Block, and copy editor Marilyn Silverman were unfailingly helpful, patient, and knowledgeable throughout the production process; the final product has benefited considerably from their professional knowledge and skill. I am especially appreciative of the help provided by my wife, Louise Sherlock Tighe, Ph.D., who read and gave incisive feedback on each chapter as it was written, patiently listening and advising on my alternative arguments, wordings, and uncertainties. The quality of the final product owes much to her input.

Chapter 1

The Growth and Impact
of Research Universities

✿

This book is about an institution that preserves and enlarges our base of knowledge, trains our scientists and scholars, educates our professional and managerial workers, creates technological innovations that drive the economy, devises medical and engineering advances that enhance our well-being, critiques our social, political, and economic institutions, recaptures our past, enriches our cultural and aesthetic lives, and informs virtually every aspect of our activities in a knowledge-based world. It is about the American research university.

Although research universities comprise a relatively small number of American colleges and universities, they nevertheless play a pivotal role in both higher education and national welfare. The United States has more than 3,500 colleges and universities of which more than 2,000 offer only associate or bachelor's degrees. Of the remainder, 125 are considered to be research universities under the commonly accepted classification system developed and employed for many years by the Carnegie Foundation for the Advancement of Teaching. The defining features of research universities are, first, that they offer graduate education through the doctorate across the arts, sciences, and professional schools, and second, that their faculties are expected to be active contributors to new knowledge in their fields and to be successful in the highly competitive arena of federally funded research, particularly within the sciences and engineering. It is important to underscore the fact that a research university embraces general education and the major areas of undergraduate education as well as graduate education and research. The comprehensiveness of this mission is at once a distinctive feature of the research university and a major challenge for these institutions.

1

While these universities comprise a well-recognized subset of America's colleges and universities, there is considerable variation among its members. They include long-established institutions that are considered to be the country's premier universities by academic peers and the public alike, for example, such well-known institutions as Harvard, Yale, Princeton, Stanford, Michigan, Berkeley, and Massachusetts Institute of Technology. They also include more recently founded and lesser-known institutions that developed rapidly in their research capabilities following World War II but whose graduate and research programs have not as yet attained the breadth and stature of their historically primary brethren. But all are alike in placing a strong emphasis on research and scholarship, mounting a broad span of doctoral degree programs, and maintaining a relatively high level of extramural research support.

These research universities are also part of a continuum of higher educational institutions, rather then being a fully discrete category. That continuum can be described in terms of progressively higher levels of education offered and correlated emphasis on research and scholarship, extending from the two-year degree programs offered by community and technical colleges, to the four-year liberal arts baccalaureate institutions, to the baccalaureate plus master's degree institutions, and finally the baccalaureate through doctoral level institutions with increasing comprehensiveness at the graduate and research level. Each type of institution plays a distinctive and extremely valuable role in higher education, and all participate in teaching and scholarly activities in varying ways and degrees. Within this continuum, the research universities can be viewed as providing the most complete, albeit not necessarily the best, expression of the teaching, research, and service functions common to all, and certainly the strongest expression of the research function. It is also tempting to ascribe a progressive or developmental aspect to this educational continuum, that is, to think of institutions as seeking to offer more advanced degree programs and to develop greater research capabilities. In fact, in the decades following World War II, a number of master's and doctoral level institutions did evolve into research universities, largely as a consequence of the major infusion of federal research funding during that period. However, the majority of community, liberal arts, and master's level colleges take justifiable pride in their primarily teaching and service missions and have little interest in expanding their research role. But it is equally clear that there are a number of master's and doctoral level institutions today that aspire, often baldly, to the status of "a research university."[1]

Perhaps the most important commonality among higher educational insitutions is the strong scholarly base of their educational programs. Even those institutions whose primary function is undergraduate teaching–the community and liberal arts colleges–will draw heavily upon the fund of specialized knowledge created and nurtured in the research universities and certainly will value scholarly attainment in their own faculties, many of whom will have received their advanced training in research universities. All of these continuities are important because they indicate that while the focus of this book is the research university, the analysis has implications for universities and higher education as a whole.

The disproportionate and pervasive impact of the research universities is succinctly expressed in the following excerpt from the report of the Boyer Commission, a panel of distinguished leaders of higher education recently convened in review of the status of undergraduate education in the research universities:

> The country's 125 research universities make up only 3 percent of the total number of institutions of higher learning, yet they confer 32 percent of the baccalaureate degrees, and 50 percent of the baccalaureates earned by recent recipients of science and engineering doctorates (1991–95). Their graduates fill the legislatures and boardrooms of the country, write the books we read, treat our ailments, litigate our issues, develop our new technologies, and provide our entertainment. To an overwhelming degree, they have furnished the cultural, intellectual, economic, and political leadership of the nation.[2]

To this it might be added that the research universities also exert a disproportionate influence on education at all levels since they are the source of many of the teachers, particularly those trained at the advanced or graduate level, as well as many of the pedagogical models and concepts, for the nation's educational system.

The critical role of these universities is further highlighted by the awareness that research and technological innovation will be increasingly important in determining a society's standing in what is now recognized as a globally competitive, knowledge-based economy. Research universities, with their focus on the production and application of knowledge, have in fact been a vital factor in this nation's social and economic development, as we shall shortly attest, and their key contributions to national and international economic development can only be expected to increase.

These institutions are also most commonly identified in the public's mind with higher education and with its perceived strengths and weaknesses. For example, it is the research university that is the acknowledged world leader in the training of scientists and professionals, and it is the research university that the public has in mind when charging higher education with neglect of teaching, irrelevant research, excessive costs, abuse of tenure, and other alleged shortcomings. And ironically in view of these charges, it is the same research university that is being called upon, particularly by the business and political communities, to expand and diversify undergraduate enrollment, to increase cutting-edge research and technology, to assist reform of K-12 education, to increase lifelong learning opportunities, to become more engaged in programs of public service, and to assist in building a multicultural and internationally sensitive society!

In sum, whatever its shortcomings, the research university has been, and is widely expected to remain, a leading player in higher education and society as a whole. Nevertheless, the thesis of this book is that it may be seriously questioned whether these universities, as presently structured and supported, can long maintain their critical role and distinctive contributions. At the root of this concern is a growing gulf between the traditional perspective and objectives of the faculty of research universities, which are primarily long-term and basic in nature, and the contemporary perspective and objectives of the university-governing structures and society at large, which tend to be short-term and applied in character. A number of factors underlie and promote this separation, which as yet is poorly understood by either party. But unless the separation is recognized, understood, and effectively addressed, the special strengths and contributions of these institutions are vulnerable.

In order to understand how we have reached this state of affairs, it will be helpful to consider first the factors that gave rise to the research university, to its distinctive character, and to its wide-ranging impact on society. Only by understanding the rationale of the research university and the conditions that fostered the growth of university research can we appreciate the dilemma that confronts us today.

The lineage of the American research university can be traced to the nineteenth century, which saw the first clear appearance of research and scholarship as a priority within American colleges and universities. Up to that point, higher education had been dominated by classical learning–the study of Greek, Latin, philosophy, history, literature, and a smattering of natural science. College education in this form was still mostly for the few and the elite, and was intended chiefly as a preparation for the ministry, the professions, and public service. In the latter part of the nineteenth century, increasing dissatisfaction with the limits of the classical curriculum, and an awareness of the growing accomplishments of the new scientific research in Europe, prompted American leaders to seek a form of higher education that would be both more rigorous and more germane to the needs of a pluralistic and pragmatic society.

In this reaction, American educators were strongly influenced by the earlier educational developments and reforms of their European counterparts, particularly the model of German universities, which had become world leaders in scientific and scholarly research within the university setting. As in America, German reform of higher education was directed against the strong hold of classical learning, which was seen as an arbitrary passport to positions of privilege and a questionable preparation for the professions. The German reformists believed that the development of more specialized fields of knowledge, based upon scholarly research, especially the new scientific research, would provide a sounder and more democratic basis for higher learning and entry into the professions. Furthermore, and most importantly, these fields were to be taught by faculty trained in methods of scholarly inquiry and actively engaged in scholarship, that is, actively engaged in the production and refinement of knowledge in their fields.

Following the German model, and with much the same purpose and objectives, American universities also began to add advanced science-based curricula and to recruit faculty trained in research methods. In 1876 Johns Hopkins University became the country's first institution devoted to graduate education and research. About this time, Yale University, Harvard University, and the University of Michigan had also begun to add programs of advanced study in the sciences. Other leading universities soon followed suit and over the early part of the twentieth century a research and scholarly emphasis was added to many of the nation's established colleges and universities, both private and state institutions. However, in important contrast to the German model, the growth of specialized fields of scholarship and teaching in American universities tended to develop at the graduate level, supplementing rather than replacing the classical liberal arts undergraduate curriculum, which remained as a traditional form of general education.

At the heart of these nineteenth-century European and closely related American reforms was the conviction that higher education at all levels should emphasize the teaching of specialized knowledge informed by scholarship and research. The knowledge to be offered by a university should go beyond that bequeathed by classical learning and tradition. It should be the product of continuing application of rigorous and objective methods of inquiry. If specialized knowledge and competence in a field were what higher education was expected to certify, then the best way to assure that knowledge and competence was by means of the scholarly foundation of the field and by the scholarly merit of its faculty. Research became the foundation of a sound education. This philosophy has been, and remains, a distinguishing feature of European and American higher education.

Research universities, then, have existed in the United States since the last quarter of the nineteenth century. In the absence of the consensual definition of "the research universities" that was later provided by the Carnegie criteria, the Association of American Universities (AAU), founded at the turn of the century, provides a measure of the number and growth of research universities over the first part of the twentieth century. The AAU was formed with the objective of raising the standards for graduate education and research in America. Its members, historically well-established and prestigious institutions, thought of themselves as research universities and were generally recognized as such. The AAU grew from fourteen founding members in 1900 to thirty-two American universities by the outset of World War II.

While relatively small in number, these early research universities nevertheless claimed a disproportionate share of both the college student population and total resources available to higher education at the time. While the inception of research as a primary feature of higher education in the United States was a consequence of adoption of the German model, the modern and distinctively American research university developed primarily as a result of several other initiatives that took the form of partnership endeavors between the federal government and the university community. These partnerships were spurred by the desire to promote the production of knowledge in areas of national self-interest and by the recognition that universities, particularly in their science base, had become a wellspring of expertise and knowledge for the nation.

The first of these initiatives began in the latter half of the nineteenth century in the form of the land grant legislation initiated by Vermont Senator Justin Morrill. The Land-Grant acts fostered the creation and development of public universities in each state that were to be accessible to all and dedicated to public needs. The land grant institutions were given a special mission to address the nation's needs in agriculture, at that time the dominant industry and occupation in America. Through the Morrill Act and through subsequent related legislative actions, these needs were addressed by the establishment of both "experiment stations," which had the explicit mission of conducting scientific research in disciplines relevant to agriculture, and "extension stations," which had the mission of directly communicating the research findings to farmers and other agricultural workers, both operating within the land grant universities. The land grant program, then, supported by federal and state funds, both strengthened basic university research across areas germane to agriculture and provided for rapid transfer and application of the research findings in the everyday world of agriculture. This was a visionary program based on the belief that large-scale support of basic university research could be a key to economic progress. The recognition of the ultimately pragmatic import of basic knowledge, which inspired the land grant movements, was succinctly conveyed by Morrill in introducing the land grant legislation:

> The modern achievements of skill, enterprise, and science, new ideas with germs of power, must be recognized, and diligently studied, as they have brought and continue to bring daily competition which must be met. If the world moves at ten knots an hour, those whose speed is but six will be left in the lurch.

"New ideas with germs of power." What a marvelous expression of the applicability and utility inherent in all knowledge!

There are today about seventy universities designated as land grant, at least one in each state. Most of these have evolved into major state institutions, and many are among our most distinguished research universities. In virtually all, the missions of the production and dissemination of knowledge in the public interest have come to characterize the programs of the institution as a whole, albeit to a less focused degree than in the agricultural colleges.

There is probably little need to document here the effect of the Morrill legislation and the federal-university partnership it embodied on the growth and productivity of American agriculture and related industries. A recent review of the impact of the colleges of agriculture at the land grant universities by the National Research Council summarizes the story very well:

> In 1860 at the dawn of the decade that would put the land grant college system in the history books, one-half of the U.S. population lived on farms and more than one-half of the labor force worked on them. . . . In the decades that followed, however, U.S. citizens left farming in massive numbers for other ways of life and alternative types of employment. By 1990 the farm population was less than one-third of what it had been in 1860 (and fell to only 2 percent of the U.S. population and 3 percent of the labor force). . . . It is important to understand that these trends, in addition to having changed the profile of the national landscape, are also indicators of economic progress. The same number of farms and farmers can feed vastly larger numbers of people today than 100 years ago. The fact that so many more people

could be fed with relatively little farm labor input meant that farm workers became available to other industries–industries that taught them different skills and paid them higher wages. Essentially, the release of labor from farm- ing fueled the growth of the rest of the U.S. economy . . . . The colleges of agriculture generated many of the scientific and management advances that contributed to the growth of productivity in U.S. agriculture. Such advances include hybrid seeds, improved farm and production management tech- niques, improved genetic stock of food animals, and sophisticated financial management strategies . . . .

The application of farm chemicals, combined with other yield- enhancing technologies such as improved crop varieties, has made it possible to produce more food and fiber on virtually the same amount of land. Yield- enhancing technologies have also helped the United States become the world's leading exporter of farm and agricultural products.[3]

There is certainly little doubt that the land grant initiative has proven spectacularly successful in raising American agricultural production and processing to its present preeminent worldwide position.

The Second World War and its aftermath produced a broader ex- pansion of the links between the federal government and the academic research enterprise. While the Civil War and World War I had fostered a recognition of the advantages of utilizing scientific expertise and research to assist the conduct of the war, it was not until World War II that the government sought to deploy toward that end the knowledge and exper- tise of public and private universities and its national research laboratories. University expertise contributed significantly to the national war effort in many key areas such as training, communications, remote sensing, trans- portation, logistics, the treatment of injury and disease, and of course the development of armaments and explosives. Probably the best-known and most powerful example was the enlistment of university scientists and re- search laboratories in the team assembled under the direction of Prof. Robert Oppenheimer in development of the atomic bomb, an effort that literally ended the war. Such striking evidence of the consequences of basic and theoretical research, upon which the project was based, helped to pro- mote a national understanding of the link between "academic" research and practical affairs.

The decisive advantage conferred by science in wartime led Presi- dent Roosevelt to request that Vannevar Bush, head of the wartime Office of Scientific Research and Development, undertake a study of how the

information, the techniques, and the research experience developed by (your office) and by the thousands of scientists in the universities and in private in- dustry, should be used in the days of peace ahead for the improvement of the national health, the creation of new enterprises bringing new jobs, and the betterment of the national standard of living.[4]

Bush's report in response to that request, entitled "Science–The Endless Frontier," was submitted in 1945. It proved to be a truly visionary and seminal document. His report outlined a new partnership between the federal government and scientific research, a partnership that more than any other factor, defined and fueled the growth of the modern research university. The premise of Bush's report was that basic scientific research directed to the continuous production of new knowledge is absolutely essential to the nation's health, security, and prosperity. While basic research by definition is not directed to practical ends, Bush argued that it is nevertheless essential to the creation of the knowledge from which practical applications inevitably arise. In Bush's words,

> Basic research . . . creates the fund from which the practical applications of knowledge must be drawn. New products and new processes do not appear full-grown. They are founded on new principles and new conceptions, which in turn are painstakingly developed by research in the purest realms of science.[5]

Accordingly,

> The government should accept new responsibilities for promoting the flow of new scientific knowledge and the development of scientific talent in our youth. These responsibilities are the proper concern of the Government, for they vitally affect our health, our jobs, and our national security. It is in keeping also with basic United States policy that the government should foster the opening of new frontiers and this is the modern way to do it.[6]

More specifically, the report called for (1) public funding of basic medical research in the medical schools and universities, hitherto dependent primarily upon private sources; (2) programs of military research conducted by civilian scientists to "continue in peacetime some portion of those contributions to national security . . . made so effectively during the war";[7] and (3) the creation of a national pool of "scientific capital" by training a significant cadre of scientists and by strengthening the nation's centers of basic research, principally its colleges, universities, and research institutes.

It is important to underscore that Bush gave colleges and universities the lead role in generating the flow of new scientific knowledge that he deemed so essential to the nation's well-being. As he stated,

> These institutions provide the environment which is most conductive to the creation of new scientific knowledge and least under pressure for immediate,

tangible results. With some notable exceptions, most research in industry and in Government involves application of existing scientific knowledge to practical problems. It is only the colleges, universities, and a few research institutes that devote most of their research efforts to expanding the frontiers of knowledge.[8]

And, as Bush emphasized, expanding the frontiers of knowledge inevitably leads to new enterprises. In further support of the logic relating university research and the production of knowledge leading to practical applications, and with reference to the earlier Morrill Act, Bush noted that "For many years the Government has wisely supported research in the agricultural colleges and the benefits have been great. The time has come when such support should be extended to other fields."[9]

To discharge these new responsibilities of federal government, the Bush report called for the creation of an agency specially designed to support basic research and to administer a program of science scholarships and fellowships, again primarily through the university structure. In the ensuing years, Congress endorsed the major postulates and proposals of the Bush report through several actions including the creation of the Atomic Energy Commission and scientific offices in each of the armed services, a significant expansion of the National Institutes of Health, and most central to the Bush report, creation of the National Science Foundation (NSF). The National Science Foundation was given broad scope and authority to promote national policies for scientific research; to foster general science education and advanced science training; and to support basic research in the natural sciences, mathematics, and engineering. The focus on the natural sciences and engineering stemmed from concern about the shortage of students in these areas who, but for the war, would have received bachelor's and advanced degrees but who were now sorely needed for the transition to a peacetime economy. Eventually the NSF fulfilled the broad conception of supporting basic research throughout the sciences when Congress directed the sponsorship of research in the social sciences in 1968.

The NSF began with a modest budget of $3.5 million in 1951 and its fifth budget was but $16 million. But its budget grew by 1960 to approximately $150 million, spurred in part by the national reaction to the launching of Russian *Sputniks* and by the perceived threat to American scientific leadership. By 1980, the NSF appropriation had expanded to $1 billion, and its research budget today is $5.0 billion. While consistently maintaining the support for basic research that characterized its early years, the NSF has greatly expanded its support across the sciences and added many important programs strategically directed to nurturing the science strength of the nation, including development of specialized national research consortia, enhancement of science instruction at all levels of education, and construction and renovation of laboratory and other support facilities in universities and research institutes. Throughout these efforts, support of university research programs and utilization of university expertise have remained centerpieces of the NSF agenda.

Equally important to the increased funding of university research has been the manner of that funding, which stressed not only basic research but research of the very highest quality as determined by competitive peer review processes, that is, by the leading scientists themselves. Furthermore, administration of the new funding followed Bush's recommendation that "Support of basic research in the public and private colleges, universities, and research institutes, . . . must leave the internal control of policy, personnel, and the method and scope of research to the institutions themselves. This is of the utmost importance".[10] In essence the NSF model, which has also characterized the National Institutes of Health and other federal agencies supporting university research, helped to foster development of a uniquely American partnership between the government and universities—what has come to be called "the social contract for science." As summarized by David H. Guston and Kenneth Keniston,

> The bargain struck between the federal government and university science . . . can be summarized in a few words: government promises to fund the basic science that peer reviewers find most worthy of support, and scientists promise that the research will be performed well and honestly and will provide a steady stream of discoveries that can be translated into new products, medicine, or weapons.[11]

Fundamental to the contract, of course, was a strong faith on the part of both parties in the practical, as well as in the intrinsic, value of fundamental knowledge.

Of course, basic and applied research are parts of a continuum, and research is thus always relatively pure or relatively applied. Inevitably, the pressures of immediate national problems have resulted in departures from a strictly basic research agenda by the NSF and by other federal agencies; and governments have always targeted and prioritized at least broad areas of research in the national interest. Calls and pressures for greater support of applied research goals are a consistent part of the political and scientific landscapes, and constitute a debated issue today. Nevertheless, support of basic research, peer merit review, free inquiry, and self-monitoring have been consistent hallmarks of the "contract" between the government and science in the United States, and virtually all quarters would agree that these have been important elements in the postwar development of American science and the research university to their current positions of worldwide preeminence.

Several additional federal initiatives also contributed in significant measure to the growth of the research universities. We have already mentioned the salutary increase in the NSF budget associated with the Russian *Sputniks*. But the *Sputniks* also produced broader federal action to counter this apparent threat to American security and presumed leadership in science and science education. The National Aeronautics and Space Act of 1958 created the National Aeronautics and Space Administration (NASA) with major funding for research on space science and technology, much of it conducted in universities. A related initiative was the National Defense Education Act of 1958, which provided large-scale funding through the Office of Education to strengthen science education and the development of scientific talent at all levels of education. Colleges and universities again played a major role. Fellowships and loans supported university students in germane fields of science, thousands of the nation's high school teachers came to university campuses to update their knowledge and strengthen their science teaching skills, and university scientists assisted the development of new curricula for the nation's schools.

Finally, Higher Education acts in 1963 and 1965 provided capital support for a broad program of facilities construction and renovation in the nation's colleges and universities, with science facilities a major part of the outlay. While *Sputnik*-related pressures played a prompting role in this action, the renewal programs proceeded from longer-standing concerns about the aging state of university and other research laboratories, a greatly expanded university enrollment (the post-World War II baby boom), and the need to keep pace with the rapid rate of scientific and technological change. A significant aspect of these efforts was a deliberate effort to broaden the ranks of "elite" science institutions by strengthening the facilities, research, and educational programs of institutions aspiring to become research universities.

The Land Grant movement, and the creation and funding of the National Science Foundation, the National Institutes of Health, and other federal agencies responsive to university research programs and needs, and the national defense and higher education acts of the '50s and '60s were the major steps on the federal level to make universities, in Dale Wolfe's phrase, "the home of science." Of course, other more specific and local actions played a significant role as well, particularly the support given to universities through systems of state and private funding. Recall that Bush had viewed strong public and private universities as constituting the environment most conducive to the creation of scientific knowledge. Bush and his colleagues recognized that the universities provided the most appropriate existing infrastructure of any real scale within which to foster the pursuit of knowledge for knowledge's sake and the development of scientific talent. But the existing infrastructure, including the availability of faculty, students, supporting academic programs, buildings and facilities, was (and still is) primarily maintained though state and private support. And of course these funding constituencies come with their own distinctive and urgent claims on the universities. Specifically, they expect of universities a strong commitment to the teaching and personal development of undergraduates, a broad array of educational programs through the professional level, and responsiveness to the social and economic needs of their regional communities. The development and accomplishments of the research universities have been all the more remarkable in view of the multiple functions demanded by its differing patrons.

Under the federal-university partnership initiatives we have described, support of university research expanded dramatically during the quarter-century following World War II, changing the landscape of university research forever and giving definition and substance to the concept of the research university. While the rate of increase in public financial support of university research slowed markedly beginning in the 1970s, overall support has remained relatively stable, and the research universities continue their distinctive and critical role in the national science agenda.

The remarkable success of the American research university has been widely recognized here and abroad. It is fair to claim that the accomplishments of scientific research in our colleges and universities is one of the great success stories of our nation. American research universities have combined the functions of teaching, research, and service in a fashion that has become a model for the rest of the world. As Varten Gregorian has noted, "As many as three quarters of the best universities in the world are located in the United States. What sector of our economy or society can make a similar claim?"[12]

Accompanying the externally visible growth of research universities was the less visible growth of a set of values that have come to characterize the faculty of these institutions. While these values have a strong link to the turn-of-the-century incorporation of scholarship into the mission of higher education, they achieved full definition only under the stimulus of the partnership initiatives and other external support we have reviewed.

Indeed, for many faculty, the "social contract" is what gave shape and legitimacy to these values.

Let us go back in time to the '40s and '50s and consider the university scientists that Bush had in mind when formulating his call for federal support of university research. First and foremost, they were *professors* who in the root sense of that word, cultivated and taught their special field of knowledge as their life's work. They fit the classic mold of the university teacher-scholar who devoted his or her life (largely his at the time) to teaching the methods and findings of their particular disciplines, to training professional scholars, and to curiosity-driven inquiry. They were "ivory tower" with little concern for application of their fields to the practical world of affairs or toward the creation of new technologies and products. Rather, their focus was scientific explanation of the natural world. Their salaries were modest and they enjoyed little of the financial support for research and few of the professional perquisites available to contemporary academic scientists. In general, the resources of the university classrooms and laboratories and the support network of academic publications and professional societies were adequate for their purposes.

Now consider from the perspective of these faculty, particularly the science faculty, the impact of the dramatic change in public financial support of university research. As indicated, prior to World War II there was little external or internal financial support of faculty research. While there were, as always, a small number of scholar stars known to the general public, federal funding was virtually nonexistent and relatively few faculty benefited from the limited support available from private foundations. While faculty were expected to be scholars in their fields, university support for research typically amounted to little more than a general recognition that research was part of a faculty member's assigned duties. There was little if any explicit provision of time for research within a demanding schedule of teaching and teaching-related responsibilities. Most faculty were left to their own devices to pursue their scholarship, which they typically accomplished through long work hours.

In contrast, after World War II university faculty were suddenly being told that what the nation now wanted—and was willing to pay for through the universities—was more scientists and more research. Now there is nothing that scientists want more than more science—that is, they want expanded opportunities to pursue their research interests and a strengthened overall science enterprise. If anything, university scientists especially fit this mold. They are, after all, individuals who have chosen to dedicate their lives to scientific research and to the teaching of science, often in its purest and most basic forms. To be told that significant funds were now available to enlarge what they most valued, providing they were willing to undergo the peer review required to prove its merits, would appeal greatly at once to their minds, hearts, and inherently competitive natures.

The university scientific community responded strongly. The bulk of the initial funding, largely channeled through competitive grant application processes, went to science faculty and science departments of what were regarded as the nation's strongest universities. And these faculty, like all faculty, were inclined to train their graduate students in their own image. That is, they produced well-trained basic scientists who tended to pursue knowledge for knowledge's sake and who generally aspired to and followed careers in university teaching and research, where they in turn imparted similar training, values, and goals to the next wave of students. With successive funding cycles, the supply and placement of well-trained researchers increased significantly and a wider range of universities were able to benefit from the funding process.

The university research enterprise grew steadily in scope and numbers with larger graduate enrollments across the sciences and significant expansion of science departments. Not only did university science departments expand, but the ranks of the research universities also themselves increased. Institutions that prior to World War II had engaged in modest or little research activity, or that had once been teacher's colleges or master's level institutions, developed into relatively robust research universities. These institutions recruited the new waves of trained scientists, and were assisted not only by federal funds but also by state governments that were convinced of the economic benefits to be expected from expanded research and technology. The obvious contributions of academic research to economic development in areas such as Silicon Valley in California and along Route 128 in Massachusetts bolstered the perception of "world-class research universities" as desirable drawing cards for business and industry, and persuaded many states to strengthen the research capacities of their universities. In fact, the enlarged university research enterprise has been critical to the development of numerous new products as well as to entire new industries. The pervasive benefits that have stemmed from university research are well summarized in the following statement of the National Association of State Universities and Land Grant Colleges.

> Since the end of World War II, federally-funded basic and applied research at universities has expanded the base of knowledge, improved American's quality of life dramatically and helped make the U.S. an economic superpower. Indeed, research accomplished at institutions of higher education has touched

the lives of almost every American. University research has improved the environment, creating cleaner energy resources and new ways to reduce or eliminate pollution. It has prompted better health, saving lives and raising the quality of life through creating new vaccines, drugs, procedures and medical equipment. And university research has boosted the economy. Reseachers have made discoveries that laid the foundation for industries such as electronics components, plastics and new materials, computers and software, telecommunications equipment and services, pharmaceutical and medical equipment, and aeronautics. These cutting-edge enterprises create millions of jobs and contribute over $600 billion per year to the economy.[13]

The Bush vision amply confirmed!

During this post-World War II period of growth there also evolved within many universities powerful reward systems that encouraged faculty to give priority to research. These rewards included increased time for faculty to pursue their deepest intellectual interests, increased weight for scholarly accomplishment in tenure and promotion decisions, the provision of improved laboratories, expanded libraries and other facilities in support of research, support for travel and participation in professional meetings, university awards and recognition for scholarly accomplishments, graduate student teaching and research assistants, and support for administration of faculty grants and contracts. Note that these university rewards offered little or nothing in the way of direct monetary benefit to the faculty. Rather they were directed chiefly toward expansion of research itself or the creation of a more supportive environment for research. These incentives not only acted to amplify the research activities of the faculty but also visibly signaled the value given to research within the whole university community. Further, and most significantly, the elevation of research as a faculty priority was not limited to the natural science areas but tended to spread across the social sciences, humanities, and arts as well. Even though the external and internal reward structures for scholarship were (and remain) much weaker outside the science areas, there grew an increased expectation within the research-oriented universities that faculty across the board should be active and accomplished scholars in their fields. Research universities today are in fact characterized by the presence of strong scholarly faculty across the academic disciplines.

In sum, from the faculty perspective, university professors did exactly what society called on them to do. That is, they significantly expanded their research activities and the production of scientists. They achieved these ends largely through their own efforts and merits, that is, by competing for the necessary resources in a rigorous peer review process. While their thrust as university scientists was naturally toward the long-term development of basic research capacities (the necessary base in Bush's strategic vision), they also responded vigorously to calls for research in areas of national interest and applied significance. Universities whose faculties were successful in the competition for funding developed stronger research programs and research environments, which in turn aided in the recruitment of research-oriented faculty. Internal reward systems were adopted that encouraged engagement in research across the disciplines, and their faculties embraced this vision. The result of the play of these factors was the elevation of research in a number of universities–in general, one could say in the research universities–to a new prominence. Indeed, in these institutions research and scholarship emerged clearly as the foundation for the whole university enterprise.

The latter observation is important. Why should a largely science-focused initiative have had such a general impact on the university? Why should strengthening scientific research have had such a spread of effect on scholarship across the disciplines? Why was the social contract interpreted in such broad fashion by the faculty? The answer is fundamental to understanding the life force of the university. It links back to the factors underlying the initial incorporation of research into higher education but proceeds most directly from the faculty's profound belief in research and scholarship as the necessary foundation for academic knowledge. Let us examine this assertion in relation to the overall mission of the university.

The three basic time-honored functions of the university–teaching, research, and public service–are all very important. Generally a research university cannot neglect any of them, and would do so at its peril, not only peril to fulfillment of its mission, but to its funding base as well. All three functions must be highly valued and nurtured. But one, in the minds of most faculty, has a clear logical primacy–and that is research, regarded as scholarship in all of its forms, whether creative activity in the arts, experimentation in the laboratories, new knowledge or interpretive studies in the humanities, or whatever the disciplinary form of inquiry and creation may be. The primacy of research stems from the recognition that the cumulative research, scholarship, and creative activity of the faculty is ultimately the source of what is taught and the source of an institution's ability to add value to society by way of public service. That is, universities teach and apply the results of long-term disciplined inquiry. They teach and apply the output of methods of study which, across the wonderful fabric of the many disciplines that comprise academia, are continually fashioned to be as free as humanly possible of error, distortion, and bias–as reasoned and objective as possible–as true as possible.

A fundamental fact of life is that all of us must depend for what we know largely upon what we learn from others, and we must depend on that received knowledge to be reliable, truthful, and useful. Nowhere is that dependency more evident than in formal education. Therefore, trust is a fundamental part of education. And in the academic world, trust must be earned and credibility based on the soundness of knowledge, and that means on the ability to produce and evaluate what is most true through continuing processes of inquiry, invention, interpretation, questioning, sifting, and refinement of knowledge—that is, through the continuing research, scholarship, and creative activity of the faculty. Research, then, is the foundation of a great university and the base of value for all of its functions. It provides the source and inspiration for outstanding pedagogy and it furnishes the knowledge base from which may be drawn answers to the myriad problems that plague society as well as inventions to improve the quality of life. To be recognized as a research university thus attests to the strong scholarly base of the university and to the overall quality of its endeavors in teaching, research, and public service. It is for these reasons that institutions and their faculties often aspire to the status of a "research university"—because that status speaks in a broadly recognizable way to the overall soundness and quality of the whole institutional enterprise.

Respect for scholarly research as the bedrock of academic knowledge, a commitment to basic knowledge but a responsiveness to research needs in the national interest, a willingness to put themselves on the line in the competition for resources and in the arena of peer evaluation, and what is at core an intrinsically motivated desire to know and understand,—these are the faculty values associated with the astonishing growth of the research universities through what arguably has been the period of greatest achievement ever in American higher education in terms of expansion in basic and applied knowledge and, simultaneously, of access to higher education. These accomplishments have provided models for the world. Society should cheer and take pride in these successes and celebrate the skills and traits that underlie them. Yet research universities and their faculties find themselves today increasingly estranged from their governing structures and society. The chapters ahead will seek to account for the causes and factors underlying that divergence, to which faculty, governing structures, and society alike have contributed.

Chapter 2

University Research

❦

Given the key role of research in higher education, it is important that the university research function be understood in some depth, particularly as it is viewed by the faculty who carry out the research. The chief aim here will be to provide a more in-depth explanation of both the essential motivation underlying university research and the unique value of university research to society.

We have used the term *research* in a very general manner to refer to all of the ways in which university faculty seek to advance knowledge. However, in everyday usage, research is often taken more narrowly to refer to inquiry as conducted within the natural sciences, that is, it is often equated with laboratory experimentation. The term *scholarship* might be a more appropriately generic term, since it refers to the knowledge of learned persons collectively, regardless of discipline. But neither the term *research* nor *scholarship* conveys reference to the creative activities of faculty in the arts or to other ways of advancing knowledge in the university setting, such as by the integration of findings across disciplines, the application of knowledge to real-life problems, or the communication and teaching of knowledge. In the absence of a better term, then, we will continue to use the word *research* in the most general way, and with the understanding that it encompasses *all* of the ways in which faculty may work to further knowledge.

For a number of reasons, faculty and administrators have done a poor job communicating the nature and significance of university research. For one thing, most faculty regard their research and scholarly activities as a self-evident good that does not require explanation. Their own long study and training in pursuit of the credentials required for a university appointment has sensitized them to research and scholarship as the indispensable pathway to the knowledge they teach. They know that every academic discipline is based upon many years, sometimes centuries, of learning accomplished through time-tested methods of inquiry, methods that are free, or as free as humanly possible, from vested interest. They proudly see their own scholarship, however modest, as part of that enduring stream of inquiry and learning. They also know that much more often than not, advances in knowledge reflect the cumulative and usually unheralded contributions of many individuals, contributions that must pass the critical test of expert peer review. And so they do not require the dramatic finding or public notice and approval to validate their work. Finally, they know that active engagement in research, while not essential to effective teaching, is probably the best way to keep abreast of new developments and to guarantee the integrity of their teaching. While these basic considerations are evident to every faculty member, they are wrong in believing that they are at all evident to the general public.

In addition, and perhaps surprisingly, faculty are for the most part not very knowledgeable about ongoing research activities in disciplines other than their own. It has been said that a good cutting edge is always narrow. For much the same reason, success in the highly competitive world of research often demands intense concentration within one's own area of endeavor, leaving little opportunity to follow developments in other fields. Besides having little time and opportunity, faculty are seldom in a position to learn about current research activities in other disciplines within their university, at least to any broad extent. In fact, very few people within the university, including its administrators, are in such a position. It is not until one gets to the level of the university provost, the chief academic officer and usually the second-ranking officer in the institution, that information about ongoing research across the disciplines of a university is brought under review. Faculty, department chairs, and deans are preoccupied with the activities of their own disciplines or, at best, activities within a limited set of disciplines. Apart from the provost and perhaps a handful of others with university-wide responsibility, one would be hard-pressed to find individuals within the university who are in regular contact with, and therefore knowledgeable about, the broad range, varied nature, and full contributions of university research.

Faculty also feel that communicating the research mission of the university to the public is not their job but rather the job of the administration. Of course, most universities do have public relations and media offices that try to keep the public informed about research at the university. However, these offices tend to focus on highly selected developments that are deemed newsworthy, a focus that tends to highlight dramatic or "good news" findings or perhaps applied research outcomes tuned to the interests of their readers. There is seldom a sustained effort to communicate the fundamental nature, scope, and vital role of research in the overall enterprise, nor do these offices typically have the background experience and knowledge required for that task.

In sum, a good reason why the university research story has not been told in more detail is that there are few within the university with the combined time, inclination, and knowledge to tell it.

Any effort to describe the nature and significance of university research must certainly convey something of the great richness and variety of the research conducted across the span of the academic disciplines. But the heart of university research cannot be reached through enumeration, but rather through links to something very basic in human nature. Therefore we begin the description of university research by writing not about universities, or about research, or even about faculty, but rather about an innate feature of human beings that precedes and predicts them all.

The most striking psychological characteristic common to every human newborn is its curiosity about the world. This curiosity is exhibited most clearly in the orienting reflex, the innate tendency of every baby to attend to novel features in its environment. So reliable and characteristic is this response that physicians have long used it in evaluating the health and vitality of the newborn. While the baby's tendency to gaze fixedly at the unfamiliar is well-known to laypeople and experts alike, only recently have we learned the full significance of this seemingly simple response. Research on babies' visual attention over the first several months of life has now established that the orienting reflex is in fact a gateway to a marvelous learning process that operates from the moment of birth and throughout life as a fundamental means to acquire knowledge about the world. We now know that during those prolonged fixations infants are forming and storing representations of the objects and events to which they attend, and by that process making them known. That is, they are spontaneously learning the world about them and to a degree that would never have been credited only a few decades ago.

The remarkable ability of babies to learn about what they attend to is revealed by the simple characteristic pattern of attention they have been found to exhibit to recurring new stimuli. To illustrate, suppose that a baby is seated comfortably in an infant seat and a simple visual stimulus that the baby has never seen before, such as a red triangle, is projected on a facing blank screen for thirty seconds. Consistent with the orienting reflex, the baby will very predictably look at this new stimulus for much of the time it is in view. With repeated exposures of the stimulus separated by brief time intervals, the baby will continue to orient to the figure upon each appearance but her fixation upon it will decline regularly over successive presentations until, after a dozen or so appearances, the figure now elicits only a momentary glance or two. If now sometime later, say, a week or two, the baby is reintroduced to the situation and to the stimulus again, the baby will be found to give it only the briefest looks, scarcely attending to it at all. This simple pattern of behavior tells us something quite profound. It tells us that during the initial session the baby *must* have learned and stored in her brain some representation and enduring memory of the stimulus because otherwise how could the baby possibly know in the later session that it was no longer novel, that it was something it had seen before? Otherwise, of course, the baby would have exhibited her typical reaction to an unfamiliar stimulus. The decline in visual attention with repeated presentations of the stimulus in the first session was not, then, as one might have concluded, a sign of fatigue or momentary boredom, but rather indicates that the baby had completed a learning process, that is, learning about that stimulus, and had stored what she learned in memory. These observations also suggest that what babies attend to, and therefore are likely to learn about, is driven by their comparing their current perception of a situation with what is stored in memory. If the incoming stimulus matches a representation the baby has learned and stored through her prior experience, then there is nothing novel to elicit sustained attention, and consequently there is little visual fixation. But if the stimulus encountered does not match the baby's memory of the situation in some respect, then that defines a novel stimulus and initiates both strong attention to the stimulus, and as we now can see, the processing and storage of information about it. Consistent with this view, if the stimulus presented in the second session had been changed in one or more of its aspects, if it were now a red circle, the infant would reliably be found to demonstrate strong attention to it. That is, the infant will respond to it as the new stimulus it is and therefore attend and learn about it.

Through many studies of the infant's pattern of initial attention to novel stimuli, attention loss with repeated exposure, and attention recovery upon stimulus change, and employing a great variety of stimulus objects and events, researchers have established that over the first months of life the infant spontaneously acquires a great deal of information about her environment through this perceptual learning process, information that constitutes much if not all of her early acquired knowledge of the world. And it has probably not escaped the reader's attention that this learning takes place without tangible rewards or external support of any kind. Rather, it is learning that proceeds spontaneously and purely for its own sake, for the sheer acquisition of knowledge about the world. The infant–every human infant the world over–comes equipped with this beautiful, fully functioning, intrinsically driven learning machine that seeks and absorbs as nourishment the new and unfamiliar. As Emily Dickinson observed, "the unknown is the largest need of the intellect."

While there is much that remains to be learned about this early but powerful form of learning and its contribution to cognitive development, we do know that all babies exhibit it from the moment of birth and that their capacity to process and store information about the world around them increases throughout infancy. We know that they learn in this manner not only basic features of the world–shapes, colors, sound patterns, and the like–but also sequences of stimuli, that is, "what leads to what" in the world. We also know that infants will work hard to get new stimuli or stimulus sequences to which they can attend. For example, they will engage for long periods in repeated effortful movements that have been arranged to trigger nothing more than the presentation of novel stimuli that they can attend to and learn about, working as it were, to produce the unknown, the raw material of learning. It is also clear that this early form of learning may steer individual and developmental differences in intellectual development, since variation in the infants' particular experiences determine what will be new and interesting and therefore what will be attended to and learned. Furthermore, there is accumulating evidence that this kind of learning taps into brain processes of a high order, as attested by studies showing that infant attentional behavior predicts later intelligence. Infants who process visual information quickly, as indicated by the rate of decline in attention to a repeatedly presented novel stimulus, have been found to become children of above average IQ in later years. We know, too, that the preference for novelty and the innate drive to explore and learn about the unfamiliar continue to be strongly manifested throughout infancy and early childhood and in fact, the evidence suggests, persist throughout life, although in less dominant fashion. Thus, if children up to the age of about five years are given a choice between a familiar object that they know contains a highly desired reward that they can have, such as candy or a toy, and a similar object that is merely novel, they will nevertheless still tend to choose and explore the novel object rather than the material reward. At later ages of childhood, however (and particularly in adults!), the rewarded alternative will invariably win out in such a competition. But strikingly, even at mature ages, if the reward is removed from the situation and if the choice is constructed to be simply between familiar and unfamiliar alternatives, the preference for the novel stimulus will continue to be manifested.

We come into the world, then, as intensely curious creatures wired to seek, attend to, and learn about the unfamiliar for no end other than to know.[1] This early learning proceeds independently of reward or other immediate external ends or consequences. But this general information-gathering about the world is, of course, of tremendous adaptive value to an organism that is designed and destined to live and achieve by its knowledge and by the power of its brain rather than by its brawn. Later in life, curiosity-driven learning must compete with, and is usually displaced by, learning that is directed toward securing some external end or reward. But the inborn pull toward the unknown and for learning for learning's sake nevertheless remain.

The argument advanced here is that much of the research conducted within the university has its roots in this innate drive to learn and know. A major function of university research is exactly what is seen in the intrinsically driven learning process exhibited by the newborn—to form a more complete, consistent, and true understanding of the world in all of its parts. The fact that the infant's inquiry and representational processes are at relatively simple levels of intellectual activity while the researcher's are much more complex is beside the point. They are related and continuous manifestations of the inborn human need to know and the fulfillment to be found in knowing. At the core, neither form of learning is directed toward immediate practical ends and both are essentially curiosity driven. But the broad body of general knowledge that is continuously established through university research has an important adaptive value for society much like the adaptive value of the knowledge inventory acquired by the infant. It provides a base of reliable information and conceptualization for the problem-solving and creative activities of society in all areas of endeavor. From this perspective, when the university leaders of the late nineteenth century sought to incorporate the findings and methods of the newly emerging sciences, they were responding in a fashion not unanalogous to the infant's attraction to, and incorporation of, new features of its world. This perspective also helps to inform our understanding of the spectacular growth of the American research university that was ignited by the federal partnerships discussed in chapter 1. The post-World War II infusion of federal funding and other forms of external support for research triggered the rapid development of research universities that took place during this period, but these were nevertheless secondary rather than the prime causal factors. These funding incentives created the favorable soil, as it were, but were not the seed of growth, as indeed the prior nineteenth-century inception of the research university attests. These incentives could not have worked without touching and amplifying the more basic life force that resides in these institutions. Indeed, it was for this reason that Vannevar Bush sought to direct federal funding to the university setting, noting that "progress on a broad front results from the free play of free intellects, working on subjects of their own choice, in the manner dictated by their curiosity for exploration of the unknown."[2] It is critical to preserve that mode of inquiry.

While contributions to human knowledge may come from many quarters of course, the university is now the only institution that supports learning directed to the advancement of basic knowledge in all areas of disciplined inquiry. Unfettered research in the interest of basic knowledge has all but disappeared from industrial and government laboratories, and is even under increasing pressure in academia. Political and business leaders express a growing impatience with nondirected scholarship that does not promise quick payback or have patent relevance to practical concerns. By definition, the curiosity-driven research pursued in universities will have little immediate utility, as the knowledge the infant pursues is of little use to an organism that cannot move about in its world. But just as the infant's intrinsically driven learning will prove of tremendous adaptive value in meeting the later demands of life, university basic research is almost invariably ultimately useful to society. That basic research has little immediate utility is really not relevant to the *preparatory* function of inquiry and learning, that is, the function of preparing the individual and society to cope with the ceaseless challenges of the world.

Since knowledge is open-ended and the human story continually unfolding, the practical application of new contributions to knowledge must often await different times or later discoveries. The history of human learning is replete with instances in which contributions to knowledge that have no immediate practical value whatsoever prove to have unexpected and great utility. For example, magnetic resonance imaging, a vital tool of modern medicine, is possible today only because decades ago physicists, largely based in universities, sought to understand the magnetic moments of nuclear spins and how these nuclear magnets interact in liquids, crystals, and molecules. Out of these quests came the knowledge that enabled a vision of an imaging technique that now promises to surpass x-rays in the power of its medical diagnostics. Similarly, the physicists who were curious about the interaction of molecules and magnetic spins with micro- and millimeter wave radiation were interested in these phenomena per se. Yet the work of these investigators led directly to the development of lasers and to the many commercial uses of lasers in fiber optic communication; surgery and medicine; printing; bar-code readers; compact disks; surveying and alignment instruments; and drilling, cutting, and welding of metals. Biotechnology, modern telecommunications, and the Internet all had their genesis in basic research conducted in university laboratories, specifically, in recombinant DNA work, in laser and fiber optic research, and in the development of the first Web browser. But to trace even more remote links between basic inquiry and application, the invention of the laser would have been inconceivable without the development of quantum theory at the turn of the century by Max Planck, a young assistant professor at the University of Berlin, and for that matter none of modern technology could have emerged without calculus, invented by Isaac Newton for investigating the motions of celestial bodies. There is probably nothing more practical than a good theory.

My favorite example of the often unlikely but perhaps inevitable linkage between basic inquiry and ultimate application, provided by Nathan Myhrvold, is dinosaur paleontology:

> . What could be more useless than studying these extinct giants? Recent work on the mysterious extinction of the dinosaurs has built a credible case that their demise was caused by the impact of an asteroid or comet. Although this explanation remains controversial among experts in the field, the inquiry has sparked the realization that a future impact by a near-earth asteroid could kill millions of people, destroy civilization, or even drive our species to extinction. Active research is now focused on this threat and on the technological means to avoid it. It is thus entirely possible that the useless study of dinosaurs might some day, decades or even centuries from now, lead to saving the human race.[3]

A final instance of the value of university research and its unexpected consequences is our brief review of the curiosity-driven research on the visual attention of infants. Where else would one find people looking at what a baby looks at! The knowledge revealed by that looking has dramatically changed our conception of the competencies of the newborn and of the contribution of early experience in cognitive development, and has obvious practical implications for improving human development.

Human experience through the ages has defined areas of inquiry that have proven useful in advancing and enriching life. These are essentially the disciplines that comprise higher education, and continued cultivation of these areas of inquiry seems a prudent strategy in dealing with an uncertain future. But even as we do, we can confidently expect that advances in knowledge will open up yet new areas for disciplinary and interdisciplinary study. As William James observed in relation to our always incomplete and never final state of knowledge, nothing can be concluded, for what has concluded that we can conclude in regard to? But perhaps one conclusion that can be safely drawn is that the more knowledge an individual or a society has the higher is the probability that that individual or society will be in a favored position when important consequences follow, as they almost. inevitably will.

Seen in this light, there is no useless research. University research, while perhaps not the self-evident good that many faculty believe it to be, is both a necessary and a utilitarian function. If it meets the test of true scholarship, that is, if it follows the rules of logic and evidence and contributes new knowledge to the field, it cannot be reduced, as some critics would argue, to just the faculty's special interests, an indulgence of idle curiosity, a labored production of irrelevance, or merely a narrow pursuit of career goals. It is rather an expression of a fundamental life force and the fulfillment of a critical human and social function.

This account emphasizes that an important component of the motivation underlying faculty research is intrinsic in nature. This is not to claim that this motivation is always present in faculty or always a factor in university research or that all faculty research is equally valuable. Human motivation is generally a mixture of multiple drives and interests and one can expect marked individual differences among faculty in the direction and intensity of their interests at different times as one would among the members of any group. Outside funding is often the game in undertaking research, and the pressure to meet publication criteria for tenure surely results in some questionable research. But the question is whether faculty as a group are specially motivated by intellectual curiosity and whether their endeavors are largely guided and sustained by that intrinsic force. A consideration of the pathway to faculty status and of the life circumstances of faculty hardly permit any other conclusion. Faculty of course share the personal characteristics common to the human condition, including all of the motivations, faults, and virtues. But if faculty have anything in common that distinguishes them as a group from the general population, it is that they are all individuals who have a commitment to the life of the mind in one form or another. That form may be study of the physical world, or of the mental world, or of world history, or of art, medicine, engineering, literature, education, business, political behavior, architecture, theater, mathematics, philosophy, and so on through the rich array of disciplines and special studies that comprise the substance of the university. Faculty are individuals who have made a major personal and financial investment in mastering some such specialized field of knowledge. For most, the striving toward that end probably had its origins in some early experience that provoked curiosity and inquiry about an aspect of the world, inquiry that they found rewarding. Those inquiries stimulated further interest and study, and ultimately led to undertaking a pathway of the formal study that is generally required for in-depth understanding of most phenomena. Finally, the continued cultivation of their interest and learning grew to a level that led them to decide to spend their lives working in the field that so compelled their interest and efforts. A sustained effort of a predominately intellectual nature has led them to a profession that offers limited opportunities for economic or other material gain. While the salaries of faculty who achieve full professor status may be considered comfortable, especially if supplemented by summer salaries for those who win competitive research grants, such salaries are certainly nowhere near the magnitude that commensurate investment of resources and effort might provide in many other professions.

In this connection, it should be noted that research is a much more demanding and tough-minded business than generally credited by the uninitiated. It is demanding in that nature does not readily yield new insights and seldom without prolonged and skillful investigation. It requires tremendous patience and persistence and a tolerance for failure. It is tough minded in that any claim to the production of new knowledge, whether empirical, theoretical, or creative in nature, must be defended in the highly critical and intensely competitive arena of peer-review and judgment. Particularly in fields that offer limited opportunities for external funding, faculty must often struggle to find the time and the means to pursue their scholarly interests within institutions and within a society that expect a primary if not a full-time commitment to teaching. For those who think academic research is a protected world without the difficulties, uncertainties, challenges, and risk of failure of "real life," I would say, "Let them try it!" They would quickly learn to appreciate the traits that are necessary to success in that arena—keen intellectual and creative abilities, a full commitment to rational modes of inquiry, hard work and persistence under limited support, and a willingness to give and receive rigorous critical assessment of truth and merit. The primary benefit of the profession faculty have chosen is that it provides a demanding livelihood that permits them to learn further about their field of interest, contribute further knowledge to it, and teach others about it. It does not seem too much to say that what faculty have at base is a love of their fields. Or as has been said about the occupation of professor, it's a lousy job–unless you love it.

Daniel Koshland, a distinguished scientist and former editor of the prestigious journal *Science* has humorously but very aptly captured the essence of the faculty researcher in a supposed interview between *Science* and a fictional expert, Dr. Noitall. While Koshland has in mind the natural scientist, with suitable modification for the characteristics of other academic disciplines, the account is fully applicable to faculty scholars in general:

Science. Could you describe the addictive personality?

Dr. Noitall. An addictive person is one who has a compulsion to behave in ways that his or her family members consider detrimental to their interest. An addictive person will frequently conceal the extent of his addiction, will lie to his family about it, is immune to logical arguments to correct the error of his ways, and foregoes income that would require abandoning the addiction.

Science. Are we talking about a dope addict or alcoholic?

Dr. Noitall. No, I am describing a scientist. It is well known that work habits of scientists are addictive, leaving their spouses in tears, their children pleading, "Come home, Mommy (or Daddy)," and involve long hours in hostile instrument laboratories or cold rooms, exposed to noxious gases and radioactivity–conditions that no sane person would choose.

Science. But surely these individuals are paid handsomely for undergoing these hazardous conditions.

Dr. Noitall. This is the peculiar paradox. The profession is poorly paid because there are hundreds of applicants for every good position. Because of the psychic income that is exploited by our oppressive society, a scientist would accept pay that would make a movie star weep.

Science. But many of these individuals are academics who have the advantages of long summers off and light teaching loads.

Dr. Noitall. Academic freedom is the freedom not to take a vacation. Far from taking summers off, these individuals would rather develop films in the darkroom than sit on the beaches of Waikiki.

Science. But surely these individuals have a record of stable homes, paying their bills, and other behavior not typical of an addict.

Dr. Noitall. That depends on how you define good behavior. These individuals tend to curl up with a copy of the *Physical Review Letters, Journal of the American Chemical Society,* or *Journal of Biological Chemistry,* rather than doing household chores or acting like good Americans who stay glued to the television set.

Science. So far, however, you have merely described an individual who works to keep his job.

Dr. Noitall. No, these individuals are definitely masochistic. They volunteer to serve on review panels that send them hundreds of incredibly detailed

project proposals which must be read and evaluated. They sit through endless thesis defenses, volunteer to edit journals, and serve on visiting committees for other schools when they have too much to do at home. They then
complain bitterly that they are too busy. . . .

   Science. Is there any behavioral characteristic that can explain this obses-
sive conduct?

   Dr. Noitall. Basically scientists have failed to grow up. They are all children, eternally curious, eternally trying to find out how the pieces of the puz-
zle fit together, eternally asking Why, and then irritatingly asking Why again
when they get the answer to the first question.[4]

   Picking up on the latter note, the psychologists David Klar and
Herbert Simon, the Nobel laureate, concluded their recent review of
decades of research on problem solving and discovery by observing, "The
more creative the problem solving, the more primitive the tools (employed). Perhaps this is why 'childlike' characteristics, such as the propen-
sity to wonder, are so often attributed to creative scientists and artists."[5]

   Lest we be accused of treacle, there is of course a dark side to academics, as there is to any human enterprise. There will be some fraction of
faculty who will abuse "the academic freedom not to take a vacation" or
time off, in whom the intrinsic motivation to learn runs out, who will give
less than full measure in teaching and collegial service, who will undertake
research of questionable merit, and even some who will exploit an environment that permits and indeed requires a good deal of individual freedom
and self-direction. But by all objective measures, and contrary to some
popular representations, that fraction is truly small. However small, that
fraction should not be tolerated, and in chapter 7 we will return to this
concern and to the corrective actions that can be taken.

   While our account of university research has emphasized research
driven primarily by the desire to expand general knowledge, it applies
equally to university research that can be classified as applied in nature,
that is, to research undertaken with more direct reference to practical
problems of everyday life. As we have seen, a strong utilitarian strain has
long been evident in American research universities. The Land Grant programs stemming from the Morrill Act are all about the production and
transfer of basic knowledge to stimulate "agriculture and the mechanical
arts," and economic development was certainly an important end product
in Bush's vision of the role of basic research. In fact, university research
comprises a broad continuum of basic to applied research ranging from the
"free play of free intellects, working on subjects of their own choice, in the
manner dictated by their curiosity" to efforts to develop or improve some
immediately, and even commercially, useful product or process. And just

as curiosity-driven research may yield unexpected practical applications, so research undertaken to address specific problems of everyday life may yield unexpected insights or discoveries that contribute to basic knowledge.

University research has historically been strongly skewed toward the "basic" end of the basic-applied continuum but virtually all is a mix of basic and applied features and both basic and applied dimensions are valued. The mix may take several forms. For example, a desire to address problems of everyday life provides the impetus to a good deal of university research, but the approach may nevertheless be through the framework of basic research. This is so in part because real-life problems are often intractable to meaningful study as they directly manifest themselves and in part because the university researcher's generic knowledge and skills provide uniquely valuable tools in analysis of real-life matters. For example, research directed to understanding the causes and treatment of cancer is necessarily conducted largely through the pathway of basic research in genetics, molecular biology, and cell physiology. Alternatively, the mix may take the form of developing theoretical models of phenomena studied in the laboratory but models with obvious implications for understanding everyday life activities, as, for example, research directed to the development of a theory of learning. The research may take the form of normative data collection undertaken without immediate practical aim that nevertheless furthers our understanding of real-life events, as, for example, the long-term collection of data on earth's climate that has enabled the detection of global warming. It may take the form of inquiry into the historical circumstances of a work of art that gives new meaning to that work, or it may take the form of experimentation with new forms of visual art that deepen and enrich our understanding of life.

While any sample of university research inevitably does serious injustice to its scope and diversity, the following list of accomplishments that may fairly be credited to faculty research may convey something of its inescapable blend of basic and applied characteristics: development of chemotherapy; discovery of planets outside our solar system; determination of the world history of humans through analysis of the DNA of people alive today; construction of nanomachines that may regulate living cells inside the body; development of survey-sampling techniques credited with "changing how the world collects information about itself"; archival research determination of the identities and backgrounds of Louisiana slaves, thereby humanizing the African diaspora; precise measurement (in atoms to parts-per-billion) of the constants in physical laws to test theoretical conceptions of the physical world; basic research on the lost world of artifacts and structures in the city of Venice that in turn now questions the viability of a multibillion-dollar plan to save the city from rising waters; determining the cause of California smog thereby alleviating a major and growing worldwide health hazard; modeling the regional economic impact of major civic and business projects; extracting from literature effective approaches to pressing issues of real life such as youth suicide, family violence, and aging; determining the three-dimensional structure of the cell part that constructs proteins (ribosomes), which at once provides insight into the nature of the earliest forms of life and a new avenue for research on antibiotics; development of electronic sensing and manipulating devices to assist the education of physically disabled people and to give them greater control over their daily lives; isolation of micro-organisms able to metabolize hydrocarbons and pollutants and thereby eliminate toxic waste; design of cost-effective high-rise buildings and bridges resistant to earthquakes; development of sustainable agriculture systems to preserve natural resources; determining sports fans' levels of physiological arousal, self-esteem, depression, and other behaviors in relation to the fortunes of their teams; development of novel stem cells with the ability to regrow the damaged human brain; bringing art to the public through creation of original literary and visual art displays on billboards; determining the wintering grounds of the beautiful monarch butterfly. And so on and on through an incredibly rich, varied, almost impossible to grasp flow of information, ideas, and applications. In these and in countless other instances of university research it does not matter where on the continuum from basic to applied the inquiry initiates; what matters is that the work produce new knowledge or perspectives about some aspect of the world, knowledge and perspectives that in some way advance the public good now or in the long run.

In recent years, however, growing ties between universities and businesses have introduced a new note which, although still insignificant in the total scale of university research, is quite different in tone. While the federal government continues to supply most of the funding for academic research, the rate of growth in federal support has declined over the past decade, as has state spending on higher education. At the same time, corporate giving to universities has increased markedly and businesses have increasingly outsourced aspects of their research and development work to universities. Businesses of course expect returns from the programs they sponsor, returns that will advance their economic competitiveness and profit margins. In addition, the Bayh-Dole Act of 1980 permitted universities to patent and license inventions developed under federally funded research, giving universities and their faculties for the first time the opportunity and incentive to develop and profit from commercially valuable ideas stemming from research. These various ties to the world of business, which tend to be centered in the biomedical, business, and engineering programs of the university, pose a clear threat to the tradition of disinterested inquiry, the hallmark of university research. For example, researchers who conduct industry-sponsored research are often asked by the industry sponsor to sign agreements to keep their work secret for a period of time so as to forestall possible competitors. Researchers may also be pressured to interpret their data in the manner most favorable to the sponsor or, for that matter if they have a royalty or equity interest at stake, may be biased by their own economic interests in the project. Issues of this nature have begun to arise with disturbing frequency. While there certainly can be significant mutual benefit from university-industry interactions, the rules of the academy and the rules of business make an uneasy mix. It is tempting to recall the earlier noted outcome when adults are given the choice between exploratory learning and learning for a material end. Universities must develop clear guidelines to insure that academic freedom and research integrity are strictly maintained in the growing interactions between industry and universities. This is one of the significant challenges to research universities to which we will return later in greater detail.

Beyond the broad descriptions of *basic* and *applied university research,* which we have noted are quite relative terms, lies the rich and varied tapestry of research within the arts, the humanities, the social sciences, and the natural sciences. The disciplines comprising these broad areas differ quite markedly in many ways: the nature of the questions posed, methods of inquiry, use of qualitative versus quantitative analyses, reliance upon discovery or reliance upon creation, primarily empirical or primarily theoretical content, basic versus applied character, support requirements, sources of funding, and still other dimensions. But although the intellectual tools and the means may differ, all disciplines work toward the same end—a more in-depth understanding and appreciation of the world and of the human condition—and all have stood the test of peer and public scrutiny of their contributions to the universe of knowledge.

In any consideration of university research as a whole, it is always temping to focus upon the sciences and engineering because these areas best fit the public stereotype of research, are the most costly, and have the most obvious application to practical affairs, particularly to economic and technological development. But it would be a serious mistake to undervalue the contribution that the nonscience areas make to both education and the world of practical affairs. Education and life itself would suffer an irreparable loss if it neglected those disciplines that place the aesthetic before the practical, the fundamental before the specific, the humanizing before the technical, the person before the occupation. As Henry David Thoreau has observed, the world is wider than anyone's view of it, and all kinds of knowledge have some use in furthering not only our understanding of that complex world but also our ability to deal with it in adaptive, critical, and innovative ways. There is broad agreement that the capacity for abstract and creative thinking, which is increasingly required in all walks of life, is fostered by broad exposure to the academic disciplines, including literature, philosophy, music, psychology, and art. And just as is the case with the sciences, the ability of those disciplines to continue to contribute life-enhancing knowledge and skills depends on continuing inquiry, expansion, and refinement of their knowledge base, that is, it depends on research.

If it is true that research is the best guarantor of the value of the knowledge conveyed by a university across its disciplines, then it is also true that the best research will convey the best knowledge. University researchers are very much aware of who is doing the best work in their field, and strive to be among the best themselves, and wish to be in universities where outstanding research is valued, and seek to attract the best scholars to their own universities. Just as competition is a driving force toward delivery of a superior product or service, so competition is a driving force to superior research, however mixed with the lure of fame and gain. Just as the desire to be the best is a driving force toward intercollegiate athletic championships in which we take pride, so the desire to be the best is a driving force toward a reputation for academic excellence in which faculty take pride. The aspiration to academic excellence is a noble aspiration, and one of far greater significance for human welfare than the aspiration toward intercollegiate athletic championships that seems, in contrast, so enthusiastically embraced by the public.

University research in the aggregate, then, is a wonderful expression of the deep-seated human desire to know. Pursued freely and apart from political and marketplace pressures, it provides the foundation for higher education and educational excellence. It is a highly specialized, complex, varied, demanding, and competitive undertaking, largely intrinsically motivated yet ultimately utilitarian in nature and directed toward the production of knowledge for the public good. It requires proper understanding of its basis, an appreciation of its function, protection of its freedom, and support of its endless quest. The question to which we turn now is, What type of administrative and governing structures oversee such an enterprise?

Chapter 3

University Governance

✿

U niversities are governed by external boards that have final authority over all university operations. The authority of boards originates from a fundamental legal source that establishes the institution as a legal entity. For public institutions, the source is usually the constitution or statutes of the state; for private institutions it is usually articles of incorporation. While the university president is delegated responsibility for day-to-day administration of the institution, boards customarily retain formal approval authority for most significant aspects of university operations, including policy formation, planning, budgets, facilities, academic programs, and tenure and promotion of the faculty. Recommendations for actions on these matters are formulated by the university leadership and presented to the board, which generally works in a supportive manner with the administration. Nevertheless, actions on these and on virtually all other major administrative matters require formal approval of the boards. Governing boards are thus in a position to exercise great power over university affairs.

Governing board members are variously called "trustees," "directors," "overseers," "regents," or less commonly, "visitors" or "curators." Private institutions will each have their own governing board, while public institutions may either be under the oversight of a board specific to a single institution or may be grouped with several other universities as a system (generally consisting of all of the public universities within a state) and placed under the oversight of a single board. Members of the latter boards are usually called "regents" and are assisted by an executive officer, or chancellor, to whom the university presidents in the system report (although in some state systems the titles of president and chancellor are reversed).

35

However, just as the presidents of freestanding universities are responsible to their governing boards, the presidents within a university system are also responsible to their board of regents through the chancellor. The final authority for all university matters, then, resides with the governing board, whatever its nomenclature or institutional span.

Considering university boards as a whole, what are their general characteristics? Governing boards of the nation's public universities are relatively small, averaging about a dozen members each; those of private universities are about twice as large. Characteristically, board members serve rather lengthy terms, usually three- to six-year minimum terms and often with their appointments renewed for terms of similar length. Public boards of course have a strong political dimension in member selection. Nearly half of all public board members are selected by gubernatorial appointment with political affiliation being a qualifying consideration in selection, and another 30% are determined by public election. Private boards select their own members and generally choose from among alumni or others with some prior affiliation with the institution and from backgrounds similar to those of current members of the board. A recent national survey found that private boards are largely white (90%) and male (74%) in composition; public boards differ only slightly (83% and 70%) in these respects. The considerable power of boards, then, is typically vested in a relatively small and stable group of like individuals.

Probably the most important question to ask about university boards concerns the knowledge and skills that board members bring to their positions. This question is best answered by considering the primary occupation or profession of board members, and boards are extremely similar in this regard. By far the largest single occupational category represented on both public and private boards across the nation is that of business executive, including executives of large corporations, small-business executives, and executives from banking, financial, insurance, real estate, and other firms. A distinctly distant second set of occupations in terms of member frequency is attorneys, accountants, and physicians. Business executives and attorneys together account for the vast majority of membership on both public and private boards. No other occupation or occupational group accounts for more than a small fraction (less than 5%) of membership in the universe of university boards. This would include students, faculty, and others in education who each constitutes about 2% or less of membership across the nation's public and private boards. University boards are essentially business boards.[1]

Expertise in university affairs, or even basic knowledge of university operations, then, has not been a consideration in appointments to university boards. To the contrary, appointment to a board of a public university is often regarded as a political plum offered in reward for demonstrated support of the party in power. Appointment to a board of a private university, particularly of a major university, is similarly regarded as a prestigious form of social recognition and acknowledgment of demonstrated or expected support, financial or otherwise, of the institution. Notwithstanding these considerations, the members of both public and private boards are nevertheless typically people who have achieved success in the world of practical affairs and who hold leadership positions in their professions and society. They tend to be very capable individuals with a commitment to public service and genuine interest in advancing higher education. They often bring business and managerial expertise relevant to the business aspects of the institutions they serve, and they may also be helpful, directly or indirectly, to the private fund-raising programs of their universities. Board members of public universities in particular may protect or advance the interests of their universities within the strong political environment in which they must operate. All of these member attributes are certainly of value to the universities served including of course research universities, the institutional category of central interest here. Nevertheless, in light of the conclusions of chapters 1–2 regarding the life force of the university and its special requirements, it is apparent that there is a fundamental mismatch between university governing boards and the institutions for which they are responsible.

None of the positive attributes noted above guarantee, or for that matter favor, an understanding of the special nature and requirements of a research university, which is a prerequisite to wise governance decisions. In fact, it can be argued that the philosophy, values, goals, and strategies of the business mentality that dominates boards are in many respects antithetical to those of the university. Businesses are perforce pragmatic, focused on material productivity and the fiscal bottom line, prescriptive in job expectations, hierarchical in decision making, and generally oriented to short-term goals and returns. Universities are idealistic, focused on the creation and dissemination of knowledge primarily as ends in themselves, committed to academic freedom and shared governance, and oriented to long-term goals in research and education. Offhand, it would be hard to imagine a less sympathetic matchup. We are left with the striking conclusion that university boards are selected and composed in a manner that virtually ensures that no one on the board will be truly knowledgeable or understanding of the enterprise they are charged with governing. This is a tough conclusion, but it is inescapable.

One might argue, of course, that notwithstanding a mismatch in the respects noted, university boards might still constitute desirably objective governing bodies from the standpoint of the public responsibilities of universities. Perhaps. But it could be asked whether this is an appropriate desideratum for private universities while noting that public universities are already generally under strong legislative oversight. And one might also ask how many businesses, particularly how many major corporations, would constitute a board of directors that was populated with individuals not knowledgeable about critical business aspects of the corporation at issue.

The nature of the formal linkage between boards and universities tends to extend the mismatch between university governance and the core values and operations of the university. One of the responsibilities of a board, and perhaps its pivotal responsibility, is to select the university president. By virtue of this selection, and by the power conferred with it, the board determines the individual who will set the overall direction and tone of the university. And university boards, like any other group, are subject to the common human tendency to select in their own image. Ambrose Bierce noted that admiration is the polite recognition of another's resemblance to ourselves. Despite the undertone of cynicism, this is a very natural and understandable dynamic. Boards can be expected to hold in high regard individuals who share, or who are at least sympathetic to, their philosophy, values, and world outlook. Boards must be fully comfortable with the individual they select as president since that individual is their only formal link between the board and the institution, that is, the president is the only member of the institution who reports to, and is responsible to, the board. The president is also the primary and certainly the determinative channel of all communication between the board and university. Boards, then, will not unreasonably tend to select presidents who share their view on university governance. This is true despite the fact that in the process of searching for and choosing a university president there is usually much ado about seeking the input of various stakeholders within and without the university. To this end, a search advisory committee is set up with representation from the faculty, university administrators, students, alumni, and various segments of the local community. The committee may be asked to advise on the position description and selection criteria, to meet the final candidates, and to present their views and advice to the presidential selection committee, composed only of board members, which makes the actual choice among candidates to be presented to the full board for approval. While this search advisory committee lends a participatory aspect to the procedures and may be helpful in screening out basically unqualified candidates, it plays only an advisory and generally weak role in the selection of finalists for the position and is not part of the final decision process. Furthermore, in recent years governing boards have increasingly turned to business firms that undertake executive search or "head-hunting" on a contract basis, firms that may bypass the advisory committee altogether in the selection of the finalists for the position.

University faculties generally and quite rightly regard the search advisory committee as window dressing in a process that effectively disenfranchises them and indeed other constituencies as well. But of course it can be argued that the governing board should have the dispositive role and final say in the selection of the president since under the rules of university governance that choice is, after all, their responsibility. The point of this discussion is that in the absence of a meaningful role for other constituencies, the board's interests and values will be fully determinant in the selection.

Another factor that may influence the board's natural propensities is the enormous growth in size and complexity of research universities, particularly public research universities, over the past several decades. From 1950 to 1995 the percentage of high school seniors continuing on to colleges and universities has increased from 20% to 60%. Enrollments of 20,000 to 50,000 increasingly diverse students are not uncommon among major universities today, a far cry from the relatively homogeneous student bodies of several thousand that typified the leading institutions of the '40s and '50s. In consequence, presidents today must pay more attention to such matters as physical plant and facilities planning; multicampus and multisite operations; residential, health, recreational, and other specialized student support services; admissions; public relations; the "university image," computer support technologies; international and multicultural programs; legal counsel and services; and police and security, to say nothing of parking and transportation. In this regard, it has been said that running a major university today is similar to running a city! A recent survey by the American Council on Education on the president's primary use of time at public and private institutions found that academic programs ranked last among six activities cited by presidents as consuming the majority of their time; furthermore, the time they actually spent on academic programs was but a small fraction of the time spent on activities such as fund-raising and planning.[2]

University interactions with external agencies have also increased in scope and number. Competition for federal grants, and responsibility for the administrative and regulatory requirements that go with those grants, require a knowledgeable and watchful eye on the policies and priorities of federal funding agencies. New technology transfer programs that license or commercialize technologies stemming from faculty research have established additional ties to the marketplace and to the legal and business communities. Economic development initiatives in partnership with local business and industry have become an expected part of the agenda of a research university, and there is scarcely a sizable community that does not want "its own research university." Twenty years ago private fund-raising was primarily the preserve of private universities and their fund-raising goals were relatively modest; today private and public universities conduct vigorous year-round fund-raising programs as well as major campaigns with targets in the half-billion to billion-dollar range. Universities also are encountering greater legislative oversight, and now must deal continually with legislative and public calls for greater productivity and accountability. In addition, the reality of marketplace competition among universities has become increasingly evident—competition for students, faculty, grant support, private funds, athletes, and prestige—and universities ignore such external competition at their peril.

While an extensive administrative infrastructure has developed to assist in all of these areas, the president remains responsible for oversight and orchestration of the broad array of internal and external activities that are part of the modern research university. In that process, today's university president faces far greater administrative demands than his or her midcentury counterparts. In short, the growth in size and complexity of research universities has placed an increasing premium on broad managerial skills in the presidency, skills that are particularly valued in the world of most board members.

As we have noted, the university president is the link between the external governance of the university and its internal governance. The most influential level of the latter consists of the university vice presidents and others who report directly to the president, all of whom are appointed solely by the president and each of whom is responsible for some significant sphere of university operations. Reflecting the increased complexity of universities, there are today about eight to ten of these officers depending upon the scope of university operations and the organizational preferences of the president. The president works primarily with this group, often called the "president's cabinet," in formulating the key decisions affecting university operations. However, all individual and collective actions of the vice presidents remain subject to approval by the president. Since the president is chosen by the board and the internal authority structure is chosen by the president, there is obviously a strong disposition toward continuity of viewpoint in the governance process.

An understanding of how this disposition projects downward into the university and of how university governance relates to the academic core of the institution requires a closer look at the officers that comprise the president's cabinet. For a major research university this group would typically include the following: (1) A vice president for academic affairs, or as this position is often called, the "provost of the university." As chief academic officer of the university, the provost is responsible for all of its teaching, research, and service programs. Often referred to as the first among vice presidents and the second in command, the provost generally represents the university in the absence of the president. (2) A vice president for financial affairs and administration, responsible for maintaining the capital and operating budgets of the university and handling general business affairs, including personnel, purchasing, contract and grants administration, and maintenance and operation of the physical plant. (3) A vice president for student affairs, responsible for residential halls, health services, and all other programs in support of student life activities. This officer is often also responsible for admissions, registration, and financial aid. (4) A vice president for university advancement, responsible for media and public relations, alumni affairs, fund-raising programs, and endowment management. (5) In universities with a medical school, the vice president for health affairs, responsible for the medical school and related clinical programs as well as allied colleges such as dentistry, nursing, and public health. (6) The director of government relations who represents the university's interest to local, state, and federal government offices. (7) The director of athletics who supervises all intra- and extramural athletic programs, facilities, and personnel including team coaches. (8) The chief legal counsel of the university. In addition, presidential cabinets are increasingly populated with one or more individuals who provide special assistance to the president in some particular capacity such as public relations or speech writing. While these aides do not exercise executive authority as such, they nevertheless report directly to the president, serve as primary advisors to the president, and can be quite influential in university policy determination.

As noted, the composition of this group and the titles employed may vary somewhat across institutions. The first five listed officers are invariably present, but the overall listing is quite representative in nature and size.

From the perspective of the present exposition, the most remarkable aspect of this high-level management group is that it contains only one member with experienced-based knowledge and understanding of university teaching and research–the provost. Provosts generally have extensive experience and strong credentials in teaching and research, and in addition are likely to have served as chairs of their academic departments and, very often, as college deans. They come from the faculty ranks and would not likely rise to the position of provost if they had not earned the respect and support of their colleagues. While other vice presidents and members of the president's cabinet will certainly have some background in higher education, it is extremely rare that they come from the faculty. Rather, and appropriate to their roles of *supporting* the core mission of the university, they are trained and experienced in areas such as business, finance, student services, development, athletics, law, journalism, and politics. With exception of the provost, then, the top-level internal management group of the university essentially replicates the board in terms of the occupational and professional skills and interests brought to the task.

While the support vice presidents do not advise the president on academic matters, the fact is that the president must consider and coordinate the needs and interests of both academic and support areas to ensure effective operation of the university. Thus when the cabinet members recommend actions to the president, whether as individual members or collectively, on such key matters as policy formation, strategic planning, budgets, and resource allocation, there is one academic voice and seven or eight voices from other backgrounds. This distribution of direct inputs to the president is also out of line with the scope of responsibilities of the various vice presidents. Typically the provost's area will include 70 percent or more of the personnel and budget of the university, with the remainder spread among the other direct reports.

The broad scope and central nature of the provost's responsibilities are recognized to some degree, as noted earlier, by its status as "first among the vice presidents" and by use of the title provost rather than simply academic vice president. However, the operational significance of such distinctions is generally very limited because presidents rarely delegate their authority over other vice presidential areas to the provost and certainly not in any broadly inclusive fashion. Recognizing the chief academic officer of the university as first among vice presidents has a gratifying symbolic ring, but in the absence of direct reporting by other vice presidents to the provost this recognition by itself imparts little if any gain to the operational priority of academic affairs. (Ironically, the effort to designate the academic vice president as having a special role by using the title of provost may actually blur the distinction since most outside the university are quite confused as to what a provost is or does!)

At the end of the day, then, and fully consistent with the charter and intention of governing boards, the president *is* the effective authority and power within the university. That pivotal individual is selected by, and must be responsive to, a governing body composed primarily of individuals from business, legal, or other nonacademic backgrounds and in turn works with an internal senior management group that is very similar in professional background. This external-internal chain of command comprises the executive authority of the university and incorporates an array of experience and expertise relevant to the many functions and interfaces that characterize the modern research university. But there is nothing about the overall character and distribution of that expertise that guarantees an understanding of the conditions necessary for the health and well-being of the academic enterprise, and in fact there is much that biases in the opposite direction, whatever the good intentions of the members. At the least, the composition of this governance structure certainly does not favor an academic perspective in central decision-making and university operations.

Apart from representation by the academic administrative leadership, the rank-and-file faculty also participate in university governance under the long-standing tradition of "shared governance." Under this principle, the university administration is expected to seek and value faculty input on all important university matters. As interpreted by the American Association of University Professors, the national faculty union organization, shared governance implies that professors should have primary authority over curriculum, research, and faculty status, and that their decisions should be overruled by the president or governing board "only in exceptional circumstance." The principle of shared governance is highly prized by the faculty, who view it as a means of injecting academic values and priorities into the decision-making processes of the university. While university administrations, and particularly the academic administrative sector, generally seek faculty input, it is much more difficult than most faculty realize to communicate administrative issues to the faculty and to secure meaningful feedback on them. In theory, one can do so through the regular academic unit structure, that is, through the academic department heads and college deans, or for that matter even by direct communication with the faculty as a whole. The reality, however, is that these are extremely uncertain and "noisy" communication channels. A comprehensive research university may have from 15 to 20 deans, 70 to 100 heads of departments or other academic units, and several thousand faculty members, all varying in their degree of attention to, and involvement in, broader university and administrative affairs and in their mix of teaching, research, and service activities. It is virtually impossible to convey through such differently tuned, multilevel, and multichannel pathways the information required for a meaningful decision and to obtain a collective view, much less a representative view, from whatever feedback is received. In fact, as universities increase in size and number of programs it is becoming more and more difficult to know what "the faculty," as a collective whole, think about anything.

In most universities the faculty senate (or university senate if representatives of constituencies other than faculty are also included) is the primary vehicle for observing the principle of shared governance. Senates are composed solely or primarily of faculty elected by their colleagues in a manner representative of the numerical distribution of faculty across the various academic units of the university. The senate's special significance to shared governance lies in the fact that it is the only faculty body authorized to represent the interests of "the faculty" to the administration. The senate normally meets monthly throughout the academic year, usually with the president and provost in attendance to provide reports on significant developments affecting the university and to respond to questions from the floor. The senate thus provides a continuing open forum in which concerns the faculty may have on any aspect of university operations may be addressed directly to the administration.

While faculty senates can be an effective means of voicing faculty views on broad philosophical matters such as tenure and academic freedom, they have proven to be very limited as a means of sharing governance in administrative decision-making. In part, the reasons are similar to those that limit communication through the academic chain of command. The complexity of administrative decision-making simply does not lend itself to the time and background limitations of the typical faculty senate. To illustrate, suppose the administration is attempting to decide on the percentage of funding in a given year's budget that should be allocated to the academic versus the support areas of the university. This is a fundamental and significant issue that should be of great interest to the faculty. In the abstract, the priority in budgeting should be given to academic affairs because that is the division of the university that directly delivers its educational, research, and service programs, and there is not a faculty senate in the nation that would not be strongly predisposed in this direction. But the fact is that academic affairs cannot long function effectively without healthy support areas. Meaningful advice on this question therefore requires knowledge of the multiplicity of educational and research needs and pressures across the many academic programs of the university as well as knowledge of all the needs and pressures within the support areas. The latter in turn will require an understanding and consideration of a host of possible consequences of inadequate support, which are likely to include academic, financial, legal, environmental, security, health and safety, and audit consequences. Each of the affected operations will in turn have a budget history and projected cost impact of differing levels of support that require examination as well. In short, an informative exposition of the question can hardly be accomplished, much less the in-depth consideration required, by a group of faculty inexperienced in budgets and administration who meet for a few hours a month on top of their regular schedule of teaching, research, and service responsibilities. While the senate will usually have a standing budget committee that is charged with making recommendations on the university budget, the members of this committee seldom have the time to master the information required for meaningful input. Therefore, the dialogues between the administration and the senate on such critical matters are likely to be collegial albeit superficial exchanges in which the administration provides information that while never misleading is perforce seldom substantive, while the faculty lack the knowledge and background to generate probing and revealing questions.

There is a second condition that limits the senate's effectiveness as a mechanism of shared governance—its questionable representativeness. The fact is that many faculty avoid service in the senate, and this is particularly characteristic of the most productive and research-oriented faculty. Faculty senates tend to be populated by faculty who have a commitment to such service and an interest in administration. A number of these faculty may be repeatedly reelected to successive terms on the senate, and thereby come to dominant its leadership. Meanwhile the vast majority of the faculty do not participate in senate elections, either as candidates or as voters, and do not attend senate meetings. Similarly, department chairs and deans, key academic leaders, are unlikely to attend meetings of the senate. The withdrawal of the faculty from this forum is part of a larger faculty withdrawal from involvement in university administration, a serious problem that we will deal with in depth in chapter 4. To the degree that the senate is not truly representative of the core faculty, it becomes difficult for the academic administration to give weight to its voice in shared governance.

It is sometimes said that the principle of shared governance gives faculty managerial power, but this is a questionable stretch. The faculty do have effective power over the curriculum and over other basically academic matters such as the academic calendar, and usually deal with these matters in a functionally autonomous manner primarily through the medium of the senate. Even here, though, the senate's actions are subject to approval by the provost and president. Neither the faculty at large nor the faculty senate have any executive authority. Their input is advisory in character, and not binding on the administration. In sum, while the executive administration will respect the principle of shared governance, welcome direct faculty input, and acknowledge its political import, nevertheless for the reasons we have reviewed, the faculty as a whole are basically nonparticipants in administrative decision-making.

University governance, then, presents a multilevel continuum that extends from external governors through the president, the latter who must attend to both external and internal governance, to the senior officers of the university, to the deans and department chairs, and finally to the faculty via the principle of shared governance. Correlated with this continuum are progressive levels of legally derived executive authority, with power weakest at the internal academic levels and strongest at the level of the board and, for state universities, the legislatures. Correspondingly, the nonacademic composition and character of the governance levels, that is, a business-political orientation, become progressively more marked as one moves from internal to external agents and from weakest to strongest power. Given these relations, any shift toward more active involvement by the external governors can be expected to have a marked impact on the overall direction of the university.

Historically, governing boards have generally eschewed direct involvement in the internal affairs of the institution, but instead have worked to support the president's decisions and priorities. Recently, however, and in contrast to the disengagement of the faculty (and perhaps in part because of it) governing boards have become much more aggressive in seeking to directly manage university operations, at times in heavy-handed fashion. Noting that the most influential governance models for higher education derive from the corporate sector, several higher-education analysts have traced the roots of this recent university board activism to the business world.[3] Traditionally, corporate boards, like university boards, were essentially honorific in nature, their membership drawn from the old boy network of supportive like-minded business leaders who rubber-stamped the actions of management while imparting an aura of external oversight and review. Although business boards are supposed to represent and protect the interests of shareholders in the corporation, they were in fact much more attuned to the perspective of company management. The dominant position of management was exacerbated by the fact that stock ownership at that time was generally broadly dispersed among shareholders who had little individual power to affect the actions of their corporations. However, beginning in the '70s and '80s stock became more consolidated in large institutional investors, notably those representing huge pension fund holdings and mutual fund investment companies, creating a new class of investors with both major interests at stake and the clout to press those interests. At the same time, there were increasing symptoms of an unhealthy business climate bespeaking questionable practices in corporate management and negligence in board oversight. Among these symptoms were plunging corporate profits, large-scale layoffs, stalled employees' wages, hostile takeovers of weakened corporations, and mergers and acquisitions of interest to managers and directors but of questionable benefit to the corporation and shareholders, all along with outrageously high executive salaries and stock ownership deals. All of this served to sharpen concern about whose interests the directors really served and to underscore the vulnerability of boards to charges of lax oversight of investor interest. With their newfound power, large institutional investors began to demand that boards be more accountable to the investor community and take more direct responsibility for the performance of companies under their oversight. Boards of directors in turn began to act, dismissing a sizable number of prominent CEOs, insisting on accountability from top management, restructuring board membership to a more "neutral" cast, initiating direct communication with investors and employees, tightening oversight of company practices, and in general better educating themselves about the nature and particulars of their company operations. The '80s and '90s saw directive power shift sharply from the executive level to the board level.[4]

Given the high proportion of business executives on university boards, it was only to be expected that the new activism of corporate boards would rapidly cross-pollinate to university boards, and that is exactly what is underway in university governance, particularly in the public sector. To illustrate, there follows a sampler of increased activism on the part of university governing boards over the past five to ten years. While not a complete account, the events noted would probably make the list of most higher education analysts. A variety of heavy-handed board actions are illustrated, including ousting university presidents, overturning university leadership positions on major policy issues, directing intervention in academic program matters, ignoring principles of shared governance, handpicking university leadership with little or no input from the university community, and channeling political pressures on university decision making. The events listed are not organized by type of action but rather appear in rough chronological order, a manner more reflective of the "all over the map" character of board activism.

The Board of Regents of the University of California acted against the advice of the university's president, its nine chancellors, and chief faculty representatives to end affirmative action in admissions, hiring, and contracting, an action widely seen as related to the governor's presidential aspirations.[5] In the process, the board threatens the job of the system's president after he suggests delaying the action on affirmative action for another year.[6]

Conflict with their governing boards results in the resignations of the chief executives (presidents or chancellors) at the State University of New York (SUNY), the University of Michigan, the University of Minnesota, and the University of Missouri at Columbia.[7] The presidents of Michigan and SUNY indicated a lack of support from their boards, the latter over his choice for provost and his resistance to budget cuts proposed by the governor. The president of the University of Minnesota found his proposal to reform remedial education overridden by the board that also questioned his choice for provost. The Missouri board fired the head of its flagship campus at Columbia for failure to eliminate programs as directed.

At the University of Iowa the new president of the board moves to eliminate programs deemed duplicative and to overhaul teaching loads without consulting faculty members.[8]

At the University of Minnesota the regents call for major revision of the tenure rules without consulting faculty, and of course encounter a storm of protest.[9]

The Chronicle of Higher Education reports that the Faculty Senate at the University of Notre Dame, voted to dissolve, frustrated by a lack of any real power or influence in the decision-making process at the university.[10] However, the senators later discovered that even their vote to dissolve may have exceeded their power, so the body may survive after all!

New York University's Board of Trustees handpick a new university president in a search process that the faculty felt was heavy-handed.[11] Before the official selection, more than one hundred fifty professors had signed a petition calling for a broader, more public search in which faculty members would play a more prominent role. The board chair's response: "We fully understand the faculty point of view, and we reject it."

Auburn University faculty express outrage over the trustees' summary dismissal of the institution's president, as soon as he took another job, charging that the board's ouster of the president culminates a decade of board micromanagement of university matters.[12]

Under strong pressure from the mayor and the governor the trustees of the City University of New York selected as president of Hunter College, one of the largest and strongest of City University's eleven four-year colleges, a candidate without experience in higher education, turning aside the university chancellor's preferred candidate, a provost at a large university.[13] A member of the search committee alleged that the successful candidate was forced through the whole search and selection process.

The policy-making body for higher education in Virginia rejects a proposed major in African-American studies at Virginia Commonwealth University despite the institution's support for the proposal, which had to pass a strong internal review process.[14]

In 1995, the Florida legislature limited all baccalaureate degree programs to 120 credit hours (the bare minimum) with any exceptions requiring approval by the Board of Regents.[15] The same legislation also limited students to taking 115 percent of the credit hours required for their degrees, with a financial penalty for exceeding that limit in the form of a higher fee per credit hour.

A SUNY system trustee upset by a conference he attended conducted by the Women's Studies Department at the New Paltz campus, publicly calls for the president's resignation.[16]

The Board of Visitors at George Mason University ignore a faculty senate decision to raise the number of credits that students receive for eight military-science courses from 6 to 10 credits and instead act to award 12 to 18 credits.[17] In taking this action, the board questions whether the faculty senate, run by tenured professors, really represents a faculty that has a substantial number of nontenured and part-time faculty.

A member of the board of James Madison University states that he is planning to go course by course in the college manual "to see what I don't like and what I think doesn't have a place on our campus."[18]

A Florida regent calls for state universities to achieve higher targets for increased number of baccalaureate degrees, noting that he would face negative consequences in his financial business if he did not increase the number of customers.[19]

Faculty members at Indiana University decry their Board of Trustees for using an outside consultant to evaluate the university president, a process that gave them less of a voice than expected under the principle of shared governance.[20] The trustees indicate that the review process was influenced by a new policy by the Association of Governing Boards of Universities and Colleges advocating a greater centralization of authority at universities in their governing boards.

A blue-ribbon panel of the Association of Governing Boards recommends that university presidents be recruited from outside the academy, and suggests business, government, the professions, the nonprofit sector, and the military as sources of presidential talent.[21] The same panel criticizes the concept of shared governance, stating that while the concept is good in theory, in practice it leads to institutional inertia.

The Chronicle of Higher Education reports that the supposed corporate know-how of college of business deans is landing them a growing number of university presidencies.[22]

University of Pennsylvania trustees publicly reprimand a president and provost for failing to sanction minority students who had confiscated a run of the student newspaper.[23]

More generally, legislatures and boards of regents all over the country are challenging the concept of tenure and requiring post-tenure review systems, instituting a variety of faculty performance measures and institutional "report cards" in the name of accountability, and mandating or considering the use of competency tests to judge the quality and educational achievement of students and institutions alike.

Other more individual, but no less revealing, instances are the takeover or attempted takeover of university presidencies by board chairs and the appointment of politicians without academic background to the presidencies of major universities.

Such actions bespeak a mistrust of universities and their traditional modes of operation and a growing impatience with the academic culture, if not an outright hostility to it. There is a strong reform-minded tone to many of these episodes with boards seeking to change the way in which universities operate even in core educational and curricular matters. These board actions also exhibit a strong unilateral character; internal governance views are overridden or simply ignored in favor of actions deemed desirable solely from the board's views and values. Perhaps what is most disturbing, is that the "my way or the highway" management style seen in a number of these episodes cannot help but make presidents and other higher-education administrators increasingly cognizant that pleasing their boards is their first obligation, with faculty interests becoming a more distant concern.

These actions illustrate that governing boards are now clearly inclined to use the legal authority they have always had but have not heretofore directly exercised. And for public universities, not only governing boards have become more aggressive but legislatures as well. In the process, legislators and trustees of both public and private institutions are acting out their business and political orientations, expecting universities to be more responsive to the political direction of the state and treating universities as entities that should operate like a business with lower cost, higher degree productivity, and greater responsiveness to "customer" preferences as top priorities. While an antiacademic intrusiveness by boards is less likely in elite institutions with well-established academic traditions, the same pressures are nevertheless at work in those institutions as well.

In summary, on top of a governance structure that by its legal and physical composition is weighted toward a business-political orientation there is now a marked shift toward more active expression of those viewpoints in the conduct of university affairs. Correspondingly, there has been a reduction in the influence of internal governance structures, particularly among those who speak most directly for the core academic values and interests of the university. At the same time, university faculty have become increasingly withdrawn from university administration, even from their own shared governance forums. Many faculty are skeptical that their interests are vigorously presented and defended by the university administration, which they regard as beholden to, if not in league with, external governance powers. Suspicious of the intentions and actions of legislators, trustees, and administrators alike, and aware of their weak position in governance, the faculty have adopted a passive and detached posture, believing they can exert little control over events and preferring to believe that "this too will pass" and that the long-standing practices and values of the academy will prevail. But the events we have reviewed indicate that that could be a serious mistake on the part of the faculty. Similarly, though, it would be a serious mistake if external governing bodies assume that, given their power and a sense of the rightness of their intentions, they can simply ignore the faculty in their zeal to reform higher education.

It is important that boards, legislators, the public and, yes, even university administrators understand that there is no getting around the fact that faculty *are* the engines of the university. They, and no one else, do the real work of the university–they do the teaching, accomplish and certify the education of its students, conduct its research, carry out its public service functions, create and present the artistic productions that enrich the community, devise technologies that stimulate the economy, and in the long run establish the academic reputation of the university. And it is the faculty, and no one else, who generate the university's income–the tuition income generated by their teaching and the research income from the competitive grants and contracts they receive. The tax dollars received by state universities are determined by a formula that heavily weighs the cost of educating each student, and the families and students who pay those dollars turn to the university for one main reason–for the knowledge and skills imparted by the faculty. Even private contributions to the university are largely traceable to faculty efforts, since apart from athletics it is the academic and research programs of the university that attract most private donations. In this day of preoccupation with titles, image, and simplifications, we are prone to identify universities and their fortunes with their publicized leaders. But at the end of the day, leaders come and go and it is the faculty who constitute the continuity, substance, and quality of the enterprise.

Therefore while governing bodies certainly have the authority to impose fundamental changes in the academy, it would be unwise to ignore the views of those who are so necessary to constructive accomplishment of such changes. Although it is hard to imagine faculty whether in public or private universities ever refusing to abide by the decisions of duly constituted authority, governing bodies should also not forget that faculty as a group are probably the most creative occupational group in the world.

Universities and their governance bodies have always been from different worlds with little by way of mutual understanding between them. As we have argued, those worlds differ very fundamentally in organizational philosophies, values, priorities, and objectives. Historically, however, these differences have not been of great consequence as governance bodies took a hands-off but supportive attitude allowing academic priorities and values to prevail in a time of simpler though developing institutions. But universities today, especially research universities, have become complex multidimensional enterprises deeply entwined with society's needs and objectives, particularly as the enabling educational pathway for an ever-increasing percentage of the population and as a source of cutting-edge science and technology vital to innovation and to a robust economy. Governance bodies now have a larger interest in the role and responsiveness of universities. Unfortunately, as they take that larger interest there is no reason to believe that they bring any improved understanding of the special nature of the academic and research base of universities—what we have called the "life force" of the university—because over the years there has been so little meaningful communication between governing bodies and that base. This is so simply because there has never been an effective platform for the core academic voice in board-university communications. Even in the internal governance structure, there is decreasing opportunity and means for input from the academic leadership, as we have seen. Therefore as governing bodies exercise their power to change and redirect universities, they are likely to do so through the framework of the business and political principles with which they are familiar. Any changes so inspired are likely to be almost reflexively resisted by the faculty as inimical to the health of the academy, a reaction that in turn will be seen by boards as confirming evidence of faculty defensiveness and resistance to needed change. At the same time, a faculty that has ignored the pressures and imperatives faced by governing bodies and that has largely withdrawn form the administrative dialogue is unlikely to contribute to the resolution of this dilemma. This is clearly an undesirable and dangerous situation. As long as this communication gulf persists, there is real risk, whatever good intentions there may be, of killing the goose that has laid many golden eggs for American society.

Before we consider how best to address this situation, it will be helpful to examine in greater depth the peculiarly distant stance that faculty have taken concerning this serious problem that has such important consequences for them, because if the problem is to be solved, that stance must change.

Chapter 4

The Faculty—An Isolated Culture

❦

What we have termed the *distant stance of the faculty* stems partly from factors inherent in the nature of the academic world and partly from the steady erosion of meaningful communication between faculty and governing authorities. A review of these conditions will be helpful in the development of a more constructive approach.

Faculty have always tended to live in a world of their own, a world that has always had a strong quality of self-definition and self-sufficiency. It is a world that to a large degree defines its own content and its own criteria for entry, accomplishment, and status. The knowledge that is held and taught in the university is, after all, knowledge that has been defined over time primarily through the cumulative learning and scholarship of faculty in the fields that compose the academy, defined through the rules of logic and evidence. While governance authorities may determine the broad goals of the institution, who else but the faculty really could or should determine what specifically is to be taught within those general objectives? Who else could or should define what constitutes the appropriate base of general education within the institution? Appropriate undergraduate and graduate education within the various fields of study? Certainly not administrators, boards, or the public. And contrary to a prevailing view that universities should be customer oriented, certainly not the students. Whether the faculty are paying enough attention to the curriculum and whether the curriculum is meeting the expectations of society may well be questioned, but what is not questioned is that we must look to the faculty to define the curriculum.

It is also the faculty who impart the training and certify the qualifications generally required for undertaking teaching and research at the university level, and it is the faculty who are still the most determinant actors in the selection of new faculty. And it is chiefly the faculty who through the process of peer review assess the quality of each faculty member's teaching and the significance of their scholarly accomplishments. So it is not unreasonable that faculty might feel that their efforts perforce define the substance and quality of the university enterprise.

The structure of the university contributes further to a sense of faculty independence and sufficiency. Faculty live and work within academic departments, the key operating units of the university responsible for delivering the teaching, research, and public service programs of each discipline or field of knowledge. The day-to-day duties of the faculty, whereby those programs are accomplished, are determined within their academic departments rather than by the administration as such. While the dean and the provost may provide broad guidelines for faculty assignments consistent with college-and university-wide objectives, the specific duties of all faculty members are assigned by department chairs. The department chair is appointed from, and continues to reside with, his or her department faculty, in contrast to the deans and the provost who are officed elsewhere as part of the central administration. Consequently, the chair will be the only person in any supervisory capacity with the direct knowledge of individual faculty strengths required to deploy their skills to their best advantage in meeting the programmatic objectives of the department. These assignments are usually determined in a consultative and collegial manner. Faculty can expect to be responsible for some segment of the curriculum appropriate to their expertise, that is, a relatively stable set of courses that are "theirs," to contribute to the research objectives of the department, and to participate in some university and public service as appropriate to the department's mission. Consistent with the principle of academic freedom, no one tells the faculty member what to teach within her assigned courses and each faculty member decides the direction and extent of her own research activities. Given the broad extent of individual or departmental determination of the faculty member's day-to-day activities, it is not surprising then that faculty often feel that they are self-or collegially directed in carrying out the essential work of the university and that they do that work with minimal involvement or even oversight from the central university administration, much less from external governing bodies. The central administration exists at considerable remove from these activities and is likely to be seen by the faculty, if attended to at all, as waving its arms in directive and exhortative conductor fashion, but unlike the symphony conductor, without expert knowledge of the production.

Another factor contributing to the independent and self-defining qualities of the faculty relates to the general elevation of research in the university mission. The significance of a faculty member's research is defined by its impact on existing knowledge in the field. Does the work advance understanding in the field and does it do so in a clear and conclusive manner? Does the work deal with significant issues in the field? Is the work an incremental contribution to existing knowledge and theory or is it truly groundbreaking in conception and substance? Such questions can only be answered convincingly by experts in the discipline, and hence the frame of reference for establishing the significance of a faculty member's research becomes the discipline at large rather than any authority in the institution itself.

Recognition within the discipline requires success in the arenas of scholarly publication and grant competition, the reviewers for which are drawn from the leading scholars in the field, and faculty are not likely to achieve such success unless they are closely following and deeply involved in the flow of research issues in their disciplines. Research grants from the National Institutes of Health and the National Science Foundation, which are highly competitive and generally regarded as a premier form of scholarly recognition in the sciences, are designated to individual investigators, thus making them unbeholden to department heads, deans, and university politics in the conduct of the research. The university really has no choice but to grant independence to grant-supported investigators in order to compete for faculty grantees and for the considerable income from the indirect cost returns attached to their grants.

As the faculty member's research reputation in the field grows, he or she becomes eligible for the rewards that accompany research distinction. Some of these rewards arise externally, for example, invited papers, editorships, professional offices, job offers, and consultancies. Other research rewards are mediated by the university, for example, advantage in decisions affecting promotion and tenure, salary increments, and research support. But eligibility for all of these is determined by the faculty member's reputation in the field, further adding to the primacy of the discipline in the faculty member's life. Indeed, a strong research standing in their discipline is one of the few effective levers a faculty member has in seeking improved salary or other benefits within his or her home institution.

Since the faculty member's disciplinary standing is such an important factor in determining not only their prestige as scholars but their worth as faculty as well, it is not surprising that many of them may identify more strongly with their discipline than with their home institution. Many higher-education observers have noted the strong disciplinary affinity of faculty, usually in somewhat critical terms. For example, the sociologists Christopher Jencks and David Riesman state that "large numbers of Ph.D.'s regard themselves as independent professionals like doctors or lawyers, responsible primarily to themselves and their colleagues rather than their employers, and committed to the advancement of knowledge rather than of any particular institution."[1] Theodore Caplow and Reece J. McGee note that

> Today, a scholar's orientation to his institution is apt to disorient him to his discipline and to affect his professional prestige unfavorably. Conversely, an orientation to his discipline will disorient him to his institution, which he will regard as a temporary shelter where he can pursue his career as a member of the discipline.[2]

In any case, there is little question that the elevation of research in universities and the strong disciplinary orientation it has fostered has lessened the identification of faculty with their home institutions and the governance authorities of those institutions, a condition, it might be added, that administrations have generally willingly aided and abetted in the interest of securing the grant income and institutional prestige associated with research prominence.

The fact that faculty see themselves as participating in the timeless and continuing construction of their field of knowledge, have the freedom to pursue their teaching and research in the manner and directions they choose consistent with the standards of their professional disciplines, and have such strong departmental and disciplinary frames of reference, all combine to create the impression that they are self-employed and have no real boss—and combine to create as well in governing authorities the generally recognized feeling that administering faculty is like herding cats. But there are still additional factors that contribute to faculty distance from the concerns of central governance bodies. Probably the most important of these is simply the preoccupation of faculty with their teaching and research, which leaves little time for administrative matters. Neither teaching nor research can be done effectively without extended effort and both tasks have an open-ended quality that invites continued improvement. Both are very public acts open to scrutiny from students, institutional colleagues, and professional peers, a circumstance that does not encourage a casual approach. Contrary to an often expressed public view, most faculty take their teaching responsibilities, as well as their research agenda, very seriously. The distribution of faculty effort to undergraduate versus graduate teaching is certainly open to question, but the data indicate that faculty are strongly dedicated to their overall teaching and research responsibilities. A 1996 survey of approximately 34,000 full-time faculty across 392 colleges and universities found that teaching was cited by 99% of the respondents as being an essential professional goal and was the most frequently cited from among six listed goals.[3] Engagement in research ranked second in essentiality at 55%. The same survey found time pressures to be the most frequently cited source of stress for faculty (86%).

Faculty are also generally adverse to the kinds of matters with which higher administration must deal, matters such as public relations, institutional image, political environment, the nuts and bolts of business relations, and budgets and the bottom line. These are seen as necessary but distasteful tasks distinctly secondary in value to the life of the mind. Just as Henry James spoke of a mind too fine to be violated by an idea, there is a sense in which faculty can be said to be too involved in the world of theory and thought to be violated by the world of practical affairs. Involvement in administrative issues and tasks not only runs counter to the theoretical and intellectual bent of the faculty but could only detract from their autonomy and ability to pursue their scholarly and teaching interests, which faculty consistently cite as the most important factors in their decision to pursue an academic career.

Furthermore, the temperament and traits that incline one toward an academic career are often inconsistent with those associated with pursuit of an administrative career. For example, higher administrators typically have strong interest in organizational issues, financial planning, relations with external constituencies, influencing the political structure, organizational control, and, yes, the power and substantially enhanced financial status that accompanies administrative positions. All of these matters are found to be of relatively low interest in repeated surveys of faculty motivation and interests. For example, in the large-scale faculty survey just referenced, influencing the political structure, being well-off financially, and participating in administrative work were among the lowest-ranking objectives of faculty.

An important related factor is the perception of many faculty that higher administrators have a different vision of the university, one that is less sympathetic, if not inimical, to academic values. A good illustration of this "different worlds" perception occurred in the author's life when, following twenty years as a full-time faculty member he accepted a *half-time* position in the university provost office to assist in academic budgets and planning. The half-time nature of the position meant that I would be continuing to teach several courses and to carry on my research activities. Nevertheless, upon encountering a longtime faculty colleague and friend the day following this appointment, I was greeted, in the most equable but serious manner, with, "I see you have gone over!" The clear implication was that I had gone to another and different side and that even as only a part-time member of the administration, I was now in a suspect category.

While all of the factors we have discussed probably contribute to this "we versus they" perception on the part of the faculty, it also stems from actions over the years by administrators and governing bodies which, whatever the pressures or good intentions may have been, run counter to academic values in the eyes of the faculty. An example of such action, but one quite representative of the differing perspectives, is the so-called 12-hour law formulated by the Florida legislature and administered through the Board of Regents of one of the nation's largest public university systems. The 12-hour law sought to set and control the amount of time faculty must spend discharging their responsibilities, with particular reference to teaching. Specifically, the rule required all faculty to teach a minimum of 12 classroom contact hours per week, that is, hours actually spent in a classroom instructing students, or to invest hours equivalent to that instructional effort on other mission activities such as research or service. Since university courses ordinarily meet 3 hours each week, the law assumes that teaching four courses a term would comprise the requisite faculty workload. Furthermore, aware that preparation time is required for each class taught, the law's formulators assumed 2 hours of preparation for each classroom contact hour plus 1 additional hour of related activity such as advising for each course. Thus the minimum requirement of "12 contact hours or the equivalent" presumes a clock-hour assignment of 40 hours per week, that is, a 40-hour workweek. The accountability mechanism was a required faculty report in which the "12 contact hours or equivalent" must be equal to a 100 percent effort, with the constituent activities expressed as percentages of that hourly defined requirement.

However clear and rational this law might appear to the governing authorities, it plays out quite differently at the level of implementation and actual academic activity. As noted, a typical course has 3 classroom contact hours per week and thus a faculty member who taught simultaneously four such courses would complete the work requirement of the rule and would be led to submit a report showing teaching as 100 percent of his or her effort and workweek. The problem of course is that while full-time faculty effort as a whole is indeed primarily devoted to teaching, most faculty also spend a good deal of time in research and/or service activities and put in considerably longer workweeks than assumed by the rule. National surveys have consistently found that full-time faculty across all types of institutions tend to work inordinately long hours, *averaging* on the order of 50 to 55 hours per week.[4] The hour-based nature of the rule thus has the effect of distorting the reporting of faculty activities in an arbitrary and quite damaging fashion. For example, a faculty member who teaches, say, three courses concurrently, a 75 percent effort involving a presumed 30-clock hours in terms of the rule, is virtually forced to underreport the actual effort he or she has spent on research and service. This would be so because the latter activities would in all probability considerably exceed a 25 percent effort as defined by the rule, that is, would likely exceed 10-clock hours per week. Consequently, that faculty member would be likely to underrepresent the effort actually spent on instruction in order to more accurately reflect the actual time spent on research or service, perhaps even underreporting those as well in order to stay within the prescribed limits of the report. The only other choice that that faculty member would have would be to underreport the time spent on research or service. The problem is exacerbated by a collective bargaining rule in the system that prohibits evaluation of any nonassigned faculty activities. Since the 12-hour rule effectively compresses, indeed curtails, assignment and reporting of faculty activities, actual achievements in significant areas may not be counted in merit determinations.

Thus while the law was intended to make faculty more accountable, it works instead to distort reports of what faculty actually do, to limit proper recognition of the full range of faculty activities and contributions, and to undermine performance and evaluation of basic faculty responsibilities. Worse, it encourages a false and pernicious perception of faculty as nonprofessionals who apportion effort across discrete teaching, research, and service activities to meet a rather minimal workweek requirement. In this way, the rule works to undermine the professional qualities that should be most expected and prized in the faculty—intrinsic motivation, creativity, love of learning in all of its expressions, and full dedication to the welfare of students. In addition, from the faculty perspective, it amounts to another centrally required report that does not appear to make much sense.

To take another example of questionable governing authority action, a number of boards and legislatures have recently formulated programs designed to increase faculty teaching. One such "teaching incentive" program provided a five-thousand-dollar increase in base salary to qualifying faculty.[5] While a purported aim of the program was to recognize excellence in teaching, eligibility for the program required the faculty member to be heavily involved in undergraduate teaching. Teaching undergraduate courses with low enrollment did not assist eligibility nor did the teaching of graduate courses. Following externally mandated guidelines, eligible faculty prepared extensive portfolios descriptive of their teaching activities, philosophy, and accomplishments that were then reviewed for "teaching excellence" by committees composed of institutional faculty colleagues. Given the limited funding made available for the program, which was allotted in proportion to the number of faculty in the various colleges, competition for the incentive awards was intense, pitting fellow faculty against one another and subjecting colleague faculty reviewers to great pressure. The program was conducted annually and recipients of a teaching incentive award could renew eligibility for the award after three years.

The program was generally viewed as a great success by the governing bodies concerned, but again the view from the faculty trenches was quite different. Of course, those faculty who received teaching incentive awards were pleased, although many lamented the arbitrariness of the qualifying criteria. But many more faculty were angry and discouraged, and the morale of the academic sector of the institution suffered considerably. Those engaged primarily in graduate teaching and thus ineligible for the program felt devalued and cheated. They know that graduate teaching is an important form of teaching, particularly in research universities, and given the strong mentoring component of graduate instruction, a highly demanding form of instruction as well. To be simply omitted from consideration was not only discriminatory, but belies the objective of determining individual teaching excellence. There was similar reaction among faculty with low-enrollment undergraduate courses, since such courses often play a critical role in the curriculum.

The mandated award process strongly rewarded portfolio preparation, and applicants were encouraged to invest great effort in preparing descriptions of their teaching philosophy and accomplishments along with supporting evaluations, syllabi, demonstrations, and other such materials, often filling several boxes. The faculty committees who struggled with this material in an effort to rank their colleagues found that task extremely difficult, and as could be expected given the selectivity that goes into faculty appointments, often found only marginal differences among the voluminous files. Among rejected applicants there grew an unhealthy suspicion of somewhat arbitrary and invidious comparisons that led to the filing of numerous formal grievances requiring extended hearing. These developments in turn made faculty reluctant to become involved in the review process, and it was difficult for deans to find faculty willing to participate. A telling statistic in this regard is that faculty applicants in the English Department typically received most of the teaching incentive awards, popularly attributed to their professional skill at the writing and preparation of such material. Since the faculty could apply for these awards annually and since a sizable number of faculty were prohibited from applying for the reasons noted earlier, there developed a kind of "get in line" mentality about the award whereby eligible faculty who did not get it one year would likely get it the next. In fact, over a three-year period almost 50 percent of the faculty received the award, an outcome that strains the conception of rewarding excellence in teaching and that increased faculty cynicism about the process.

By making teaching more of a means to an end rather than an end in itself, the program also appealed to the extrinsic motivations of faculty, and some faculty sought to withdraw from graduate teaching and small undergraduate classes. With renewal of eligibility following an initial award, a sizable number of faculty received a second award in their fourth year. This meant that some faculty members primarily involved in undergraduate teaching achieved a ten-thousand-dollar increase in base salary for which those more involved in graduate teaching, and therefore in research as well, could not even be considered. For some faculty, such an increase might amount to a 25 percent increase in salary. In addition to the gross unfairness of such differential treatment of faculty colleagues, this outcome could only serve to drive a wedge between the graduate and undergraduate functions of the university where, if anything, a greater interaction is desired.

Finally, there is the dubious wisdom of offering faculty, who are generally hired primarily to teach, an incentive to do what they were hired to do! A question that was patent to the faculty but not apparently to the governing authorities.

Examples like these indicate that governing authorities fail to appreciate some fairly basic features of the academic world such as the professionalism of faculty, the extent of the faculty work effort, the ways in which the faculty must distribute their activities to accomplish the university mission, the equally valuable contribution that different kinds of teaching make to education, and the intertwined nature of research and graduate education. Furthermore, they indicate a piecemeal conception of the academic workplace that fails to appreciate that teaching, research, and service are at base integral and mutually reinforcing functions. Actions like the twelve-hour law and the teaching incentive program, even though undertaken with valid concerns and reasonable objectives, make many faculty skeptical about the understanding that governing authorities have of the nature of the academic enterprise and therefore mistrustful of their intentions.

It is important to note that there is no reason to believe that the governing bodies involved in the twelve-hour rule and teaching incentive program had any knowledge of the ensuing realities of implementation or the negative faculty reactions. There is no record of expressed presidential concern about these programs, if indeed there was full awareness at that level. Nor is there any reason to doubt that the governing bodies firmly believed that they had in fact increased faculty accountability and faculty teaching. The reality, however, was that the twelve-hour rule worked to underreport and distort accounts of faculty activity, while the teaching incentive program likely had the effect of simply redistributing teaching efforts among a portion of the faculty at a cost of considerable grief, rather than increasing the overall teaching efforts of the faculty. One has the impression of two different worlds pursuing different intentions, experiencing different consequences, and drawing different conclusions.

While faculty are certainly aware that such differences in perspective exist, the disconnect between faculty and management is much greater than most faculty realize, even within the confines of their own institutions. Indeed, in-depth experience in both spheres—the academic world and the administrative world—may be required in order to appreciate the degree to which faculty have become a negligible factor in the key decision making within their universities. No one set out to create this state of affairs, but it is nonetheless widespread, and perhaps under present conditions, inevitable. The situation has been well described by Richard Breslin who became fully conscious of the degree of separation only after he returned to the faculty after extended high-level administrative service:

Although I realized that I was moving away from issues of concern to academics, I wasn't truly conscious of the distance that I'd traveled until I went full circle and returned to the faculty. Now that I'm back in the ranks as a professor, I'm struck by the wide gulf between faculty members and administrators. In fact, from my new vantage point in the trenches, I can see how both sides suffer from restricted fields of vision.

Presidents and other senior staff members assume that the faculty has little comprehension of the world in which the administration needs to function in order to accomplish institutional goals. In many ways, that assumption is correct. Professors have become so specialized, so focused on their individual disciplines, that they no longer see the institution as a whole.

I realize now, however, that administrators can have equally narrow perspectives. As I served in various senior administrative posts, including the presidency of two universities, I thought I had an intimate knowledge of the workings of higher-education institutions and was in touch with the big picture. However, the more I focused on the "critical issues" of administration, the more removed I became from the day-to-day activities of the typical faculty member. Inexorably, like most administrators, I didn't focus enough on what is known in higher education as "the business of the business." One does not set out to do this. As administrators, we say that the faculty is our most important constituency and that teaching and research are central to our mission. But as higher education has become more complex, and the bureaucracy has burgeoned, teaching has increasingly lost priority in the hurly-burly of the daily work world. Administrators are so busy planning ahead, seeking the resources that enable our collective dreams to come true, that money is now perceived as the root of all excellence. With our focus on the bottom line, we've increasingly regarded the faculty as an obstacle to our objectives.

Thus, a growing number of decisions are made by senior staff members who see nothing wrong with their control of finances and information. Not only do they "own" the data, but they are comfortable making pronouncements about those decisions as if no one else had been involved in the process. The faculty plays a diminishing role—if it plays one at all.

Although many of us in the faculty see the problems in that approach, as a senior administrator, I viewed it as business as usual. Other presidents and administrators whom I knew also accepted that state of affairs without question. The more time we spend in our own ivory tower, and the higher we went, the more we made decisions in isolation, guided principally by the market forces that were driving our institutions.[6]

The market-force-driven decisions made in isolation that are probably of greatest consequence to the faculty are those affecting resource allocation, not resource allocation at the level of academic departments, generally a matter of allocating chronically small sums among a host of competing needs, but resource allocation at the institution-wide level. It is the latter decisions that drive what will be available for the needs of the departments, but they are invariably made in isolation from the faculty. For example, institutions with flexible endowment funds may return all of their investment income to those funds or allocate some portion to the operating needs of the institution. This is a judgment call in which investment to meet anticipated future needs must be considered against investment to meet current needs, and it is often made without consultation with the academic administration, much less with the faculty. Yet given a sizable endowment, a slight turn of the operating budget spigot—a percent or two difference in return to operating budget—could make an enormous difference in the ongoing departmental teaching and research programs. To take another example, many institutions are now investing millions of dollars in computing technologies and support staff for administrative functions, particularly in the areas of finance, accounting, admissions, and registration, often borrowing heavily against the future to enable immediate purchase. Clearly, the more outlay for administrative technology, the less available for direct academic uses. A perceived need to keep up with the competition is the primary driver of these investments, which again are made by the administration with minimal if any input from the faculty. Or as a final example, consider decisions regarding institutional enrollment and admissions. Enrollment is a major source of revenue for all universities as well as a significant cost factor. Given the finite resources available for support of higher education, it is always tempting for university-governing authorities to increase enrollment income when market opportunities are favorable, while attempting to control or minimize the attendant costs, for example, by the addition of part-time rather than regular faculty. Such an institutional strategy can make a major difference in both the institution's operating budget and the quality and climate of its educational programs. But while the faculty are primary recipients of the impact of such a strategy, they have little involvement in the annual determination of admissions targets. Rather, these are set by the admissions specialists in conjunction with the higher administration, and the targets are likely to be based on financial factors, market opportunities, and the desire to keep up with the competition rather than on consideration of the capacity of the academic programs and the impact on their quality.

The point here is not to question that the final decision in such matters is properly a responsibility of the senior administration, but that the faculty should be a meaningful part of the decision process. Issues of the type we have illustrated pose complex judgment calls on which no one has perfect wisdom, and it is therefore important to have the benefit of all pertinent perspectives. But not only are the faculty increasingly detached from the administration, by their own and the administration's doing, but they are basically "out of it" in terms of having any real understanding of how administrators approach decisions of this nature and the terms of the dialogue, which as Breslin noted, tend to be those of the market. In the absence of continuous strong representation of the academic perspective, institutional strategies become treated as essentially business strategies. But while it would be a serious mistake to ever ignore the business aspects of universities, it would be fatal to treat universities like a business.

The disengagement of faculty from their institutions and institutional governance authorities has taken place over a period that has seen a tremendous increase in demand for university services. Part of this increase stems from a growing population with higher expectations for educational attainment, straining the capacities of institutions designed for a smaller and more select clientele. This increase also stems from the very success of the social contract that made universities the home of science and led to increased public awareness of the vital connections between university research, technology, and economic development. More than ever before universities are being asked to tune their programs to the social and economic interests of their communities. Yet as these various pressures impact the university, challenging and changing traditional ways of doing business, we have the spectacle of a faculty largely preoccupied with their professional interests and detached from the administrative and governance decision-making through which these external forces must be filtered. It is this situation–the self-centeredness and passivity of the faculty in the face of strong and changing demands on the universities–that underlies and fuels so much of what is awry with higher education and the frequent harsh criticisms of university faculty. Universities are facing difficult dilemmas that are unlikely to be constructively resolved unless faculty take greater responsibility for the welfare of their institutions and contribute what they uniquely can contribute. This is not to say either that the faculty are responsible for what is amiss with higher education or that the changing demands and expectations should be accommodated, but that the latter should be squarely faced with full engagement of the faculty.

Consider this statement in relation to several critical problems facing universities today. One major problem, which has probably drawn the most commentary from critics of higher education, is university admissions. It is no secret that American colleges and universities are accepting almost all applicants with a high school diploma. Fewer than 10% of America's more than 3,500 colleges and universities have truly selective admission policies; the remainder are essentially open admission institutions.[7] Some 63% of high school graduates in America now go on to at least begin some form of further education, up from a World War II base of less than 20%.[8] In terms of numbers, for four-year institutions alone this represents an increase from 2.4 million students in 1946 to 9 million full-time students today plus several million more part-time students. This change has resulted in a large number of poorly prepared students in the universities. Eighty-one percent of four-year public institutions and 63% of four-year private institutions now offer remedial courses in reading, writing, or mathematics for students who were inadequately prepared by their high schools.[9] Over all types of institutions 30% of entering freshmen enroll in such courses. Even elite institutions that claim they do not offer remedial courses or accept underprepared students typically provide help in different guises. Harvard and Yale, for example, offer peer tutors and a writing center to assist some beginning students, and other major institutions offer special precollege summer programs that give selected students a head start on college work. In short, many high school graduates are really not prepared for college. Albert Shanker, the former president of the American Federation of Teachers, noted that more than half of the students going on to college in America would not qualify for admission to colleges in Europe or Japan.[10]

In order to reduce student failure and drop out rates, many institutions have eased requirements within entry courses that students found too difficult, such as beginning mathematics, chemistry, and English composition. Grade inflation has risen to notorious levels even in elite universities.[11] Harvey Mansfield, professor of government at Harvard and a strong critic of Harvard's grade distribution in which half of all undergraduate grades are now A's or A-'s, drew national attention recently by giving his students two grades, one that conforms to the university's distribution and one that gives his evaluation of how well each student *really* did. But even with relaxed requirements and grades, degree completion and six-year graduation rates remain dismally low in many four-year institutions, the latter averaging only about 50% nationally. The burgeoning numbers of students has made more plain what has probably always been true, namely, that most students seek a college degree as a means to improved economic prospects rather than out of a desire for knowledge per se. This utilitarian attitude has been reflected in a notable decrease in course and major selections within the arts and sciences and a corresponding increase in business and vocationally related disciplines and majors. Requirements for the major have also been relaxed in areas generally regarded as difficult for many students, such as the physical and biological sciences, and the number and range of courses required for the college degree have also been relaxed. In addition, students are demanding–and getting–courses that more directly reflect what they desire to learn about rather than courses selected on criteria of intellectual growth and preparation for the demands of life. Finally, the loose admissions policies of our universities contribute in no small measure to our serious problems in secondary education; if preparation for a higher and more demanding level of learning is not required for college entrance, why bother?

How has this dismal situation developed? Contributing factors include increased demand for higher education as the gateway to participation in a knowledge-based economy, direct pressures from legislatures and the public for more open policies, increased availability of paying students generously assisted by federal and state financial aid policies, and the institutions' own eagerness for enrollment growth and the income it brings. But what of setting and maintaining educational standards required for college work? Who is responsible for these actions? It's definitely not the admissions officers who simply follow guidelines set by the institution. Of course, the president and higher administration have responsibility, but their actions are likely to be driven by political, financial, and market forces. If any group in the university has responsibility for the integrity of the educational process it is surely the faculty, but recall that the faculty have no executive authority and cannot directly formulate institutional policy.

Faculty have certainly been aware that their classes are becoming populated by large numbers of ill-prepared students, and generally will bemoan that condition at the slightest opportunity. The 1995 national survey of full-time faculty cited earlier found that only 24 percent of the 34,000 professors canvassed felt their students were well prepared academically, a number in striking agreement with surveys of employers regarding their view of the capabilities of high school graduates. Nevertheless the faculty have taken no programmatic action nor made any concerted protest of this appalling situation. Of course, faculty can maintain standards within the courses they teach, and those who do so in required "difficult" introductory courses routinely fail huge numbers of students every year. But is it right to admit unprepared students and then force them to almost certainly undergo damaging failure experiences that force them to drop out of college?

While faculty, lacking executive authority, cannot be held formally responsible for institutional admissions policies, they are certainly the group most knowledgeable about the standards required for college work and the educational effects of the failure to maintain those standards. Within the university, then, the faculty is the body that should be most expected to vigorously champion sound admissions policies. But, consistent with their detachment from institutional governance, they have failed to do so, and this is very serious.

The admissions problem, like other problems facing universities, does not have a simple right or wrong answer. There are legitimate forces pressing for greater access to higher education. In the interest of promoting a plural and economically competitive society, a number of states have provided free or greatly reduced tuition to all graduating high school students whose grade point averages exceed a relatively modest level. What university is likely to turn down applicants upon whom funds have been bestowed with a promise of access? If a legislature, interested in promoting the economic competitiveness of the state, calls for greater production of baccalaureate degrees and specifically funds universities to produce them, the universities have little choice but to comply. But at some point someone must vigorously question the value of a thousand more baccalaureates if they are not intellectually capable baccalaureates. Where is the line to be drawn on quantity versus quality of graduates? This is a judgment call on which reasonable people can take different positions. But this debate is unlikely to arise in the legislature, and presidents and their administrations will not force it. The initiation of this debate is properly a faculty responsibility, and they have shirked it shamelessly.

The increasingly heavy reliance of universities on part-time faculty is another serious problem with similar overtones. A 1993 survey by the National Center for Education Statistics (NCES) found that 42% of the instructional staff in colleges and universities in the fall of 1992 worked part-time, up from 33% in the 1987 NCES survey report and nearly double the percent (22) in 1970.[12] More recently, a survey of humanities and social science disciplines by a coalition of twenty-five disciplinary associations found that nontenure track instructors (basically, part-time faculty and graduate teaching assistants) make up almost half of the teaching staff in many of those disciplines, and that only 48% of the introductory undergraduate course instructors in those disciplines are full-time tenure-track faculty.[13]

Faced with large numbers of students and limited resources, it makes economic sense for administrators to rely more on part-timers who can handle many more courses at lower cost than full-time faculty and who can be hired or released semester by semester. Critics argue that extensive use of part-time faculty reduces the quality of undergraduate education, where they are chiefly employed, by reducing the stability and continuity of the educational environment and the instructor's availability to students. While many part-timers are excellent teachers, most will have divided loyalties in the workplace and it seems inevitable that their commitment to the institution's educational programs, students, and objectives will be less than that of full-time faculty. Whatever their merits, the increasing reliance on part-time faculty is transforming the academic workplace with little heed being paid to the consequences.

Again, full-time professors have done little beside watch and wring their hands as this change has taken place. Furthermore, full-time professors, particularly within research universities, are often reluctant to teach labor-intensive lower-division classes, and therefore are often not unwilling to have those duties handled by part-time faculty and graduate students. The part-time faculty situation also interacts with another significant problem, namely, the oversupply of frustrated Ph.D.'s unable to find full-time faculty positions, thereby providing a continuing supply of low-cost part-time labor for the universities.

In the absence of careful examination of the academic consequences of extensive reliance on part-time faculty, it seems certain that institutions will continue to make heavy usage of them. University administrators will continue to find the economic benefits of part-time instructors simply too great to forego. A concern for the academic consequences of part-time faculty usage will not come from university governance authorities, much less a demand for their determination. This call must come from the faculty, if it is to come at all. But here, too, the faculty have failed to press the case.

Similar analyses can be made of a number of additional problems commonly held to afflict higher education. These include overemphasis on research at the expense of teaching, resistance to accountability, resistance to change and new technologies, abuse of tenure, "meaningless" research and publications, lightweight courses that pander to student tastes, politicization of the curriculum, overproduction of Ph.D.'s, toleration of poorly performing faculty, student rudeness in the classroom, undue corporate influence on research, and the unseemly priority given to athletics. These and other concerns have been treated in highly critical if somewhat one-sided terms in a number of well-known books the titles of which convey the harsh tone of their judgment on higher education: *The Closing of the American Mind: How Higher Education Has Failed Democracy and Impoverished the Souls of Today's Students; Killing the Spirit: Higher Education in America; Profscam: Professors and the Demise of Higher Education; The Moral Collapse of the University; Inside American Education: The Decline, the Deception, the Dogmas; Illiberal Education: The Politics of Race and Sex on Campus; In the Company of Scholars: The Struggle for the Soul of Higher Education; Up the University; Impostors in the Temple;* and *The Shadow University: The Betrayal of Liberty on America's Campuses.*

Common to many of these and other critical treatments is the view that faculty control is responsible for the ills of higher education, that self-governance has essentially become nongovernance and poor governance.[14] But self-governance without power amounts to little more than the option to ignore the true governance of the institution. In fact faculty do not control their institutions. As we have pointed out, faculty do not have executive authority—the power to determine the policies and practices of the institution. They do not administer the institution. But they do have a voice in the affairs of the institution, and critics of the faculty are right in condemning their failure to give concerned and forceful expression to that voice.

Despite nationally visible bad press, and despite the fact that the behavior of faculty is the focus of most of the concerns expressed, the faculty have remained silent. The failure of the faculty to address these issues, either by way of explanation and defense or by way of suggested reform and resolution, is a serious omission from the national debate. They have the only deeply authentic academic voice and therefore have a special responsibility to their students, their institutions, and the public to either refute the criticisms or acknowledge their validity and work toward change. The need for faculty engagement has been eloquently expressed by William H. Danforth:

> If it was ever true that faculty members' pursuit of individual interests automatically created a great university, it is certainly not so now. Rather, the loosening of institutional ties has become a major risk, for today's successful university requires effective internal operations aimed at agreed-upon goals. Because faculty do the essential work of teaching and research, their participation and leadership are key. Also, faculty must embody and serve as guardians of the values that should permeate the institutional culture, including, at a minimum, freedom of exploration and expressions, commitment to excellence in scholarship and teaching, and tolerance for differences. Promotion of such values requires time, effort, and devotion. . . .
>
> Whether universities will adapt successfully to the present environment will, in my view, depend on whether individual faculty members correctly read the needs of the era and take personal responsibility for the success of their institutions. I can think of nothing more important or rewarding than to help preserve our research universities for the next generations, so that they may continue to represent the highest aspirations of the American people.[15]

Constructive resolution of the many challenges facing universities today must have engagement of the faculty, the constituency with the greatest personal investment in the university—their lives and livelihoods, and the most at stake—their academic professions and professional values. But if the faculty do not become effectively engaged, the governance authorities will address these challenges and act anyway, because they have no other choice. Right now only one side is playing.

Our review of factors underlying the isolation of the faculty made clear not only that faculty disengagement from the governance of their institutions has multiple roots but also that it is a deeply ingrained mode of behavior. If that behavior is to be changed and if faculty are to take greater responsibility for the welfare of their institutions, more will be required than simply exhorting the faculty to become more fully engaged with their institutions and with the governance process. Structural change will be required.

Chapter 5

Shared Governance Revisited

There is an urgent need for faculty to become an effective part of university governance. It is unlikely that this can be accomplished by any existing structure or practice within the university. The faculty senates that represent the formal expression of the principle of shared governance were fine for a simpler age and simpler institutions, an age when teaching and research were virtually the sole functions of the university, when university administrations were weighted toward academic leadership and academic issues, when faculty found their professional fulfillment largely within their own institutions, and when communication was simply a matter of calling a meeting of the faculty. But in today's complex, diffuse, multifaceted institutions, beset by strong business and political pressures, faculty senates do not have the knowledge, time, or representational muscle to be able to contribute in a meaningful or timely way to the driving governance issues. Faculty senates do play and must continue to play a dispositive role in a number of vital academic matters, such as oversight of the curriculum and general education, academic regulations, and scholastic honors and awards. But for the reasons elaborated in chapter 3, the complexity of university-wide governance issues has outstripped the senates' capabilities for effective participation. On substantive matters of university-wide policy and priorities, they have become little more than a vehicle for largely rhetorical expression of academic principles and ideals, or even worse, an administrative means of "officially" communicating to the faculty largely predetermined governance actions.

Governance bodies also appear to be dissatisfied with university senates as a means of representing faculty views on governance issues. The Association of Governing Boards of Universities and Colleges (AGB) has argued that the current environment requires speed in administrative decision making and that the traditional mechanisms of shared governance, that is, essentially, the university senates, have become "dysfunctional" and unable to keep up.[1] As an alternative, the AGB has called for strengthening the power of the presidency and even eschewing use of the term *shared governance*. But to abandon or minimize the principle of shared governance would remove faculty even further from decision making.

In addition to communication with faculty senates, other steps are sometimes taken by governing authorities in the general spirit of shared governance and communication with the faculty. As one such action, university administrations and governing boards sometimes attempt to secure a faculty perspective by inviting individual faculty or small groups of faculty to visit and briefly participate in their administrative councils. For example, it is not uncommon for a university president to periodically invite an individual faculty member to meet with the administrative leadership and to present a brief report on their activities or perhaps on the programs of their department. Similarly, individual faculty (usually faculty "stars") may be invited to make similar show and tell presentations to boards of trustees. While there may be some benefit to such exchanges as gestures of goodwill or as public relations actions, they are virtually worthless, if not actually harmful and misleading, as a means of securing insight into the faculty world or assessing the vitality of the institution's academic and research programs, although it would probably be hard to convince governance bodies of that. Faculty are usually pleased to have such an opportunity, although often are somewhat bewildered as to why they rather than any of the hundreds of their colleagues were invited (generally there was some recent incident that brought them to the attention of the administration). Straining to make some meaningful point in the usual five minutes allowed for speaking, and often misreading the opportunity as an invitation to make the case for additional resources for their unit, the faculty member presents a few highlights and some pressing needs and then departs, vaguely hoping that some change may ensue (it never does). The administrative leadership (apart from the provost) or governing board have a good feeling of having communicated with the faculty and perhaps have the illusion of further understanding the academic enterprise, the scope, complexity, sophistication, nuances, and needs of which cannot of course even begin to be conveyed by such essentially random and anecdotal episodes.

Perhaps one step from such exchanges, but whether up or down is debatable, is the appointment of a faculty assistant to the president. This is an individual plucked from the faculty who serves as a general aide to the president, usually accompanies the president to campus meetings, and often participates in cabinet sessions, presumably to lend a faculty perspective to the discussions. While there is perhaps a political plus for the president in having such a visible link to the faculty, it is a most tenuous one. Such faculty appointees lack the knowledge and experience to meaningfully assist administrative decision making and usually end up functioning primarily as presidential gofers. In any case, they can represent only some very limited aspect of the academic community, and invariably bring their own idiosyncratic views to the discussions when what is needed is a broad and integrative grasp of the academic spectrum.

It is interesting to note that although it has not been uncommon for governing boards to take the still more meaningful action of including one or two students as members of the board of trustees, faculty representation on boards is very rare in comparison to student representation, particularly in public universities. James Duderstadt, past president of the University of Michigan, has recently proposed putting professors on governing boards, noting correctly that "the real governance does not occur in the senate, but in the governance body."[2] Duderstadt is concerned that faculties will turn to unionizing more often in the absence of an effective governance mechanism, and that is a very real concern. While the inclusion of faculty on boards could be a step in the right direction, it is highly unlikely that boards will agree to such action, at least to any substantial degree, as recent actions of boards and the ABG attest. Further, unless faculty populated the board in some real numbers–a situation impossible to imagine and a questionable legal and political action in any case, the appointment of one or two faculty might well have all the shortcomings of the faculty show-and-tell exchanges or the faculty assistant to the president, namely, a token, unrepresentative, and ineffectual presence.

In sum, there are no existing viable mechanisms of shared governance. There is clearly a need for a new approach that will effectively incorporate the faculty perspective into university governance. Just as it has been said that war is too important to be left to the generals, so education and research are too important to be left to the governance bodies. While that may appear to some to be a strained analogy, it is fully apt in the sense that university research and education are so important to society as to merit the broadest possible care and concern. And surely those who actually carry out these functions and have the most direct knowledge of them have an essential contribution to make to their wise management, however reluctant they may be to make it.

Reluctant or not, it is time for the faculty to drop the posture that management of the academic enterprise is someone else's problem and not theirs. What faculty care about most is their day-to-day teaching and research and the environment of support that is provided for those activities. But it is management who largely determines the possible climate of support for teaching and research by virtue of its control of institutional strategies, resource allocation, and public and governmental relations. As university administrators now struggle to shape sound strategic directions that will advance the enterprise, allocate limited resources among many competing needs, and make the case for public and private support, it is vital that those with the deepest understanding and commitment to the best traditions of teaching and research be part of these efforts.

It is also time for the faculty to abandon the naive belief that their overseers should somehow divine the faculty perspective and arrive unaided at a shared understanding of the academic world, and it is also time for faculty to stop complaining when that belief inevitably falls short of expectations. Governance bodies are doubtless no less wise and perceptive than faculty but they are certainly less knowledgeable about academics and less democratic in both spirit and action. Unless the faculty vigorously and directly press their concerns at the highest level, they are likely to remain largely unknown.

It is also time for the faculty to drop the attitude that administrative involvement is somehow a suspect activity of lesser value. The central task now faced by governance bodies and administrations is extraordinarily difficult, complex, and consequential. It is nothing less than how best to adapt universities to the production, dissemination, and application of knowledge on a scale unprecedented in history. Higher education is rapidly becoming universal, continuous research and technological development is becoming indispensable, and public service by universities is becoming a much higher expectation. As a result, universities are being asked to take on an ever-increasing set of tasks and responsibilities. Even just a partial list of these new or expanded responsibilities would include providing increased access for graduating high school students, providing off-campus lifelong learning opportunities for adults, developing more flexible educational programming for nontraditional and part-time students, undertaking more active programs of community outreach and social service, fostering improved understanding of our cultural diversity, developing programs of international education and research, serving as a think tank, undertaking contract research for the government and for the business community, promoting economic development, and developing technology transfer programs.

All of this in addition to carrying on the core residential undergraduate and graduate programs of the institution, where universities are also under pressure to improve the quality and efficiency of instruction. While these many pressures and expectations are eloquent testimony to the centrality of universities in an increasingly knowledge-based world, society's resources nevertheless remain as constrained and contentious as ever. This situation poses a host of management problems for universities that are every bit as intellectually challenging as teaching and research. How these problems are resolved will define the future of higher education and the research universities. Faculty should be willing to play an active role in their wise resolution, and indeed may be indispensable to their wise resolution.

It is also time for faculty to stop ignoring the harsh journalistic attacks on the universities, as if they had no role in their origin and no stake in their effects. Given the scope and sometimes vitriolic nature of these assaults, it is surprising that there have not been more spontaneous reactions from faculty. Perhaps this is because individual faculty may justifiably feel little responsibility for some of these criticisms. Or perhaps faculty who are stung by such faultfinding may feel they have no right or means to speak for faculty as a whole. Or perhaps it is simply easiest to look the other way. But a public primed to conclude the worst about faculty and university education and research is a public primed to interpret faculty silence as acquiescence and agreement. If, as even some strong academics have argued, teaching has slipped, academic rigor has been relaxed, some areas of the curriculum have become politicized or trivialized, and athletics has become too dominating, then it is not unreasonable for the public to assume that such changes would not have come about without faculty complicity and to hold faculty responsible for initiating the necessary reforms. An honest and thoughtful faculty-based response to attacks on the integrity of the academic enterprise is long overdue.

Finally, it is time for faculty to reciprocate more closely in kind the commitment their institutions make to them in the form of tenure. When an institution awards tenure to a faculty member, it commits a lifetime of professional support and full salaried employment in that institution. In financial terms, this is the equivalent of setting up an endowment sufficient to support the faculty member for his or her lifetime, an endowment on the order of several million dollars for the average faculty member of today. The faculty member, however, makes no like reciprocal commitment to the institution and is free to leave any time a more favorable opportunity materializes. Of course, faculty members must earn tenure by meeting high standards of performance in teaching and research, and the concept of tenure can certainly be justified under principles of academic freedom. Nevertheless, from the viewpoint of up-front financial investment, security, and loyalty, the institutional commitment is extraordinarily one-sided. In the highly competitive marketplace for intellectual talent that is the academic world, it would be neither prudent nor feasible to ask faculty to commit to a single institution for a lifetime. But it would not be unreasonable to expect faculty to invest some greater portion of their professional lives in assisting the welfare and governance of their home institutions, and collectively thereby, the welfare and governance of the academy as a whole.

In short, it is time for the faculty to seek a new model of shared governance and to do their part to make it work. Of course, not all faculty can or need become directly involved in the governance of their institutions. Direct participation is not a task for all talents and tastes nor for all times in a faculty member's career. Direct participation must necessarily fall to some designated portion or group of the faculty acting on behalf of the whole. But all of the faculty can and should take a more active interest in the governance of their institutions and can work to support those who do become directly involved.

In light of the many factors reviewed in chapter 4 that act to detach faculty from university governance, it is evident that if the faculty are to support and participate in any new approach, they must be persuaded that it will be an effective means of conveying the academic perspective. At the same time, governance bodies must be assured that a new process would address their perceptions of current dysfunction in faculty governance. More specifically, both faculty and boards would want a process capable of providing a balanced and representative presentation of faculty views and interests. Faculty would want several additional assurances: that input could be provided not only on matters of policy and institutional strategy but on substantive operational matters as well, notably on budget priorities and resource allocation; that faculty input be determined and conveyed by representatives who are highly respected in the faculty community; and that the input be truly and fully considered in the decision processes. For their part, boards would want assurance that the process is capable of providing input in a timely fashion and that it be cognizant of administrative, fiscal, and political realities. All of this is a tall order indeed, but nevertheless one quite possible to fill given a mutual willingness to entertain a fresh approach.

What kind of process would meet these concerns? Our premise has been that there is a need to reinforce the faculty perspective in university decision making, so the first and foremost requirement is that the input proceeds directly and authentically from the faculty. Given the deficiencies of existing means of faculty participation in governance, this can only be accomplished by the creation of a new faculty council especially composed to speak with authority and credibility on behalf of the faculty of the institution. To be able to deal with the complex issues of governance in a truly effective and timely manner, the members of this council–let us call it the "faculty council on governance"–must undertake their charge as a major, if not in fact their primary, responsibility during their term of service in the group. As we have noted, one of the limitations of faculty senates, whose members simultaneously carry on their regular faculty responsibilities, is that that body simply does not have the time to develop the knowledge base and analytic work required for useful input. Given the major time requirement of the task, this is not a service that should be expected of untenured junior faculty who are under strong pressures to meet the standards for award of tenure and who have relatively little experience in the university. Rather, the group should be composed of carefully selected senior members of the faculty who are able and willing to give extensive time to the task. They must be prepared to invest the time required to learn about and fully understand the administrative and governance functions of their institution, the perspectives of management, and the political and financial environment of higher education. They must be willing to become, for all practical purposes, part of the administrative and governance structure of the university. The faculty who so serve should be relieved of equivalent effort in their regular responsibilities so as to permit adequate attention to their new roles. In this regard, it might be noted that faculty who represent faculty unions are regularly relieved of academic responsibilities in recognition of such service. In comparison, the members of the new faculty council would perform a much more critical and significant service for their institutions and for higher education as a whole.

The council members should of course be representative of the faculty but not in the simple "size of unit" manner that characterizes the composition of faculty senates. Senate membership is usually apportioned equally among all the academic colleges and campuses based on the number of members of the general faculty in each college or campus, with a total membership that might then reach quite sizable numbers, for instance, fifty to sixty members. Further, the membership may come from all faculty ranks, including non-tenure-track faculty, with the only other criterion for membership being a willingness to stand for election by fellow members of the unit. These conditions are likely to exclude faculty who are strongly committed to research and scholarship and to bias toward the selection of faculty interested in university service and administration, as well as toward the inclusion of inexperienced junior faculty. In contrast, the new council should represent all academic functions in a balanced manner and should be a "leaner and meaner" body, the latter in part in the interest of promoting greater responsiveness and efficiency and in part because its function simply does not require representation from every academic unit of the university. Rather, faculty representation would be drawn equally from the four major academic divisions of the university–the arts and humanities, the social sciences, the natural sciences, and the professional schools. The much more important consideration in composing the council membership is that it insure the inclusion of faculty who are highly knowledgeable and committed within each area of the tripartite university mission–teaching, research, and service–and in proportion to the significance of these functions in the mission of the institution. For example, in a research university, 45% of the council might be composed of faculty chosen primarily on the basis of accomplishments in research, 35% primarily in recognition of their contributions to teaching, and 20% for public service. While virtually all tenured faculty will participate in each of these activities, their knowledge and experience within each can be expected to vary considerably, and thus selection without regard to these functions could well yield a body that does not properly represent the chief academic functions of the university. The academic area and faculty function categories noted would likely yield a council membership of about twenty-five to thirty faculty.

The council members should of course be chosen by the faculty rather than by the administration, but also not solely by virtue of simple popularity or public reputation. One possibility would be to have department chairs within each of the broad academic areas to be represented, nominate slates of candidates within the proportions designated for each academic function. Department chairs undoubtedly have the keenest knowledge and appreciation of the individual abilities and accomplishments of the faculty working under their leadership. Membership on the council would then be decided by vote of the tenure-track faculty holding appointment within the academic areas of the candidate slates. Terms of service should be of sufficient duration to insure that council members have the opportunity to become thoroughly familiar with the governance and administrative functions of the university and with the specific issues they undertake to address. Three- or four-year terms would probably be required to meet this consideration, with the terms of the initial members staggered to insure a continuing core of experienced council members as individual members complete their terms.

The council should focus its work on several areas. First, it should provide input on university budget priorities and allocations. It is extremely important that the council participate in the budget process of the university because that is invariably where the action is. University administrations always provide eloquent expression of lofty academic goals and values; every university leader with a desk and a pen is in the academic excellence business. But it is the budget of the university that provides the clearest statement of its priorities. The budget is the means, and the only means, whereby the institution carries out its plans and actions. Where the funds are put, that is where the institutional action will be, and the extent and strength of the activity will be directly proportional to the amount of funding provided. So to know what the institution is doing, what it values, and where it is going, one must know where the money is going.

Discrepancies between verbally expressed and budgeted priorities do not necessarily reflect insincerity but rather the difficulties and uncertainties inherent in the typical university budgeting process, which invariably pits numerous and worthy financial claims against far too few resources. No one person or group has unimpeachable wisdom on how to budget available resources across the many academic and support functions of the university in order to best accomplish its mission. It is a matter of making many difficult decisions and judgment calls among a large number of possible activities about which there is at best imperfect information. At the end of the day, and if only because of the magnitude and time constraints of the task, those decisions and calls are more likely to be guided by general intentions, beliefs, and attitudes than by careful calculation of costs and returns or by rigorous examination of past or projected outcomes. So it is all the more important that the intentions, beliefs, and attitudes of the academic sector be strongly represented in these decisions.

The council should also provide input on institutional policies and strategies impacting academic affairs. These might be matters selected by the council for study or matters on which the administration or the board has specifically requested council input. It is not difficult to generate a list of topics that would benefit from in-depth analysis from a truly faculty perspective. Admissions policies, guidelines on part-time faculty appointments, faculty and university accountability mechanisms, teaching-research relations, university relations with the corporate sector, and post-tenure review are among the topics on which it would be helpful to have a reliable and representative expression of faculty views and recommendations.

Finally, but at a lower priority than the foregoing activities, the council may provide a vehicle for faculty response to the attacks on higher education in the media. In the best tradition of academic freedom, which holds that all subjects are open to investigation, the council should investigate the university itself to determine whether its many critics might not have some valid points. This role would doubtless require criticism of university and faculty practice, but being critical is at the heart of caring. While the views of any single council on one or more of these contentious issues would have little impact on the national press and public views, the cumulative expressions of faculty councils across the country could well have a significant and visible impact. Further, as this mechanism takes hold it is tempting to envision a national network of such bodies that could serve as a forum for national discussion of these issues and as a catalyst for reform of faculty or university practices where that is indicated.

In reflecting on these several activities of the council it is important to underscore that the work of the council will be the primary if not single responsibility of its members. The council will thus be able to invest the time and effort necessary to accomplish thorough analyses of the matters on its agenda, to formulate sound recommendations, and to become a truly substantive and effective part of university governance.

Faculty have always been willing to participate in the governance of their institutions and traditionally have tried to carry out that responsibility. But they have not generally felt some related important responsibilities–a responsibility for the welfare of their institution, a responsibility to respond to criticisms of the university and of themselves, and a responsibility to speak out strongly in the interest of the academic ideals that underpin the university. As we have seen, they no longer have an effective means of exercising the first responsibility and they have never had a platform or even a strong sense of obligation to exercise the latter. The proposed council would provide a means to address all of these responsibilities.

It is extremely important that faculty respond to the opportunity to serve on the council and that they regard such service as both an obligation and an honor of the highest order. The stakes are high; as Danforth stated, nothing less than the preservation of the research university. Tenured faculty especially should feel a keen obligation to represent the deeper needs of education and research and to vigorously represent the ideal of the university. Nevertheless, it will be difficult for faculty who are deeply engaged in teaching, research, or public service to draw back from such involvement for the sake of what may appear at first blush as a difficult and distracting, and perhaps even suspect "administrative chore." This will be particularly true of faculty who are deeply involved in research, which above all else rewards persistence and punishes interruption. But the very passion and commitment such faculty have for their research and creative activities is what makes their involvement in the mission of the council so desirable and necessary. To a large degree, they represent the motivation, knowledge, concerns, and perspective that have been missing from the dialogues to date. Therefore, to encourage faculty participation and to further the work of the council, special support and incentives should be provided council members during their terms of service. In addition to reducing the faculty member's teaching responsibilities, consideration should be given to providing special assistance that could enable continuation of their research programs whenever such action is feasible, as, for example, research assistants to enable continued data collection or assistance with preparation of grant applications. In addition, every effort should be made by the university's administrative staff to provide information and technical assistance pertinent to the council's work. While the provision of time and support for the work of the council represents a substantial financial investment, the significance and complexity of the council's task more than warrant this commitment.

While such incentives are appropriate to encourage faculty to give precedence to council service over strong professional interests, the primary motivation for faculty service should really be a concern for the good of their institutions and the academy. The words that James Lincoln Collier has used in urging resistance to the rise of selfishness in America could well be applied to university faculty. Faculty must come to see that the university—and the university community at large—comprise *their* community, and that, as members of it, they and that community are going to be damaged one way or another if they do not from time to time put the interests of the whole above their own concerns. "A people who will not sacrifice for the common good cannot expect to have any common good."[3]

The weight and respect accorded the work of this council by the governance authorities is probably the best guarantor of the significance that faculty will assign to such service. In part for this reason, the council should report directly to the external governance body since, as James Duderstadt observed, that is where the real governance takes place. If we are going to have shared governance, then it should be the real thing as well, that is, we should make it meaningful and truly shared governance. The council's observations and recommendations should always be in written form and as public documents would be broadly circulated through the internal and external university communities. More important, to provide assurance that the work of the council is truly considered and respected by the governance body, that body should feel an obligation to respond in writing to the council's recommendations, providing specific reasons for acceptance or rejection of those recommendations. The governance body's response would also be given broad circulation and visibility. Faculty of course are accustomed to public disclosure and criticism of their work–after all that is how they pursue their research and how the value of their work is determined. But governance boards are not accustomed to giving exposition of their reasoning or to justifying their decisions, and may find this last proposal somewhat difficult to swallow. But from the viewpoint of the faculty, the governance body's willingness to provide response to their input and to explain the basis of its decisions will be the litmus test of the board's concern and respect for faculty participation in governance and probably an essential condition for effective operation of the council.

In this connection, while the council is proposed as a means of revitalizing shared governance, it can also be seen as proposing a form of paired governance in the sense that governing boards would be receiving input from both the faculty and the administrative leadership of the university and would be communicating directly with both. However, this should not pose a problem for the university leadership since there would be no compromise of its executive function. The council's input would be advisory in nature and all executive power would remain vested in the board except that delegated to the president of the university, which is the present state of affairs. But the direct council-board reporting relation would greatly elevate the significance of the council in the eyes of the faculty, the administration, and the general public and would energize the work of its members. These direct exchanges would also help to give council members a better understanding of the nature and perspectives of the governing body, an understanding that will facilitate its work and communication. Often, people know very little about the systems and forces that really determine the conditions under which they live and work, and faculty are no exception in this regard. How better can they come to learn about and understand the governing system and its dynamics than by being a part of it? At the same time, the governing body would similarly become better educated about the academic world as a result of direct and substantive exchanges with those working in its trenches. The elevation of the faculty council in the governance hierarchy would effectively make it a *political factor* in the best pragmatic sense of that term–a factor that the governance authorities could not lightly dismiss or ignore.

The desirability of regular direct faculty-trustee interaction on meaningful issues has been similarly argued by Richard Chait, professor of higher education at Harvard University and a well-known observer of the higher-education scene, whose words are worth quoting in this connection:

> Unfortunately, many trustees (and more than a few college presidents) are apprehensive that regular, two-way communication between faculty members and board members could lead professors to engage in a stampede of end runs and constant complaints that would undermine administrative authority. But if I can generalize from 25 years as a board consultant and facilitator, the greater the extent to which board members and professors work together, through agendas and channels designed with the president, to resolve crucial issues of common concern, the more productive and congenial the faculty member-trustee relationships will be. Even if I have inadvertently reversed cause and effect, the correlation still stands.
>
> As in other situations, isolation perpetuates stereotypes, and interaction debunks them . . . .
>
> Substantive discussions may pose dangers, but the potential payoffs include richer dialogues, better ideas, and healthier relationships. Wouldn't a continuous conversation about major, unresolved issues of mission, strategy, and values be far preferable to sporadic confrontations about motives, personalities, and presidential tenures?[4]

The faculty council might also play a useful role in a number of other administrative and governance actions. As a standing body that would be highly knowledgeable about both faculty and administrative perspectives, it could lend some substance to otherwise often superficial reviews of candidates for university leadership positions, including the presidency. The council could also provide advice and recommendations on a variety of important operational matters, such as capital facility needs and priorities, fund-raising goals, and major contracts with external entities.

University administrations and governing boards should welcome a mechanism of the type proposed here as a means of securing faculty input on issues of policy and governance. We have earlier commented on the frustration experienced by presidents and provosts in seeking reliable and representative faculty views on critical issues facing their institutions. Governing boards themselves have not objected to the principle of shared governance per se but rather but to perceived weaknesses in the manner in which that principle is currently implemented. In general, boards see the faculty as unable to get their act together, largely indifferent to the concerns of society, ignorant of the political and financial environment within which universities operate, and unable to make decisions and provide input in a timely manner. However, the proposed council of senior, representative, highly respected faculty with the time and resources required to become knowledgeable about critical governance issues and to generate timely input on them would meet all of these concerns. By virtue of its charge and reporting relation, it would also be a visible and welcome expression of the engagement of the faculty with the destiny of their institutions and the challenges facing universities today.

The faculty council on governance would also complement several accompaniments of the new activism of university governing boards, which as noted in chapter 3 has been patterned after the corporate board reform movement of the '70s and '80s. During this period, under pressure from large institutional investors, corporate boards began to acknowledge their ultimate accountability for the performance of companies under their oversight and, accordingly, became much more active in exercising their director responsibilities. Company executives were held to stricter standards of board review and oversight and board members began to educate themselves about the particulars of company operations, the latter efforts extending even to initiating direct and independent communication with company employees, stockholders, and customers. Such exchanges had previously been viewed as poor business practice by company executives and boards of directors alike on the grounds that it might undermine company management. But by initiating independent communication with company constituents, board members were able to free themselves from virtually absolute dependence upon the executive leadership for their information about company performance and operations. Given the tendency for university boards to model themselves after corporate boards, such direct two-way exchanges between university board members and students, faculty, or other university constituents can be expected as newly active board members seek information relevant to their responsibilities. In fact, such exchanges already take place in a number of institutions and seem likely to become more commonplace in the future. But in undertaking such communication with the general faculty, board members will face the same problem encountered by university presidents and provosts in seeking to secure representative views from a highly heterogeneous and withdrawn faculty. With which faculty would board members communicate? Those encountered in campus tours? Individual faculty who volunteer information? The typically uninformed standing faculty committee? Randomly selected faculty? The campus politicians? Open-door sessions to hear every gripe and complaint? There may well be bits and pieces of provocative opinion or titillating information in such exchanges, but nothing that could be very helpful in guiding decisions on substantive matters of policy or operation. Direct board-faculty exchanges are likely to be helpful in educating board members about the faculty perspective and the status of academic operations to the degree that they involve faculty who are representative of the faculty at large, knowledgeable about their institution, attuned to current administrative and governance issues, and authorized and prepared to speak for the faculty. The proposed faculty council on governance meets all of these criteria and would be an excellent group to include in trustee-faculty dialogues. If direct dialogues between faculty and trustees do become more common as several prominent educational analysts have predicted, this could only be a helpful development providing they involve faculty groups such as the proposed council. Over time, and for the first time, such dialogues could lead to a mutual understanding of the systems and pressures under which each party lives.

One additional aspect of the corporate board reform movement could provide an important lesson for university governance. As part of the new corporate board activism, a number of corporations have restructured their boards to reduce the number of "insiders," that is, the number of board members drawn from the company leadership itself, thereby imparting a more objective and independent cast to the board. While there is no ready parallel to "insiders" on university boards, the principle of seeking knowledgeable and independent directors who are likely to act solely in the best interests of the organization is certainly applicable to university boards. As noted in chapter 3, expertise in university affairs or even a basic knowledge of university operations has not been a criterion for university board membership. It would certainly be appropriate, then, for university governance authorities to consider reserving some portion of board membership for individuals who are not drawn from local sources and who would bring in-depth knowledge of academics and higher education to their governing responsibilities. Just as there have been repeated calls for scientists to become directly involved in guiding government decisions in the interest of informed science policy making, so the inclusion on university boards of individuals with proven records of leadership in higher education would assist informed policy making in university governance. Such appointees could be recruited nationally, assuring a large pool of highly capable candidates. There are any number of present or past chancellors, presidents, or provosts who would very likely be willing to serve in such a capacity not only in the interest of the institution but in the larger public and national interest as well. The presence of even a few such individuals on the board would add a more knowledgeable, global, and impartial perspective to board discussions and decision making, while at the same time providing a helpful link in communications between the faculty council on governance and the board.

In concluding this chapter, let us reemphasize why it is so important to reengage the faculty in a meaningful way in the governance of their institutions. Earlier we noted that all universities aspire to academic excellence and proclaim that heady state as their primary goal. The readiness with which they so proclaim is clear recognition that the long-run strength and reputation of a university rest above all else on the quality of its academic programs. However, while academic excellence is surely a commendable goal, institutions seldom make clear just what it means and exactly how they are striving to achieve it. Many factors contribute to the quality of an institution's academic programs, but few are under the sole or direct control of the institution as such. For example, the amount of public and private financial support an institution receives is of course an important factor but one that is decided primarily by outside parties. What specifically, then, should an institution *itself* do to achieve academic excellence with regard to those factors over which it has direct and full control? The answer is clear. It should promote the quality and work of its faculty because all else follows from that. When you consistently attract and retain faculty who are highly knowledgeable, skilled, and dedicated to the creation and transmission of knowledge in their fields, it follows as day follows night that you will attract, prepare, and graduate students who are knowledgeable and skilled and who will bring these attributes to the larger society. It also follows that new knowledge and technologies will be forthcoming from that institution in the arts and sciences, engineering, business, and medicine; that new intellectual expertise and resources will be infused into the community and region; that federal, state, and private grant funding will be attracted to the university; that well-prepared and loyal alumni will graduate; and that private donors will want to support educational and research programs of growing quality, enabling outstanding libraries, museums, laboratories, and other critical support facilities. All of these effects will also feed back on themselves and augment one another on the principle of nothing succeeding like success.

Of course these developments do not occur overnight. But if the institution maintains focus on building the quality of its faculty, they will take place more rapidly than one might expect in common hours because the quality of the faculty is inescapably the biggest factor determining the quality of its teaching, research, and service programs. That institutional focus begins with faculty recruitment, which for most universities proceeds nationally and, these days, even internationally. It is all a question of attracting good brains–bringing smart, creative, and dedicated people to the institution and structuring an environment that allows them to work productively. The competition for the best faculty is strong, but it is a competition that can spur growth and excellence in all institutions. The aim should always be to recruit the best possible faculty and to avoid the faculty (and very human) tendency to recruit in their own image. The focus on faculty quality extends further to insistence upon rigorous standards in teaching and research for the award of tenure and faculty promotion. Mediocre performance should never be tolerated. High standards attract outstanding faculty because the best want to be where they can do their best–where it is clear that the best are recognized and valued. Finally, the focus extends to providing a good environment for the work of the faculty, that is, a good environment for teaching and research, and that means giving priority in resource allocation to facilities and staff who work in *direct* support of teaching and research. The driving principle behind academic excellence is clear but it is not always easily implemented given the vagaries of the political and financial climate within which most universities must operate and the many needs and interests of a university community. But adherence to the principle over time will surely produce the product.

In short, academic programs can be excellent only with excellent faculty, and thus building such a faculty should be the first priority of the institution that is striving for excellence, a priority that in turn should drive its standards and operating decisions.

The centrality of the faculty to the work and quality of the institution is why it is so important to reconnect them in a truly meaningful and influential way to the governance of their institutions. It is particularly important to reengage faculty in governance at this time when universities are facing many new demands for service and pressures for change. The external entities that present those demands and pressures interact with the university's governance authorities, not with the faculty. And it is in the governance process that institutions will come to grips with those demands and pressures, deciding when and how to accommodate and when to resist. Only by active participation in governance can faculty really understand the contemporary challenges to traditional ways of operating, understand what is being asked of universities, what is at stake, what has already been lost and what is vulnerable, and how their own behavior has contributed to that loss and vulnerability. Only by being a meaningful part of the governance process can faculty help to preserve the best of the traditional while necessary adaptations are fashioned to a changed environment. And only by the inclusion of a strong faculty presence in governance are universities likely to remain centered on the virtues and values that underlay the successful growth and development of the research universities. Sometimes it is necessary to look back to go forward.

Chapter 6

The Teaching-Research Relation

This chapter and chapters 7 through 9 examine in some depth several topics in higher education that are currently of concern to university governing bodies, matters that one hopes will also shortly be addressed by faculty councils on governance. These topics include the relation between research and teaching; the question of tenure; university and faculty accountability; and relations between universities and the corporate sector. Each of these topics has received a good deal of attention in the higher-education literature, as well as in the popular press. The intention here is not to summarize the many analyses and recommendations that have been offered on these topics. Rather, the aim is simply to illustrate approaches that might be taken to these matters from a faculty perspective and, more importantly, to show how "top-down" solutions are likely to play out in the context of actual day-to-day academic operations. It is the latter perspective that urges the wisdom of insuring that the faculty be involved directly and fully in the resolutions of such issues.

With respect to research universities, perhaps no issue has been so widely and frequently discussed as the effects on teaching of a strong faculty emphasis on research. While teaching remains the predominant activity of most university faculty, the question is whether growing faculty attention to research has reached a point that is harmful to undergraduate education. There is no doubt that the increased opportunities and rewards for faculty engagement in research that began in earnest under the new social contract in the '60s and '70s have resulted in an overall increase in the average faculty effort devoted to research as opposed to teaching, especially undergraduate teaching. For example, surveys of faculty teaching loads show that full-time faculty in research universities, where of course the expectations and rewards for engagement in research are strongest, teach fewer undergraduate courses than their counterparts in less research-oriented universities and colleges. For example, an analysis of data from the 1992–1993 National Study of Postsecondary Faculty found that faculty in four-year doctoral institutions teach one-third fewer undergraduate classes than their counterparts in four-year nondoctoral institutions.[1] Correlated with this difference, faculty in research institutions are likely to spend less time with undergraduates in ancillary educational activities such as advising, mentoring, or simply being in contact with undergraduates. Furthermore, a national survey of science and engineering faculty at research universities found that the portion of those faculty reporting research as their primary responsibility increased from 19% in 1973 to 33% in 1993, while the portion reporting teaching as their primary responsibility declined from 69% to 53% over this period.[2] These and similar data, amplified unfortunately by largely anecdotal reports of faculty forsaking teaching responsibilities in avid pursuit of research goals, have been treated in the popular press in a somewhat sensationalistic manner. Recent stories present a picture of the general faculty fleeing from the classroom, leaving teaching to graduate students (usually with deficient English-speaking skills), using external grant funds to buy out of teaching responsibilities, shirking responsibilities to general education in favor of specialized research-oriented course offerings, and achieving tenure and promotion primarily on the basis of the number of their research grants and publications, the latter usually characterized as of questionable utility. Less harsh but still strong criticism has come even from within the academic community. For example, the Boyer Commission on Educating Undergraduates in the Research University, composed of prominent leaders in higher education, states in its 1998 report:

> We believe that the state of undergraduate education at research universities is (in) a crisis, an issue of such magnitude and volatility that universities must galvanize themselves to respond. . . .
>
> Again and again, universities are guilty of an advertising practice they would condemn in the commercial world. Recruitment materials display proudly the world-famous professors, the splendid facilities and the ground-breaking research that goes on within them, but thousands of students graduate without ever seeing the world-famous professors or tasting genuine research. Some of their instructors are likely to be badly trained or even untrained teaching assistants who are groping their way toward a teaching technique; some others may be tenured drones who deliver set lectures from yellowed notes, making no effort to engage the bored minds of the students in front of them. . . .

Advanced research and undergraduate teaching have existed (within the research universities) on two quite different planes, the first a source of pleasure, recognition, and reward, and the latter a burden shouldered more or less reluctantly to maintain the viability of the institution.[3]

Others within the academic community have observed that since good research and good teaching each take a great deal of time, it is hard for any faculty member to do justice to both, and therefore an institution that places strong emphasis on research will almost inevitably relegate teaching to a distinctly second-place status. The time requirements to be competitive in research within these institutions, it is argued, lead to large impersonal undergraduate classes taught by graduate assistants and part-time faculty, the abandonment of undergraduate student advising and mentoring by regular faculty, and other reported displacements of undergraduate education by research activities. A concern that faculty engagement in research takes place at the expense of undergraduate education has even prompted a number of states to institute minimum requirements for classroom teaching time and office hours for faculty at public universities, as illustrated in the Florida "twelve-hour law," or to institute financial rewards for increased undergraduate teaching by regular faculty, as in the Florida Teaching Incentive Program.

The concern that research conflicts with education is somewhat ironic in view of the fact that putting research and teaching together is often cited both here and abroad as the special achievement and strength of the American university system. The former Soviet Union and many parts of Asia and Europe have followed a different model, placing research in special institutes separate from the university teaching function, an approach now widely recognized as limiting both the effectiveness of teaching and the development of research. Joining the creation of knowledge and the teaching of knowledge is held to vitalize and enrich both functions. As Massachusetts Institute of Technology president Charles Vest observed,

The most valuable and farsighted concept to emerge from the original (Vannevar) Bush vision was that by supporting research in the universities, the government would also be investing in the education of the next generation—a beautiful and efficient concept. In short, every dollar spent would be doing double duty. This integration of teaching and research is at the heart of America's unique system of research universities.[4]

Of course, this productive synergy of research and teaching is best realized at the graduate level, where the student and teacher are relatively close in subject knowledge and interest and where acquaintance with the latest findings and techniques directly serves the student's professional preparation and aspirations. However, it is generally assumed that undergraduate education can be similarly enriched by the presence of research faculty who infuse their teaching with the latest advances in knowledge and their own enthusiasm for discovery. But critics of the research universities insist that whatever may be the benefits of a research-oriented faculty, they are far outweighed by the disadvantages at the undergraduate level. They argue that the emphasis on research has gone too far, often resulting even in the removal of regular faculty from undergraduate teaching.

Has the emphasis on research gone too far? Has faculty attention become too focused on research to the detriment of teaching? Should regular research-oriented faculty be forced to spend more time in the undergraduate classroom? To answer these questions requires first that we complicate our thinking beyond two assumptions that pervade popular views of the teaching-research relation. The first is that the faculty are the prime agents in this dynamic, that is, that the teaching-research relation is set solely or primarily by the faculty and therefore if it is awry, the correct adjustment can be achieved simply by changing faculty behavior. The second assumption is that of a simple trade-off between teaching and research, that is, that an expanded faculty effort on research necessarily subtracts from the quality of teaching and education. To correct the first assumption we need only recall society's explicit and continual call and strong support for faculty research as expressed under the land grant programs, under the university-federal social contract following World War II, and under the contemporary pressures for university-driven economic development. In these major initiatives university faculty have been more response than stimulus, willing responders to be sure because research and scholarship is their natural strong inclination. But nevertheless the pressures and rewards for research have been more set by external and institutional agencies than by faculty, and from this perspective faculty have behaved in entirely rational and helpful ways.

The second assumption, that expanded faculty effort on research detracts from teaching, similarly attributes a more determinate role to the faculty than they possess. As Harold Shapiro, president of Princeton University has pointed out in a cogent analysis of this issue, how much time a given faculty member spends on his or her research has, in itself, no necessary implication whatsoever for the quality of the student's overall educational experience. If a faculty member does spend less time in the classroom because of engagement in research, the institution could always hire additional faculty to replace that lost effort and thereby maintain the quality of its teaching. Of course, this would increase the cost of operating the university, and the key question is how this expanded commitment to scholarship is to be financed. Quoting President Shapiro,

> My own view on this matter is that all the patrons of the university (government, students and their families, private foundations, university endowments–etc.) have shared this burden, and the critical question is whether costs have been shared in some way proportionate to the benefits received. This is a critical issue which may lie behind a good deal of current criticism and has not been adequately studied.[5]

In short, external agencies and the institution are more controlling than faculty of both the nature of the teaching-research relation and its cost attributions. From this perspective, the faculty are caught between–rather than being prime movers of–the pressure to produce new knowledge for the benefit of society and to enhance institutional resources and prestige and the pressure to maintain quality educational programs for a growing student body, to say nothing of the additional pressure to deliver both products at bargain cost. This perspective also shows the shortsightedness of attempts by governing authorities to deal with the teaching-research issue by simply requiring faculty to teach more. It is a considerably more complicated matter involving other factors and players.

But putting aside these considerations for a moment, there is also no clear evidence that a simple trade-off does in fact exist between a faculty member's involvement in research and the quality of instruction. While a good deal of research has been addressed regarding this issue, the overall results are equivocal, doubtless owing to the complexities and nuances of the relations between teaching and research and between faculty and students.[6] For example, some student surveys have found a modest positive correlation between a faculty member's research involvement and effectiveness as a teacher and advisor but other surveys have found either no correlation or a negative correlation. Similarly, studies of the relation between the research orientation of an institution's faculty and student satisfaction with the quality of their instruction and overall college experience also do not permit a consistent conclusion. The research that has been conducted, then, does not enable us to conclude that strong involvement in research either enhances or detracts from the quality of teaching.

But nevertheless few would dispute the fact that over the past several decades the average proportion of the full-time faculty member's time devoted to teaching and advising has decreased significantly while the time devoted to research has increased, certainly within the research universities.

And few would dispute that this period has also seen changes in under-graduate education that most would regard as undesirable, including less undergraduate contact with regular faculty and more with graduate students and part-time faculty, larger classes, lower graduation rates, relaxed curricular requirements, grade inflation, and a general withdrawal of faculty from student advising. The popular mind may be quick to link the greater research involvement of the faculty to these deleterious developments, but are they linked?

As for so many other important questions concerning human activity, the answer is that life has no control groups. That is, there has been no otherwise constant world against which one might estimate the impact of the change in faculty behavior, specifically, their increased commitment to research. This same period has seen many other significant developments that could produce the changes just noted in undergraduate education. Thus, while faculty have shifted their efforts to research during this period, the number of faculty members per student has actually increased, although in many public institutions this has been accomplished by adding lower-cost part-time faculty. The net effect of these developments is less exposure to regular full-time faculty, but the key factor is an institutional decision about resource allocation. The increase in larger, more impersonal classes almost certainly derives more from the dramatic growth in the percentage of students continuing from high school to college coupled with the failure of state and other funding sources to keep pace with the cost of maintaining smaller class size. Lower graduation rates are linked to profound social changes over this period that make the traditional residential four-year college experience almost uncommon today and part-time, intermittent student attendance more the norm, particularly in urban institutions. With the exception of a handful of elite residential universities, the average proportion of students who today graduate within six years after beginning their university education is only about 60 percent, a figure that reflects changed student behavior rather than faculty actions. The chief relaxation in curricular requirements during this period occurred as a consequence of student reaction against authorities and the establishment that took place as part of the social and political upheavals associated with the Vietnam War protests. While one may argue that the faculty should have held the academic center better at that time, certainly much more potent forces were at work in remolding the structure of undergraduate education. As for grade inflation, faculty of course are the mediators of altered standards here and have too often taken the easy way, but hardly as a sop for any shift in teaching and research effort. Other factors have played a role as well. It would be foolish to deny the dilemmas posed by the influx of less well-prepared students, and pressure from administrators to minimize student loss is certainly not unknown. Finally, Shapiro has pointed out that the decline in faculty advising and mentoring activities can be seen as part of a much larger cultural change in community life. Quoting again from the same source,

> . . . the nostalgic image of the avuncular "prof" who became confidante, moral mentor and surrogate parent to his "boys" (and I use the term advisedly) no longer holds true, and some may lament its passing. Yet for many others–students and faculty–the thought of such a relationship is no longer even desirable. In any case, many of the cultural functions which might once have taken place in an after-hours chat or at a dinner or afternoon tea served up by the prof's agreeable wife are today undertaken–if at all–by professional counselors and advisors of various types, specifically trained to provide particular services. This new division of labor reflects, among other things, the contemporary realities of family life, the new role of women in the workplace, and the very different urban communities within which most of us now reside.[7]

Still other factors complicate evaluation of the teaching-research trade-off assumption, including the effects of curricular shifts associated with a research-oriented faculty, the greater variety of educational options offered today's student (e.g., accelerated degree programs, undergraduate research opportunities, and study abroad), and the increasing role of technology in the teacher-student relation, to name but some. The teaching-research relation, then, is considerably more complex than has been credited and we need to be skeptical of the assumptions and conclusions that characterize many discussions of this issue. In addition, it seems clear that any top-down "corrective" approach that focuses on one agent or variable (as top-down efforts invariably seem to do) is apt to be misguided and may well accomplish more harm than good. Policy that is not based on the facts of the matter cannot coerce reality.

Nothing in the foregoing analysis should be interpreted as indicating that we should be satisfied with the status quo or that the current distribution of faculty effort and resources allocated to research and undergraduate teaching should not be adjusted. Rather, it is simply that we need to complicate our thinking about this issue, as well as about other controversial issues in higher education, so that governance actions can proceed from a more sophisticated, logical, and accurate base of understanding. In particular, we need to be skeptical of simplistic, blame-oriented single-agent approaches and instead realize that all parts of the governance chain contribute to problem areas of university operations and must contribute to their resolution as well.

However, for reasons we have earlier noted, it is unlikely that either external governing authorities or university administrations can or will take the lead in "complicating our thinking," at least in core academic areas; they are too far removed and too preoccupied with day-to-day managerial pressures. But the proposed faculty councils on governance would be an excellent body to take the leadership, in Shapiro's words, "in defining more precisely and thinking more carefully about the complexity of some of the issues which face us." Defining precisely and thinking carefully are precisely the faculty's forte. Nor should we be concerned that faculty councils would simply leave us buried in thought. Rather, they would be expected to formulate recommended actions as well as analyses, recommendations that would then engage full response from the highest authorities.

While we cannot readily draw firm conclusions about the trade-off between faculty research and the quality of teaching and education, we can nevertheless acknowledge and address the questionable features of undergraduate education in research universities noted earlier, whatever their causes. What approaches might be suggested or endorsed by faculty councils to improve undergraduate education?

The recent report of the Boyer Commission on Educating Undergraduates in the Research University outlines one possible pathway. The report notes that the present-day situation is a legacy of the way in which research universities developed. When advanced research became incorporated into the American university at the end of the nineteenth century, it was essentially grafted onto the existing undergraduate liberal arts core mission and little effort was made to integrate these functions. Instead, graduate education and research and undergraduate teaching, involving essentially the same faculty, were brought into coexistence on largely disconnected planes, the first focused on inquiry and discovery and the latter on existing knowledge and general education. The premise of the commission's approach, however, is that inquiry and discovery lie at the heart of *all* learning, including advanced research and undergraduate teaching alike, and therefore these functions can and should be better integrated than historical legacy has inclined. In the commission's words, we need to recognize

that inquiry, investigation, and discovery are the heart of the (university) enterprise, whether in funded research projects or in undergraduate classrooms or graduate apprenticeships. Everyone at a university should be a discoverer, a learner . . . learning is based on discovery guided by mentoring rather than on the transmission of information. Inherent in inquiry-based learning is an element of reciprocity: faculty can learn from students as students are learning from faculty.[8]

Therefore, the commission concluded, the way to improve undergraduate education within the research university is to better integrate the research skills and activities of the faculty into the curriculum and classrooms in order to create a unique research-based learning environment, rather than striving to mimic the special environment of the liberal arts colleges.

Applying these general ideas, the commission recommends a number of specific actions to turn the unique resources of the research university to pedagogical advantage. In general, large classes should be replaced by more individualized forms of instruction, guided by discovery and mentoring; ideally, there should be a mentor for every student. Beginning in the freshman year, students should be able to engage in research in as many courses as possible, with training in effective oral and written communication a prominent and continuing feature of their education. The focal point of the first year should be a small seminar taught by experienced faculty who begin to foster an inquiry-based approach to learning. Wherever possible, instruction at all levels should combine groups of students and faculty in collaborative and interdisciplinary fashion and in block courses organized around major topics. New reward structures should be put in place to encourage faculty to engage in such collaborative efforts. Traditional lecturing to large classes should no longer be the dominant mode of instruction in a research university. Undergraduate education should culminate with a capstone experience, a major project that utilizes the research and communication skills learned in earlier semesters. Furthermore, there should be no remediation in a research university; students should have, upon entry, the skills required to take advantage of the inquiry-based learning to be provided therein. Also, graduate education should be redesigned to prepare students to handle their undergraduate teaching responsibilities, training that would also benefit their later professional work as college and university teachers. Finally, research universities should commit themselves to the highest standards in teaching and create the faculty reward structures that validate that commitment.

Probably few would question the commission's view that the research and undergraduate teaching missions of the American research university have never been well integrated or the view that inquiry and discovery are in fact fundamental features of all learning. And few would question that the commission's recommended actions could greatly strengthen and enrich undergraduate education. However, many probably would question the cost and feasibility of their recommendations. Implementation of most of these recommendations would require a very low ratio of students to full-time faculty in the university, probably on the order of 10 to 1, whereas existing student-faculty ratios in research universities are 20 to 1 or higher, even with inclusion of part-time faculty. The recommendations appear to require that the reformatted introductory and general education courses be taught primarily by experienced regular faculty members, whereas in many research universities as many as 50 percent of general education courses are presently taught by non-tenure-track faculty. The instructional formats recommended–collaborative, interdisciplinary, inquiry-based, and blocked courses–are extremely time-intensive to teach, and that factor alone would require a significant increase in faculty lines. These observations indicate that implementation of the commission's recommendations would require an enormous investment in additional faculty lines at most research universities, and one must question whether their private and public patrons would be prepared to pay the necessary price. As we have seen, the funding for regular faculty lines at most public research universities, the most costly faculty in higher education, has already failed to keep pace with enrollment increases. In addition, the commission's "no remediation" recommendation flies in the face of the fact that at all but a handful of elite universities substantial remedial education is offered to entering students, and one must wonder whether there exists the political will to adopt more selective admission policies.

It is interesting to compare the commission's recommendations with actions recently proposed by Murray Sperber, a professor of English at Indiana University, who similarly decries the quality of undergraduate education in the large public universities.[9] Sperber criticizes what he views as the essential falseness of the common practice among universities of touting honors programs that offer a small number of students special educational opportunities of the kind recommended by the commission while denying those opportunities to ordinary students, who are generally consigned to large lecture classes. Would not all students, rather than a select few, prefer and benefit from small classes, personal contact with professors, individual attention, and research opportunities, asks Sperber? Shouldn't any university be a single community of learners whose members all have equal access to its educational resources? What prevents such "special" educational opportunities being available to all in large public universities, he argues, are faulty admission policies coupled with financial constraints in which the costly pursuit of research prestige looms large. Sperber therefore proposes turning all undergraduate education "into one large honors program" through two quite radical actions: large-scale reductions in enrollment by refusing admission to students who require remedial help, and a wholesale redirection of university funding from graduate research programs to undergraduate teaching.

Sperber and the commission start from the same point–they are persuaded of the inadequacy of undergraduate education in the research university–and they arrive at the same point–a more individualized, inquiry-based, faculty-intensive form of undergraduate instruction. To achieve this end, both would reduce enrollment through more selective admissions while dramatically increasing funding for undergraduate education. The major difference is that the commission views faculty research as a special strength to be exploited for the benefit of undergraduate education, while Sperber views faculty research as preempting the priority due to teaching and as a major source of the new funding required to strengthen undergraduate education. There are telling points and worthy arguments in each of these analyses, but many are likely to question both the merits and the feasibility of undertaking the large enrollment reductions and funding changes envisioned under these proposals.

Is there another route to educational reform that might achieve some of the ends sought by the commission and by Sperber but without the costs inherent in those approaches? Richard Felder, a professor of engineering at North Carolina State University, has suggested a strategy that might allow universities to maintain a distinctive research mission yet permit some significant redirection of faculty effort to undergraduate education.[10] The approach proceeds from the view that the traditional university model of faculty performance and evaluation works to seriously distort the natural distribution of faculty interests and effort. Under that model faculty are expected to engage substantially in both teaching and research and to excel in both in order to qualify for tenure. Relatively little trade-off in performance is allowed between these activities. Most universities will require outstanding performance in either teaching or research and at least strong or superior performance in the other. But the reality is that *very* few faculty have either the talent or the time required to excel in both of these activities. Therefore faculty must give priority to one or the other in order to maximize their chance of achieving the highest standard while also striving to at least suffice in the other. Under the existing academic incentive and reward system, the only viable priority choice for most faculty is research, whatever their personal preference and interests might be. Not only are there many strong incentives and rewards for putting research first, as described in chapter 4, but because research accomplishments enhance the university's reputation and financial status and are more readily measurable than teaching accomplishments, research invariably receives greater weight in the tenure review process.

The young faculty member entering the research university and striving for a favorable tenure judgment six years later quickly learns these contingencies and proceeds to focus on research, giving as much time and energy as she has left over to teaching. Nor does the constrained priority to research cease with the award of tenure. The next hurdle is review for promotion to full professor, usually held after another six years, in which the primary if not sole criterion for a favorable decision is attainment of a national or international reputation in the candidate's field of research. Together these extended evaluation periods comprise the shaping period of the faculty's member's career. The result, says Felder, is that much undergraduate teaching is done by professors who either have little interest in it or cannot afford to take the time to do it well, and much research is done by professors who might rather dedicate themselves to education if they had the choice. Consequently, the quality of both teaching and research suffers.

To address this situation Felder proposes a new model for faculty advancement that would allow them to focus their careers on either research or teaching, reflecting their deepest interests. The proposal establishes two broad and distinctly differently pathways for advancement: a research pathway and an education pathway. The research pathway would emphasize and value activity in any form of research, including basic and/or applied, multidisciplinary, or socially engaged scholarship. Faculty in this track would also be expected to teach graduate and undergraduate courses as a rule. The criteria for advancement (tenure and promotion) along this pathway would be essentially those now effect in research universities, with superior performance being required in research and at least satisfactory performance in teaching. (At present, no research university would permit published standards for tenure allowing merely satisfactory performance in any activity.) In contrast, the education pathway would emphasize teaching and closely related activities, including an emphasis on undergraduate teaching, advising, and mentoring, curriculum improvement, development of innovative teaching methods, preparation of undergraduate textbooks, participation in educational conferences, and publication in teaching-oriented journals. Advancement on this pathway would require superior teaching performance as measured by student, alumni, and peer evaluations. A department in a research university might allocate, say, 75 percent of their full-time faculty lines to the research pathway and 25 percent to education-pathway positions, a distribution that should have minimal effects on costs. In the system as proposed, the education pathway would be largely filled by known outstanding teachers, and new Ph.D.'s without teaching experience would not be permitted to enter the pathway until they had demonstrated their potential to meet the criteria for advancement. A critical feature of the proposal is that no distinction should exist between the two pathways in status, perquisites, or opportunities for tenure, promotion, and salary increments.

Felder believes this policy would have major benefits for both undergraduate education and research. First and foremost, undergraduate classes would be taught be a higher proportion of faculty who have a strong commitment to teaching and proven instructional skills. These professors would also have more time for the many tasks that undergird a quality undergraduate education, tasks presently unattended or reluctantly pursued by an overworked faculty, such as course and curriculum planning, preparation of instructional materials, collaborative teaching efforts, undergraduate advising, and mentoring of junior faculty. Faculty in the research pathway would have reduced undergraduate teaching responsibilities and therefore should be able to increase their research and grant productivity, which in turn would produce increased financial and other benefits to the university. At the same time, reduced research activity among education-pathway faculty would produce financial savings that could be redirected to education. In addition, tenure and promotion reviews could focus on the activities most relevant to the candidate's distinctive contribution to the university mission, with a by-product of fewer less essential faculty publications.[11]

Felder notes that his system is consistent with, and builds upon, a reconceptualization of faculty work roles proposed by Ernest Boyer in a 1990 book that has stirred national debate.[12] Boyer proposed that the definition of faculty scholarship or research be broadened beyond the traditional forms of research directed to the production of new knowledge. His redefinition would also include as scholarly work the integration of knowledge within or across disciplines, the application of knowledge to real-life problems, and teaching itself. He argues that although each of these scholarly functions is important to the well-being of the university and society, the current university reward system values only scholarship directed to the discovery of knowledge. Boyer then proposed that we establish new faculty work arrangements that would make it possible for faculty to concentrate on any of the four scholarly functions at different points in their career. Felder's proposal can be seen as an explicit and strong expression of such a system.

A comprehensive restructuring of faculty work-life into distinct educational and research pathways of the form proposed by Felder is as yet untried. An underlying assumption of the system, of course, is that a substantial proportion of faculty presently work on either research or teaching against their strongest talents and interests, and therefore a better matching of work assignments to those talents and interests would produce substantial gains in overall efficiency and work quality in both areas of endeavor. This is surely a reasonable and attractive hypothesis, but its validity can only be known by testing. A further positive feature of the system is that it does not appear to require increased funding, and might even result in overall financial gain to the institution.

In addition to proposals that seek to improve undergraduate education through broad restructuring of the university, different commentators have suggested a variety of other actions of a more specific nature. These include, for example, providing financial and other rewards in recognition of special teaching efforts and accomplishments; requiring external peer reviews of teaching comparable to such existing review of research; supporting programs to define and measure desired student-learning outcomes; providing resources for the improvement of teaching and teaching materials; requiring grant applicants to provide a statement of the pedagogical impact of their proposed research; providing funds for collaborative and interdisciplinary teaching; extending research participation opportunities to undergraduates; and improving the evaluation of teaching so that it can be better recognized and weighted in the promotion and tenure process. A number of universities have implemented or are considering one or another of these actions, which if adopted may have some salutary local benefit to undergraduate education. However, none of these actions, nor any of the system-based proposals, has approached the degree of general support required to effect significant overall change in the status quo, nor are they likely to do so without both broad faculty endorsement and approval by governing authorities. As we have seen, there is no present mechanism for such collaborative dialogue and action by faculty and governance authorities. It is on just such matters that faculty councils on governance could make a key contribution to advancing constructive and broadly supported change. Further, by virtue of their intimate knowledge of the academic workplace, it is likely that faculty councils once so engaged would contribute additional useful ideas to the mix. For example, consider the following simple, zero-cost change in faculty recruitment practice that could significantly enhance the climate for undergraduate teaching.

As part of the job interview process, candidates for faculty positions are usually asked to give an hour-long talk on their research to the department faculty; this presentation is a critical factor, and often the deciding factor, in judging the candidate's suitability for the position. The simple change would be to ask the candidate to give an additional similar talk on a topic that would appear in an introductory course in the field, and to make that presentation to a group of undergraduate students as well as to the faculty. The point is to sample the candidate's teaching potential as well as their research potential. A research presentation has quite limited use in assessing undergraduate teaching potential. The candidate of course knows her own research better than anybody in the world (especially if it is her doctoral thesis), and is presenting it to a sophisticated, like-minded, interested audience (the faculty) familiar with the field, its concepts and terminology, and related findings. There is no need to educate. It amounts to inside shoptalk between professionals on an advanced topic. On the other hand, an introductory topic presentation to undergraduates is a much more difficult matter. No prior understanding or interest can be assumed. One must make the topic clear and compelling to someone approaching it for the first time. Mere statement of the key concepts, terminology, and findings will not be enough. They must be made meaningful to the listener by thoughtfully chosen examples, parallels, and questions that sustain attention, establish relevance, and motivate interest and engagement. This in turn requires at least some knowledge and consideration of the listener and his world and usually many hours of "thinking through" possible approaches and pathways of effective communication. Although one would not expect to hear polished lectures in this setting, particularly from new Ph.D.'s, such a presentation could surely be helpful in judging the candidate's potential for teaching while specifying her or his actual entering level of teaching skill.

In addition to its use in selecting future faculty, requiring such an introductory topic presentation would give a powerful signal to the candidate about the value the department and university place on teaching and undergraduate education. And it would be a powerful signal as well to graduate schools that they should start preparing their students to be teachers as well as researchers. At present there is no such message given in either graduate training or in the recruitment process. In fact, graduate education is a powerful socializing force to think highly only of research. Finally, undergraduates would doubtless be pleased by the attention and value given to their views in the selection of faculty for whom they will be a captive audience.

Of course, the suggested change in faculty recruitment practice would be only one meaningful step toward altering the university teaching culture. However, a culture is not changed by edict but by changing the basic practices that define the culture. The point of the illustration is that the necessary changes in basic practice are more likely to be identified by faculty than by those farther removed from, and therefore less knowledgeable about, the defining practices of the academic workplace.

In concluding this chapter on the teaching-research relation, it may be helpful to consider a story from the earliest days of the university. When Galileo moved from his academic position at the University of Padua to the University of Pisa in 1610, he arranged that his new appointment would entail no teaching duties, leaving him free to devote himself fully to research and publishing, a freedom he had never known in his earlier academic appointments.[13] At the time of his new appointment, Galileo had already achieved fame through his experimental approach to physics and through the most startling astronomical discoveries ever claimed by a single individual, discoveries that were to require new conceptions of the world and our place in it. Who would question the sense of an arrangement that allowed the father of modern physics and astronomy to focus on research studies that shape to this day the teaching of scientific method and understanding of the universe?

The Galileo story tells us, first, that the teaching-research issue has always been with us. As the Yale University historian Edmund Morgan said, "scholarship begins in curiosity, but it ends in communication."[14] Research and teaching are part of a conflicted continuum, and there will always be some tension and struggle between the imperative to produce new knowledge and the need to communicate knowledge. For the research universities, the challenge has been and will remain how to best prepare students for the challenges of life while staying at the cutting-edge of knowledge, knowing that the latter is essential to the former. And that touches on the second message in the Galileo story—the importance of research to education. Just as Galileo's research studies have become a cornerstone of what we teach today, so research in all areas provides the foundation of a great university and a sound education. Putting research and teaching together in the free environment of the university has been good for discovery and good for pedagogy. However, there is no magic formula that predicts the right mix of emphases. But as in Galileo's case, the pull and excitement of inquiry and discovery is so strong that the best barometer of imbalance probably resides in the pedagogical area. We have seen that distinguished observers of the research universities, including the members of the Boyer Commission, Sperber, Felder, and many others believe we should now take steps to strengthen undergraduate teaching, and it is hard to dispute their concern. But to redress the balance will require contribution from all levels of the governance chain, and especially from the faculty.

Chapter 7

The Question of Tenure

❦

Faculty tenure is another university practice that is currently under great scrutiny with many arguing that it is time to abandon tenure. However, as in discussions of the teaching-research relation, the public debate on tenure has often proceeded without awareness of some important particulars of the process. We begin our discussion, then, with a brief primer for the general reader on the nature and conditions of tenure.

Tenure is a status that may be awarded to a faculty member that provides continuing protection from summary dismissal. As a very rarely excepted rule, only full-time regular faculty are eligible for the award of tenure. Part-time faculty, adjunct faculty members, and even full-time faculty who are not appointed to a "tenure-track" position, that is, to a position with explicitly authorized eligibility for tenure, may not be considered for tenure. Faculty in tenured or tenure-track positions, then, comprise the continuing core of the university in terms of both programmatic substance and long-term financial commitment. The number of positions so defined and budgeted is therefore of critical importance to the faculty and administration alike.

As another infrequently excepted rule, faculty are considered for the award of tenure only after a probationary period of performance, usually about seven years for a new inexperienced faculty member. During this period the faculty member receives annual evaluations that should include feedback on his or her progress toward meeting the criteria for tenure. Then in the final probationary year, the candidate undergoes a comprehensive and very intensive review explicitly designed to enable a decision on the award of tenure. Specifically, the candidate's overall achievements in teaching, research, and service are independently evaluated by his or her departmental colleagues, the department chair, a college-wide faculty committee, the college dean, often a university-wide faculty committee, external reviewers in their field of research, and the provost and the president. Those who survive this multileveled review are then recommended for tenure to the board of trustees who formally authorize the award.

It is difficult to give an estimate of the probability that a faculty member in general will be awarded tenure through this process since there are no studies on the frequency of favorable tenure judgments across universities and individual universities have not made such data available and in fact seldom compile such information. However, some data relevant to this question has been provided by the author who in his capacity as an academic administrator at an Ivy League institution studied the career-course of all of the faculty appointed over a ten-year period within that institution. Only faculty who joined the university as their first post-Ph.D. appointment were included in the analysis. The study found that 33 percent of the newly appointed Ph.D.'s were awarded tenure at the end of their probationary period, which was uniformly in their seventh year of appointment. The remaining two thirds either were denied tenure or had resigned at some earlier point during their probationary period, some to take an academic position elsewhere and some leaving the academy. In a number of cases, the resignations were very likely prompted by annual evaluations that indicated that the individual was at significant risk of an unfavorable tenure judgment.

The fact that only a third of those in the "new faculty pipeline" succeeded to tenure at this institution bespeaks a rigorous selection process. Of course, an Ivy League institution is not representative of universities in general or for that matter of research universities. But even if one were to assume liberally that the probability of tenure for a beginning Ph.D. at most other universities is double that found in the author's study, the point is that tenure is hardly a sure thing. Further, based on interviews with faculty and administrators in institutions around the country, the *Chronicle of Higher Education* recently reported that the bar for tenure is rising even further at major research universities and teaching institutions alike.[1] Given the average ten-year period of preparatory academic training that precedes an initial faculty appointment and the seven-year probationary period that typically follows, it is clear that the pathway to tenure is long, arduous, and uncertain. Working with survey data provided by the U.S. Education Department, the American Association of University Professors (AAUP) found that among full-time professors on campuses nationwide, 52 percent held tenure in 1995, about the same proportion as in 1975.[2]

Many people mistakenly believe that tenure is an employment guarantee for life. It is not. The protection afforded by tenure extends *only* to academic freedom, the freedom of faculty to teach, inquire, and learn without interference. Tenure does not protect the faculty member from being terminated for a variety of reasons, such as incompetence, neglect of responsibilities, insubordination, unprofessional conduct, or financial exigency leading to program elimination. As stated in the "Statement of Principles on Academic Freedom and Tenure" formulated by the AAUP, a document that serves as the guideline on tenure for most institutions today, "The teacher is entitled to full freedom in research and the publication of the results, *subject to adequate performance of his other academic duties*" (emphasis added).[3] The AAUP estimates that in a typical year, fifty professors across the country are terminated for various forms of unprofessional conduct, a number that depending on one's view of the general character of the faculty can be read as either surprisingly large or surprisingly small.[4]

The concept of tenure arose in the United States in the later part of the nineteenth century. It served then, as it serves now, to protect faculty who may be threatened with dismissal for speaking out on controversial matters, as, for example, advancing unpopular but logically defensible ideas in the classroom or criticizing an institution's corporate mission or an institution's speech code. There are well-known cases that illustrate the necessity of such protection. For example, Joycelyn Elders was almost denied the right to return to her tenured medical school faculty position because of the views she expressed as surgeon general on such politically sensitive topics as decriminalization of drugs, and tenure protected Anita Hill against legislators' efforts to have her fired from her law faculty position after her Senate testimony. In a particularly notorious episode, Florida legislative committee investigations in the 1960s, searching for communists, homosexuals, and others considered dangerous, led to the withdrawal of one university professor's appointment offer and the pressured resignation of another professor.[5] But for every such high-profile case, any experienced provost will be aware of additional instances where tenure has helped them to shield individual faculty against inappropriate pressure from people in powerful positions. More generally but equally vital to academic freedom, the protection afforded by tenure contributes to a broad institutional climate of free expression that proponents of tenure believe is vital to the integrity of university teaching and research. As Alan Charles Kors and Harvey Silvergate attest in their 1998 book *The Shadow University*, freedom of both student and faculty expression, particularly in regard to matters of race and gender, are currently threatened by a deteriorating climate of "censorship, indoctrination, intimidation, official group identity, and groupthink."[6] The protection of tenure also makes it possible for faculty to speak up without fear and with conviction about university policies and university leadership, a protection essential to the effective participation of faculty in university governance that we have urged. In short, most faculty see tenure as inseparable from academic freedom. The case for tenure is essentially the case for freedom of inquiry and expression within the academy.

There have been many strong statements in defense of tenure. The following two passages present faculty perspectives that are particularly applicable to the current university environment. The first, by Dominique Homberger and A. Ravi P. Rau, professors, respectively, of biological sciences and physics and astronomy at Louisiana State University, speaks to the core role of tenure in protecting academic freedom in academic research and inquiry, while the second by Saunders Mac Lane, a professor of mathematics at the University of Chicago, speaks to somewhat more general but equally important protections of tenure:

> Today, knowledge, its critical analysis, its creation, and its transmission, have come to rest overwhelmingly in our universities. It is the importance of this function that has led to, and justifies, the institution of tenure for professorial faculty. Tenure is an integral part of university culture, specifically its spirit of free inquiry to follow ideas where they may lead, even if this be out of favor with or anathema to society and governments of the time.
>
> This spirit of free inquiry is a habit of the mind, a way of approaching all questions to get closer to truth and understanding, whether convenient or not. Tenure is needed to nurture this habit and to sustain a campus culture that values such inquiry, not just tolerates it. You cannot be free when you have to fear for your job, whether from political and other pressures from outside the academy or from differing styles and ideological pressures from within academic units themselves. A habit of critical inquiry that is free of concerns for personal safety is particularly necessary in a profession that analyses received knowledge critically and generates new ideas—both of these activities, by their very nature, may upset the status quo.
>
> There are many examples of ideas, inventions, and basic research that at one time were seen as esoteric, academic, and devoid of any relevance to society but later became absolutely central to society and to our lives. History also provides countless examples of ideas that at first were part of unorthodox thinking prevailing eventually over established opinions. Predictions being fallible, society or academic units themselves must not censor creative and critical inquiry. Every professorial faculty member needs to be free to pursue a particular line of research even if it does not follow the current bandwagon.[7]

After speaking to the role of tenure in the protection of academic free speech, Mac Lane addresses the more general role of tenure in promoting a broad institutional climate of free direction and expression:

> But the provision of academic freedom is by no means the only consideration. With tenure, faculty members can embark on long-term, adventurous research projects–trying out difficult experiments or devoting years to preparing a book. In other words, tenure protects the faculty in their chosen activities.
>
> This is of crucial importance at the present time, when professors need to be free to speak up on current policy changes. Today, professors in universities are often called upon to do a wide variety of timely and useful things: to aid the handicapped, to teach more courses, to act as mentors, to help reform education K-12, to serve society, to advance competitiveness, to listen to authority, and to be correct, politically or otherwise. This downbeat of approved instructions and orders tends to obscure the primary task of the professors: to ignore distractions, to think deeply on scholarly issues, and to report truthfully the results of that thought.
>
> The professor is there both to expound past thoughts and to anticipate future ideas. There is no greater achievement than a sparkling new and effective idea, and there can be many difficult steps on the way to discovering and formulating such an idea. But ideas do not come from committees or from peer reviews or from reports or from official policies. Ultimately, these important ideas come from individuals following their own leads and building up new insights while protected in that vital task by the provision of tenure. Tenure for faculty is essential to the work of the university. Unthinking attackers of tenure are to be firmly resisted.[8]

Having stated the essentials of the case for tenure, what are the critical features of the case against tenure, or as might more accurately be said, of the attacks on tenure? The strongly vituperative nature of much of the literature questioning tenure makes it somewhat difficult to distill the substantive arguments that might be fairly advanced. For example, the following are some of the phrases that have been actually used in that literature to describe tenure and its claimed negative effects: "is an absolute scam," "is the equivalent of welfare," "turns faculty jobs into sinecures," "raises costs," "inhibits competition," "makes tuition excessive," "protects little more than professors' paychecks," "fossilizes departments," "lowers productivity," "protects incompetence," and "unfairly prevents faculty from suffering like other workers." Such language has surely helped to give tenure a bad name in the public mind, and bespeaks strong resentment of a practice seen as outmoded and unjustified. Nevertheless, one can detect even in these loaded phrases several valid grounds for questioning the concept of tenure.

The major contentions are that tenure prevents the discharge of faculty who are incompetent or unproductive ("protects incompetence," and "is the equivalent of welfare"; "turns faculty jobs into sinecures," and "lowers productivity"); prevents or constricts the flow of new talent and new ideas into department teaching and research ("fossilizes departments," and "inhibits competition"); and prevents the reduction of faculty positions when cost cuts are required or students' tastes change ("protects faculty paychecks," and "raises costs," and "makes tuition excessive"). The presumptions underlying these criticisms of course are that tenured faculty *are* in fact less productive and accountable than they would otherwise be if not tenured and that the practice of tenure excessively constricts the flow of new blood into the faculty ranks and unduly prevents reduction of the faculty roster as a means of accommodating financial cutbacks and enrollment shifts. It is reasonable to make these points, but they bear scrutiny.

Although the idea that faculty become less productive after tenure is often expressed, one never hears it asked whether there are studies actually bearing on that proposition. In fact there are such data and they provide a pretty convincing answer. It should first be noted that the question of diminished productivity does not really arise in connection with teaching. Faculty are hired primarily to teach and their teaching duties tend to be relatively fixed and well monitored. Peer pressure alone will generally ensure that they contribute their share of effort to the curricular needs and enrollment demands on their department. And faculty simply do not have an option whether or not to teach assigned classes; any dereliction of that very public responsibility would be immediately noticed and dealt with swiftly. In contrast, scholarly work is unscheduled, self-selected work accomplished voluntarily and usually privately at whatever hours. In particular, writing and publication are self-driven and solitary activities. The nature of scholarly work, then, certainly affords faculty an opportunity to be more or less productive with very little social or supervisory consequence, at least for prolonged periods. Thus if research and publication are significantly tied to the quest for tenure, as is often assumed, one might well expect decreased scholarly productivity after tenure is granted.

Studies examining this question have tracked publication by faculty beginning with their initial appointment and through the end of their careers.[9] Publication, of course, is the end product of scholarship and is generally employed as the standard measure of research productivity. In general, this research has looked at faculty within Ph.D.-granting institutions, tabulating the number of articles or books published each year by the faculty member and/or the number of times the faculty member's published research is cited annually in other independently published research papers. As one might expect, these studies have found marked individual and discipline differences in faculty productivity rates, but they also have found a characteristic hump-shaped pattern of career-length productivity that transcends those differences. Essentially, publication rates in general are found to climb sharply in the early career stages, level off and decline gradually in midcareer, and then decline more steeply in late career as retirement approaches (these studies were done when faculty faced mandatory retirement at age sixty-five; retirement is uncapped today). The overall pattern indicates that publication rates of university faculty in general either remain high over the course of their careers or peak relatively late in their careers, that is, peak beyond the average tenure-decision age. There is no evidence in the data that tenure is associated with a general decline in productivity. In fact, publications tend to increase somewhat following the award of tenure and to become more variable in rate suggesting increased risk-taking in research, something that tenure is designed in part to encourage.

The fact that productivity tends to remain relatively high after tenure should not really be surprising. The best predictor of future behavior is past behavior. What else should one expect from the collective behavior of individuals motivated in some significant part by intrinsic interests who enter their post-tenure years after an average of seventeen years of academic preparation and professional work including seven years of intense productivity in the tenure track? The largely autonomous nature of faculty motivation has been well expressed by Myles Brand, president and professor of philosophy at Indiana University, a major research university:

> Those who argue that tenure leads to declining productivity do not understand the motivation of faculty members. Professors are far more interested in gaining knowledge and communicating it to others than they are in high salaries. It does not matter if the knowledge is a scientific breakthrough, a new interpretation of a text, or a noteworthy performance of a classical score. It is the activity itself and sharing one's results with students and colleagues that faculty members find rewarding. Being a faculty member is not a job, it's a life.[10]

Evidence that faculty in general remain productive after tenure does not, of course, deny that some tenured faculty may slacken and neglect their responsibilities in various ways, perhaps even to the degree of becoming totally unproductive or even counterproductive as professional colleagues. But as pointed out earlier, tenure itself does *not* protect such faculty. This is an important point because much of the animus against tenure appears to be fueled by the perception that tenure confers unconditional lifelong economic security and job protection. The feeling appears to be that other workers in society are vulnerable to job insecurity and therefore faculty should also be vulnerable. While this is an ungenerous view, it is an all too human reaction, and universities should therefore make clear in pronouncement and practice that the protection of tenure is strictly limited to matters of academic freedom. However, in fairness to critics of tenure, universities in fact often have been reluctant to terminate tenured faculty, in large part because the courts have recognized that tenure carries a property interest and therefore stringent due process must be followed to remove it. But if circumstances warrant and if there is clear resolve, the termination process can surely be implemented. In the final analysis, unsatisfactory performance by tenured faculty, to the extent that it exists, is not protected by tenure per se but by a failure of institutional policy. How institutional policy and practice might be strengthened in this regard is an important question that will be considered later in this chapter.

Does tenure lead to the "fossilization of departments"? That claim is not supported by the data we have just reviewed, which indicate that tenured faculty on the whole continue to be energetic contributors to the literature in their fields and indeed may be even more likely to try novel or risky approaches than their untenured colleagues. While there are no comparable data bearing on post-tenure teaching performance, it would not be unreasonable to assume that the same characteristics infuse the teaching of tenured faculty. And again, should tenured faculty become unproductive or counterproductive in behavior, they *can* be held accountable through the annual evaluations that determine their salary increments and through administrative disciplinary actions. Finally, if 52 percent of the faculty in the average university department is tenured, as indicated by the earlier cited AAUP data, this would seem to permit a generally acceptable rate of turnover and infusion of "new blood" and updating of faculty competencies.[11] However, universities that permit relatively high institution-wide levels of tenured faculty, for example 80 percent or more, and there certainly are such instances, are clearly vulnerable to the fossilization charge. In this connection, it might be observed that the percent of faculty on tenure in any department, and more importantly the quality, productivity, and dedication of the faculty on tenure, are determined by the standards imposed by the faculty and administration in making judgments on the award on tenure. In fact, it can be argued that the post-tenure concerns we have discussed reflect to some significant degree poor decisions on tenure. For this reason, the tenure decision should always be made with the greatest possible care, and the tenure procedures of a university should be continuously reviewed to insure the most rigorous and objective possible process.

The argument that tenure prevents or constrains reduction in senior faculty in response to sudden financial downturns or enrollment shifts is certainly true for all practical purposes. While faculty layoffs are possible under conditions of financial exigency, one would have to make a strong and time-consuming case for the urgency and necessity of that course of action. Therefore cutting tenured faculty is not a readily available or very viable cost management option to be utilized in order to meet unanticipated shortfalls in institutional budgets. But there are other effective ways to control faculty costs that can be quickly implemented. The simplest is to impose a partial or total freeze on the hiring of new faculty and staff. That is, it may be difficult to lay off incumbent tenured faculty, but it is easy to simply delay bringing new additional or replacement faculty on board. This action can be taken at any time by administrative fiat and without legal restriction of any sort, and in fact is not uncommonly taken as a means of dealing with sudden financial cutbacks. Personnel salaries usually comprise about 80 percent of a university budget with faculty salaries by far the largest component. Given the annual rate of turnover in any sizable university, even a relatively short-term freeze on hiring is likely to generate sig-nificant savings, generally enough to cope with even sizable revenue shortfalls. A protracted freeze in faculty hiring will of course pose hardship for departments, but seldom enough to cripple academic programs in the near term. But should the hiring freeze be insufficient as a means of controlling faculty costs, one can alternatively reduce other instructional appointments that are not protected by tenure–graduate assistants, lecturers, adjunct faculty and other part-time faculty, full-time faculty in nontenure tracks, and finally faculty in tenure-track appointments. Therefore, the criticism that tenure prevents cost-saving cuts in regular faculty during financial downturns, and therefore necessitates increased tuition, has little practical significance in light of other effective means of controlling faculty costs. As for cutting faculty resources in response to enrollment shifts, most such shifts are not sudden but rather are gradual changes that can be readily accommodated through adjustment of faculty hiring and replacement plans. Moreover, there is not a simple one-to-one coupling between enrollment and faculty resources. For example, a required course that is normally offered with a hundred students but that undergoes, say, a 75 percent loss of enrollment must still be taught. In summary, the arguments that tenure leads to lower productivity, prevents incompetent or poorly performing faculty from being discharged or otherwise held accountable, unduly limits the flow of new talent and ideas into department programs, and prevents the reduction of faculty positions when cost cuts are required or students' tastes change, are at best questionable contentions.

A more recent argument has been that tenure is no longer needed to protect academic freedom because the First Amendment forbids the state to infringe upon free-speech rights. Such protection would only clearly apply to state colleges and universities, but proponents of this argument claim that private colleges and universities are sufficiently public in function, and receive so much financial support from the government, that they would also likely fall under this First Amendment protection. But they acknowledge that this point is not settled legally, that is, that there is insufficient case law to infer how the courts would act. Another major point of uncertainty in the First Amendment argument is whether courts would interpret the legal category of speech as also including the wide range of activities that academic freedom currently covers, activities that are critical to free academic function. For example, would "speech" cover curriculum design and content, textbook selection, syllabus construction, admission decisions, grading, research and scholarly activities, and the various forms of community service currently being pressed on faculty such as contributing to regional economic development objectives? There is no way to answer this question other than to try abandoning tenure and then determine how the courts would rule on the inevitable legal tests of such activities as instances of free speech. But that would be a very risky experiment indeed.

A related argument is that if the large number of part-time faculty and other limited-term faculty are presumably freely carrying out their university work with only First Amendment protection, then why is tenure needed for regular faculty? Do these temporary faculty not represent a de facto uncoupling of tenure and academic freedom? One should be very cautious in so concluding because we do not know the number of times temporary faculty were let go because they expressed unpopular or politically incorrect views. Nor can that number ever be known because administrators have the option of simply not renewing such temporary faculty appointments solely at their discretion. But it is probably very safe to conclude that the number is *not* zero.

As noted, the fact that tenure does not protect the growing number of temporary university faculty has been used in arguments against the concept of tenure, but that same growth phenomenon represents a more lethal form of opposition to tenure that might be termed *death by stealth.* We earlier noted that part-time faculty, who are all employed on limited-term contracts, grew from 22% of instructors nationwide in 1970 to 43% of instructors today. But even more disturbing are recent analyses by

Jay Chronister and Roger Baldwin, working with survey data provided by the U.S. Education Department, showing that the proportion of *full-time faculty* working on temporary contracts climbed from 19% in 1975 to 28% in 1995 while the proportion of full-time faculty on the tenure track fell from 29% to 20%.[12] Add to these reports the fact that some forty institutions around the country have now adopted contract systems for all new faculty hires, often in connection with the start-up of new institutions.[13] Under such systems, the regular full-time faculty member is given a time-limited employment contract, normally for three to five years. While that contract may be renewed for other limited periods of time, the institution has no commitment to do so and the faculty member will never be considered for tenure. These several observations make clear that as faculty lines have come open or as new ones have been created, administrators have been increasingly likely to fill them with temporary faculty, part-time and full-time, instead of with tenure-track professors. At this point, the appointment of full-time faculty to temporary positions has primarily impacted positions in the tenure-track category, but as faculty who are currently in tenured positions retire, this development will inevitably show as a significant erosion of tenure. The movement toward the appointment of contract-faculty rather than tenure-track faculty has been incremental and not linked with any explicit repudiation of tenure, leading some to label this trend a *silent killer*.

As a rule, faculty appointments off the tenure track cost universities a lot less in salary and benefits than those within tenured ranks. Faculty hired on temporary appointments can also be used in very targeted ways rather than carrying out the full teaching, research, and service responsibilities expected of regular faculty. Full-time temporary faculty are usually expected *only* to teach and generally carry heavy course loads. They have few if any rights and privileges. They can be let go as soon as their contracts expire, have no vote in the faculty senate and, as we have seen, little protection of their academic freedom. They tend, understandably, not to become identified with, or become full participants in, the university community. In creating this growing body of temporary faculty, then, universities have instituted a category of second-class faculty who can be hired, assigned, and fired at will while providing a relatively cheap, targeted, and flexible means of meeting immediate productivity needs. Is it any wonder that some faculty have concluded that this development is a direct reflection of the business orientation of boards and administrators—an emphasis on the deployment of resources to achieve short-term educational objectives while minimizing bottom-line impact? This view has been forcefully expressed by Cary Nelson, a professor of English at the University of Illinois. After characterizing the highly targeted, short-term employment needs of corporations, Professor Nelson states:

> If such activities are high priorities, then the presence on campus of full-time faculty members devoted to the institution may at best be an inconvenience, at worst an impediment to "progress". Better to hire people to perform narrowly defined tasks: Teach this class segment, design this course, grade these exams, supervise these lab technicians, evaluate these teachers, carry out this research contract, review these application files, write this syllabus, advise these students, hire these part-timers. The war against the faculty entails identifying and separating all the roles that faculty members perform, eliminating those that inconvenience administrators, and contracting for the others as piecework.[14]

Whether the growth in temporary faculty is a reflection of corporate ideology, or of inadequate funding of higher enrollments, or of a deliberate attempt to do away with tenure, or a matter of protecting the research time of tenured faculty with their concurrence, or whatever combination of factors may be operating, a change of this fundamental nature should not be taking place silently and without full awareness of all constituents. Clearly, there are major consequences of shrinking the proportion of the faculty workforce protected by tenure and having an increasing amount of the work of the academy carried out by temporary faculty. As stated earlier, temporary faculty cannot be expected to bring the full commitment of regular faculty and are unable to contribute to the scholarship that forms the backbone of a strong university. And as the core of tenured faculty at the center of the enterprise shrinks, so does the protection of free speech and the power of faculty within the institution as a whole. The trend toward replacement of tenured faculty by temporary faculty and its likely impact on the academy should be broadly and vigorously discussed and debated. This is a prime task for individual and collective treatment by the proposed faculty councils.

Another recent development that faculty are strongly inclined to view as part of a move against tenure is so-called post-tenure review, that is, in-depth reviews of the performance of all tenured professors. According to a regent of one university system that has adopted a post-tenure review process, these reviews are intended to make it easier to fire tenured professors who are "driving through their careers on autopilot."[15] Again, the presumption is that "autopiloting" goes on after tenure and therefore a new system of review must be imposed to detect and weed it out. As earlier noted, the discussions surrounding such presumptions have not been characterized by systematic examination of the relevant data but rather have been fed by largely anecdotal reports of underperforming faculty. Whatever the impetus to the post-tenure review movement, it has clearly gained a foothold. This movement is now underway in one form or another in thirty-seven states, including many private as well as public institutions.[16]

Proposals for post-tenure review have often arisen in the context of attempts to do away with tenure itself, and can thus be seen as a compromise or fall-back position from that more sweeping proposal or as a first and more readily achievable step toward the eventual abolition of tenure. Given the significance of such review to the question of tenure, and more generally to the presumption of underperforming faculty that underlies both, it will be helpful to consider a case history of the development of such a review process.

In 1996 the Florida Board of Regents voted to require tenured professors in the state-university system to undergo regular performance evaluations. The plan, adopted after two years of study, called for every one of the approximately six thousand tenured faculty within the system's ten universities to be given an in-depth evaluation at least once every seven years. Consistent with the "eliminate auto-piloting" intention, it was envisaged that professors who received poor reviews could be subject to disciplinary action, including dismissal from their university positions. Before considering details of the review process, it is important to understand the baseline process for evaluation of tenured faculty upon which this new post-tenure review system was imposed.

Most universities require all full-time faculty to undergo annual evaluations of performance, whether they hold a tenured or tenure-track or even a non-tenure-track position. These annual performance evaluations, which are conducted at the department level, are used primarily for decisions on merit salary increments (when such funds are available), but they also provide an occasion for reporting unsatisfactory faculty performance. The process in place within the Florida university system, which is quite typical, calls for each faculty member's annual accomplishments in teaching, research, service, academic advising, and administrative activity to be reviewed by a committee of departmental faculty colleagues who assign a rating of outstanding, strong, satisfactory, weak, or unacceptable within each category of assigned activity. A similar review and evaluation is also independently conducted by the chair of the department. Finally, these evaluations are forwarded to the college dean along with recommendations from both the faculty committee and the chair regarding the appropriate level of any available discretionary salary increment, recommendations that typically would range in several steps from "no increment" to "high increment."

Since a system of this nature already provides an opportunity for assessing and reporting unsatisfactory performance by any faculty member, why did the regents seek a new system of review that specifically targets tenured faculty? The answer is that departments view the annual evaluation process primarily in relation to salary recommendations and tend to direct the process to that purpose. The focus is on scaling above average performance, and the evaluative categories of satisfactory, strong, and outstanding are adequate to the typically small salary increments available. In fact, ratings below satisfactory are very seldom given. The process, then, is flawed as a means of reporting inadequacies in performance, and does not approach the in-depth evaluation of teaching, research, and service that characterizes the review required for the tenure decision. Therefore, the regents sought a post-tenure process that would parallel the tenure review and be just as rigorous. The regents' proposal immediately brought opposition from the statewide faculty union that argued that if already tenured faculty are to be held every seven years to the same standards as those in the review for tenure, then tenure amounts to nothing more than a seven-year contract. The stage was set, then, for contention between the regents' position that a post-tenure review process was needed to weed out tenured faculty deadwood and the union's view that such a process would be a de facto elimination of tenure. The manner in which this matter was resolved in the final action of the regents is a case study in how not to manage academics, notwithstanding the doubtless good intentions of the regents.

As noted earlier, a post-tenure review process was in fact established as part of the new collective bargaining agreement ratified by the Board of Regents, although the process was renamed "sustained performance evaluation" in deference to the sensitivities associated with use of the displaced phrase. Also as originally planned by the regents, the process requires tenured faculty members to be evaluated on their *cumulative* performance every seven years, that is, on performance over the previous six years. The process thus meets the regents' original intention to conduct an extensive review of tenured faculty to document sustained performance after the award of tenure. However, beyond these features, the newly enacted process bears little resemblance to the regents' original conception of the nature and objectives of this review. The primary reason for this departure are two provisions in the plan as finally enacted: first, that the sole basis for the review would be the faculty member's annual evaluations and, second, that faculty who received satisfactory annual evaluations during the review period could not be rated deficient in the overall post-tenure review. But as we have noted, the annual evaluation process focuses on salary recommendations and rarely yields less than satisfactory performance ratings at any time. Further, even if a faculty member were to receive an overall unsatisfactory rating in the analysis of his or her six-year file of annual evaluations, the action to be taken is not dismissal or even disciplinary action. Instead a "Performance Improvement Plan" is to be developed for such faculty that sets targets for improvement over a relatively generous time period. Finally, in still further erosion of the original concept, a faculty member who is rated unsatisfactory in some respect over the six-year review period does not necessarily require even a Performance Improvement Plan. Such a plan is to be required only if the faculty member has been *consistently* evaluated as being below satisfactory throughout the full period of review, an outcome which, given the infrequency of an unsatisfactory rating in any single annual evaluation, is extremely remote.

This post-tenure or sustained performance review process has been in place in the state university system for three years now, and of the roughly six thousand tenured faculty who have undergone evaluation only a handful have been asked to develop a Performance Improvement Plan, itself a procedure without any clearly specified consequence. Thus the process, while ambitious in conception, has proven virtually devoid of impact. Worse, it has exacted high costs. First, it creates a significant additional administrative workload that must be carried annually by faculty committees designated to review the extensive files involved in conjunction with their department chairs. Second, and a much higher cost, the faculty know that the process as ultimately conceived and implemented is essentially meaningless. As such, it stands in their perception as a palpable sign of the poor understanding governance authorities have of the academic workplace. And it also stands as continuing evidence of the lack of trust of the governance authorities in the dedication and integrity of those who have passed the most rigorous test of academic professionalism.

A post-tenure review program that creates a lot of work and weeds out nobody is a ludicrous process that reflects discredit on all involved. While the union may feel that it scored a "victory" in this matter, the final outcome creates meaningless work for the faculty that reduces their time for teaching and research while further eroding their confidence in the academic leadership of the board and higher administration. These are not outcomes of which to be proud. For its part, the board attempted to do what it thought was right in the public interest, but jumped to poorly grounded conclusions about the necessity for its actions and betrayed its ignorance of the existing faculty evaluation structure. The university presidents displayed little leadership in the matter and remained publicly silent throughout the process. Efforts were made by a provost or two to promote a more meaningful process, but having little influence at the governing board level, their proposals were swept aside. In short, nobody distinguished themselves and the entire enterprise was diminished.

The final irony is that no new process was needed to address the regent's concern because there already existed a means that could be used to identify unsatisfactory faculty performance, namely, the annual evaluations. That the annual evaluation process has not been used for this purpose is not because it cannot be, but because departments simply have not been inclined to so use it. And this inclination reflects a lack of clear institutional policy, directives, and standards, rather than any uncooperativeness on the part of department faculty or chairs.

While departments will usually seek disciplinary action and even dismissal of tenured faculty who display explicitly unacceptable conduct or incompetence, they are likely to tolerate, at least for a period, less extreme but still troublesome inadequacies in tenured faculty performance. The reasons are several. As previously noted, the long-practiced behaviors that earn tenure tend to generate continued strong performance, as attested by the evidence on sustained faculty productivity after tenure. The very infrequency and unexpectedness of inadequate performance, then, dispose against an immediate move to discipline or dismiss. The first response of department chairs to an emerging problem in faculty performance is not to report the faculty member, who probably has been a long-time colleague, but to try to work with that individual to attempt to correct the deficiency. This supportive attitude, however, would not preclude the award of minimal or zero salary increments through the annual evaluation process, a consequence that in the scale of faculty salaries can be quite painful. But even if the problem behavior persists, the chair may still be reluctant to initiate the formal disciplinary process, and the public discussion, litigation, and grief that go with it, if the higher administration has not expressed a zero tolerance policy regarding such behavior and made clear that it can be relied upon to back efforts to discipline or dismiss. And administrators, who may also have concerns about the negative publicity and "bad image" attendant upon faculty disciplinary actions, typically have not done so.

Nothing in these observations should be taken to conclude that inadequate faculty performance should be tolerated, however infrequent it may be. If the public is wrong in generalizing about reported or even experienced unprofessional behavior on the part of faculty, they are right about some professors' abuse of their privileges. Faculty who fail to properly meet their responsibilities violate the implicit social contract with students, the university and society, and have a disproportionately negative impact on public opinion and the reputation of the faculty as a whole. The faculty in general thus have a strong interest and personal stake in assuring that their colleagues perform up to standards and carry their share of the load. Tenured professors in particular have a responsibility to speak out against unprofessional behavior on the part of colleagues if they are to deserve the freedoms that tenure provides. No new process or authorization is required to address any concerns there may be in this area. What is needed is a clear statement of the standards defining satisfactory performance and of the disciplinary processes to be followed when those standards are found to have been violated in the annual evaluation, and then the resolve to follow those disciplinary processes, including action to terminate when conditions warrant. These desiderata should be established through collegial dialogue between faculty and governance authorities and explicitly incorporated into the annual evaluation process. Virtually all faculty would support an approach of this nature.

The faculty councils could be most helpful in creating such a dialogue. In fact, it is unlikely that the Florida post-tenure review process would have developed as it did if faculty councils had been in place as a standing feature of the governance structure. Regular communication between councils and the governing authorities would almost certainly have fostered a better information base for the decisions and a better climate for discussion of this sensitive issue. In contrast to the adversarial and doctrinaire approach that characterizes faculty unions, the councils would have afforded an opportunity for a more collegial exchange with faculty less oriented to a protective stance while still committed to the highest standards of faculty performance.

Chapter 8

Accountability

❦

A*ccountability* is the latest buzzword in higher education. It has a fine ring to it. Who would argue that individuals and organizations should not be answerable for their actions and obligations? In fact, it has such a fine ring to it that governing boards, legislatures, and governors are usually described as not just seeking accountability from universities but as downright demanding accountability. One understands the temptation of those in leadership positions to be firmly on the side of the unassailable–they get so few opportunities–but "demanding" also implies a call for something that is being willfully withheld and universities in fact have never failed to be accountable. If by accountability one means reporting regularly on all financial and programmatic actions and responding to innumerable year-round ad hoc requests for information from governing authorities and their staffs on virtually any aspect of institutional objectives and operations, then universities may be the most accountable organizations in the history of humanity. In this regard, it is instructive to look at an actual record of the accounting that a particular but representative public research university was expected to provide in its annual report twelve years ago, well before the current wave of accountability concerns.[1] The report format required the university to both estimate its expected level of performance on a variety of program measures (i.e., estimated prior to the beginning of the year) and then provide the actual year-end figures for each measure. Since the estimated activity for each program guided funding allocations to the university, a comparison of estimated to actual figures would gauge whether funding was spent for the purposes allocated. The data the university was required to provide included number of degrees and certificates conferred by type; percent of entering freshmen

124

retained to the fourth year; percent of entering freshmen graduated within five years; total full-time equivalent student enrollment; total full-time equivalent faculty; student-faculty ratio; research expenditures by source (state, federal, and private); number of grant proposals submitted; number of cooperative extension contacts; number of fine arts events and attendance at each broken down by on-campus and off-campus location; number of pubic service programs conducted and attendance, broken down by state and nonstate participants served; school districts served; number of teachers trained; number of museum programs and attendance; total computer system users by type; computer terminals by number and site; number of personal computer laboratories, users, and sites; library acquisitions by type; library hours of service and number of daily users; number of interlibrary loans and public borrowers; number of university-sponsored events for students with attendance at each; number of student-initiated events and attendance; athletic teams with participants, events, and attendance for each team; number of financial aid applications processed by type and awards; number of daily client health-services; listing of employers recruiting on university campuses; total applications for admissions by level of study; number of admissions and final enrollment; listing of public safety incidents; number of purchase orders issued by type; number of outgoing mail pieces; facilities maintenance costs; facilities square feet per custodian; acres maintained per grounds keeper; all capital construction projects and expenditures; all major program operating budgets; and expenditures and balances on all fund sources.

Along with such annual stock taking, public universities ordinarily must provide many additional regular reports to their overseers during the year. For example, one large state university system required more than a hundred fifty such reports from its individual member institutions annually.[2] While many of these are routine status reports on such matters as personnel and payroll rosters, operating budget expenditures, enrollments, and course assignments by instructor, they nevertheless indicate the high degree of scrutiny under which public universities operate and the constancy of institutional accounting. In fact, reporting is such a ubiquitous feature of university management that university systems have been known to do a report on reporting, that is, an analysis of the completeness and timeliness of institutional report submissions, with institutions then being required to submit a report explaining any improper reporting![3]

In addition to such regular monitoring of activity, universities are periodically evaluated by national accrediting bodies to assure maintenance of the standards required to qualify graduates for admission to higher levels of education or to professional practice. Institutional accreditation is a two-year ordeal that covers all aspects of the university's academic degree, administrative, and educational support programs. The first step in this process is an exhaustive self-study, both descriptive and evaluative in nature, which is then subject to examination by an externally selected team of perhaps thirty to forty educators who spend several weeks on campus reviewing all materials and interviewing administrators, faculty, and students. The full body of final reports and evaluative material is then reviewed by the standing national accrediting commission itself, which makes the final decisions on accreditation.

In addition to such university-wide accreditation, universities must also secure separate re-accreditation every five to seven years for all professional academic programs, such as engineering, medicine, nursing, business, law, computer science, and physical therapy. The accreditation or re-accreditation of each professional program typically requires a year-long self-study covering all aspects of program operations and resources, which is then subject to review by an externally selected visiting team of specialists charged to safeguard the standards of the profession and the public interest.

Both institution-wide and professional program accreditation evaluations are taken very seriously by universities, since failure to maintain accreditation or even an issued warning of possible loss of accreditation can seriously impact student enrollment. Eligibility for federal financial aid for students is also dependent on institutional accreditation. Finally, most university systems and even individual universities themselves additionally conduct periodic reviews of all academic programs that are not subject to external accreditation review, usually employing outside evaluators in the process.

Universities are also mandated to provide annual reports to the National Center for Education Statistics, a federal entity that collects and analyzes data from all postsecondary educational institutions on a variety of institutional characteristics and performance variables such as degrees awarded, enrollment, graduation rates, facilities, and financial information.[4] And there are still other special federal reports that universities must provide for public consumption or maintain on file for inspection, such as data on campus crime and security and faculty effort reports on federal grant projects.

There is yet another round of intensive reporting beyond that at the institutional level. Individual faculty in public institutions must report on their specific activities in teaching, research, and service every semester, reports that are subject to audit by system and institutional auditors. Every department and academic unit must provide an annual report of its activities and accomplishments to the president; these of course are public documents. Individual faculty are evaluated annually by peer committees and by their department chairs, chairs are evaluated by their deans, and the deans are evaluated by the provost, utilizing annual reports of accomplishments against goals assigned at the beginning of the year.

In sum, universities and their faculties have hardly been functioning as entities unto themselves. To the contrary, they are under constant pressure to report and account for their activities, to demonstrate progress toward goals, to defend the quality of their programs, and basically to justify their uses of public and private resources. The pressure is greatest in public universities, but it is present as well in private institutions. Small wonder that some faculty and administrators have been known to observe that the more time you have to spend reporting on what you are doing, the less time you have for doing it. Probably the same ones who question why there is no reverse consideration of state and board accountability *to* higher education, as, for example, measures of the proportion of costs shifted to the student. In this connection, it might be noted that in 1986–1987, 41.6 percent of public university revenues came from state appropriations, but by 1997 that number had shrunk to 32.5 percent.

Accounting for faculty and institutional activities has thus long been an omnipresent fact of university life. What, then, has changed to elevate accountability to its newly visible status? What accounts for the present preoccupation of governance authorities with "making universities accountable?" The answer is that while being accountable has not changed, the *terms* of the desired accountability have changed. In the parlance of today's governing authorities, universities are now being asked to be accountable in terms of *outputs* rather than *inputs*. Essentially, this is a shift from the historical practice of evaluating universities on the basis of what is *put into* the educational process to evaluating universities on the basis of what that process *produces,* and more pointedly, to what that process immediately produces.

Consider first, the traditional input model of accountability. In this approach, institutional performance is evaluated by considering two basic types of inputs. The first includes such factors as the scholarly quality of the faculty (generally the preeminent factor), the number of full-time faculty relative to the number of students, the scope and depth of the academic degree programs, the amount of time students are in class, the size and quality of the library, the quality of instructional laboratories and other educational support facilities, and the research and research-support environment. These factors all bespeak a favorable environment for learning and can be quantified or otherwise scaled in much the same way across universities, allowing for ready comparison. The second type of input considered in traditional evaluation concerns the quality of the processes or specific operations by which teaching and learning are carried out. Processes are not as easily measured as environmental factors but nevertheless can still be subject to evaluation. For example, how well a professor teaches is hard to quantify because teaching is such an abstract and variable matter, but nevertheless teaching effectiveness can be judged by such means as student course evaluations, observation by visiting faculty colleagues, feedback from graduates and employers, or examination of syllabi and other course material within "teaching portfolios." Another and very important example of a process factor is the construction and maintenance of curricula. How this process proceeds is worth treating here in some depth because it illustrates well the importance of considering less quantifiable forms of accountability as well as those that can be readily scaled.

Our discussion of curriculum construction will focus on general education because it is central to the mission of any university, but construction of disciplinary curricula follow similar though more circumscribed steps. The task of curriculum construction, and by extension the whole question of accountability, should be considered in the context of an important aspect of the acquisition of knowledge, an aspect that while perhaps obvious, is often overlooked. As noted in chapter 1, it has been observed that all of us in acquiring our knowledge *must rely upon others,* generally to a significant degree, and we cannot dispense with that reliance. This means that knowledge acquisition or learning involves *trust*–the confident belief, if you will,–that those from whom we acquire knowledge have sought to create and convey that knowledge with integrity and truth. Nowhere is the relation of trust to knowledge acquisition more evident than in formal education, and nowhere in formal education is it more evident than in higher education, which students *elect* to pursue, trusting that the curriculum that has been created will best prepare them to achieve their aspirations for a full and rewarding life.

Looked at in this way, what an awesome responsibility is the creation of a curriculum! And what a difficult task, for within the student's brief span of four years of study and the limits of credit hours, universities can at best offer but a portion of the accumulated wisdom of the ages and the vast body of disciplinary knowledge. The task of creating that "best curriculum" falls of course to the faculty. It is a task that can never be done to the satisfaction of all, nor is it a task ever finished. Nevertheless, the student *does* trust, explicitly or implicitly–that the faculty have selected and deliberated with great care, in the most informed and reasoned manner, and have sought to create a curriculum that achieves the best possible balance between specialized knowledge and general knowledge.

In the construction of a general education curriculum there are increasing pressures for faculty to choose specialized over general knowledge instead of maintaining a balance between the two. The enormous growth of new knowledge and techniques and the resulting demand for specialization and skill acquisition have led to a greater emphasis on vocational and professional education in the university curriculum. In addition, recent externally imposed limits on "credit hours to degree," that is, limits on the number of credit hours students are permitted to take to attain the baccalaureate degree, further erode the base of general education. The danger, of course, is that the undergraduate curriculum will lose its liberal arts roots, and that students will lack exposure to fundamental knowledge and fail to acquire the most basic–and the most broadly applicable–intellectual skills.

While specialized education is essential to both state and national needs, higher education would suffer an irreparable loss if it neglected those other portions of the curriculum that place the person before the occupation, the fundamental before the specific, the humanizing before the technical. Because, at the end of the day, despite the pressures toward specialization and despite the greater rewards of specialization even for the faculty themselves, universities profess to *educate*–that is, to produce an educated person.

And so, the age-old question persists, rendered more urgent by these pressures, What should every educated person know? How do we best balance the needs for general and for specialized knowledge? In particular, how do we best define and select that body of general knowledge and skills? What is most true to the intellectual needs of this generation of students?

Construction of a general education curriculum is an effort to answer those questions and to provide a framework to continually address those questions, which as noted earlier are ceaseless. The faculty who work on construction and maintenance of the general education curriculum, generally under the direction and guidance of the faculty senates, are drawn from across the university and work together to carry out one of the most difficult and important responsibilities of the university. It is certainly an easier matter, for example, to define the relevant curriculum within the faculty member's specific areas of expertise, just as it is easier to teach those who have elected to pursue advanced or major study in the faculty member's own area of interest. It is far harder, and more humbling, to attempt to reexamine and augment the accumulated wisdom of history and to define relations among different areas of knowledge. But it is only through such an arduous process of sifting and relating, retention and change, in the context of reasoned debate and discussion, that consensus can be forged about the "best" body of general knowledge. And it is through this process, too, that there is built a much-needed sense of community among students and faculty–the sense that there is a body of knowledge to be valued by all, that there are ideas and ideals to which we can all subscribe, and that there are themes and values that transcend race, gender, and social circumstance.

In working on the development of curricula, whether general education or their own disciplinary curricula, faculty are being true to the trust inherent in the knowledge relation. It is work driven primarily by the professionalism and commitment of the faculty. Such endeavor is not a quantifiable form of accountability, and it is seldom acknowledged, much less understood, by governance authorities or even by many university administrators. Yet it would be remiss not to recognize such endeavor, along with many other "process" efforts in education, as perhaps the highest form of accountability. Finally, it should be noted that general education curricula, like most disciplinary curricula, are subject to formal external evaluation as an explicit part of the institutional accrediting process.

The foregoing curriculum construction process is described in ideal terms, and there are many faculty who willingly contribute long hours to such effort. But there are more faculty, often those with strong research and scholarly agendas, who consistently avoid this responsibility, though their input would be of great value. Furthermore, there is strong evidence that faculty senates have allowed significant slippage in the balance and rigor essential to a sound general education. Examining the course catalogs of the top fifty undergraduate institutions as rated by *U.S. News and World Report* in 1989, the National Association of Scholars has documented a general loosening of the structure, content, and rigor of the general education requirement offered by those institutions, particularly in the latter part of the twentieth century.[4] For example, between 1964 and 1993, the average percentage of the general education requirement from which exemptions were not permitted dropped from 62% to 29%, the percentage of institutions with English composition or other writing requirements dropped from 89% to 36%, the percentage of institutions according special curricular status to humanities subjects dropped from an average of about

45% to virtually 0%, the exemption possibilities from English composition or other writing requirements dropped from 42% to 4%, and the exemption possibilities from natural science requirements rose from 40% to 74%. These findings clearly indicate the need for greater internal and external attention to this usually overlooked form of accountability.

Accountability in terms of inputs, then, focuses on environmental and process factors in evaluating academic success. The rationale is that superior ingredients and conditions of learning mediated by a strong faculty dedicated to excellence will produce a superior education. These terms of accountability, although not set by the faculty, are nevertheless consistent with their educational philosophy, which values the scholarly training and accomplishments brought to the process, sound programs of general and disciplinary education, strong standards of learning and assessment, and the quality of educational support facilities. All in all a sound approach, but an approach which, according to today's critics, places too much emphasis on inputs to the educational process and not enough on specifiable educational outcomes. For these critics, the key question in accountability is whether universities are efficiently producing outputs that are relevant to state and regional needs, and they believe new measures of university performance are needed to make that determination.

The impetus to the shift in the terms of accountability from inputs to outputs is not hard to discern. It stems from a combination of factors–the demands of the new knowledge-based economy, the marked increase in those seeking higher education as the pathway to the benefits of that economy, the concomitant increase in society's investment in higher education, and the ever-present limits in society's resources. These pressures have led governing authorities to seek more specific assurance of what they deem to be pertinent return on investment. Accordingly, the last decade has seen a steady stream of efforts, initiated by governors, legislatures, and governing boards alike, to devise measures of university outputs. This movement has been primarily within the public domain, although given the similar philosophical orientations of public and private boards, private universities have not been immune from the new accountability concerns. Roughly 50% of the states have now experimented with or have actually adopted some form of output-oriented accountability systems and other states have similar systems under development.

There is considerable variation across states in the output measures that have been developed but among the most commonly used measures are graduation rates, usually defined as the percentage of first-time-in-college students who graduate in six years and the percentage of community college transfers who graduate in four years; faculty workload or productivity, usually defined in terms of the number of classroom contact hours or number of courses taught; number of undergraduate and graduate degrees awarded per year; numerical match between actual enrollment and funded enrollment; number of credit hours taken by students in completing their degrees (the aim being to minimize these hours); cost per student by level of study; graduates' pass rates on state licensure or certification exams for selected disciplines; job placement data on graduates (sometimes expressed as the number of graduates holding jobs of a certain dollar value within the state); number and percentage of accredited programs; ratio of external or sponsored research funding to state funded research expenditures; and student satisfaction studies. Productivity, efficiency, practical returns, and "customer" satisfaction are the themes of this list, all captured in simple quantitative terms. The list characterizes well what has been said to be an ongoing shift away from the long-held tenet of what the state should do for the colleges and universities to one of what colleges and universities can do for the state.[5]

In addition, many states are experimenting with ways to link such performance measures to institutional funding either by considering the institution's overall performance on such measures as a factor in campus budget allocations or by tying state money directly to specific performance outcomes on specific measures. As an example of the latter, colleges and universities in Tennessee today can earn up to 5 percent above institutional appropriations based on such outputs as improving graduation rates for minority and other students, testing students for general education outcomes, and increasing favorable responses on student satisfaction surveys. Similarly, Colorado designates about 2 percent of total funding to reward institutions for achievements in five policy areas: productivity, work-force training, K-12 linkages, use of new technology, and undergraduate education. By tying dollars to results, performance-based funding tightens both the specificity of accountability and external control of institutional operations.

The movement to output measures of accountability and performance-based budgeting has encountered some resentment and resistance in the higher-education community, particularly within the institutions affected. Governing authorities tend to view this reception as a typical defensive posture on the part of an enterprise that is finally being properly called to account, while university leaders see deficiencies in the new approach that they believe will be harmful to proper objectives of higher education. Critics complain that the new accountability models negate important institutional processes or quality factors, ignore special institutional missions, encourage misleading comparisons between institutions, constrain institutional autonomy, and force institutions to adjust continually to shifts in political priorities rather then focusing on long-range goals. The simple, quantitative, "no-nonsense" character of output measures is viewed as being achieved only by ignoring the real complexities of university operations. Consequently, the measures themselves are argued to be simplistic if not actually misleading indicators of institutional performance. As an example, consider the seemingly straightforward measure of graduation rate, the percentage of students graduating within a specified time period following entry to the university. The presumption is that the higher an institution's graduation rate the better the job that institution is doing in retaining and successfully educating their students. However, research on predictors of educational success suggest that retention and graduation rates have a lot more to do with who an institution admits than its effectiveness in educating students. Regardless of where they attend college, the least-well-prepared students, for example, those with lower high school grade point averages or those without college-track math courses, are found to be far more likely to drop out or take longer to complete graduation requirements than the best-prepared students. Therefore graduation rate by itself says little about an institution's effectiveness in moving students along and can be meaningfully interpreted to that end only in light of information about the qualifications of the entering students. Even then, one at best has an indirect and questionable estimate of the institution's contribution.

Other aspects of student body composition confound simple measures of institutional productivity and efficiency. Urban universities in particular have a mission to serve part-time students who differ in many significant ways from the full-time residential students that tend to characterize older and more traditional institutions. Part-time students are more likely to be employed during college, to be married or have other family responsibilities, to be independent of parental financial support, to come from lower socioeconomic backgrounds, and to have higher-living expenses, all factors that operate to slow their educational progress. As much as 50 percent of the enrollment of an urban university may consist of part-time students while a more traditional residential university may have only 5 percent part-time enrollment. Clearly, any comparison of such institutions on measures such as retention, graduation rates, hours to degree, or cost per student would be seriously confounded. Even comparison of such measures *within* an institution can be confounded by external factors such as fluctuation in external employment opportunities. While adjustments can be made for the part-time student factor in interpreting educational output measures, there is no clear agreement on how to best do so.

Output measures have also been resisted on philosophical and pedagogical grounds as well on methodological grounds. For example, implicit in the cost per student measure is the view that lower cost is obviously the better outcome. But one could ask the question, Is it good for education to be cheap or is it good for education to be expensive? A quality university education is inherently inefficient and expensive in many respects. Particularly in the arts and humanities it requires a good deal of personal faculty contact with individual students, thoughtfully prepared educational requirements and challenges, extensive student writing opportunities, careful reading and grading of those written products, small class sizes, advising on course selection, and career counseling, and other forms of individual student-faculty exchange. Using students as modular production units against an aggregate cost figure, a standard measure in output models, entirely ignores whether these costly and inefficient, but also most valuable, educational experiences have been provided to the student.

Another example is the "hours to degree" measure that reports the number of credit hours taken by students in the course of completing their undergraduate degree requirements. If students complete their degrees with their total course credit hours within or only slightly exceeding the credit hours required for graduation, education can be said to be efficiently delivered in that respect. Excessive hours might reflect such inefficiencies as poor course scheduling, poor student advising, or poor planning on the part of students themselves. In fact, some states feel so strongly about controlling hours-to-degree that they impose financial penalties on students and institutions for hours-to-degree that exceed rather narrowly defined limits. However, one of the major reasons why students take extra hours in the course of completing their undergraduate work is because they change their major area of study. Many students enter college with preconceived ideas about their major but find as their studies progress that other newly experienced areas are more interesting to them or are a better fit to their intellectual strengths. Other more highly motivated and intellectually capable students may seek to accomplish double majors or take advantage of the opportunity to sample a variety of disciplinary areas during their undergraduate years. While many would argue that undergraduate education should permit and even encourage such forms of intellectual exploration and testing, the hours-to-degree measure clearly discourages such learning and may even discourage students from pursuing more adaptive career choices. On the other hand, in a resource-constrained society, excessive use of a publicly supported program is a legitimate concern.

The shift in the terms of university accountability, then, has stirred a good deal of debate and controversy over the past decade as governing bodies have sought to respond to public demand for greater accountability, or at least for new forms of accountability. Progress in developing new measures has been uneven, with frequent changes from year to year as measurement confounds or as other shortcomings have been identified or as public priorities have shifted. Nevertheless, output measures of accountability and performance-based budgeting are not going away and if anything appear to be gaining strength.

Perhaps the most remarkable feature of the move to redefine accountability has been the almost complete uninvolvement of the faculty. The measurement controversies have largely swirled above the heads of the faculty and in fact even beyond the awareness of many faculty. The protracted discussion of performance measurement and performance-based budgeting has essentially been a dialogue between university administrations on the one hand and legislatures and governing boards on the other hand. Furthermore, even though new measures of performance have been developed and put in place for many institutions, there has been little awareness of these changes on the part of the rank-and-file institutional faculty member and little if any change in faculty work-life. Again, we see the phenomenon of two different worlds—on the one hand, the world of governance authorities and higher administration making decisions about the primary objectives and operation of the university, and on the other hand, the world of faculty for whom those decisions are, at least in the short term, of little significance. Eventually, however, and particularly if university funding is progressively altered, the new accountability approach will bring about important changes in how faculty work and therefore how universities work.

The absence of faculty input reflects in large part the basic disconnect between faculty and governing authorities discussed at length in chapter 4. In addition, faculty simply do not have access to the raw material necessary to this debate. Only the administration could command the university-wide data and analytic work required to participate in development of the performance measures at issue. Finally, it may be that university administrations have wished to buffer or spare the faculty from a debate that has frequently shifted terms and which, like many a management initiative, might prove to be a passing fad. Whatever the reasons, the omission of the faculty from the accountability discussions is particularly ironic because it is the work of the faculty that drives virtually every performance measure at issue–graduation rates, teaching productivity, degrees awarded, external funding, and so forth. More importantly, the omission of the faculty is wrong because the shift in accountability terms will ultimately impact the faculty and academic sector more than any other part of the university. For example, the strong emphasis in new accountability models on rate of degree production, fewer hours-to-degree, and lower cost per student will inevitably shift concern from a focus on the quality of the education represented by those degrees to a focus on producing more, faster, and cheaper degrees, particularly if funding is tied to these measures of output. Similarly, defining and rewarding teaching productivity in terms of class time or class size will discourage other important kinds of teaching activity; defining and rewarding research in terms of external dollars generated may discourage other important forms of scholarship; and emphasizing job placement data on graduates will encourage training for the market rather than educating for life. It may be that imperatives of economics and the new demographics require a shift of this nature in university operations, but it should not take place without direct involvement of the faculty.

An indication of how faculty themselves might approach accountability reporting can be seen in a model that was devised prior to the current wave of output measures.[6] The model was developed by a faculty planning group within a sizable land grant research university of approximately 22,000 students and 1,300 full-time faculty. The aim of the planning group was, in their words, "to give substantive meaning to the phrase excellence in teaching, research, and service by developing measures of the quantity and quality of the university's principal products in each of these core activities." While thus essentially an output model, there are several features of the approach that distinguishes it from current governance-generated output models. First, the model focused on the activities of the disciplinary departments rather than the institution as a whole. The rationale was that it is the academic departments that are really responsible for the university's principal products in teaching, research, and service, and it is important to move accountability for outputs to the level of those who produce them. This action also works to secure greater faculty identification with the process while assuring that the accountability measures are sensitive to the important differences among the disciplines. Second, the planning group was convinced that the development of useful and acceptable measures of performance had to be accomplished through debate and discussion with department faculty themselves. While this seems to be an arduous task to pursue across all departments, the planning group employed two rules that greatly facilitated the process. The first rule was that the planning group would not use any performance measure to which a department objected; the second rule was that a department could not refuse to have measures applied. That is, if a department felt that a proposed measure did not validly reflect some aspects of its performance in teaching, research, or service, it was free to reject that measure but was requested to propose an alternative valid for the discipline at issue. In this way, the planning group was able to secure a more willing and thoughtful involvement of department faculty in the measurement process. Finally, the planning group undertook the task as an explicitly evolutionary process, seeking refinement of the measures through annual testing and an expanding base of information before application of the model. This experimental approach also helped assure faculty involvement and support.

The measures that emerged after several years of work quantified each department's standing within seven basic categories of activity: undergraduate teaching; graduate teaching; creative productivity (research and scholarship); scholarly reputation; external funding; service to the university, state, and nation; and degree of centrality to university, state, and societal needs. By "centrality" is meant how essential the work of the department is to the mission of the university and to the needs of the state and society.

Performance within each of the seven basic categories was measured quantitatively on a number of vital component activities that were defined through careful debate and discussion with the department faculties. The undergraduate teaching category included such measures as number of degrees conferred relative to the number of entering juniors, number of majors per faculty, number of nonmajor course enrollments per faculty, advising and mentoring activities, student ratings of faculty teaching, Scholastic Aptitude Test (SAT) scores of graduating seniors, faculty teaching awards (external to the department), and job placement of majors in career-related positions or in graduate or professional schools. Graduate teaching measures included Graduate Record Examination scores, graduation rates of master's and doctoral candidates, student ratings of faculty, faculty teaching awards, number of extramural (national) predoctoral fellowships awarded, and percent of graduates successfully placed in postdoctoral positions. Creative productivity measures were shaped to the individual disciplines but in general included number per faculty of publications (books, refereed articles, conference proceedings, etc); software packages; patents and licenses; and artistic performances, exhibitions, and compositions. Scholarly reputation included such measures as editorships of major journals or of national or international conferences; major offices in professional societies; membership in federal agency peer review committees or advisory councils; major national or international research recognition and awards (e.g., National Academy of Science memberships); national consultancies; and commissioned works of art, music, or drama. External funding measures included grant dollars awarded per faculty member, percentage of faculty with external funding, and number of grant applications submitted per faculty. The service metrics included the frequency of various forms of university service per faculty member, e.g., committee memberships and administrative appointments; state and community service, e.g., service on state government committees; consultation for state and local agencies and contributions or presentations to community groups; and national service, e.g., professional society committees or offices, government committees, and consultation to government agencies or to national or international business and industry organizations. Finally, measures of the department's centrality to the university included utilization of the department program by other university fields and units, while measures of the department's centrality to state and/or societal needs included ratings of the department's importance in providing trained manpower or research expertise to essential public and private industries in the state and nation, the department's importance in providing cultural enrichment and/or public service to the region, and the availability of the program in the region.

Every department's annual output or standing in each of the foregoing aspects was measured and rated on a scale of zero to five, where a rating of five represented the output of an outstanding department at the very best of a carefully selected comparison group of major state universities. These ratings were then weighted to reflect the judged importance of each activity to the performance category at issue and then combined to yield a single overall performance score within each of the seven categories. Of course, the scaling of the category activities, the values of which index both the level of performance, and by reference to the standard group, the relative merit or degree of excellence of the performance, is a critical aspect of the process. While the planning group served as the primary mechanism for these judgments and for the weighting of dimensions, the judgments involved extensive debate and discussion with the department heads and faculties leading to very broadly based determinations.

The final category scores present a picture or profile of each department's performance in the seven critical areas of activity. It is unlikely, of course, that the profiles of any two departments would be identical, given the differing missions and special features of the various units. The scores serve primarily as a tool to measure current standing and historical progress within a department, rather than to support comparisons between departments. In particular, the metrics are intended to be used longitudinally to determine progress toward goals set by the department and by the institution. The department's profile scores will eventually be directly sensitive to the effects of the strategies undertaken to improve targeted performance goals. The metrics and resulting profiles thus gauge institutional excellence in teaching, research, and service in quite specific terms, while changes in profile scores over time provide a mechanism for accountability of resource use in categories having face validity to both internal and external audiences.

It is notable that this essentially faculty-generated model bears a strong family resemblance to output models not only in its focus on specific products but also in its emphasis on teaching and on various forms of service to society. Not surprisingly, the faculty model places greater emphasis on creative productivity and scholarly reputation, but overall there is more agreement than disagreement in these approaches. The faculty model also offers several unique advantages. We have noted that if faculty are directly involved in the development of the accountability measures they are more likely to be supportive of the process and of the resource allocation decisions guided by it. In addition, moving accountability to the department level enables a much more effective coupling between the academic performance goals set by governance authorities and by those who actually do the academic work. The faculty model also respects the important individual differences among academic disciplines, differences that tend to be overlooked or blurred in cruder institution-wide measures. For example, the overall grant funding of a university is an important datum but it is much more useful to know which units of the university are responsible for that funding and whether they are performing up to their capabilities. Or as another example, most governance-generated models entirely overlook important creative products and impacts on society generated by the arts and humanities departments. Finally and most important, the faculty model includes measures of quality as well as "amount" in performance. Quality is captured both by giving greater weight to more distinctive achievements and by scaling the level of output on the various measures in relation to recognized models of excellence.

The aim here is not to argue the superiority of the faculty accountability model, or for that matter the superiority of any of the approaches discussed. Each has strengths and weaknesses and each speaks to important facets of accountability. But the fact is that while governing authorities have consistently tried to hold universities accountable, and universities have consistently tried to be accountable, we simply do not know how best to do so. We have at best indirect and incomplete measures of the effectiveness of university education and its contribution to society. Input models stress the quality of inputs to a university's educational and scholarly programs on the assumption that these best predict excellence in education and the ultimate impact of the institution. The weakness of these models is that they speak primarily in general rather than specific terms about the nature of the returns on investment. (But then, no one seems to worry about Harvard University's accountability!) In contrast, output models provide quantitative measures of immediate practical returns on investment, but on the downside, pay scant attention to inputs, particularly quality processes in education, and to the significant longer-term growth impacts of universities. The faculty model incorporates both quantitative and qualitative measures but does so in a fashion that would probably not please all quarters. It is also a relatively inefficient process, since it requires continual exchange with the faculty. But, then, there are those who would see that as its best feature.

As in many other areas of higher education, there is no simple "best" answer to the accountability dilemma. It is tempting to invoke again the dictum that "life has no control groups." There is literally no way to know how best to measure the performance of universities to be assured that one has maximized the practical and life enrichment returns to individuals and to the larger society. It is a matter of attempting to devise measures that balance the many and often conflicting goals and expectations that society has of universities. But in attempting to construct that balance, it is surely important to engage directly those most responsible for delivering it.

Chapter 9

Universities and the Corporate Sector

❧

Historically, the production and practical application of specialized knowledge has been a driving factor in social and economic development, and universities have always been an important part of that dynamic. Universities in particular have long viewed contributions to economic development as a significant aspect of their mission, as seen in the land grant programs and in the pursuit of basic research as "the fund from which the practical applications of knowledge must be drawn" (V. Bush). In the latter part of the twentieth century the linkage between new knowledge and economic vitality became much more evident, immediate, and pressing as a national priority. Beyond the well-recognized shift from an economy based on agriculture and heavy industry toward a knowledge-based economy, there were several specific developments that gave rise to much closer ties and interdependencies between universities and the world of business.

Perhaps the biggest single stimulus was the passage of the Bayh-Dole Act in 1980, which authorized universities to patent and license discoveries stemming from federally funded research. At the time, Congress was concerned about declining national productivity and rising technological competition from Japan and from other countries. The aim of Bayh-Dole was to encourage a more rapid movement of research findings from the laboratory to the marketplace. If a federally sponsored research project produced findings of potential commercial value, universities could now license the rights to such discoveries to U.S. companies that could then develop them for the marketplace in return for royalty and other payments to the universities. Over the next twenty years the Act resulted in a sea change in the way in which universities and their faculties viewed the results of research and their relations with the business world.

141

Prior to the Bayh-Dole Act the typical faculty member gave little if any thought to the possible commercial value of their research findings. The results of research were to be disseminated freely for the benefit of the field and of the public at large, and the return was the recognition of one's peers and perhaps on occasion the interest and appreciation of a larger audience. But with this act, faculty and their institutions became much more aware of the possible economic value of what has come to be termed *intellectual property,* that is, the ideas and discoveries emanating from research and creative activities. While it was of course widely recognized that many industrial products had important origins in freely given university research, most faculty nevertheless viewed the commercial exploitation of research findings as a matter for the profit-seeking world to consider and pursue, not the academy. But now here was Bayh-Dole highlighting the commercial significance of university research and providing universities and their faculties with opportunities and financial incentives to partner with business and industry in further development of their research findings. At this time, too, universities were entering a period of decline in the rate of growth in federal research support and a decline in state support of higher education. A possible new source of revenue was thus especially attractive. The business and industry sector, for its part, was making its own cutbacks in expenditures for in-house research and development, and saw in Bayh-Dole a new source of tax-supported research findings that could give them a competitive edge, if not indeed whole new product lines. It was a marriage made in Las Vegas.

Under the stimulus of Bayh-Dole, universities began to urge their faculties to disclose findings of possible commercial value to newly created "technology transfer" offices that were charged to facilitate the movement of research discoveries to the practical world of affairs. Those discoveries might take the form of ideas, products or product prototypes, processes, or techniques, which collectively came to be termed *technologies.* The job of the technology transfer office was to evaluate faculty disclosures; secure protection (i.e., patents) for those deemed of potential value; and license the rights to those discoveries to companies interested in their commercial application. In return for those rights, companies compensated universities in various ways, including license fees, royalties on earnings attributable to the technology at issue, and sometimes an equity interest in the technology-based business. The faculty researcher who produced the new technology stood to benefit handsomely if the technology proved commercially viable since universities typically commit 35% to 45% of the royalty income to the faculty inventor. License fees and the remainder of royalty income are used at the university's discretion, although patent and licensing is a high-cost operation.

Today, twenty-three years after Bayh-Dole, every major research university has a technology transfer office and almost all have a sizable record of accomplishment in contracting university-based technologies to the private sector, primarily technologies emerging from the sciences, engineering, and medicine. In addition, many universities now participate in business incubators designed to nurture faculty discoveries into companies, and some even participate in venture funding and equity stakes in these companies. The U.S. Patent Office has reported a steady increase in the annual number of utility patents assigned to academic institutions, reaching 3,340 in 1999, up from just 589 in the mid-1980s.[1] Further assessment of the impact of this act is provided through the annual survey of the more than 300 members of the Association of University Technology Managers, a consortium consisting largely of universities or university-affiliated institutions that engage in technology transfer.[2] The survey indicates that since 1980 at least 2,922 new companies have been formed based on licenses that had their genesis in an academic institution. Furthermore, overall technology transfer from universities to industry was estimated to have contributed $40.9 billion to the economy in 1999, supporting 270,900 jobs and forming hundreds of new companies based on academic inventions. University income from licenses and options in this same year was $862 million. Columbia University alone received $96 million in licensing fees and royalties under the Bayh-Dole Act, ranking it first among universities in income from inventions in 1999.[3] These numbers on patent activity, economic impact of university technology transfer, and university income have been increasing steadily with no sign of slowing. There is little doubt that Bayh-Dole achieved its objective of accelerating the transfer of research discoveries to the marketplace, and in the process fostered much closer relations between universities and the business sector.

To fully understand the impact of these new relations requires a closer look at the university-industry interface in the technology transfer process. The technology disclosures that emerge from university research are seldom if ever in a form suitable for immediate commercial use. They are better thought of as seeds of products or processes that with further development might prove of economic value in a business application. Frequently, a faculty disclosure will not be suitable for licensing but a company might be interested in investing in further faculty research on the finding. Even when appropriate for licensing, usually much additional research and development (R & D) is required before the discovery can be developed into a commercial product and return a profit. It is frequently to the interest of both the company and the university to have the faculty originator play a continuing role in R & D. The company will often find it advantageous to enlist the special expertise that gave rise to the technology, while from the university perspective continuing faculty involvement helps assure aggressive development of a technology in which the university now has a financial interest. That continuing engagement may take the form of awarding research contracts to the faculty member, hiring the faculty member as a consultant to the company, stock ownership or stock options for the faculty member, and perhaps even putting the faculty member on the company board of directors. Inevitably, other aspects of the faculty member's research program, for instance, university facilities, technical staff, and students, are likely to become implicated in the university-company relation. Technology transfer, then, often goes well beyond a simple contract for a deliverable between discrete entities pursuing different objectives. Rather, it is likely to cultivate a highly interdependent and entrepreneurial relationship centered on a for-profit objective.

The technology transfer relationships stimulated by Bayh-Dole have also evolved into much larger and pro-active alliances between universities and industry. For example, in 1998 the University of California at Berkeley signed an agreement with Novartis, a Swiss pharmaceutical firm and producer of genetically engineered crops, whereby Novartis gave the university $25 million to fund research in its Department of Plant and Microbial Biology, and Berkeley in return granted Novartis first right to licenses on one third of the department's research discoveries during the period of the agreement.[4] The agreement applies to all discoveries emanating from the department's research programs including research supported by state and federal funds as well as that conducted under Novartis's funding. Furthermore, the agreement gives Novartis two of five seats on the department's research committee, which determines how the firm's money is to be spent in research. Basically, Novartis and the university have collaborated on venture capital funding of the department's research, and of course both would realize financial return should the findings produced under that funding prove of commercial value—an outcome that Novartis clearly feels is highly probable. A number of other major universities and research institutions, including Harvard University, the University of California at Irvine, and the Scripps Research Institute, have struck similar "block" technology transfer agreements of this type with specific industries, granting rights to research findings in exchange for "up-front" research support or for the funding of research laboratory buildings and other facilities. Arrangements of this nature are becoming increasingly attractive to universities in the face of declining public support of higher education, aging facilities, and the increasing cost of doing research. Even bolder and more entrepreneurial are recent proposals from the private sector to provide large-scale venture funding to a research university in return for first rights to *all* emerging technologies plus a major say in how the funds are to be invested in the institution's research programs. Clearly, in any such arrangement it would be hard to convince the skeptic that the university would remain a fully free and independent determiner of its research directions.

Separate but closely related developments in the economics of health care and medical schools have also contributed significantly to expanding university-business relations. The basic science and clinical expertise within university medical schools, coupled with their access to patient populations, have long made them fertile ground for clinical-trial studies of medicines and medical devices, supported both by federal research grants and private industry. However, in recent years increasing competition for federal research dollars, the financial pressures of managed health care, and the Balanced Budget Act of 1997 have led hard-pressed medical schools to be more aggressive in seeking funds from industry, particularly from the pharmaceutical industry, the research budget of which now outpaces that of the National Institutes of Health. For its part, the pharmaceutical industry, spurred by rapid advances in molecular biology and biochemistry, has been eager to enlist the skills and cachet of university medical scientists and clinicians in the development and testing of new drugs and the fierce war for market share. Many research universities have now developed relatively large-scale clinical-trial programs funded by the pharmaceutical industry in which thousands of patient volunteers are recruited annually in the assessment of new medicines. These clinical-trial programs comprise a substantial part of the grants and contracts of research universities with medical centers. The development and marketing of new drugs is an extremely expensive, risky, and competitive business with a lot of money at stake, and the academic physicians involved in clinical-trial research, who are likely to be opinion leaders in their fields, are thus brought into contact with a high-pressure business environment. From the academic physician's point of view, these programs offer an opportunity to do research that can advance medical science and improve patient care, in many cases research that otherwise might never be done. But this marriage between academia and business is a risky act of balancing the aims of commerce and the aims of science and the clinic.

Another factor contributing to closer university-business ties has been a marked increase in corporate donations, owing in significant part to another piece of legislation, the 1981 Recovery Tax Act that increased the tax deductions corporations can claim for donations to universities. A prominent form of corporate giving has been the financing of endowed chairs and professorships, which often carry the corporation name. These are faculty positions filled by distinguished scholars with strong backgrounds in teaching and scholarship and supported by the return on investment of the donated endowment funds. The size of the endowment required to create a chaired position will vary but ordinarily an endowment in the range of $1 to $3 million would be required to underwrite the chair-holder's salary and research activities. Endowed faculty positions are highly valued by universities and are apt to be a major fund-raising objective in any capital campaign. They allow the university to redirect the state or tuition-based funding that would normally be required to pay the faculty member's salary. They are a powerful tool for recruiting outstanding faculty since they typically enable some enhancement of the normal faculty salary rate and provide the chair-holder with assured research support funds. Finally, endowed chairs and professorships are a visible sign of the university's commitment to teaching and research excellence in the endowed field of study. From the viewpoint of the corporations, these chairs are instruments of goodwill and favorable publicity and a means of promoting research in areas pertinent to their business interests. These interests are apparent in the very names of many endowed chairs, for instance, the University of Minnesota General Mills Chair of Cereal Chemistry and Technology, the Yahoo! Chair of Information-Systems Technology at Stanford University, Kmart's Chair of Marketing at Wayne State University, and the University of Memphis FedEx Chair of Information-Management Systems.[5] In addition, universities may accept endowed chairs that place more specific requirements on the chair-holder. For example, Kmart has an endowed a Chair in Management at West Virginia University that requires its holder to spend up to thirty days a year training assistant store managers. There is nothing intrinsically wrong with research or teaching activities that address interests of the chair donor as long as these activities are congruent with the educational and research objectives of the university. Nevertheless, the past decade has seen literally scores of new corporation-endowed chairs created annually, most to promote work in areas of interest to the business world, and a directive influence of this university-industry nexus seems inevitable.

Yet another but more diffuse development that is drawing universities and businesses closer together is the growing expectation on the part of many legislators and communities that universities, and particularly research universities, should take an active role in the development of their regional economies. This expectation has been fostered by well-known examples of university-impacted regional economic growth, such as the Stanford-Silicon Valley connection, the presence of Harvard, Massachusetts Institute of Technology, and other major universities ringing Route 128 in the Boston area, and the North Carolina Research Triangle anchored by Duke University, the University of North Carolina, and North Carolina State University. While the presence of research universities was certainly not the only factor giving rise to these well-known centers of economic activity and technology, their critical contribution seems incontrovertible. For example, a 1994 study found that in 1988 fifty Stanford-based firms, that is, firms formed by faculty or alumni of Stanford, accounted for more than half of the total revenue of Silicon Valley, at that time a figure in excess of $50 billion and today probably twice that amount.[6] Similarly, a 1997 study of the financial impact of MIT on the state of Massachusetts[7] reported that 1,065 MIT-related firms headquartered in the state employed 353,000 people worldwide and 125,000 in the state, generated worldwide sales of $53 billion, and represented 5 percent of total state employment and 10 percent of the state's economic base. MIT-related companies were firms whose founders include an MIT graduate or a member of the faculty or staff, or companies that were spun off from an MIT lab or were founded based on licensed MIT technologies.

Beyond such important business thrusts, universities are now becoming involved in more coordinated, pro-active, and broadly based approaches to economic development. These take the form of collaborations with state and local governments, economic development organizations, and the private sector in strategic plans targeted to business objectives of the state and region. For example, in the early 1990s the Connecticut legislature allocated $24 million to the University of Connecticut to support basic and applied research in five areas of emerging technology deemed vital to the state's economic recovery from the collapse of its defense industry economy following the end of the cold war. These research thrusts were selected, designed, and carried out in active collaboration with state agencies, key industries, and other public and private educational institutions in the state. In the mid-1990s Florida committed more than $100 million to support the expansion of microelectronics and related technology industries in the central Florida region. Critical aspects of this economic development plan were direct allocations to regional research universities, the University of South Florida and the University of Central Florida, to support university training and research pertinent to those industries, and a sales tax rebate on equipment purchases by the microelectronics industry that if invested in university research would be fully matched by additional state dollars to the universities. In the year 2000 the state of California announced the most ambitious university-based economic development plan to date,[8] launching the California institutes for science and innovation to be underwritten by $300 million in state funds over four years and more than twice that amount in matching funds from private industries. The new institutes are the Nanosystems Institute at the University of California at Los Angeles in collaboration with the University of California at Santa Barbara, which will focus on the development of miniaturized technologies; the Institute for Bioengineering, Biotechnology, and Quantitative Biomedicine at the University of California at San Francisco in collaboration with the University of California at Berkeley and the University of California at Santa Cruz; and the Institute of Telecommunications and Information Technology at the University of California at San Diego in collaboration with the University of California at Irvine, which will focus on the development of wireless technologies. This visionary and extremely ambitious state-university-private sector collaboration essentially replicates the post-World War II role of the federal government in funding university research as a seed ground of technological advances and industrial development. As Governor Gray Davis said in announcing this initiative, "The most important thing a state government can do to improve local economies is to support research universities."[9] A particularly important feature of this initiative is the relatively open-ended nature of the research financing whereby the institutes will pursue both basic and applied science objectives.

The foregoing review of ties between universities and the world of business reveals a variety, scope, and directness of interaction that would have been impossible to imagine thirty years ago. At the heart of all of these interactions is the enlistment of faculty knowledge and expertise to assist commercial objectives, whether in the form of technology transfer, evidence-based medicine, or state and regional economic goals. There is no question that these partnerships have brought substantial benefits to the private and public sectors alike. We earlier noted the major financial and job-creation impact of university-born technologies. Clinical trials sponsored by industry now drive much of the development of new medical products and processes, with academic scientists setting important standards for quality and objectivity. And Governor Davis has aptly characterized the return to state economies from strategic investment in research universities. There have been clear benefits to the universities as well. There is the discretionary income that accrues from the commercialization of intellectual property, although to this point technology transfer has brought substantial financial gain to only a relatively small number of universities and faculty. Much more important has been the direct research support provided by private industry, which has helped to maintain and broaden the scope of university research, build necessary research infrastructure, and create valuable training opportunities for students. Industry research and development (R & D) expenditures at universities and colleges have increased from $1.4 billion in 1993 to $2.2 billion in 2000, and virtually match R & D expenditures at universities and colleges by state and local government.[10] Correlated with the growth of technology transfer and research-focused partnerships is an even higher level of corporate donations to universities, which rose from $2.8 billion in 1996 to $4.1 billion in 2000 and $4.3 billion in 2001.[11]

But in spite of the undoubted benefits of the new academic-business partnerships, they pose serious problems for the universities. All of these ties, in varying ways and to varying degrees, bring into direct conflict the opposing values and practices of the business and academic worlds. In essence, businesses are profit oriented, secretive, and narrowly focused, while universities are public spirited, open, and broadly encompassing. Further, while the practices of business are not susceptible to change, those of universities are. That is, business would not remain business if it were not profit-oriented, concerned about ownership, and highly focused on specific functions, but universities can operate in more or less public-spirited, open, and encompassing ways. The concern, then, is that the mix of cultures will work to erode the values of the academy, specifically the long-standing traditions of disinterested inquiry, free sharing of information, and broad and balanced pursuit of knowledge. The evidence to date suggests that the concern is well grounded.

The most apparent and perhaps most disturbing impact on university practice associated with industry-supported research concerns the dissemination of research results. With the rare exception of classified research conducted in the national interest, universities have always supported unrestricted and immediate publication of the research and scholarship of their faculties. But in paying for university research, businesses are paying for knowledge that they hope will confer commercial advantage and therefore want that knowledge to be protected from competitors. For this reason, industry contracts for research usually prohibit publication of findings beyond the time required to file a patent, a one- to two-month delay by National Institutes of Health guidelines. While secrecy in any form is undesirable in a university environment, delays of this order would not be a major concern. However, large-scale surveys of the both life-science industries and university life-scientists indicate that much longer delays, including outright prohibition of publication, have now become common.

A 1996 survey of several hundred life-science companies, including Fortune 500 and international firms, confirmed that the great majority of these companies required academic researchers to keep information confidential in order to allow filing of a patent application.[12] But in addition, the survey found that 58% of the companies set the patent application period at more than six months, and more than half of the respondents said their agreements with universities sometimes required that research findings be kept confidential even beyond the patenting process. The survey also showed that graduate students and postdoctoral fellows are particularly vulnerable to industry policies on secrecy. These beginning researchers rely on prompt publication of research findings in order to secure their first jobs after completing their training, but 57% of the companies reported that their sponsorship of graduate students and postdoctoral fellows involved work of a proprietary nature.

In a related survey of several thousand academic life-science faculty in fifty universities ranked highest in NIH funding, almost 20% of more than two thousand respondents said they had delayed publication of data by more than six months, generally for reasons linked to commercial stakes and most commonly to prepare a patent application.[13] Disturbingly, some 28% also reported that they had to "slow dissemination of undesired results."

The latter point is central to the well-publicized industry experience of Dr. Betty Dong, a pharmacy professor at the University of California at San Francisco, which provides an extreme but nonetheless real example of the damage that industry-controlled publication can wreak on science and the public interest.[14] Boots Pharmaceuticals had contracted with the university and Professor Dong to test its popular thyroid drug against a rival brand and two lower-cost generics on the market. Dong and her research team found that the generic substitutes worked just as well as the Boots drug in controlling thyroid problems, and concluded that eight million Americans could save as much as $365 million a year by switching to the cheaper generic versions. When the findings were shared with Boots officials, they charged that the study was flawed. However, independent reviews by investigators in the field, some with ties to Boots, concluded that the research report was acceptable for publication in the *Journal of the American Medical Association.* At this point, Boots called on the university to stop publication of the paper, citing a provision in the research contract that the data could be published only with the company's permission.

Although the university complied with this contract restriction, the episode became known several months later when the *The Wall Street Journal* ran a front-page article on the entire matter. After the media storm had subsided, Knoll Pharmaceuticals, which had bought Boots the year before, agreed to allow publication of the paper, almost seven years after the first objection to the findings and suppression of publication.

Other apparent efforts to suppress or alter the presentation of industry-supported studies have begun to plague universities across the country. In Providence, Rhode Island, an occupational health physician at a Brown University-affiliated teaching hospital contracted to study a possible outbreak of lung disease at a local textile plant.[15] When he sought to publish his subsequent finding of a high incidence of the disease among the workers, the plant tried to suppress the report, citing a confidentiality agreement to protect the company's "trade secrets." The researcher, who moved to publish his results anyway, claimed that the hospital then closed his clinic in retaliation. In another case, a drug manufacturer demanded up to $10 million from an AIDS researcher and from the University of California at San Francisco over a study that concluded that the company's drug is ineffective against HIV, the virus that causes AIDS.[16] The company, which paid for the study, charged that the researcher had omitted favorable data in his report and also had violated a confidentiality agreement. The principal investigator argued that company officials were simply trying to intimidate him into withholding his findings, which of course ran counter to the firm's commercial interests. These and similar intellectual property disputes are beginning to take a familiar form. The university researcher claims that the company seeks to delay, suppress, or alter presentation of findings in a manner that benefits the company, and the company argues that they are maintaining a confidentiality agreement, that the data are flawed, or that they are seeking a more balanced report of the findings. In the absence of a full review of the research and data by independent experts, it is difficult to prove editorial heavy-handedness. But in the university tradition, the principal investigator would have final responsibility for presentation and interpretation of the findings. The full extent of such seeming corporation attempts to influence published reports is difficult to assess since disclosure generally depends upon a voluntary report by the researchers. But any such effort, or for that matter even the appearance of such an effort, is cause for grave concern.

The foregoing observations suggest that commercialism and competition are destroying the once open and congenial atmosphere of university laboratories and impeding access to university-generated knowledge. Of course, these changes are not due solely to the expansion of industry partnerships. Under the stimulus of Bayh-Dole, universities themselves are increasingly likely to place publication restrictions on university-funded faculty discoveries for which patents are being sought. While such publication delay is under direct university control and presumably of a more limited nature, it is at best nonetheless as inimical to freedom of information principles as industry-imposed secrecy.

In addition to fostering greater secrecy and contention in the university environment, university-industry partnerships have also significantly increased opportunities for conflict of interest among the faculty, conflicts that work to erode both the university tradition of disinterested inquiry and public confidence in that tradition. Faculty who undertake work for industry as consultants or research investigators usually benefit substantially in the form of expanded research capabilities and augmented income. At the most elemental level, conflict is induced between the faculty member's responsibilities to the university and those to the external company. Universities have attempted to minimize such conflict through policies that limit the amount of time faculty may consult and by insuring that contract research does not interfere with the delivery of instructional programs. Nevertheless, as in any dual employment situation, some conflict of interest is inescapable. But a more specific and troublesome conflict of interest is posed by the faculty member's awareness that renewal of industry contracts, and the research opportunities and financial gains they bring, is contingent on producing results that are useful to the business entity, an awareness that can lead to bias in the collection and reporting of research results even in the most methodologically careful faculty. The possibility of such bias in the design, conduct, or reporting of research becomes still greater when the faculty member has financial interests in the company that go beyond being compensated for the research performed. As noted earlier, faculty who enter research relations with companies, particularly in further development of new technologies, will often have some other financial involvement with the company, such as stock ownership, royalty entitlement, or company gifts.

Conflicts of interest that threaten the principle of disinterested inquiry surely are not unique to university-industry ties. Disinterested inquiry is always at some risk if only from the inescapable frailties of faculty as human beings. Even in the absence of any direct link to a profit motive, the search for truth is probably always in some conflict with other objectives or with other forms of personal benefit. For example, a faculty member pursuing a federally funded project, or for that matter even an unfunded research project, could be biased in the collection and reporting of results by a desire for scholarly fame or peer recognition, either as ends in themselves or because they are a recognized means to enhanced professional opportunities and income. The values and practices of the university are all about minimizing such conflicts of interest through careful training in methods of objective inquiry, rigorous application of the rules of logic and evidence, critical peer review, and in the sciences, objective methodologies and independent replication of findings.

While conflicts of interest in university research are thus not unique to industry-university partnerships, it seems clear that by explicitly linking research to direct financial gain for the researcher, the opportunities for conflict of interest and the threat to disinterested inquiry are significantly increased. Studies indicate that financial ties between faculty and industry are becoming widespread, particularly in the area of biomedical research. A 1996 review of the publications of more than a thousand scientists at universities in Massachusetts in fourteen leading journals of biomedical science found that slightly more than a third of these articles had one or more chief authors who stood to gain financially from the results they were reporting.[17] That is, they were patent holders, board members, stockholders, or had some other relationship to companies that would commercially pursue the results. Further, the financial interests of these authors were not mentioned in the publications. Industry "gifts" to researchers, usually with strings attached, are another common form of linkage. A survey of life scientists in the fifty top-funded research universities found that 43 percent of these investigators had recently received an industry gift–typically biomaterials, laboratory equipment, trips, or money–which they characterized as important to their work.[18] More than half of the recipients stated that the donor in turn expected to exert influence over their work, including review of academic papers before publication and patent rights.

The ubiquity of connections between researchers and corporations is underscored by a recent wryly humorous observation in the journal *Science*.[19] They reported that the *New England Journal of Medicine*, a leader in screening potential conflicts of interest among its authors, found so many industry ties in a large-scale twenty-nine-author drug study that for lack of space in the journal it was forced to list them on its website. The lead author alone had served as a consultant to nine companies, received grants from nine, and served on thirteen corporate advisory boards. *Science* editors quipped that the journal might save space in the future with a simple disclaimer: "Assume multi-drug company ties unless otherwise indicated."

But do such ties influence the investigator's opinion or behavior? The typical faculty researcher's reaction to this question is likely to be one of indignation. They are confident and sincere in the belief that the methods of science together with their own rigorous training and basic honesty protects against possible conflicts of interest. Furthermore, they are keenly aware that their reputation for reliable science is the most important possession they have. Nevertheless, any scientist will tell you that they must always be on guard against possible sources of error in the design, conduct, and interpretation of experiments, and modern experimental psychology has convincingly demonstrated how expectations and motives may induce selectivity in perception and thinking, even without the individual's awareness.

Several studies have put the question of industry influence on investigators' views to an empirical test. One of the most comprehensive was conducted by a team of Canadian researchers who sought to determine whether there was any relation between investigators' published positions on the controversial clinical question of the safety of calcium-channel blockers as a way to treat hypertension and angina and their financial ties with drug companies that make the blockers.[20] Seventy published articles, primarily review articles and "letters to the editor" rather than reports of original research, dealing with this issue were reviewed and classified as being supportive, neutral, or critical with respect to the use of calcium-channel antagonists. The reviewers had no knowledge of the authors' financial relationships with pharmaceutical companies. The authors of the articles were then independently asked about their financial relationships with manufacturers of these blockers and with manufacturers of competing products. Specifically, they were asked whether they had received any of five types of funding in the past five years from these manufacturers: support to attend a symposium, an honorarium to speak at a symposium, support to organize an educational program, support to perform research, and employment or consultation. When the authors' positions on the use of calcium-channel blockers were correlated with their financial ties, the researchers found that 96% of the supportive authors had received one or more of the types of funding from manufacturers of these blockers as compared with 60% of the neutral authors and 37% of the critical authors, a highly significant difference.

Another relatively large-scale study examined the published outcomes of research studies evaluating the effectiveness of various drugs in relation to whether the research was done under drug company support (40 such articles) or without such support (112 studies).[21] Research done under company support would of course be concerned with evaluating drugs of direct interest to the company. Research studies that acknowledged support by the pharmaceutical industry were found to be significantly more likely to report results that favored the drug of interest (98% of the articles) than were articles that did not acknowledge pharmaceutical industry involvement (79%). Several other clinical trial studies have reported outcomes of a similar nature.[22]

While these few studies are certainly disturbing, we should be careful about drawing hard conclusions from them regarding the extent to which industry ties may influence the opinions of clinicians and researchers. For one thing, as in any research, there may be possible confounding variables. For example, there is reason to believe that for-profit companies are less likely than independent research institutions to sponsor drug studies unless some evidence already suggests that a particular drug may be effective. If so, this factor could underlie the observed higher percentage of positive outcomes in drug research sponsored by industry. And again, the experimenters in these studies doubtless did their best to pursue objective inquiries, analyses, and judgments. But it would be very naive of universities and their faculties to assume that the general public would not be both very disturbed by such findings and most uncomfortable if it knew the extent of undisclosed financial ties between university scientists and industry. The gravest threat of all from extensive industry ties to university researchers may be the erosion of confidence in universities as centers of disinterested inquiry in the public interest.

Some argue that this threat might be countered in good part if university investigators simply fully disclosed their financial relationships with industry in the course of publishing or otherwise communicating their research findings. Other investigators in the field, and the general public as well, could then evaluate the merits of research reports in the light of the authors' disclosure of possible conflicts of interest. Although there is now a belated and growing concern to require such disclosure, universities, granting agencies, and journals have not yet developed effective policies on reporting conflicts of interest. Current guidelines tend to be vaguely worded and poorly enforced by universities and journals alike. Faculty generally believe that financial sponsorship does not influence their investigative work, and tend to feel that while conflict of interest concerns may apply to others, they are certainly not valid in *their* case. A survey of more than 60,000 papers appearing in 181 peer-reviewed journals in 1997 found that only 5 percent of those papers contained information about authors' financial ties, a figure that is surely but a small fraction of the actual relationships.[23] While a survey of current publications would probably yield a somewhat higher disclosure rate, conflicts of interest disclosure is clearly a long way from being the norm in research institutions and journal practice.

The concerns about industry-funded research apply as well to the proliferation of industry-endowed chairs and industry-funded research centers, although the tendency to attach company names to chairs and centers diminishes the disclosure issue. Corporations view such support as investments to promote study in areas important to their business concerns, and these concerns are usually short-term and profit-oriented. As Paul Berg, the Stanford Nobel Prize-winning biochemist has observed, industry will support biotechnology projects that might make a profit but not the basic research that made biotechnology possible. They are even less likely to fund a chair in, say, medieval studies, philosophy, or the poetry of Emily Dickinson, nor are university development officers likely to press such scholarly areas on corporate donors. There is a much larger "appetite for giving," to use a fund-raising phrase, to applied areas of university endeavor, such as medicine and engineering.

Since chair endowments always act to augment teaching and scholarship in areas important to the donor, something that cannot be assured for other areas of endeavor, industry funding of chairs can influence the institution's academic priorities. Further, there is always the potential for chair donors to attempt to influence as well the selection of the chair-holder or even the incumbent's specific research and teaching activities. Several disturbing episodes in this vein have been documented, although to this point it appears that most universities have kept donors at "arm's length" in selection of chair-holders and the incumbent's activities. The harshest critics of corporation-donated chairs argue that the donors are motivated more by market savvy than by public-spiritedness. These critics charge that corporation-endowed chairs or business-related research centers essentially use the university to enhance public perception of the corporation and its products by association with the university reputation for objectivity and integrity. The danger, they argue, is that the transfer will inevitably be two-way. That is, by association with commercial enterprises, the university will lose the public perception of being outside the marketplace and thus will lose as well the positive image and confidence in their objectivity that makes them attractive to corporations in the first place. This is a cynical view, but it certainly exists within the ranks of the academy.

There is also concern that the growing pressures on universities to contribute to regional economic development programs may similarly bias the academic program profile. Consider, for example, the thrust of the several university-state-industry economic development programs noted earlier.

Connecticut provided special funding in five university program areas: materials science, pharmaceuticals and biotechnology, environmental technology, marine science, and photonics. The Florida program invested heavily in microelectronics and related technologies. The California program will focus on nanosystems, biotechnology and biomedicine, and telecommunications and information technology. Emily Dickinson loses again.

The selection of these educational and research areas for special investment is certainly understandable. They comprise the most fertile ground for translational research, that is, for research likely to produce technologies that can be moved quickly to the marketplace and provide immediate payoff. But differential expenditures of the magnitudes involved will have sizable differential effects. A visit to any research university today is likely to find ongoing construction, the best educational and research facilities–and the majority of students–in these highly funded areas. In chapter 4 we noted that an increasing utilitarian attitude of students has been reflected in a notable decrease in course and major selections within the arts and sciences and a corresponding increase in business and vocationally related disciplines and majors. A recently reported national study of this question found that from 1970 to 1994 the number of bachelor's degrees in English, foreign languages, philosophy, and religion all declined, while there was a five- to tenfold increase in degrees in computer and information sciences, changes that the study authors attributed to the new "Market-Model University."[24] Ironically, this skewing of academic program priorities runs directly counter to what the business community in repeated surveys has indicated as their greatest need–graduates with strong critical thinking, perspective-taking, and communication skills and the ability to work in cross-functional and cross-cultural teams, all capabilities to which the humanities and liberal arts contribute significantly. The risks of an overly strong business orientation in higher education has been eloquently expressed by Michele Tolela Myers, the president of Sarah Lawrence College:

> We borrow the language of business because we are forced to operate like businesses. Higher education has become more and more expensive at the same time it has become increasingly necessary. As we look for ways to operate efficiently and make the most of our assets, we begin learning about outsourcing, for-profit ventures, the buying and selling of intellectual property. . . .
>
> As we in the academy begin to use business-speak fluently, we become accustomed to thinking in commercialized terms about education. We talk no longer as public intellectuals, but as entrepreneurs. And we thus encourage instead of fight the disturbing trend that makes education a consumer good rather than a public good. If we think this way, our decisions will be

driven, at least in part, by consumers' tastes. Are we ready to think that we should only teach what students want or be driven out of business?

Physics is hard, it is costly, it is undersubscribed. Should it be taught only in engineering schools? I don't think so. Should we not teach math because everyone can get a cheap calculator? Should we stop teaching foreign languages because English has become the international language? And what about the arts, literature, philosophy? Many might think them impractical. I think we have a responsibility to insist that education is more than learning job skills, that is also the bedrock of a democracy. I think we must be very careful that in the race to become wealthier, more prestigious, and to be ranked Number One, we don't lose sight of the real purpose of education, which is to make people free–to give them the grounding they need to think for themselves and participate as intelligent members of a free society.[25]

The central tendency of the array of university-industry interactions reviewed in this chapter has evoked such arresting phrases as "the corporatization of the university," "the commercialization of the campus," and "the kept university." A good summary of the import of these phrases–and of this chapter, is contained in a statement by James Robert Brown, a professor of philosophy at the University of Toronto:

> What do these notions mean? To me, they involve an increased dependence on industry and philanthropy for operating the university; an increased amount of our resources being directed to applied or so-called practical subjects, both in teaching and in research; a proprietary treatment of research results, with the commercial interest in secrecy overriding the public's interest in free, shared knowledge; and an attempt to run the university more like a business that treats industry and students as clients and ourselves as service providers with something to sell. We pay increasing attention to the immediate needs and demands of our "customers" and, as the old saw goes, "the customer is always right." Privatization is particularly frightening from the point of view of public well-being.[26]

In summary, although university-industry partnerships bring substantial benefits they also pose grave risks to the revered university traditions of disinterested inquiry, free sharing of information, and broad and balanced pursuit of knowledge. There are those who argue strongly that the risks are not worth the gains, that universities should be overwhelmingly funded from the public purse, or from the private purse without strings, and that we should just say no to any form of philanthropy with its own ax to grind. On the other hand, the university research and scholarly enterprise may have grown in breadth and cost beyond the willingness or even the capacity of public funding to support it. Over the past several decades, universities have gone from exploring private funding, to experiencing its benefits, to depending on it, and that is a hard course to reverse. In this dilemma, it is tempting to offer the solution of welcoming corporate support while attempting to studiously draw the line on anything that risks the ideals of the university, recognizing that in real life, maintenance of principles is often a matter of degree and common sense.

Is such an approach too risky? One might think so from the popular press, which has generally depicted "the corporatization of the university" as a matter of a strong corporate sector luring an overburdened and resource-hungry academic community to its bidding with the promise of research support and profits, with universities a reluctant but ultimately led partner. But it is important to realize that at the end of the day there can be *no* partnership agreements without the university signature–no technology transfer agreements, no endowed chair agreements, no clinical-trial contracts, and no economic development programs. And it is equally important to realize that in the marriage of business and academia, the primary suitor is business, not academia. True, there are needs on both sides but the needs are greater in business than in academia, particularly in the new knowledge-based economy. There are risks on both sides too, but the risks are far less for business. No business ever went broke paying royalties on the sales of new technologies, endowing chairs, or contracting for research. These are all investments with calculated greater returns. But there is the real risk that academia could lose what business is paying for–knowledge and expertise of unparalleled quality, breadth, objectivity and credibility. The assets of business are replaceable, but those of the academy are not, and in that sense they are priceless. Universities are therefore actually in the stronger position in the negotiation of business-academic partnerships, if they but fully realize it. It is in those negotiations, that is, in the negotiation of actual agreements and contracts, and in the formulation of the policies that condition them, that the defense of academic principles must lie. And in those negotiations, who now represents the university to protect its values and objectives? Not in any effective way the faculty, whose efforts lie at the base of every agreement, but the governance authorities of the university. This does not mean that boards and university presidents are not genuinely concerned with protecting university values or do not attempt to consult faculty in the process. But the fact of the matter, as our analysis of university governance has shown, is that the center of gravity of governance is now strongly biased to the values and objectives of business, and mechanisms for meaningful faculty consultation are virtually nonexistent.

That agreement on policies for university-industry interactions is urgently needed is seen in sharply different views within existing practice. Harvard Medical School, worried that they might have trouble recruiting and retaining faculty who thought they could make more money at other schools with more lenient conflict of interest policies, recently considered loosening its rules to permit faculty to own more stock in companies that sponsor their research and to earn more money consulting for such companies.[27] After receiving fire from ethicists, Harvard withdrew these proposals, while urging a national dialogue on the issue involving universities, government, and industry. About the same time, Marcia Angell, a lecturer at Harvard Medical School, a former editor of the *New England Journal of Medicine,* and a prominent critic of conflict of interest in industry-sponsored medical research, argued that the best way to restore public confidence in the scientific enterprise is for universities and scientists to *altogether* eschew financial ties with companies that sponsor their research—no consultancies, no equity interests, and no roles as paid speakers for the companies.[28] The fact that such closely associated influential sources have such diametrically opposed views clearly indicates the need for broad debate and consensus on this critical matter. In that debate, the proposed faculty councils on governance could play a most valuable role in representing and advocating the views of the full faculties of their universities.

Specifically, consideration should be given to the following guidelines for industry-university partnerships in the interest of preserving academic freedom: refusing to accept contract research that prohibits disclosure of results; protecting the right to publish with at most a ninety-day delay allowed for patenting; forbidding professors to have financial ties to companies sponsoring their research and universities from investing in those companies; requiring faculty and universities to disclose at the time of publication any conflict of interest that could bear on the research or views reported, and requiring as well clinical-trial investigators to disclose such conflicts to patient subjects; assigning students only to industry-sponsored projects that are fully consistent with their educational goals and training needs; scrupulously protecting students against proprietary restrictions on publication of their work; maintaining "no strings" endowed chair and research center agreements; keeping university-paid faculty time in for-profit activities within current consulting time limits; and prohibiting universities and their scientists from selling or purchasing stock in any company working to commercialize a university invention until well after the product is on the market (Johns Hopkins University has such a restriction to prevent possible manipulation of research results to influence stock value).

In a broader vein, faculty councils could also be helpful to university governance authorities in making the case for legislative and social policies that work to protect unfettered inquiry in the public interest even as university-industry partnerships are pursued–for example, the case for preserving and enlarging public support for the freest possible dissemination of information, for placing the considered educational needs of students above the interests of business or philanthropy, and most of all, for understanding that the discoveries with the greatest social and economic impact have come from research *not* oriented to market objectives. They might also consider recommending some innovative ways to ease the strains of directed research. One example might be to pursue university-government-private industry collaborations that target research areas important to the public interest but leave substantial freedom for individual investigators in the selection of the research approach and certainly in the conduct and reporting of the research. Another example might be a policy to provide matching financial investment, from state or private dollars, for those university areas that do not benefit from extra funding for economic development or marketplace objectives. The proportionate investment necessary to keep up in these areas would be trivial compared to the millions now flowing to programs more relevant to the marketplace, and as President Meyers of Sarah Lawrence College has pointed out, would serve as well the most important educational needs of a free and advanced society.

Chapter 10

A Summing-Up and Final Word

🦋

R esearch universities comprise a wellspring of knowledge and ideas that have advanced and enriched virtually every aspect of our society. We have argued that the ultimate source of that wellspring is the cumulative scholarship and research of the faculty, that is, the specialized knowledge and largely intrinsically driven inquiry and creativity of the faculty. The growth and major economic impact of the research universities under the stimulus of the historic federal-university partnerships reinforce the view that research and scholarship are the foundation of a great contributing university, the necessary underpinning of both educational excellence and effective service in the public interest.

It is vital to maintain the ideal of the university as a place where intrinsically driven learning and research are supported, where logic and evidence are prized in the determination of what is true, and where what is taught and applied is based only on sound scholarship and inquiry free from self-interest. The fact that these ideals–like any human ideals–are imperfectly realized does not gainsay the importance of striving to protect and nurture them, because they are the source of the university's ability to truly educate and serve the public good.

Ironically, the very success of research universities in assisting the growth and meeting the needs of society now threatens the traditions of basic scholarship and academic freedom that have been so integral to that development. In attempting to meet greatly increased and varied demands for educational access, contract research services, and new partnerships with the private and public sectors, as well as a myriad of other pressures, research universities have become large multifunction institutions with diminishing focus on academic core functions.

The increased demand for the university's educational services has been met in significant part by reliance on part-time and temporary faculty and graduate student instruction, eroding the inherent connection between scholarship and educational quality and eroding as well the scholarly base of the university's teaching and research functions. While the research activities of full-time faculty have indeed increased, particularly under the stimulus of governmental and private support, the overall research function of the university has not grown in proportion to its educational and public service functions because the full-time faculty base has not been so expanded. Furthermore, the pressures for scholarship and research more directly tuned to short-term social and economic development goals threatens the survival of inquiry driven primarily by the desire for knowledge and better understanding, the vital role of which has never been well-supported or well-understood.

Correlated with the increase in size and complexity of research universities are important changes in their governance structures and processes. As we have recounted, the upper level of university governance has changed dramatically over the past several decades while the lower level, that is, the faculty shared-governance mechanism, has remained the same in structure and process. Thirty years ago the senior administration likely consisted of the president and a few other high-level administrators, all or most drawn from the faculty, often including the president. Today there may be a dozen or more high-level administrators at the vice presidential level drawn from business, finance, law, or other nonacademic backgrounds, almost none of whom are likely to have experience-based knowledge of academics. Essentially, university higher administration has become just another business–the business of managing universities. Meetings of the president's cabinet are like company meetings–more frequent, perhaps, but probably just as dull. The agenda is consumed with managerial issues–reports and discussions on physical plant problems, land acquisition issues, ongoing litigation cases, public relations, government relations, audit issues, athletic highlights, fundraising, enrollment plans, marketing, dormitory development, and the like. There is seldom a meaningful discussion of academic matters per se. In such a setting it is difficult, if not impossible, to accomplish an in-depth treatment of such topics as the adequacy of the institution's tenure standards or the content and quality of its general education curriculum. Yet academics remain the heart of the university and the basis of its capacity to truly serve the deepest needs of its students and society.

Of course the faculty senates, at the lowest level of the governance structure, do continue to provide a forum for treatment of key academic matters, but that forum is now essentially divorced from the power structure. There is a great need to inject the faculty perspective into the highest levels of governance and to promote at that level discussion, understanding, and action on core academic matters of the university, action that might then be more likely to become a regular part of the "business of the university."

The enlargement and strengthening at the top of the university organization has not been an inappropriate development in light of the increased size, complexity, and managerial concerns of universities. But in the process of these changes the higher university administration has become business oriented and more distant from the academic process, while the faculty voice has become muted and weaker in matters of university policy, priorities, and resource allocation. Add to this circumstance the strong business-political orientation and increasing activism of governing boards and legislatures, and the mismatch between the higher and lower levels of university governance becomes even more obvious—one group focused upon maintaining the traditions of academic freedom, disinterested inquiry, and broad pursuit of knowledge and the other upon achieving higher productivity, managerial flexibility, cost saving, and immediate economic and community goals. Furthermore, it is only the higher governance levels that directly and routinely interface with legislative and societal bodies and concerns. In contrast, the faculty, focused on their departmental and professional activities and all but isolated by the autonomous character of the faculty world and by a nonfunctional shared-governance mechanism, are essentially omitted from dialogues on the need for change.

The problem in university governance is not a case of "worth on foot and rascals in the coach"—a dedicated but powerless faculty working in the trenches and insensitive boards and administrators wielding power. Rascals and much worth appear in both places. We earlier noted that board members, for example, are generally capable and successful individuals with a commitment to public service and with a genuine interest in advancing higher education. If they have a rascally attribute, it is a predilection to assume that they know more than they do about the faculty and academic world, particularly about research and scholarship and its proper role in the academy. It is a kind of unwitting ignorance, but ignorance in any form is particularly dangerous when combined with power. To quote Justice Louis Brandeis, "The greatest dangers to liberty lurk in insidious encroachment by men of zeal, well-meaning, but without understanding." And if we were to talk of rascally qualities in the faculty, these would surely be their reflexive dismissal of criticism and strong focus on their individual concerns rather than the welfare of the institution.

No, the basic problem in university governance is not a matter of worth versus rascals. Rather, the problem is the lack of meaningful communication between the faculty and governing authorities at a time of major challenges to traditional university operations. Demographic, economic, and technological changes in our society over the past several decades have already impacted the composition and operation of universities, placing new demands and expectations on them, and bringing into question many of the traditional practices of the academy. In particular, legislatures, governing boards, and university administrations have begun to show an increasingly common interest in reengineering universities in more direct service of the goals of internal and external constituencies and away from the traditionally faculty-determined production, dissemination and application of knowledge. Some changes in this direction have already taken place, such as the new view of students as customers, the weakening of tenure, the vocational drift in the curriculum, the increased focus on productivity and the bottom line, and the pressures for more directed forms of faculty research and public service. More changes of this nature will certainly be pressed. The argument here is not that there should be no change in traditional university operations, but rather that adaptations to new demands and expectations be made with proper protection of the academic practices and values that have made universities great. No one doubts that presidents and provosts are concerned about protecting those values, but the drift in governance power toward business and political perspectives is so strong that there is need for a balancing infusion of the academic perspective in the decision-making process, and how better than from those who actually live the academic life. In this time of challenge and change, the communication gulf between the faculty, those who do the essential work of the institution, and their governing authorities is clearly dysfunctional. The preceding chapters on controversial issues in higher education illustrated how dysfunctions may result from governance actions that fail to adequately consider the faculty perspective, and illustrated as well how greater faculty involvement might assist progress on such issues. There are many needed improvements and changes in higher education on which faculty input is sorely needed if not essential, for example, how to measure better the *transferable* knowledge and skills that students acquire, how to give teaching greater weight in the tenure process, how to best use the new technologies in teaching, how to best incorporate training in teaching into graduate education, how to foster interdisciplinary research in face of the rigid and narrow department structure of universities, how to define accountability measures congenial to both legislators and academics, how best to monitor financial relationships between faculty and industry, and so on.

There is therefore an urgent need to establish better communication between the faculty and governing authorities, internal and external, and to strengthen the "bottom" of the governance chain to a degree commensurate with the growth that has taken place at the top. Our proposal is that faculty representatives be given the means and authority to become engaged as full participants at the highest levels of university governance. The faculty councils that we have proposed as a means of restoring truly shared governance will likely meet with skepticism in some quarters. There will be those who will doubt that faculty can be made to overcome their aversion to deep administrative involvement, particularly those faculty who are highly committed to research and scholarship but whose involvement is so important to effective council representation. But it is interesting to note that the faculty commentaries on the higher education scene that have begun to appear in the literature are generally by active and distinguished scholars deeply concerned about the current state and direction of the university. With some inventiveness and goodwill on the part of governing authorities and the faculty, it should be possible to enlist the full engagement of such concerned faculty, who are certainly "out there" but who are now without effective voice in governance. Others will feel that, regardless of the faculty's commitment to council service, they would bring a naive, idealistic perspective to the task and lack the measure of hardheaded political and business acumen required to work effectively with governance authorities. Initially perhaps, but recall that the proposal would require protracted involvement of the faculty in the governance issues affecting their institutions, and there is no reason to believe that their learning curve for these matters would be any different than for their demanding professional fields of endeavor. For that matter, one should probably wonder if governing authorities would have an equally rapid learning curve for the perspective and concerns of the faculty world.

The proposed faculty councils may not be the best way to accomplish the restorative strengthening of academics in university governance, but the councils or some similar means of engaging and empowering the best and brightest of the faculty in a collegial fashion must be instituted. Otherwise, what are the alternatives? One is the status quo. This would maintain the spectacle of a faculty largely preoccupied with their professional interests as external forces work ineluctably to reshape the university, a faculty essentially detached from the administrative and governance decision-making processes through which those external forces must be filtered. In fact, it is this situation–the self-preoccupation and passivity of the faculty in the face of strong and changing expectations on the universities that underlies so much of what is awry with higher education and that fuels so much of the harsh criticisms of university faculty. Absent a meaningful restoration of shared governance, there is no reason to believe that faculty isolation, the criticism, and the drift toward "corporatization of the university" would not continue.

Another alternative is that in the absence of an effective means of shared governance, faculty will turn to unionizing. There are already signs that faculty are beginning to look to unions as a means of protecting their interests in the growing estrangement from governing authorities, and there are signs as well that unions are becoming more active in their efforts to organize faculty. In responding to the attacks on tenure and imposition of post-tenure review systems, faculty commentaries almost invariably cite, with evident admiration and appreciation, the work of the American Association of University Professors (AAUP), the national faculty union, in formulating and advancing the principles of tenure. Certainly the AAUP has a laudable record as a defender of academic freedom. Faculty senates, too, have begun to find common ground with union representatives, and in universities that contain faculty union chapters, senate leadership and union leadership are now often identical. This development is partly a matter of the average faculty member's aversion to administrative service, but it can also be seen as faculty deference to the union's willingness to seek leverage against a distant administration. There are also vigorous new movements by part-time faculty members and graduate assistants to seek unionization. A recent *New York Times* op-editorial article by Ellen Willis, a professor of journalism and president of the AAUP chapter at New York University, is a virtual call to arms–to union arms. Willis's comments illustrate well a growing militant view among some faculty. She notes that in 1980 the Supreme Court, citing the collegial structure of the medieval university, ruled that Yeshiva University need not recognize its faculty union because professors are part of management. In so ruling, the court was of course proceeding on the premise that the historic principle of shared governance was still alive and well. But as Willis observed, even in 1980 the Yeshiva decision was anachronistic. Citing many of the same points that have been elaborated in this book, she continues.

> Today it's undeniable that universities, public or private, are modeled not on medieval guilds, governed by their members, but on modern corporations. Policy is made by a president (read chief executive) and administrative bureaucracy accountable not to a community of scholars but to funders and

the board of trustees. The corporate university is obsessed with its bottom line. Faculty members are regarded as employees who must be pressured to increase "productivity" by teaching more and larger classes at less pay and financing their own programs with outside grant money. Students and parents are seen as customers to be satisfied.

From the corporate viewpoint, traditional notions of shared governance and faculty autonomy are a nuisance that impedes administrative "flexibility". Tenure is particularly galling, protecting both the "unproductive" and the insubordinate. So university administrators are doing their best to reduce faculty power. The number of tenured professors is rapidly shrinking relative to low-paid part-time and non-tenure-track instructors–who are excluded from academic governance–while a large percentage of undergraduate teaching is done by graduate students. Faculty "authority" over hiring and promotion amounts to the right to make recommendations that are frequently overridden; professors are increasingly denied a role in appointing administrators. "Merit pay" has largely become "market pay", based not on professors' scholarly achievements as judged by their peers but on the demand for their services at other institutions.[1]

After citing these and other abrogations of principles of faculty governance and shared governance, as well as some heavy-handed board actions at her own university, Willis concludes: "There's an old labor movement saying: 'The boss organizes the shop.' It promises to be as true of the academy as of the factory." She may be right.

History shows that unions do indeed gain a foothold where workers have been poorly treated by management, and the history of universities that have become home to faculty unions appears no different. Unions have in fact improved faculty salaries in some institutions where pay was egregiously low and the faculty turned to organized labor for redress. The collective strength that unions offer, particularly when that strength can be combined with external political clout, may well appeal to faculty who have a growing sense of disenfranchisement. But the downside of unions is that they would inevitably make the academy more like the factory, and in the process work against the very qualities that have made universities such singular and great institutions.

The philosophy and practices of unions are fundamentally inimical to the traditions and ideals of the academy. Unions treat faculty as employees whose interests are to be represented in common denominator fashion with one voice speaking for all. But faculty comprise a collection of highly differing individuals who have never been considered to be *employees* in the traditional sense of the word, although boards and legislatures now often refer to them as such. They neither punch a time clock nor report to a supervisor on a regular basis. Instead, faculty members are professionals, most possessing doctoral degrees in a specialized field. They work independently to meet class schedules, set office hours, advise and mentor students, carry out research and scholarship, and perform service to the university and the community. The qualities that characterize faculty endeavor are the highly individual qualities of intelligence, imagination, creativity, judgment, dedication, integrity, and professional training and accomplishment, qualities that cannot be bargained or reduced to rules of work. The "work condition" most valued by faculty is the intellectual autonomy and flexibility they enjoy to carry out their teaching and research in the manner they see best fit. While faculty of course perform prescribed responsibilities in exchange for salaries, their finest efforts are motivated by their natural interest in their fields and by their desire to produce new knowledge, by the intrinsic challenges of learning, creation, and problem solving, by the satisfactions in teaching, and by care and concern for their students. Universities should always prize and reward these qualities in their faculties, but such action would hardly be encouraged by union representation, which typically advances longevity and seniority in position as preferred measures of worth. The thrust in union negotiation is by definition communal, and that means treating everyone the same and rewarding everyone the same, rather than encouraging singular achievement, dedication, and excellence. Furthermore, by its very nature, collective bargaining assumes competing interests and thus tends to create conflict between faculty and governing authorities. The confrontational atmosphere between faculty and the administration inherent in collective bargaining is especially unfortunate given the collegial relationship between faculty and administrations that was strongly fostered in the early history of shared governance.

Far more preferable than the alternatives we have noted would be to restore the principle and practice of shared governance by instituting the faculty councils or a similar process that more strongly injects the academic voice, values, and passions directly into decision making at the highest levels. Universities are facing difficult challenges that are unlikely to be constructively resolved unless faculty are empowered and persuaded to take greater responsibility for the welfare of their institutions and to contribute what only they can contribute. Strong forces are working to change the traditional academic culture, and those forces will not disappear. Some change is inevitable and even desirable. But the ideals of the research university and the contributions to society that stem directly from those ideals are far too important to allow the threat to their continuation to go unattended.

Notes

❦

Chapter 1   The Growth and Impact of Research Universities

1. *But it is equally clear.* In 2000, the Carnegie Foundation presented a new classification system that emphasizes teaching and focuses on the number and type of degrees an institution awards as a primary basis for classification, rather than research funding. In the new system, Research I and II universities are termed *Doctoral Extensive universities* and comprise the bulk of that grouping. The revision was prompted by the foundation's concerns that the former categories weighed institutions' research activities too heavily and that the system had come to be used as a means of ranking universities, which indeed was often the case. While the foundation's desire to encourage attention to the broader educational functions of universities is laudable, the research classification has been in use so long and has been so emulated by many institutions, that the "research university" descriptor will doubtless continue to find currency for many years. In this connection, it is instructive to consider the outcome of the recent effort by the chancellor of the Florida university system to classify its ten universities in a manner that denied the "research university" status to the bulk of its institutions. Following the former Carnegie criteria, the classification proposed a tier comprised of three research universities and two other tiers under labels such as *comprehensive universities* grouped on the basis of their relatively greater emphasis on undergraduate education. The outcry from the latter groupings, both from the institutions themselves and from their regional communities and supporters, was intense, with the result that the term *'tier'* was quickly replaced by the more neutral term *classification,* followed shortly by a new classification into Research I and Research II institutions, and followed finally by the acknowledgment that all ten institutions were potential Research I institutions and could ultimately so progress to that status. As Roger Bacon said, man may make distinctions, but nature isn't obliged to recognize them.

An excellent statement of the defining characteristics of the research university is presented in *The Top American Research Universities,* a report published in

170

2001 by *TheCenter* at the University of Florida at Gainsville, and available through its website at *http://thecenter.ufl.edu.*

2. *"The country's 125 research universities make up only 3 percent of the total number of institutions of higher learning."* "Reinventing Undergraduate Education: A Blueprint for America's Research Universities," Report of the Boyer Commission on Educating Undergraduates in the Research University, State University of New York, Stony Brook, 1998, Overview, p. 1, *http://www.stonybrook.edu/boyerreport.*

3. *"In 1860 at the dawn of the decade." Colleges of Agriculture at the Land Grant Universities: A Profile,* Washington, D.C.: National Academy Press, 1995, pp. 18–19.

4. *Undertake a study of how the "information, the techniques, and the research experience developed by (your office) and by the thousands of scientists in the universities and in private industry, should be used in the days of peace ahead."* Letter from President Franklin D. Roosevelt to Dr. Vannevar Bush, November 17, 1944, in *Science, The Endless Frontier,* Report to the President on a Program for Postwar Scientific Research, July 1945. Reprinted July 1960, National Science Foundation, Washington, D.C., p. 3.

5. *"Basic research creates the fund."* Vannevar Bush, Ibid., p. 19.

6. *"The government should accept new responsibilities."* Ibid., p. 8.

7. *"continue in peacetime."* Ibid., p. 6.

8. *"These institutions provide the environment,"* Ibid., p. 6.

9. *"For many years the Government,"* Ibid., p. 22.

10. *"Support of basic research in the public and private colleges, universities, and research institutes must leave the internal control of policy."* Ibid., p. 33.

11. *"The bargain struck between the federal government and university science."* David H. Guston and Kenneth Keniston, "Introduction: The Social Contract for Science," in Guston and Keniston (Eds.), *The Fragile Contract: University Science and the Federal Government,* Cambridge: Massachusetts Institute of Technology Press, 1994, pp. 1–2.

12. *"As many as three quarters."* Vartan Gregorian quoted in Frank Rich, 'The Unkindest Cut,' *New York Times,* Op-Ed page, May 21, 1995.

13. *"Since the end of World War II."* "University Research: Touching the Lives of All Americans," Report of the National Association of State Universities and Land-Grant Colleges, Washington, D.C., 1996, p. 2.

Chapter 2   University Research

1. *We come into the world, then, as intensely curious creatures.* A general overview of the perceptual and cognitive competencies of the infant can be found in Marc H. Bornstein and Michael E. Lamb, *Development in Infancy,* 3rd ed., New York: McGraw-Hill Higher Education, 1992. A more specialized review is given in Leslie B. Cohen and Cara H. Cashon, "Infant Perception and Cognition," in R. Lerner, A. Easterbrooks,

and J. Mistry (Eds.), *Comprehensive Handbook of Psychology, vol. 6, Developmental Psychology, II, Infancy,* New York: Wiley, in press. An early demonstration that infants will work for new visual stimuli is found in E. R. Siqueland and C. A. DeLucia, "Visual Reinforcement of Nonnutritive Sucking in Human Infants," *Science,* 1969, vol. 165, 1144–1146. The relation between early infant attention and learning and later development is described in M. Sigman, S. E. Cohen, and L. Beckwith, "Why Does Infant Attention Predict Adolescent Intelligence?" *Infant Behavior and Development,* 1997, vol. 20. The developmental course of the early preference for novelty versus extrinsically driven performance is traced by David Zeaman in "The Ubiquity of Novelty-Familiarity (Habituation?) Effects," in T. J. Tighe and R. N. Leaton (Eds.), *Habituation: Perspectives from Child Development, Animal Behavior, and Neurophysiology,* New Jersey: Lawrence Erlbaum Associates, 1976, pp. 297–320.

2. *"progress on a broad front."* Science, *The Endless Frontier,* July 1945. Reprinted July 1960, National Science Foundation, Washington, D.C., p. 12.

3. *"What could be more useless."* Nathan Myhrvold, "Supporting Science," *Science,* 1998, vol. 282, 621.

4. *"Could you describe the addictive personality?"* Daniel E. Koshland, "The Addictive Personality," *Science,* 1990, vol. 250, 1193.

5. *"The more creative the problem solving."* David Klar and Herbert A. Simon, "What Have Psychologists (And Others) Discovered about the Process of Scientific Discovery?" *Current Directions in Psychological Science,* 2001, vol. 10, 79.

Chapter 3   University Governance

1. *University boards are essentially business boards.* Information on the composition and other characteristics of university governing boards is derived from surveys of nearly eleven hundred governing boards of independent and public colleges and universities conducted by the Association of Governing Boards of Universities and Colleges (the AGB) and reported in two papers by Holly Madsen published in 1998 by the AGB, Washington, D.C. These reports are the "Composition of Governing Boards of Independent Colleges and Universities," Occasional Paper no. 36, 1997, and the "Composition of Governing Boards of Public Colleges and Universities," Occasional Paper no. 37, 1997.

2. *A recent survey . . . on the president's primary use of time.* "College Presidents Say Planning, Fundraising, Budgeting, and Personnel Issues Occupy Much of Their Time," in *Higher Education and National Affairs,* American Council on Education, October 9, 2000, vol. 49, no. 18. p. 2.

3. *Several higher education analysts.* The linkage of university board activism to the business world outlined here draws upon papers by Marvin Lazerson, "Who Owns Higher Education? The Changing Face of Governance," *Change,* March–April 1997, vol. 29, no. 2. p. 10 and Richard Chait, "The New Activism of Corporate Boards and the Implications for Campus Governance," *Association of Governing Boards,* Occasional Paper no. 26, 1995.

4. *The 80s and 90s saw directive power shift sharply from the executive level to the board level.* The Enron scandal would suggest that the shift has hardly been sufficient to offset the manager-friendly bias of business boards.

5. *The Board of Regents of the University of California acts against.* Joan Wallach Scott, "Defending the Tradition of Shared Governance," *Chronicle of Higher Education,* August 9, 1996.

6. *In the process, the board threatens the job of the system's president.* Patrick Healy, "Critics Say New Trustees Are Politicizing Presidential Searches," Ibid.

7. *Conflict with their governing boards.* Lazerson, "Who Owns Higher Education?" Healy, "Critics Say New Trustees Are Politicizing Presidential Searches." Ibid.

8. *At the University of Iowa the new president of the board moves to eliminate programs.* Scott, "Defending the Tradition of Shared Governance." Ibid.

9. *At the University of Minnesota the regents call for major revision of the tenure rules.* Denise K. Magner, "Minnesota Professors Irate Over Plans They Say Threaten Tenure," Ibid., May 17, 1996. Magner, "Minnesota Regents' Proposals Stir Controversy with Faculty," Ibid., September 20, 1996.

10. *The Chronicle of Higher Education reports that the Faculty Senate at the University of Notre Dame.* Alex P. Kellogg, "Faculty Senate at Notre Dame, Angry over Lack of Clout, Votes to Dissolve," Ibid., May 18, 2002.

11. *New York University's Board of Trustees handpick a new university president.* Peer Review, Ibid., May 18, 2001.

12. *Auburn University faculty express outrage.* Julianne Basinger, "Trustees' Ouster of President at Auburn Fuels Widespread Anger," Ibid., March 16, 2001.

13. *Under strong pressure from the Mayor.* Karen W. Arenson, "Mayor's Choice Picked to Run Hunter College," *New York Times,* January 30, 2001.

14. *The policy-making body for higher education in Virginia.* Catherine R. Stimpson, "Activist Trustees Wield Power Gone Awry," *Chronicle of Higher Education,* January 16, 1998.

15. *In 1995 the Florida legislature limited all baccalaureate degree programs to 120 credit hours.* Florida Senate Bill 2330 enacted in the 1995 legislative session.

16. *A SUNY system trustee upset by a conference.* Stimpson, "Activist Trustees Wield Power Gone Awry." *The Chronicle of Higher Education,* January 16, 1998.

17. *The Board of Visitors at George Mason University.* Magner, "Battle over Academic Control Pits Faculty Against Governing Board at George Mason U." Ibid., June 18, 1999.

18. *A member of the board of James Madison University.* Stimson, "Activists Trustees Wield Power Gone Awry".

19. *A Florida regent calls for state universities to achieve higher targets.* Statement in a 1999 public meeting of the Florida Board of Regents in relation to board policy and directions on university accountability.

20. *Faculty members at Indiana University decry.* Basinger, "In Evaluating the College President, Governing Boards Assert More Authority," *Chronicle of Higher Education,* August 13, 1999.

21. *A blue-ribbon panel of the Association of Governing Boards.* "Renewing the Academic Presidency: Stronger Leadership for Tougher Times," Report of the Commission on the Academic Presidency. Association of Governing Boards, Washington, D.C., 1996.

22. *The Chronicle of Higher Education reports.* Katherine S. Mangan, "Corporate Know-How Lands Presidencies for a Growing Number of Business Deans," *Chronicle of Higher Education,* March 27, 1998.

23. *University of Pennsylvania trustees publicly reprimand.* Lazerson, "Who Owns Higher Education?".

Chapter 4   The Faculty–An Isolated Culture

1. *"large numbers of Ph.D.'s regard themselves as independent professionals."* Christopher Jencks and David Riesman, *The Academic Revolution,* Chicago: University of Chicago Press, 1977, p. 14.

2. *"Today, a scholar's orientation to his institution."* Theodore Caplow and Reece J. McGee, *The Academic Marketplace,* New York: Basic, 1958, p. 85.

3. *A 1996 survey of approximately 34,000 full-time faculty across 392 colleges and universities.* "The American College Teacher: National Norms for the 1995–96 H. E. R. I. Faculty Survey," University of California at Los Angeles Higher Education Research Institute.

4. *National surveys have consistently found that full-time faculty across all types of institutions tend to work inordinately long hours.* "Background Characteristics, Work Activities, and Compensation of Faculty and Instructional Staff in Postsecondary Institutions: Fall 1998," 1999 National Study of Postsecondary Faculty, National Center for Education Statistics, U.S. Department of Education, Washington, D.C.

5. *One such "teaching incentive" program.* The program discussed here is the Teaching Incentive Program, familiarly known as TIP, initiated by the Florida legislature and implemented by the Board of Regents. TIP was in effect for the state's ten-university system for a good part of the 1990s.

6. *"Although I realized that I was moving away from issues of concern to academics."* Richard D. Breslin, "Lessons from the Presidential Trenches," *Chronicle of Higher Education,* November 10, 2000.

7. *Fewer than 10% of America's more than 3,500 colleges and universities have truly selective admissions policies.* Chester E. Finn Jr. and Bruno V. Manno, "What's Wrong with the American University?: Behind the Curtain," *Wilson Quarterly,* Winter 1996, pp. 44–53.

8. *Some 63% of high school graduates in America now go on to at least begin some form of further education.* U.S. Bureau of the Census. *Statistical Abstract of the United States,* 118th ed., U.S. Government Printing Office, Washington, D.C., 1998.

9. *Eighty-one percent of four-year public institutions and 63% of four-year private institutions now offer remedial courses.* "Remedial Education of Higher Education Institutions in Fall 1995," Postsecondary Education Quick Information System, National Center for Education Statistics, U.S. Department of Education, Washington, D.C.

10. *Albert Shanker . . . noted that more than half of the students going on to college in America would not qualify for admission to colleges in Europe or Japan.* As reported by Marc Tucker in "Many U. S. Colleges Are Really Inefficient, High-Priced Secondary Schools," *Chronicle of Higher Education,* June 5, 1991.

11. *Grade inflation has risen to notorious levels even in elite universities.* Harvey C. Mansfield, "Grade Inflation: It's Time to Face the Facts," Ibid., April 6, 2001.

12. *A 1993 survey by the National Center for Education Statistics.* "Instructional Faculty and Staff in Higher Education Institutions: Fall 1987 and Fall 1992," 1993 National Study of Postsecondary Faculty, National Center for Education Statistics, U.S. Department of Education. Washington, D.C.: Robin Wilson, "Contracts Replace the Tenure Track for a Growing Number of Professors," *Chronicle of Higher Education,* June 12, 1998.

13. *a survey of humanities and social science disciplines.* Ana Marie Cox, "Study Shows Colleges' Dependence on Their Part-Time Instructors," Ibid., December 1, 2000.

14. *Common to many of these and other critical treatments is the view that faculty control is responsible for the ills of higher education.* This argument is well expressed by Alan Wolfe in "What's Wrong with the American University?: The Feudal Culture of the Postmodern University," *Wilson Quarterly,* Winter 1996 pp. 54–66.

15. *"If it was ever true that faculty members' pursuit of individual interests."* William H. Danforth, "Universities Are Our Responsibility," *Science,* 1995, vol. 269, 1651.

Chapter 5   Shared Governance Revisited

1. *The Association of Governing Boards of Universities and Colleges (AGB) has argued that the current environment requires speed in administrative decision making.* Courtney Leatherman, "Shared Governance under Siege," *Chronicle of Higher Education,* January 30, 1998. "Renewing the Academic Presidency: Stronger Leadership for Tougher Times." Report of the Commission on the Presidency. Association of Governing Boards, Washington, D.C.: 1996.

2. *"the real governance does not occur in the senate."* James Duderstadt quoted in Leatherman, "Shared Governance under Siege." Ibid.

3. *"A people who will not sacrifice for the common good cannot expect to have any common good."* James Lincoln Collier, *The Rise of Selfishness in America,* New York, Oxford University Press, 1991, p. 262.

4. *"Unfortunately, many trustees (and more than a few college presidents) are apprehensive."* Richard Chait, "Trustees and Professors: So Often at Odds, So Much Alike," *Chronicle of Higher Education,* August 4, 2000.

Chapter 6   The Teaching-Research Relation

1. *an analysis of data from the 1992–1993 National Study of Postsecondary Faculty found.* "Instructional Faculty and Staff in Higher Education Institutions Who Taught Classes to Undergraduates: Fall 1992," National Center for Education Statistics, U.S. Department of Education, Washington, D.C.

2. *Furthermore, a national survey of science and engineering faculty at research universities.* National Science Board, *Science and Engineering Indicators,* 1996 (NSB 96-21), U.S. Government Printing Office, Washington, D.C., 1996.

3. *"We believe that the state of undergraduate education at research universities is (in) a crisis."* "Reinventing Undergraduate Education: A Blueprint for America's Research Universities," Report of the Boyer Commission on Educating Undergraduates in the Research University, State University of New York at Stony Brook, 1998, Conclusion, p. 1, Overview, pp. 2–3, *http://www.stonybrook.edu/boyerreport.*

4. *"The most valuable and farsighted concept to emerge from the original* (Vannevar) *Bush vision."* C. M. Vest, "Research Universities: Overextended, Under-focused, Overstressed, Underfunded," Speech delivered at the Cornell Symposium on the American University, May 22, 1995, p. 4.

5. *"all the patrons of the university . . . have shared this burden."* Harold T. Shapiro, "Notes on the American University in a Changing World," Presentation given at the First Richard A. Harvill Conference on Higher Education, University of Arizona at Tuscon, November 23, 1992.

6. *While a good deal of research has been addressed regarding this issue, the overall results are equivocal."* M. J. Finkelstein, *The American Academic Profession,* Columbus: Ohio State Press, 1984. K. A. Feldman, "Research Productivity and Scholarly Accomplishment of College Teachers as Related to Their Instructional Effectiveness: A Review and Exploration," *Research in Higher Education,* 1987, vol. 26, pp. 227–298. A. W. Astin, *What Matters in College,* San Francisco, Jossey-Bass, 1993.

7. *"the nostalgic image of the avuncular 'prof'."* Shapiro, "Notes on the American University in a Changing World."

8. *we need to recognize "that inquiry, investigation, and discovery are the heart of the (university) enterprise."* "Reinventing Undergraduate Education: A Blueprint for America's Research Universities," Report of the Boyer Commission on Educating Undergraduates in the Research University, State University of New York at Stony Brook, 1998, Section: The University as Ecosystem, p. 1; Section: Make Research-Based Learning the Standard, p. 1, *http://www.stonybrook.edu/boyerreport.*

9. *It is interesting to compare the commission's recommendations with actions recently proposed by Murray Sperber."* Sperber, "End the Mediocrity of Our Public Universities," *Chronicle of Higher Education,* October 20, 2000.

10. *Richard Felder . . . has suggested a strategy.* Felder, "The Myth of the Super-human Professor," *Journal of Engineering Education,* April 1994, pp. 105–110.

11. *with a by-product of fewer less essential faculty publications.* The idea that the tenure process, as well as pressures to increase institutional prestige and win grant

money, have increased the amount of "trivial" research is fairly widespread. To counter such pressures and achieve a better balance between teaching and research, Donald Kennedy, then president of Stanford University, proposed in 1991 that Stanford limit the number of publications that candidates for tenure and promotion can submit to the panels that evaluate them, thereby shifting the review focus from quantity of publications to their quality. While this idea surely merits consideration and was hailed by many academics at the time, it has resulted in little if any action from administrators or faculty in America's universities. Again, it is exactly the kind of constructive idea that could well be rescued and furthered by the proposed faculty councils. For further discussion of Kennedy's proposal, see "Efforts to Limit "Trivial" Scholarship Win Backing from Many Academics," by Carolyn J. Mooney, *Chronicle of Higher Education*, May 22, 1991.

12. *A reconceptualization of faculty work roles proposed by Ernest Boyer.* Ernest Boyer, *Scholarship Reconsidered: Priorities of the Professoriate*, Special Report of the Carnegie Foundation for the Advancement of Teaching, Princeton, N.J.: Princeton University Press, 1990.

13. *When Galileo moved from his academic position at the University of Padua.* Dava Sobel, *Galileo's Daughter*, New York: Penguin Books, 2000, p. 36.

14. *"scholarship begins in curiosity, but it ends in communication."* Edmund S. Morgan, address to a freshman class at Yale, quoted in Jacob Neusner, "On Submitting to the Process of Education," *Transaction Periodicals Consortium*, a Publication of the National Association of Scholars, Rutgers–The State University, New Brunswick, N. J., 1998, vol. 11, 11.

Chapter 7   The Question of Tenure

1. *the bar for tenure is rising even further.* Robin Wilson, "A Higher Bar for Earning Tenure," *Chronicle of Higher Education*, January 5, 2001.

2. *Working with survey data provided by the U.S. Education Department, the American Association of University Professors (AAUP) found.* Ernst Benjamin, "Disparities in the Salaries and Appointments of Academic Women and Men," *Academe*, January–February 1999, pp. 60–62.

3. *"The teacher is entitled to full freedom in research and the publication of the results."* Louis Joughin (Ed.), *Academic Freedom and Tenure: A Handbook of the American Association of University Professors*, Madison: University of Wisconsin Press, 1967, p. 35.

4. *The AAUP estimates that in a typical year.* As estimated by Jordan Kurland of the national office of the American Association of University Professors, Washington, D.C., based on forty years experience. Personal communication.

5. *Florida legislative committee investigations in the 1960s.* James A. Schnur, "Cold Warriors in the Hot Sunshine: USF and the Johns Committee," *Sunland Tribune*, November, 1992, pp. 9–15. Schnur, "Cold Warriors in the Hot Sunshine: The Johns Committee's Assault on Civil Liberties in Florida, 1956–1965," Master's thesis, 1995, Department of History, University of South Florida, University of South Florida library.

6. *As Alan Charles Kors and Harvey Silvergate attest.* Kors and Silvergate, *The Shadow University: The Betrayal of Liberty on America's Campuses,* New York: Free Press, 1998, p. 5.

7. *"Today, knowledge, its critical analysis, its creation, and its transmission."* Dominique G. Homberger and A. Ravi P. Rau, "Preserve the Roles of Tenure, Teaching, and Research," *Scientist,* May 11, 1998, 8.

8. *"But the provision of academic freedom is by no means the only consideration."* Saunders Mac Lane, "The Travail of the University," *Perspectives in Biology and Medicine,* 1997, vol. 41, 5.

9. *Studies examining this question have tracked publication by faculty beginning with their initial appointment and through the end of their careers.* Nancy Stern, "Age and Achievement in Mathematics: A Case-Study in the Sociology of Science," *Social Studies of Science,* 1978, vol. 8, pp. 127–140. Stephen Cole, "Age and Scientific Performance," *American Journal of Sociology,* 1979, vol. 84, 958–977. Arthur Diamond Jr., "The Life-Cycle Research Productivity of Mathematicians and Scientists," *Journal of Gerontology,* 1986, vol. 41, 520–525. Thomas H. Goodwin and Raymond D. Sauer, "Life Cycle Productivity in Academic Research: Evidence from Cumulative Publication Histories of Academic Economists," *Southern Economic Journal,* 1995, vol. 61, 728–743.

10. *"Those who argue that tenure leads to declining productivity."* Myles Brand, "Why Tenure Is Indispensable," *Chronicle of Higher Education,* April 2, 1999.

11. *if 52 percent of the faculty in the average university department is tenured.* The percentage of full-time faculty on tenure in public research universities is somewhat higher (63) and somewhat lower in private research universities (50), according to the U.S. Department of Education, 1993 National Study of Postsecondary Faculty. But this variation does not question the conclusion advanced here regarding generally acceptable rates of faculty turnover.

12. *But even more disturbing are recent analyses by Jay Chronister and Roger Baldwin.* As reported by Courtney Leatherman, "Growth in Positions Off the Tenure Track Is a Trend that's Here to Stay, Study Finds," *Chronicle of Higher Education,* April 9, 1999.

13. *some forty institutions around the country have now adopted contract systems.* Wilson, "Contracts Replace the Tenure Track for a Growing Number of Professors," Ibid., June 12, 1998.

14. *"If such activities are high priorities."* Cary Nelson, "The War Against the Faculty," Ibid., April 16, 1999.

15. *"driving through their careers on autopilot."* Karla Haworth, "Florida Regents Approve Post-Tenure Reviews for All Professors," Ibid., October 11, 1996.

16. *This movement is now underway in one form or another in thirty-seven states.* *Post-Tenure Faculty Review and Renewal: Experienced Voices,* Christine M. Licata and Joseph C. Morreale (Eds.), American Association for Higher Education, Washington, D.C., 2002.

Chapter 8   Accountability

1. *an actual record of the accounting that a particular but representative public research university was expected to provide.* The performance measures listed are from the annual report of the University of Connecticut submitted in 1990 to the Governor's Office and to the state legislature following a format that had been in place for many years.

2. *one large state university system required more than a hundred and fifty such reports from its individual member institutions annually.* This number is based on a count of the number of individual reports submitted by a member institution of the state university system of Florida in 2000.

3. *a report on reporting.* Such a report was required by the Chancellor's Office of the state university system of Florida in 2000 in an effort to reduce perceived errors and late submissions in the voluminous reports required of the member institutions.

4. *the National Association of Scholars has documented a general loosening of the structure, content, and rigor of the general education requirement. The Dissolution of General Education: 1914–1993,* Princeton, N. J.: National Association of Scholars, 1996.

5. *The list characterizes well what has been said to be an ongoing shift.* In addition to the productivity-type measures of output listed here, there is a related but quite different move to assess student learning in public colleges and universities through means other than the usual course final examinations. The objective is to develop standardized tests or other independent assessments of students' acquired competencies in general education and in their majors. In part this movement has arisen from institutional efforts, with encouragement from accrediting bodies, to improve university teaching and learning by measuring learning outcomes in relation to preestablished goals. More recently, a number of state legislatures and system boards have shown interest in enacting some form of assessment of postsecondary student learning as another means of establishing accountability for colleges and universities, in much the same manner that the national-standards movement in K-12 education is being used to establish accountability for the schools. While assessment of learning outcomes as a means of improving teaching and learning is likely to grow, especially since this practice is being reinforced by accrediting bodies, it is too soon to predict whether a national-standards type program will develop in postsecondary education. Several states have experimented with statewide assessments of college students only to abandon such efforts.

6. *An indication of how faculty themselves might approach accountability reporting can be seen in a model.* The model outlined here was developed at the University of Connecticut in the early 1990s and is described in a report published by the University of Connecticut Provost Office in 1993. The model is also described by the author in an article published in *Assessment and Accountability Forum,* 2000, vol. 10, 5–7, 18.

Chapter 9   Universities and the Corporate Sector

1. *The U.S. Patent Office has reported a steady increase in the annual number of utility patents assigned to academic institutions.* "Technology Assessment and Forecast

Report: U.S. Colleges and Universities–Utility Patent Grants 1969–1999, U.S. Patent and Trademark Office, Office of Information Dissemination Service, Technology Assessment and Forecast Program, Washington, D.C., September 2000.

2. *Further assessment of the impact of this act is provided through the annual survey of the* ... *members of the Association of University Technology Managers*, Association of University Technology Managers, *AUTM Licensing Survey, FY 1999 Survey Summary*, Northbrook, Illinois.

3. *Columbia University alone received $96 million in licensing fees and royalties* ... *in 1999.* Karen W. Arenson, "Columbia Leads Academic Pack in Turning Profit from Research," *New York Times*, August 2, 2000, A1, A25.

4. *The University of California at Berkeley signed an agreement with Novartis.* Goldie Blumenstyk, "A Vilified Corporate Partnership Produces Little Change (Except Better Facilities)," *Chronicle of Higher Education*, June 22, 2001.

5. *These interests are apparent in the very names of many endowed chairs* ... *the past decade has seen literally scores of new corporation-endowed chairs created annually.* Julianne Basinger, "Increase in Number of Chairs Endowed by Corporations Prompts New Concerns," Ibid., April 24, 1998.

6. *a 1994 study found that in 1988 fifty Stanford-based firms.* James F. Gibbon, "Silicon Valley: Startups, Strategies, and the Stanford Connection," *MRS Bulletin, A Publication of the Materials Research Society*, 1994, vol. 19, 4–10.

7. *Similarly, a 1997 study of the financial impact of MIT on the state of Massachusetts.* "MIT: The Impact of Innovation," Economics Department, BankBoston, Boston, March 1997.

8. *the state of California announced the most ambitious university-based economic development plan to date.* John Markoff, "California Sets up Centers for Basic Scientific Research," *New York Times*, December 8, 2000, A20.

9. *"The most important thing a state government can do to improve local economies."* Governor Gray Davis as quoted by Markoff, "California Sets up Centers for Basic Scientific Research."

10. *Industry research and development (R & D) expenditures at universities and colleges have increased.* National Science Foundation, Division of Science Resources Statistics, *Academic Research and Development Expenditures: Fiscal Years 2000*, NSF 02-308, Project Officer, M. Marge Machen, Arlington, Virginia, 2002.

11. *an even higher level of corporate donations to universities. Voluntary Support of Education, 2001.* New York: Council for Aid to Education, 2002.

12. *A 1996 survey of several hundred life-science companies.* David Blumenthal, Nancyanne Causino, Eric G. Campbell, and Karen Seashore Louis, "Relationships Between Academic Institutions and Industry in the Life Sciences–An Industry Survey," *New England Journal of Medicine*, 1996, vol. 334, 368–373.

13. *In a related survey of several thousand academic life-science faculty.* Blumenthal, Campbell, Melissa Anderson, Causino, and Louis, "Withholding Research

Results in Academic Life Science: Evidence from a National Survey of Faculty," *Journal of the American Medical Association,* 1997, vol. 277, 1224–1228.

14. *the well publicized industry experience of Dr. Betty Dong.* Ralph T. King Jr., "How a Drug Firm Paid for University Study, Then Undermined It," *Wall Street Journal,* April 25, 1996, 1. Gretchen Vogel, "Long-Suppresed Study Finally Sees Light of Day," *Science,* 1997, vol. 276, 525–526.

15. *In Providence, Rhode Island, an occupational health physician at a Brown University-affiliated teaching hospital.* Wade Roush, "Publishing Sensitive Data: Who Calls the Shots?" *Science,* 1997, vol. 276, 523–524.

16. *"In another case, a drug manufacturer demanded up to $10 million from an AIDS researcher."* Katherine S. Mangan, "Company Seeks $10 million from Scientist and University," *Chronicle of Higher Education,* November 17, 2000.

17. *A 1996 review of the publications of more than a thousand scientists at universities in Massachusetts.* S. Krimsky, L. S. Rothenberg, P. Stott, and G. Kyle, "Financial Interests of Authors in Scientific Journals: A Pilot Study of 14 Publications," *Science and Engineering Ethics,* 1996, vol. 2, 395–410.

18. *A survey of life scientists in the fifty top-funded research universities.* Campbell, Louis, and Blumenthal, "Looking a Gift Horse in the Mouth," *Journal of the American Medical Association,* 1998, vol. 279, 995–999.

19. *a recent wryly humorous observation in the journal Science.* "The Burden of Baring All," *Science,* 2000, vol. 288, 1331.

20. *One of the most comprehensive was conducted by a team of Canadian researchers.* Henry Thomas Stelfox, Grace Chua, Keith O'Rourke, and Allan S. Detsky, "Conflict of Interest in the Debate Over Calcium-Channel Antagonists," *New England Journal of Medicine,* 1998, vol. 338, 101–106.

21. *Another relatively large-scale study examined the published outcomes of research studies . . . in relation to whether the research was done under drug company support or without such support.* Mildred K. Cho and Lisa A. Bero, "The Qualtiy of Drug Studies Published in Symposium Proceedings," *Annals of Internal Medicine,* 1996, vol. 124, 485–489.

22. *Several other clinical trials studies have reported outcomes of a similar nature.* R. A. Davidson, "Source of Funding and Outcome of Clinical Trials," *Journal of General Internal Medicine,* 1986, vol. 1, 155–158. P. A. Rochon, J. H. Gurwitz, R. W. Simms, P. R. Fortin, D. T. Felson, K. L. Minaker, and T. C. Chalmers, "A Study of Manufacturer-Supported Trials of Nonsteroidal Anti-Inflammatory Drugs in the Treatment of Arthritis," *Archives of Internal Medicine,* 1994, vol. 154, 157–163.

23. *A survey of more than 60,000 papers appearing in 181 peer-reviewed journals in 1997.* Krimsky and Rothenberg, "Conflict of Interest Policies in Science and Medical Journals: Editorial Practices and Author Disclosures," *Science and Engineering Ethics,* 2001, vol. 7, 205–211.

24. *A recently reported study of this question found that from 1970 to 1994 the number of bachelor's degrees in English, foreign languages, philosophy, and religion all*

declined. James Engell and Anthony Dangerfield, "The Market-Model University: Humanities in the Age of Money," *Harvard Magazine,* May–June 1998, pp. 48–55.

25. *"We borrow the language of business because we are forced to operate like businesses."* Michele Tolela Myers, "A Student Is Not an Input," *New York Times,* Op-Ed page, March 26, 2001.

26. *"What do these notions mean? To me, they involve an increased dependence on industry and philanthropy for operating the university."* James Robert Brown, "Privatizing the University–the New Tragedy of the Commons," *Science,* 2000, vol. 290, 1701.

27. *Harvard Medical School, worried that they might have trouble recruiting and retaining faculty.* Mangan, "Harvard Medical School Opts Not to Ease Its Conflict-of-Interest Policies," *Chronicle of Higher Education,* June 9, 2000.

28. *Marcia Angell, . . . argued that the best way to restore public confidence in the scientific enterprise.* Mangan and Goldie Blumenstyk, "Conflict Rules Are Criticized for Vagueness," ibid., November 17, 2000. Jeffrey Brainard, "The Ties that Blind?" Ibid., September 8, 2000.

Chapter 10   A Summing-Up and Final Word

1. *"Today it's undeniable that universities, public or private, are modeled not on medieval guilds, governed by their members, but on modern corporations."* Ellen Willis, "Why Professors Turn to Organized Labor," *New York Times,* Op-Ed page, May 28, 2001.

Index